Corporate Control, Corporate Power

The Twentieth Century Fund is an independent research foundation that undertakes policy studies of economic, political, and social institutions and issues. The Fund was founded in 1919 and endowed by Edward A. Filene.

Corporate Control, Corporate Power

A Twentieth Century Fund Study

EDWARD S. HERMAN

Professor of Finance
Wharton School, University of Pennsylvania

CAMBRIDGE UNIVERSITY PRESS

CAMBRIDGE

LONDON   NEW YORK   NEW ROCHELLE

MELBOURNE   SYDNEY

81-1529

Published by the Press Syndicate of the University of Cambridge
The Pitt Building, Trumpington Street, Cambridge CB2 1RP
32 East 57th Street, New York, NY 10022, USA
296 Beaconsfield Parade, Middle Park, Melbourne 3206, Australia

First published 1981

Printed in the United States of America
Typeset, printed, and bound by Vail-Ballou Press, Inc.,
Binghamton, New York

Library of Congress Cataloging in Publication Data
Herman, Edward S
Corporate control, corporate power.
"A Twentieth Century Fund study."
Includes bibliographical references and index.
1. Corporations – United States.
2. Big Business – United States.
3. Industry – Social aspects – United States.
4. Industry and state – United States.
I. Title.
HD2785.H46   338.7'4'0973   80-29447
ISBN 0 521 23996 6

Contents

Tables and Figure

vii

Foreword

The giant corporation, which is one of the most publicized features of modern capitalism, has been a source of criticism as well as praise since the nineteenth century. Now, in the latter part of the twentieth century, its power and influence remain the subject of controversy. The Trustees of the Twentieth Century Fund, who have long been interested in the relations between big business and big government, were receptive to Edward S. Herman's proposal for a fresh inquiry into the accountability and control of the nation's large corporations. Its receptivity, admittedly, was heightened by the fact that the late Adolf A. Berle, who with Gardiner C. Means wrote the landmark study on the managerial revolution – the shift of control from owners to managers – over 50 years ago, was the longtime chairman of the Fund and had frequently voiced the hope for a reappraisal of corporate power.

Herman's study reassesses Berle and Means in light of the vast changes that have taken place over the post-World War II decades. During this period, corporations have grown immensely in size and in reach, a growth accompanied by an increase in government regulation and other efforts to make corporate management more responsible to society at large. The movement to tame the corporation has intensified in recent years, aroused by illegal corporate activity, as well as by heightened awareness of corporate power and its role, intentional and unintentional, in our society. As a consequence, higher standards of corporate behavior have been enacted. But the debate has continued, with corporations and their supporters claiming that regulation is now excessively rigid and their critics charging that corporations have managed to evade their alleged obligations to society.

In this study, Herman traces the changing structure of the corporation, analyzing its responsiveness to outside controls. He has found that the power of government to restrict or limit corporate action is exaggerated and the influence that financial institutions once held over corporate decision making has declined. He also argues that corporations have remained faithful to their basic objective, which is to maximize profits, and that they continue to be relatively impervious to the demands that they have a responsibility for the public welfare.

These findings may add fresh fuel to the debate, not tamp it down. But it must be pointed out that Herman has amassed a wealth of evidence in support of his position. In all the studies sponsored by the Fund, our authors have complete freedom in expressing their views so long as they are substantiated. Herman, a careful and thoughtful scholar, has met this test. Although his findings may provoke controversy, he has provided valuable new material that must be taken into account in assessing the place of the large corporation in our society.

The Fund is grateful to Edward S. Herman for his comprehensive study. I hope that it will stir debate on a higher plane, which in itself is a significant contribution.

M. J. Rossant, Director
The Twentieth Century Fund
October 1980

Preface

The 1960s and 1970s witnessed a great increase in political and social activism in the United States, sparked in part by new or greatly intensified concerns over environmental pollution, urban decay, and other maladjustments that were attributed partly to government ineptitude, partly to corporate irresponsibility. For some, government ineptitude was seen as a *product* of corporate irresponsibility. Interest in these issues was given special impetus by the Watergate and foreign bribery scandals of the mid-1970s and the Love Canal and Three Mile Island episodes of the latter part of the decade. This period was also one of increased academic interest in the limitations of market processes (market failure), the growing demand for and importance of so-called public goods, and the need for and limits of "corporate responsibility." There was a parallel surge during these years in government activities and programs designed to provide individual and group income security, as well as to protect against the various perceived forms of market failure.

This expansion of government activity was not well received by the business community in the United States. And although the growth of government helped to cope with some social problems (income and medical insecurity, environmental degradation), others were not only unresolved but were even exacerbated. Inflation worsened, productivity growth continued to decline, unemployment rose, and fragmentation and social divisiveness became increasingly evident. We are now in the midst of a period in which "Big Government" is blamed and castigated for numerous social ills, waste, and ineffectiveness; but at the same time, government is being asked to deal with many of these identical problems. The attacks on government further the process of fragmentation and weaken its authority and power to act – especially efficiently and rationally.

The efficiency, rationality, power, and ends of government are greatly affected by the specific character of the corporate order and larger society within which government functions. In the United States, Japan, and Sweden, the degrees of accommodation, coordination, and conflict between the private corporate world and that of government are significantly different. These variations are of enormous importance, as government in every industrialized state is not only large but has also been assigned (or has assumed) significant responsibilities. Effective management can provide stability and alleviate social distress, whereas government ineptitude, corruption, or fanaticism can inflict serious damage, and in extreme cases even pose a threat to community survival (e.g., Nazi Germany).

This book is about the corporate order in the United States and some of its special characteristics that affect its relationships with government, its capacity for reform, its responsiveness to external pressures, and its likely short- and medium-term evolution. These matters are addressed from the vantage point of how they are affected by the control of the large corporation; the interests and objectives of those who control it; and the constraints and linkages, internal and external to the firm, that help shape those objectives. In a sense, this book is a reappraisal of the postulate of a "managerial revolution," with a more explicit concern than appears in much of the earlier writing on this subject with the forces that shape and limit managerial discretion.

On some questions central to this work – the evolution and present status of control of the large corporation; the changing ownership position of individuals, families, and financial institutions; the role of financial institutions in corporate control; and the structure of ties among companies – significant fresh data are presented in Chapters 3, 4, and 6. The focus on corporate control allows detailed treatment of many controversial issues – the alleged attrition of the profit motive as a consequence of managerial control, the resurgence of the control power of the banks, government encroachment on corporate decision making, and the extent to which intercorporate ties and interest groupings (e.g., interlocking directors and joint ventures) have compromised corporate autonomy and unified the business community. Analysis of these issues sets the stage for an appraisal of the concept of corporate responsibility and various proposals for making the large firm more responsive to changing community priorities.

This book is a product of the author's long interest in the centralizing tendencies and effects of corporate and financial power,

and in the broader question of the possibilities and limits of reform and social change. Although my own concern with and
study of these issues go further back, the Patman Report of 1968,
which described in dramatic fashion the extensive stock ownership by bank trust departments, was a landmark in provoking
controversy and research (including my own) on the issue of the
centralization of corporate control and the role played by banks
and other financial institutions in this process. Based on this interest, I prepared a research study, also sponsored by the Twentieth Century Fund, on commercial bank trust departments.
From this study, which was concerned in part with the control
powers of banks arising out of stock ownership, came the present, broader inquiry into the control of large firms.

The author wishes to acknowledge his indebtedness to Josh
Markel, Adam Finnerty, and Michael Marchino, who served as
research assistants during the preparation of this work and contributed much useful advice on both technical details and the
broader issues considered here. Donald Goldstein provided invaluable assistance in the analysis of director characteristics
(Chapter 2) and interlocks and other ties among large firms
(Chapter 6). Many helpful comments were made by Joel Dirlam
and Vic Reinemer, who read the original manuscript. Thanks are
owing the Twentieth Century Fund for financial assistance and
to its Director, M. J. Rossant, for his patience and encouragement. Editing by Pamela Gilfond greatly improved the readabil-
ity of this book, and many valuable substantive comments were
made by Masha Sinnreich, also at the Twentieth Century Fund.

Edward S. Herman

1

Corporate Control: Background and Issues

The large corporation and its impact

A central feature of economic development during the past century has been the rise of the large corporation, both nationally and internationally, to a strategically important position. Large firms have grown enormously in absolute size, and those economic sectors dominated by large firms, such as manufacturing and utilities, have increased at the expense of other economic sectors, particularly agriculture (see Table 6.1). In the late 1970s more than 60 percent of the assets of all nonfinancial corporations in the United States were owned by companies with $250 million or greater in assets, and in the important manufacturing sector, the 200 largest firms controlled 60 percent of all assets in 1977, up from 45 percent in 1945.[1]

Whether concentration and market power have increased since 1900 is still subject to debate; the changes in output composition, the increased geographic scope of markets, the higher rate of product innovation, the greater importance of advertising, and other complexities make comparisons difficult. Still, authorities on these matters agree that concentration had already attained quite high levels 75 to 80 years ago and that significant market control prevailed in many industries following the great merger movement around the turn of the century (if not before).[2] Thus whatever the *trend* of market control since 1900, its level was substantial then and is substantial in 1980. The long-established norm of market structure and behavior has been that of *oligopoly,* that is, the constrained rivalry of a few interdependent sellers who compete mainly by means of product differentiation.[3]

An economy dominated by oligopoly is one in which the market still operates, but under conditions far removed from Adam Smith's "obvious and simple system of natural liberty." The range of variations found in oligopolistic industries in degree of competition and in the adequacy of market results is wide.[4] Under some circumstances, where they are subject to competitive challenges,[5] internal pressures,[6] or a favorable cultural milieu, large oligopolistic firms may skillfully adapt and develop products, techniques, and social policies according to market changes and community demands. In other contexts, oligopolists may be technologically lethargic, quick to resort to restrictive practices and seek protection when subject to competitive threats, and socially and politically regressive. These differences are conspicuous among nations, but extremes of oligopoly can be found among large corporations within a given country – witness the dynamism of the computer and semiconductor businesses in the United States, on the one hand, and the lethargy of the automobile–steel–rubber tire businesses, on the other.

Lethargy is partly a function of the maturity and size of an industry, as well as of the age, size, and bureaucratic character of the dominant individual firms. Old and very large firms may lose their flexibility as a result of bureaucraticization, technological vested interests, and habituation to limited competition and protectionism.[7] They may be able to get away with this – at least for a while – if their market power is great and entry barriers are substantial. They may even have enough economic and political clout, given their networks of related supplier–customer interests, to be able to command social resources that enlarge and protect such vested interests, to the long-run detriment of society at large. In the United States this point has been raised with respect to both the automobile industry[8] and the "weapons culture."[9]

Another urgent issue in this age of rapid technological change is the proliferation of what economists call "externalities," "spill-over," or "neighborhood" effects. These are unintended impacts of production or consumption on others, effects that are excluded from the cost and revenue calculations of the originating sources; that is, they are not "internalized" and taken into account through market processes. Their importance has increased with growing numbers of people, greater economic interdependence, and an outpouring of chemicals and industrial products of uncertain environmental effect – on consumers using products containing, say, nitrites; workers absorbing new chemicals in the workplace; the general public affected by waste residues interacting with one another in the environment. Where these external effects produce deleterious results, the externalities are properly regarded as negative outputs and associated final products are underpriced and produced to excess.[10] When external effects would be positive (e.g., public education, or mass inoculation by law to combat a serious contagious disease), privately produced outputs tend to be too small and overpriced. In the case of outputs designated "public goods," external benefits are spread over many people – perhaps the entire population. Prices cannot be readily assigned or charged to such goods,[11] like national defense and national parks, which private enterprise does not provide in economically efficient quantities. Such goods have been increasing in importance in the total spectrum of goods demanded by the public.[12]

Problems such as negative externalities and a deficiency of public goods output are hardly attributable to the rise of the large corporation, although insofar as the large corporation has accelerated modern industrialization, has assumed industrial leadership, and wields political power, at the very least it shares responsibility as a causal agent. The large corporation may also contribute more directly to negative externalities as a result of its size, geographic dispersion, and mobility, which give it greater freedom to select technologies and business strategies that add to its internal efficiency but that may involve an unfavorable trade-off between costs and benefits to society.[13] Nonetheless, it is clear that the problems of externalities and public goods deficiencies would not be resolved by a return to a world of small-scale enterprise. Their resolution will depend, however, on an efficient political response to the new demands that are not being met by market forces alone.

Problems that *are* directly associated with size and market control might be solved by a return to a world of smaller enterprise (although this is by no means certain),[14] but size and market power are almost surely irreversible developments – society is not going to return to a small, perhaps mythically beautiful, world, barring a revolution in values and power hard to envisage emerging out of present structures and trends, or an international catastrophe that would bring a regression to mere survival. Thus room for policy maneuver may be painfully narrow. It is partly for this reason that the bulk of social commentary addressed to the large firm, its impact and reform, operates within the very limited framework of what appears to be practically possible. There are utopians at the extremes, urging massive decentralization to quasi-laissez-faire, on the one hand, and broad-scale nationalization of the commanding heights of private enterprise, on the other. But most reformers call for marginal changes that recognize current realities; namely, that the large corporation is here to stay and that change will come through some combination of corporate initiatives, shaped to a greater or lesser degree by external pressure, and government intervention, direct and indirect.

Given the traditional economic assumptions of unrestricted competition and a goal of profit maximization, "corporate initiatives" are clear and simple and the very idea of corporate "responsiveness" is meaningless – corporate behavior will always be based on adapting available means to a profitability end. With restricted competition, however, the pressure to maximize is relieved, and it becomes possible for nonprofit goals to emerge – the monopolist may choose the "quiet life,"[15] and yet other ends may be pursued by managers, their subordinates, and employees. With the profit-maximization goal still intact, the discretion allowed by restricted competition may not be realized – the monopolist may continue to pursue a strenuous life, and any outcropping of ends incompatible with profits may be strongly discouraged or quashed by the profit-seeking control group.

Whether the profitability goal is preserved, and the intensity with which it is sought, depends not only on competitive pressures but also on who controls the corporation. The traditional assumption was that owners control, directly or through their representatives on the board of directors; the board and the top managers were either the owners themselves or controlled agents and fiduciaries obligated by law to serve stockholders' interest. This interest has been assumed to be material gain and the postulated objective has therefore been profit maximization. The rise of the large corporation, however, has been associated with a diffusion of ownership interest and an enlargement in the power and discretion of professional managers. It is widely believed, and has become part of the conventional wisdom, that there has been a "managerial revolution" during the twentieth century, characterized by a massive shift in the control of corporation from the owners to nonowning managers. If true, the question of corporate goals takes on a different complexion. The assumption of profit maximization would appear more precariously based than in circumstances of direct or assured owner control. It becomes more plausible that the managers might evolve into a new, powerful elite of technocrats who can take real initiatives and bend more flexibly to social needs.

Whatever the truth of the matter, the separation of ownership and control in the large firm has raised new questions about corporate goals. And the objectives of the large corporation; its internal drives, choices, and power; and its responsiveness, actual and potential, to external demands and social control are major issues today. This book is directed to these issues. The main focus is on the evolution of the control and objectives of large corporations, especially the extent to which goals and behavior have been affected by the growth in importance of professional managers in the top echelons of power, the increase in company size and bureaucratization, the evolving patterns of intercorporate linkages, and the changing role of financial institutions and government in the decision-making processes of the giant corporation.

The Modern Corporation and Private Property

The rise in importance of the large corporation and its implications for ownership and control were described in a very effective way by A. A. Berle, Jr., and Gardiner C. Means in their classic, *The Modern Corporation and Private Property,* first published in 1932.[16] They portrayed an economy, in 1929 and 1930, that was already dominated by the 200 largest nonfinancial corporations, and they offered a cautious forecast of greater domination in the future, as part of a long-term trend toward increasing corporate size and centralization.[17]

With larger corporate size comes a greater dispersion of stock ownership, a steady reduction in the power and interest of the shareholder, and a gradual enhancement of managerial authority, that is, a separation of ownership from control. This process reaches its extreme in the case of corporations subject to "management control," where effective decision-making power rests with inside officers with "negligible"[18] ownership interests in their companies. For 1929–1930 Berle and Means found 44 percent of the 200 largest nonfinancial companies by number, 58 percent by wealth, to be subject to management control; another 21 percent by number and 22 percent by wealth were found to be controlled by a legal device.[19] Thus the aggregate of nonownership control of large companies was 65 percent by number, 80 percent by total wealth.

Berle and Means claimed that this transformation to management control – with nominal ownership divorced completely from control and de facto power in the hands of self-perpetuating management groups – amounted to a revolutionary change in property relations, as momentous as the shift from feudalism to capitalism. With these "new princes" in power, the link between ownership profits and the producing and investing decision-making processes was severed. Berle and Means suggested that the possible negative effects of this "splitting of the property atom" were: a diversion of resources from owners to managerial use, an unwarranted and uneconomic growth in firm size (and greater centralization) in the interests of managerial prestige and power, and an efficiency loss. These ill effects were only hinted at, and the impact of separation and centralization on the willingness to incur risk, and on price, output, investment, dividend, and borrowing policy, was not seriously discussed.

Although Berle and Means described with drama and insight the growth in the overall importance of large firms and, especially, the separation of ownership and control in the large corporation, they had almost nothing to say about the effects of these changes on market concentration and market power. At various points they even added a positive note to the list of possibilities, suggesting that the new managerial elite might well assume broader responsibilities than private profit making and bridge the gap between the narrowness of profit-seeking enterprise and the growing social needs of a complex society.[20] But basically they did little beyond establishing the trends and rationales for these developments (obviously important subjects in their own right).

The Modern Corporation and Private Property presented ideas that had been emerging and circulating in various forms for a great many years. A significant degree of separation of ownership and control was implicit in the manipulations and rip-offs of the "robber barons" of the late nineteenth and early twentieth centuries. Many of their exploits were at the expense of creditors, but the stockholders came in for their share of victimization by insiders. In the case of the railroads, which bulked large as security issuers (and giant corporations) in the late nineteenth century, a phrase quoted by Newton Booth in 1873 was that "every tie in the road is the grave of a small stockholder."[21] The promoters and managers of the railroads generally put in very little if any capital, extracting it from governments, bondholders, and potential railroad users cajoled into investing in their own economic interest. Under the usual plan, "the only men in the community who are absolutely certain not to contribute any money are those who own and control it when finished."[22] In describing the struggle over control of the Erie Railroad in the late 1860s, Charles Francis

Adams, Jr., wrote that "It was something new to see a host of adventurers, men of fortune, without character and without credit, possess themselves of an artery of commerce more important than was ever the Appian Way . . ."[23] Adams observed that the idea of any inquiries by the ordinary stockholder into the affairs of the Erie "were looked upon by the ring in control as downright impertinence."[24]

In the famous Pujo Committee report of 1913, the separation of ownership and control and the loss of power by the ordinary stockholder were clearly described as general characteristics of the large corporation.

> None of the witnesses called was able to name an instance in the history of the country in which the stockholders had succeeded in overthrowing an existing management in any large corporation, nor does it appear that stockholders have ever even succeeded in so far as to secure the investigation of an existing management of a corporation to ascertain whether it has been well or honestly managed . . . The situation that exists with respect to the control of the so-called mutual companies is in a modified way illustrative of all great corporations with numerous and widely scattered stockholders. The management is virtually self-perpetuating and is able through the power of patronage, the indifference of stockholders and other influences to control a majority of stock.[25]

The committee went on to discuss the ease with which *bankers* could control large companies, given their strategic position as promoters and lenders, and great attention was given to the power of J. P. Morgan and his close-knit coterie of commercial and investment banking associates.[26] The maintenance of control with a limited interest in a company in the pre-World War I era was known, in fact, as the "Morgan theory" of control. According to Edwin P. Hoyt, Jr., "The principle was put into practice by J. Pierpont Morgan to suit the convenience of William Henry Vanderbilt, who wanted to safeguard his fortune by selling large blocks of New York Central Railroad stock, yet maintain control of the railroad with a minority interest. Morgan showed Vanderbilt how it could be done."[27]

As early as 1904 Thorstein Veblen wrote that "the management is separated from the ownership or property, more and more widely as the size of corporation finance widens," and he made much of the conflict of interest between managers and *both* stockholders and the larger community.[28] Writing on the basis of late nineteenth century experience, Veblen not only took separation as a premise, but took the managerial *norm* to be the use of control for short-term transient gain.[29] In the 1920s Veblen made less of manipulative gain but saw the conflict broaden, identifying the separable interests of the dominant financial or absentee owners, ordinary owners, hired managers who he assumed to be nonowners with a production-technological bent, and the general public bringing up the rear. The holding company was seen as having created "a more perfect order of absenteeism," with "effectual control and management . . . passed into the hands of a relatively smaller minority of the ultimate owners," with the ordinary shareholder left with "a correspondingly slighter chance of personally influencing any action taken by management." Veblen was also impressed by Morgan's financiering of mergers and holding companies and the general growth of investment banker influence in the 1890s, which provided "the means by which the needful running collusion in the further conduct of the business was to be enforced and regulated."[30]

In the 1920s there was a great increase in the number of shareholders and a further diffusion of stock ownership.[31] In addition, there were innovative developments in the use of nonvoting, fractional-voting, and multiple-voting stocks, and the pyramiding of intercorporate holdings to facilitate insider control, thus supplementing the advantages of top management position with various types of legal disenfranchisement of the general run of preferred and common stockholders.[32] These developments were observed and debated at the time, and many of them were discussed with sophistication in William Z. Ripley's *Main Street and Wall Street.* With reference to the phenomenon of separation of management from ownership, Ripley said:

> What an amazing tangle this makes of the theory that ownership of property and responsibility for its efficient, farsighted, and public-spirited management shall be linked the one to the other. Even the whole theory of business profits, so painstakingly evolved through years of academic ratiocination, goes by the board. All the managers, that is to say the operating men, are working on salary, their returns, except on the side, being largely independent of the net result of company operation year by year. The motive of self-interest may even have been thrown into the reverse, occasionally, so far as long-time upbuilding in contradistinction to quick turnover in corporate affairs is concerned.[33]

J. M. Keynes also wrote with insight and prescience on these issues in the 1920s, pointing to the "tendency of big business to socialize itself," with shareholders "almost totally dissociated from the management" and managements more concerned with "the general stability and reputation of the institution" than with any maximizing of owner profits. "The shareholders must be satisfied by conventionally adequate dividends, but once this is secured, the direct interest of the management often consists in avoiding criticism . . ."[34] He saw the large organization as vulnerable to external attacks because of its great size and semimonopolistic position. Thus Keynes gives the rudiments of a theory of meeting minimum profit standards ("satisficing" in contemporary jargon) and the basis for a doctrine of corporate responsibility. He even saw that "the same causes promote conservatism and a waning of enterprise," with a "natural line of evolution" from a bureaucratized capitalism to state socialism. "The battle of Socialism against unlimited private profit is being won in detail hour by hour."[35] Keynes's insights on the impact of the rise of the large corporation follow a long British tradition that goes back at least as far as Adam Smith, who wrote with vehemence on the abusive tendencies of joint stock companies and their inability to compete against "private adventurers" (i.e., smaller, owner-dominated companies) in the absence of grants of exclusive privilege.[36]

The triumph of managerialism

Although subject to a great deal of criticism from 1932 up to the present on the score of method, inferences, and policy conclusions, the central theme of *The Modern Corporation and Private Property* – that ownership and control in the large corporation have been separated, with effective discretionary power in the hands of the active management rather than stockholders – has become part of the conventional wisdom, accepted by conservatives like H. G. Manne, liberals like R. A. Gordon and J. K. Galbraith, and even Marxists like Paul A. Baran and Paul M. Sweezy.[37]

The management control premise, referred to here as *managerialism,* has spawned a wide array of hypotheses, most of them focusing on managerial objectives, behavior constraints, and performance. If managers have discretion, to what ends will they use it? Insofar as managers are free of owner constraints, and assuming that they are "economic men" trying to maximize their own net advantages, we have the basis for a theory of "expense preference" or constrained expense maximization (expenses including managerial salaries, staff, and amenities).[38] Other hypotheses focus on size or growth in size as corporate objectives best meeting managerial preferences.[39] Another major line of departure from the traditional assumption of profit maximization – that of the behaviorist school of Simon, Cyert, and March – uses a managerialist premise in its theories on how organization affects business objectives and behavior. According to these analysts, firms tend to seek satisfactory rather than maximum profits, and they adapt to the pressures of environmental opportunities and threats (rather than engaging in a profit search of great and unchanging intensity). It is not clear that a high degree of separation of ownership and control, as opposed to mere large size and structural complexity, is required for the behaviorist theories, but separation fits nicely into the downgrading of the profit motive as the preeminent corporate objective.

It is also evident that the varying objectives of a managerial group could influence business performance – that is, affect prices, outputs, profits, expense ratios, payout ratios, growth rates, and the willingness to take risks and innovate – in ways that might be at the expense of some or all of the owners of the companies. A large, and inconclusive, literature has arisen on this matter.[40] Similarly, the policy implications of these various conjectures and revisions have also been left quite vague. Those who claim to have established a case for departures from classic profit mazimization have made little effort to assess the direction or magnitude of the social costs involved in these tendencies, if any, or their impact on the main drift of the corporate system as a whole, let alone appropriate policy responses.[41]

The triumph of managerialism has also led to a process of reconciliation between it and older doctrines in conflict with or threatened by the newly established truths. For example, the discretion of management and the possibility of nonprofit-maximizing behavior call into question the efficient properties of a free market in a system of managerial enterprise. The response of some devotees of the free market has been an outright denial of the validity of the managerial hypothesis.[42] But others have integrated it nicely into free enterprise logic via the theory of takeovers and the "market for corporate control" – inefficient managers, if not responsible to, and subject to displacement by, owners directly, can be removed by stockholders' acceptance of takeover bids induced by poor performance and a consequent reduction in stock value.[43] Here, reconciliation is achieved by showing that the scope of market discipline is wider than had been previously recognized. This same gap has been bridged in official corporate pronouncements, and in some academic analyses, by a theory of an evolving recognition of corporate social responsibility and trusteeship.[44] Here, the market mechanism is conceded to be deficient, but its defects are remedied over time by a nonmarket system of managerial noblesse oblige, conscience, intelligent self-interest, and outside pressures. Other less sanguine liberal analysts have denounced the system of noblesse oblige both as inadequate and a public relations cover for business opposition to needed government intervention, and some of them have used managerialism to build a case for changes in corporate structure and rules of governance and positive government actions to bridge a widening gap between private power and the public interest.[45]

For Marxists, and others on the left, managerialism posed the problem of how to reconcile management control with the class character of capitalism and capitalist control of the economic process. The concept of managers as "a purely neutral technocracy"[46] suggested that a new leadership had emerged, separate from capital and the owning class, that might rise above class conflict and direct capitalism from a disinterested trustee perspective. This implication led to the vehement rejection of managerialism by many Marxists. For others reconciliation was achieved by a denial of the "neutral technocracy" idea and a focus on the ownership and other linkages that make the managerial elite merely "the leading echelon of the property owning class."[47] In a sense, this is a rejection of separation rather than a reconciliation, as ownership interests still dominate a control group that represents ownership and controls only within a narrow range of profit-oriented choices. On this point there is a fusion of ideas between left and right, with Milton Friedman also contending that formal separation has not altered the fundamental orientation of management in the owners' interests.[48]

Whereas some observers accepted managerialism and tried to work it into existing frameworks, others responded with attacks on its assumptions, facts, and inferences. Most of these attacks have had little effect on the institutionalization of the major managerial premise, but some have raised important questions about the meaning and significance of the managerial triumph. From the very first, the Berle and Means measures of the 200 largest nonfinancial corporations were subject to criticism. Their universe included regulated as well as unregulated firms – that is, firms whose power was already circumscribed by government control, along with those not so controlled. The regulated sector (telephone companies, electric and gas utilities, railroads) is capital intensive, so that an asset-based computation tends to exaggerate the importance of the controlled sector. The controlled sector also tends to be more concentrated as well as more limited in freedom of action, containing as it does a number of "natural monopolies." In an early criticism of Berle and Means, William Leonard Crum pointed out that public utility, railroad, and traction companies accounted for five-eighths of the Berle and Means total; he also noted that, taking industrial assets alone, only 30 percent of the relevant assets were controlled by the 106 largest industrials, whereas 49 percent of nonfinancial assets were controlled by Berle and Means's 200 largest.[49] Thus the biases inherent in the Berle and Means selection were questioned early and continue to be at issue.

Another continuing thread of criticism has revolved around the meaning and significance of any measure of "aggregate concentration," a concept popularized by Berle and Means. The proportion of assets and net income controlled by the 200 largest nonfinancials is an index of overall, not market, concentration. Traditionally, the focus of economists has been on "market concentration," and many have been dubious of aggregate concentration as a meaningful rubric of analysis. Rejection of the usefulness of aggregate concentration, and even market concentration, and counterfactual studies of trends in both overall and market concentration have been important features of the conservative response to Berle and Means.[50] Many things can be happening *within* a global aggregate, even a narrower aggregate, such as all manufacturing industry (which has been the basis for a number of studies of miniaggregate concentration trends). On the other hand, it is difficult to avoid the suspicion that an upward trend in the absolute, and especially the relative, importance of large units is devoid of economic or social significance.

An important left-oriented school of criticism, which has ebbed and flowed since 1932, has argued that managerial analyses have underestimated ownership and family control and overrated management control. This line of criticism was given powerful impetus by the Temporary National Economic Committee Monograph No. 29, *The Distribution of Ownership in the 200 Largest Nonfinancial Corporations,* prepared by the Securities and Exchange Commission (SEC) under the direction of Raymond W. Goldsmith and Rexford C. Parmelee, and published in 1940. This invaluable study is the only one ever produced in which Congress used its powers to gather extensive ownership data from a wide spectrum of large corporations. Based on fairly full information on the 20 largest holders of each of the 200 largest companies, with a detailed look behind record ownership to beneficial interests, and with a major effort to connect family and other interest group linkages, Monograph No. 29 found ownership and family control substantially more important than did Berle and Means. The latter found only 34 percent of the 200 largest to be subject to owner/family control. Monograph No. 29 showed 46 percent of the largest firms to be owner/family controlled, although many of these owners turned out to be other corporations.[51] More recently, Philip H. Burch, Jr. effectively attacked the original Berle and Means data and came up with his own finding that owner and family control, although subject to a historical downtrend, is far more important than Berle and Means realized. Using a 450-firm sample, Burch found management control and family control at an approximate standoff in numbers – 41 percent management, 42 percent family, 17 percent uncertain.[52] Burch was not talking about the largest 200, however, and his own definitions and methods are not beyond criticism.[53]

Another major basis of continuing criticism of managerial analyses has been an alleged neglect of the power of financial institutions as centralizing control vehicles. As Crum observed in 1934, "Full examination of the degree of concentration of economic power, would by all means cover the relation of financial institutions – incorporated or otherwise – to non-financial units."[54] In the Berle and Means study, financial control was obscured by their use of the category "control by means of a legal device" (a technique frequently employed by financial interests in the late 1920s), and they gave little attention to nonownership bases of financial control, such as creditor status. Monograph No. 29 also confined itself to ownership facts (including owner participation in management), noting that "no account, however, will be taken in this chapter of control by bankers or control of officers and directors if it is not also reflected in stock ownership."[55]

The concept of financial control, in fairly refined form, dates back at least to the Pujo Committee report (1913) of the Morgan–Baker era, Louis D. Brandeis's *Other People's Money, and How the Bankers Use It* (1914), Rudolf Hilferding's *Das Finanzkapital* (1910), and Lenin's *Imperialism* (1916).[56] The 1939 National

Resources Committee study, *The Structure of the American Economy, Part I, Basic Characteristics*[57] added 50 financial institutions to Berle and Means's 200 largest nonfinancial corporations and dealt at length with interlocking directorates and interest groups. Appendix 13 of the 1939 study described 13 interest group systems, several centering in investment and commercial banks. More recently, the Patman Report of 1968, entitled *Commercial Banks and Their Trust Activities: Emerging Influence on the American Economy,*[58] gave further impetus to the stress on the importance of financial institutions in corporate control, showing the extensiveness of large holdings of corporate stock by bank trust departments.

Corporate control: overview and prospectus

Despite the persistence of these various lines of criticism of managerialism, its position has strengthened over time, and, at this juncture, its triumph is virtually complete. That top managers generally control large corporations is an established truth, which serves as a premise – not as something to be proved – in most serious analyses in the field of industrial organization and policy. Among the explanations for this triumph, the most important is surely that enhanced managerial discretion and power are a reality. There is, however, an ambiguity in the managerialist premise, which tells us that management *controls,* but leaves open the question of the *determinants* of and the *limits* to managerial authority. The premise is thus sufficiently elastic to accommodate a range of possibilities, extending from unrestricted management discretion to levels of constraint that raise questions about the extent and even the reality of management control. This vagueness traces back to the original Berle and Means formulation, which was very sketchy on managerial interests and, especially, on managerial power. Their managers either controlled or did not control; any gradations or limits were pretty much ignored. It was from this simple dichotomy that Berle and Means arrived at their notion that the controlling managers might eventually serve as neutral technocrats. Unrestricted management control was also implicit in James Burnham's fuzzy vision of a "managerial revolution."[59] Managerialism, however, is a broad concept in which these theories of managers as autonomous technocrats are only special cases. The managerialist perspective developed in this book, for example, which incorporates a number of internal and external constraints, finds managers to be a far cry from neutral technocrats.

The analysis here concludes, in fact, that the profit motive has suffered no discernible eclipse as a result of the rise of management control.

In developing this argument in the chapters that follow, I begin with a discussion of the concepts of control and strategic position and put forward a theory of control based on the importance of strategic position. I show how this theory fits in with the role of the board of directors as it has evolved in the United States (Chapter 2). This theory of control is amplified in Chapter 3, which describes the decline in ownership control and factors underlying that decline, but which treats at length the ways in which ownership persists as a powerful influence and constraint on managerial ends and behavior. This line of argument is supplemented with a discussion of the internal structural changes and rules of behavior that developed out of a search for order and rationality in these sprawling giants – arrangements that preserve and reinforce a profitability goal. Chapter 3 also provides a classification and description of the control status of the large corporation as it has evolved from 1900 to the mid-1970s.

Having developed a theory of constrained managerial control of the large corporation in Chapters 2 and 3, in the succeeding chapters I turn to a closer examination of sources of potential influence or control that are external to the firm – mainly financial institutions and government. Chapter 4 analyzes lender and institutional investor influence, describing in detail the reasons for the decline in financial control over the large firm during the past 70 to 80 years. Financial power is shown to be real, but exercised as a constraint and an ideological influence rather than by direct control over the large corporation. In Chapter 5, the role of the government is examined, as both a participant in the world of large firms and a regulator. The government's position as a member of the universe of large firms is shown to be extremely modest. More surprising – and more controversial – its role as a regulator is found to be overrated, at least as regards scope and impact on business decision making. Large firms subject to extensive regulation by commission have declined in relative importance over the past half century (particularly, the railroads), with a resultant decline in the proportion of large firms directly regulated by government. The new social regulation has clearly expanded in scope and is often not trivial in effect, but in a number of areas the government agencies responsible for enforcement have been underfunded and ineffectual, and overall they are most properly regarded as providing a slowly expanding set of constraints on key corporate decisions, which are still made with great freedom of maneuver.

In Chapter 6, I turn from the external threats to managerial autonomy (banks and governments)[60] to the looser ties and bases of coordination among large firms and to the broader question of centralization of corporate control and power. I treat briefly the changes in aggregate concentration and large-firm market control – concluding that both have increased somewhat in recent decades over substantial levels in the past. The chapter examines mainly the various forms of ownership, business, and personal linkages among large firms, their changes over time, their strength, and the extent to which these ties are likely to affect the autonomy and behavior of large corporations. The primary conclusion from this inquiry – very tentative, given the great complexity of the subject – is that large firms in the United States are probably, on average, as independent of outside domination now as 80 years ago. Strong and tightly knit interest groups effectively integrating large firms have declined in importance; and although the large number of ties that are shown to link together large firms (including financial institutions) are a factor serving to mitigate competition, such ties are only one factor in a complex setting.

In the final chapter an attempt is made to apply the earlier analysis of corporate control, objectives, and power to contemporary problems and proposed avenues of change. I discuss in detail the prospects of change through voluntary managerial assumption of larger social responsibilities, through external pressures on corporations by interested individuals and community or public interest groups, and through improved disclosure and changes in the composition and duties of boards of directors. These are all shown to be extremely feeble mechanisms for bringing about change in the short run, with long-run effects that are highly uncertain. It is argued here that more significant change might follow from a turn toward public ownership (rather than regulation), which, by enlarging the role of government as a producer, would reduce business leverage. But the evolution of the corporate order in the United States and the structure of interests and power that it has produced have muted pressures for public ownership while furthering the drift toward centralization. The conclusion stresses the immobility of this corporate order in the face of escalating social and economic problems and presents some plausible scenarios for the next decade or so.

2

Control and Strategic Position

The basis of management control is strategic position, and the essence of a managerial theory of control must be an explanation of how strategic position conveys power, how management comes to command it, and why its importance has grown over time. By *strategic position* I mean a role and status in an organization – usually associated with high executive office, a directorship, and high official committee positions in the bureaucratic structure – that enable their possessors to participate in the making of key decisions. In the first part of this chapter I examine the concept of control and the problems of applying it to the large corporation. In the section that follows the focus is on how strategic position is attained, why it gravitates into the hands of an inside management group as concentrated entrepreneurial ownership positions gradually shrink, and why and how strategic position provides a basis of power and control. Attention is next directed to the board of directors – the immediate and legal locus of control – to see how this important institution fits into the control puzzle. A further section is devoted to an examination of the interplay between board and management power and the stability of corporate control when strategic position is its prime basis.

The concept of control

Control Versus Constraint

Control is a term used in many disciplines as well as in common parlance. It relates to power – the capacity to initiate, constrain, circumscribe, or terminate action, either directly or by influence exercised on those with immediate decision-making authority. The concept is elusive in the social sciences because power is elusive. In the giant corporation the number of actions over which power can be exercised is great and the number of potential influences on those actions is also very large. There is no one locus of power, and the power loci vary in importance by type of action.[1]

Many decisions within a large organization are influenced, often decisively, by its own internally dictated set of drives, momenta, and constraints in some sort of dynamic equilibrium.[2] Bureaucratic organization and decentralization of decision making, if not extremely well controlled from the top, may also allow the emergence of subgoals within departments and divisions that protect and enlarge their interests at the expense of overall organization goals.[3] What appear to be decisions by top officers and the board alone may be dictated by pressures from below, and the failure of corporate leaders to take some particular action may be based on a recognition of negative responses from within the organization that would have made otherwise sensible actions unfeasible.[4]

Similarly, external factors affect the making of important corporate decisions. Unions bargain on wages and working conditions, and their presence, strength, and negotiating position and terms can have profound effects on a variety of corporate decisions (including investment and divestment in particular locations).[5] Various levels of government tax, subsidize, restrict, and control business, in some cases impinging directly on matters as basic as pricing (rate regulation, informal interventions into price setting) and the direction of investment (zoning, required pollution control devices, limits on acquisitions). Community pressures arising out of the interests of parents, environmentalists, and other consumer and public interest organizations, affect business directly and through induced or threatened governmental actions. The large corporation also interacts extensively with other business firms that lend it money, sell its securities, buy its goods, supply it with raw materials, and join with it or its officials in political and social activities. External corporate interests predominate as outside representatives on boards of directors. They are "coopted" to some degree by the relationship, but obtain power in exchange. The discretion of the insiders of a corporation is constrained to a greater or lesser degree by these external interests that are linked with the organization.[6]

The assumption made here is that the more remote and relatively fixed background constraints can be reasonably ignored in trying to identify the control of a large corporation. That is, the corporation and its control can be analyzed in a useful first approximation as a "closed system."[7] This still leaves open serious problems concerning the weight to be given potential decision makers and constraining elements that are not very remote, such as the managers of subdivisions within the larger entity or bankers lending money under restrictive convenants and serving on the board or large owners hovering in the background.

In these large complex organizations the highest echelon of leaders frequently farms out to its various operating units considerable administrative and operational discretion. But the top management almost always retains and normally exercises final authority over long-term strategic planning: capital allocations among various corporate activities; major geographic and product moves; and decisions on top personnel hirings, firings, and promotions.[8] In a great many cases the installation of a new top management is followed by substantial changes – firings, functional and divisional realignments, lopping off of divisions and subsidiaries, undertaking new domestic and overseas ventures, a policy of systematic acquisitions. In short, whatever the constraints on the corporate leadership by outsiders and the internal interest groups within the organization itself, the leadership can usually make significant moves that will affect internal discipline, morale, objectives, and material direction and well-being.

A distinction will be made in this study between literal control and the exercise of a constraining influence, although the line between the two is narrow and somewhat arbitrary. *Literal control* as used here means the power to make the key decisions of a company, which include choices of products, major markets, volume and direction of investment, larger commercial and political strategies, and selection of top personnel. The *power to constrain* is used to mean the power to limit certain decision choices, as in a ceiling on dollars that may be spent on new facilities or paid out in dividends, or a power of veto over personnel choices. The two terms are not mutually exclusive as defined here. A constraint is a form of control even if only negative in exercise, as it shapes the decisions made by limiting the scope of choice. In many cases the power of veto is accompanied by the power to consult and a positive say in what is to be done. A constraint also merges into control when it extends to the power to displace the active management. But constraints usually involve power over only one or a narrow range of corporate activities, so that they amount to partial control rather than control over the entire spectrum of major decisions. The frequent pattern in the large corporation is for power over a wide range of decisions to be held by a dominant insider coalition, subject to constraints or partial control by others in some decision areas (e.g., bankers in regard to volume of borrowing and perhaps investment).

There are also important constraints on managers that arise out of the profit, risk-taking, and growth expectations of the board members, large owners, financial community, and working members of the organization itself – expectations that may be formalized into rules and plans, and internalized in managerial objectives and understandings. It may be argued that if the system of constraints forces managers to choose policies within a narrow range of profit opportunities compatible with stockholders or creditor interests, the constraints may be as, or more, important than the specific discretionary choices of managers in determining corporate objectives and actions. If these constraints grow, the discretion of control groups could actually shrink over time. It is one of the main themes of this book that the managerial revolution has been one of increasing, but sharply constrained, management control, with the controlling managers operating within behavior boundaries that have not widened over time.

Active Versus Latent Power

Closely paralleling the distinction between control and constraint is that between active and latent power. With control by owner/managers (Ford Motor Company before 1979) or by a nonowner management (American Telephone and Telegraph Company) *active* power and control are merged; but where some power is still held by large owners who are no longer part of the working management, or by financial interests that promoted the company, the extent of decision-making power retained by the nonmanagement groups becomes harder to assess. It is possible that they still make the decisions directly or select the top managers and then instruct them and monitor their actions closely, but more often their power is less directly maintained; they recede farther into the background, sometimes only to intervene when something goes seriously astray. Their power is then *latent,* but it may still be effective as a constraint. There are many stages between the extremes of active direction from behind the scenes and withdrawal into a latent and constraining role. The exact state of affairs is often hard to determine, as it may not be put to the test over a long period during which the power structure is evolving in sometimes subtle ways. The problematic cases are frequently those of declining family/owner power, where the family's stockholdings and influence on the board are dwindling and the strength of the active top insiders is growing. The residual, latent power of the family/owner may depend on circumstances, and even in times of transition is sometimes elusive.

In the case of Allied Chemical, for example, the Solvay group of Belgium has had a large minority interest for many years (20.3 percent in 1937, 9.7 percent in 1979), but it has usually had only one indirect representative on the board, and no overt control, despite both this large holding and the absence of any comparably large minority blocks in other hands. Nevertheless, in 1967, after a period of declining earnings, Jacques Solvay requested and obtained a seat on the board, and shortly thereafter a new top management group was installed with John Connor brought in as chief executive officer (CEO).

This would appear to be impressive evidence of Solvay latent power and ability to control, but the impression would be somewhat misleading. The management displacement occurred at a time of serious company malaise, so that the latent power exercised then might not have been decisive under different company circumstances. And Solvay did not act alone in the 1967 turnover; other powerful forces were at work. In fact, the Meyer and Nichols family interests were long predominant in the power alignments of Allied Chemical,[9] despite smaller stockholdings than Solvay, and both were still directly represented on the Allied Chemical board in 1967. Their power came from early strategic position, personal – as opposed to Solvay's represented – presence on the board, and some Solvay reticence based on antitrust and foreign status complications.

The business success of Allied Chemical under Connor, between 1967 and 1978, almost surely reduced the latent power of the Solvay interests relative to the inside management group and strong board. An interesting aside on the Solvay role was the 1977 contingent agreement by Solvay to sell its entire holding in Allied Chemical to Textron, represented on the Allied Chemical board at that time by G. William Miller, then CEO of Textron. The reason for this offer was reportedly to provide funds for a contemplated expansion of Solvay facilities in the United States. Despite joint ventures and other business relationships with Allied, plus its formidable holding of Allied stock, it is evident that Solvay did not regard Allied Chemical as a controlled arm capable of meeting Solvay's needs in the United States.

In the case of S. S. Kresge, as another example, the Kresge family owned 37 percent of the company's stock in 1964 and occupied several top managerial posts. In 1975 only Stanley Kresge, a non-officer, remained on the board of 17 as a family representative, and his personal holdings amounted to only 855,672 shares (0.7 percent of an outstanding total of 120,238,158). The Kresge Foundation, probably still under Kresge control, had almost 10 million shares in early 1975, so that the Kresge family was still in a position to vote at least 9.7 percent of the company's stock. S. S. Kresge had grown into a major retail force only since 1962, under the direction of very successful hired managers. The enormous expansion of Kresge greatly increased the stock outstanding and reduced the relative holdings of the Kresges. The success of these hired managers tended to consolidate their power over the corporation. In a symbolic episode occurring at the 1977 annual meeting of S. S. Kresge, the management proposed and won a vote for changing the company's name from S. S. Kresge to K Mart. This move was commented upon at the meeting by Stanley Kresge, speaking from the floor as a now retired director. He was not happy with the change but would not oppose it.

Latent power may also rest with banks and other institutional investors, based on stockholdings, credit extensions, loan agreements, indentures, influence over the availability of future credit, and so forth. The power of these important outsiders is likely to depend not only on past business and personal connections but also on the magnitude of capital demands imposed by technology, marketing costs, growth plans, and growth rate of the company and industry.[10] The financial well-being of the company in question has always been another critical factor, with external power increasing as the company approaches credit limits and violations of loan agreement terms. As noted earlier, lender power is often negative in character, derived in part from lender rights under credit agreements, in part from management's unwillingness to proceed on programs looked upon with disfavor by institutions whose goodwill is important. This veto power usually applies only to certain spheres of company activity (forms and quantity of borrowing, dividend payout rates, sale of underlying assets), although there is great variation running from negligible creditor power to the power to displace the active management. For very large corporations, creditor and other institutional investor power is usually latent rather than active, part of a system of constraints, and, at the same time, part of a system of interlocking power that is more often supportive than threatening to dominant management groups.

Shareholders in general can be said to have some sort of latent power over large corporations, but the diffusion of ownership is such that ordinary stockholders do not directly threaten management displacement. Important differences among owners in wealth, tax factors, investment objectives, attitudes toward dividend payout rates, and desired degree of risk in investment undertakings further weaken the power of ordinary investors. Their latent power, therefore, constitutes a background constraint that is of concern to the control group in that disenchanted owners will contribute to depressed stock prices, will welcome tender offers, and may possibly harass the management in other ways.[11] The potential for loss of control through tender offers and disclosure and public relations concerns have increased management sensitivities to the latent threat of ordinary shareholders.

The board of directors "controls" the corporation in a formal legal sense, because the bylaws give it the power to make key decisions by majority vote. But, as discussed more fully later in this chapter, top inside managers normally dominate the board selection *and* decision-making processes and the board and outside directors are best viewed as having various degrees of latent power. Outsiders on the board normally defer to and support the top inside managers, but they do have legal responsibilities to the company's owners and often represent outside interests of great power. Under some circumstances, therefore, top management nonperformance, malfeasance, or disarray activates the outsiders and induces them to exercise their legal powers.

Those possessing latent power share it with those who have active power, which is exercisable within limits, under constraints, and on a contingent basis. Shared power is the general case in complex organizations, because a wide spectrum of interest groups invariably impinge on the decision-making process. In a sense, therefore, "a complex decision is like a great river, drawing from its many tributaries the innumerable component premises of which it is constituted."[12] Its "tributaries" include owner and creditor expectations and rights, government rules, and organizational pressures and imperatives. Nonetheless, virtually all the major corporate decisions are shared in or finally decided upon by a small group of high-level leaders of the organization, whereas outsiders with influence usually exercise it in a much narrower sphere.

The Mechanisms Versus the Locus of Control

There are two related but different aspects of control: *how* control is maintained (the mechanics or instruments of control)[13] and *who* controls (i.e., the distribution of power between owners, managers, banks, etc.). Ownership is often both a mechanism of control and the locus of control; but in the numerous and important cases where minority ownership concentrations run from 1 to 15 percent, the overlapping of how and who becomes less assured. As a mechanism whereby control is achieved and maintained, a 5 to 6 percent holding may or may not be relevant, depending on circumstances. Somebody may own 6 percent of a company's voting shares and have no power whatsoever in its affairs, as in the case of Richard Gruner's purchase of 5.6 percent of the voting shares of American Airlines in the early 1970s or of a great many holdings of comparable size by institutional investors. If, on the other hand, a control group holds 6 percent of the stock of a company but would easily control by strategic position with no stock ownership whatsoever, the 6 percent holding is not the *means* of control. Of course, one of the claims for the significance of the rise of managerial control is that the control groups tend to have no important ownership stake in their companies and 6 percent of the stock is a substantial interest in absolute terms, even if proportionately small (and possibly irrelevant as a mechanism of control). In large companies even small fractions of stock are quite important in magnitude of dollar investment – Armand Hammer, with only 1.8 percent of the stock of Occidental Petroleum and John Kendall with 2.8 percent of Colgate-Palmolive had investments valued at $13 million and $44.3 million, respectively, at the low market levels of December 1974. It is possible to have a large stake without that stake being especially important in explaining how control was established and how it is maintained.

The failure to separate how control is maintained and who controls has probably led to an overrating of ownership as a mechanism of control, but it may well have caused an undervaluation of the importance of the ownership stake of control groups and of ownership as a constraint factor.

It is a fallacy, sometimes put forward by those anxious to establish the continued importance of ownership as a vehicle of control, that the diffusion of ownership eventually makes possible the control of large corporations with very small stockholdings, say, 1 to 5 percent. This represents a confusion between *who* controls and *how* control is obtained and maintained. There is no case known to this author where the acquisition of 1 to 5 percent of the stock of a large corporation by an outsider gave the purchaser control; from this I infer that without initial strategic position, 1 to 5 percent has little bearing on control. It also suggests that if persons who do control have 1 to 5 percent, it is not the stock that is critical to their control position; at best it strengthens strategic position.

The identification of control *groups,* that is, cases where separate blocks of stock should be considered to be unified from the standpoint of their impact on control, also presents problems. In a sense, all owners of a given company have a unified interest – which may be even more valid and pertinent for all *small* holders of common stock – but the small, absolute and relative size of their holdings, their impersonal and distant relationship to the organization, and the high cost of obtaining detailed knowledge about a company and communication among numerous stockholders normally limit the cohesion and power of ordinary owners. At the other extreme is a set of owners such as the five individual directors of Weyerhaeuser who each controlled 500,000 or more shares in the late 1970s (although with holdings still totaling only a little over 5 percent of the outstanding). These investors are knowledgeable, in close communication with one another, and interested in corporate affairs because of the size of their holdings and their active involvement. There is, therefore, a potential unity among this group, although it is obvious that there also could be conflict. But a primary basis of unification for the formation of meaningful control groups is organizational role and shared power.

Contemporary debate over the existence of group power commonly focuses on large owners with both substantial interests and the capacity to communicate with one another, but with no apparent organizational role, a frequent large number and diversity of such interests, and relationships with both other owners and the managements of the companies owned. The large institutional investors are the most important of such owners. Do ten bank trust departments, five insurance companies, and five mutual funds, together owning 35 percent of the stock of a large corporation, constitute a "group" from the standpoint of cohesiveness bearing on control? Two criteria are used in this study: (1) Do these institutions use their voting powers, directly or by threat, in a collective manner, designed to influence the selection of boards of directors? (2) Does their use or threat of use of the power to buy and sell stock on a collective basis (whether tacit or explicit) allow them to exercise a decisive or substantial influence over corporate decision making? The answer to the first question, on voting power, is a clear negative; the answer to the second is that groups of owning institutions rarely work together to discipline managements, but they do think alike and emulate one another and their behavior does exercise a real influence. But this form of influence is more accurately described as a form of constraint than control.

Strategic position as the basis of control

In cases where companies are closely held or subject to majority ownership control, the dominant owners occupy the top offices themselves, or they select (and can readily displace) those who do – with the result that strategic position, in the form of occupancy of high office, is not a significant source of independent power. But with diffused ownership in large companies, occupancy of the top positions becomes an independent source of power that can be built up by deliberate strategies and passed on to successors. As noted earlier, strategic position as a basis of power is at the heart of managerialist theories; how strategic positions are attained and the reasons for their importance as a power base are considered in the balance of this section.

Strategic position typically has been attained by one of the following routes: (1) initial possession of a large stock ownership position or a major stock acquisition; (2) a role in organization and promotion (sometimes associated with the acquisition of significant stockholdings);[14] (3) management changes or more far-reaching reorganizations following serious financial difficulties; and (4) the gradual accretion of power from within the organization.

The numerous railroad and other business failures in the depression of the 1890s and the combination movement around the turn of the century and in the 1920s greatly increased the importance and strategic position of promoters and bankers. But these original positions of power eroded fairly rapidly as hired managers struggled for, and obtained, substantial autonomy for the organization and its active management. Because the largest corporations normally have not been dependent on individual commercial and investment banks for corporate necessities, the preservation of control positions by promoters or bankers would have had to rest on an aggressive monopolization of high office by themselves or through reliable dependents. But the domination of high office by bankers is not conducive to business efficiency, and "reliable" dependents may cease to be so in a newly established organization where their functional interests diverge from those of outsiders. Furthermore, in contrast with Germany and Japan, banker control has always been suspect in the United States and subject to periodic waves of adverse publicity and government-imposed limits that have made the preservation of strategic position by bankers more difficult; the appearance of autonomy has been obligatory, and without any permanent basis of real control; this has contributed to the emergence of genuine autonomy.

Although more durable than banker control, direct ownership control has also tended to decline, partly because of an attrition of entrepreneurial stock positions under conditions of rapid growth,[15] and also because entrepreneurial skill often does not extend to the second and third generation (or, even if it does, is unlikely to be the best obtainable)[16] and strategic position is relinquished in the interest of higher profits through more effective management. In the Kresge case, for example, it was the hired managers that brought the firm from modest affluence to preeminence in prestige and profits. Thus top-level positions are gradually occupied by hired managers, even in cases of dominant (if declining) ownership. Over time, and with corporate success and substantial growth, significant power gravitates into the hands of the hired managers. The normal, but not uniform, trend is for the "hired managers" eventually to be hiring themselves, at which point *cooptation* rather than *hiring* becomes the relevant concept.

Ownership has been and remains an important basis for obtaining strategic position; it has a solidity as a power base beyond that available to the promoter and banker, assuming retention of a large proportionate interest. Stock-based power and strategic position reinforce each other. But with the rapid growth in corporate size, the sales of new issues in the public market, and the divestment of stock by the former dominant owners, the retention of control by the former owner group will depend increasingly on the power derived from strategic position – occupational role and status – rather than on ownership.

In the case of Federated Department Stores, for example, the relatively large Lazarus family holdings had fallen to 0.8 percent of the outstanding by 1980, but there was little question that Ralph Lazarus was the key decision maker and final authority. His power, which had arisen out of significant family ownership plus occupancy of many key positions, now rested almost entirely on strategic position. Somebody from the outside buying 384,375 shares (0.8 percent) of Federated *might* be able to get a representative on the board of directors but certainly would not be able to gain control. It was recognized in the organization that Ralph Lazarus's retirement would rapidly transform Federated from the last stages of family control to one more case of management control. This would not be so if the Lazarus stock ownership rather than the family's strategic position were critical to control.

The strategic position and power of the management (the top full-time officers of the organization, some of whom are usually on the board of directors) stem in large part from its authority and dominance over day-to-day operations, the disposition of company resources, and the planning and long-term decisions of the company. The top officers and their employee subordinates devote full time to doing the business of the company, assessing its problems and prospects, and making and implementing plans for its improvement. By virtue of this concentrated effort and presence, they have special command over the technical details essential to an intelligent consideration of company problems.[17] They also must of necessity make a great many immediate decisions that require experience, knowledge, and on-the-spot presence. Most of the specific decisions involved in day-to-day operations are made by middle managers, but those at the top call the tune, set the parameters within which choices are made, and make some of the important specific decisions (including the compensation, promotion, and ouster of those below them in the managerial hierarchy). These are the built-in advantages of top management that give it a structure of dependencies both within the organization and outside (customers and suppliers), and thus give it power. This power extends to the board selection process and board decisionmaking (described more fully in the next section). Domination of the board and proxy machinery of the corporation is the link between the de facto power of the managerial leadership and the legal but nominal power of the diffused ownership.

If the company is doing well, employee morale is high, and the various cogs in the large machine are geared together in working order, then the power of the management is further enhanced, because interference with or displacement of the top management would involve a serious loss of efficiency and profits. Interests potentially capable of ousting a management, such as large stockholders and lenders, would find it difficult to convince others of the need to replace management under such circumstances and would be threatening their own economic interests by disturbing a favorable set of arrangements.[18] Business success, therefore, enlarges managerial freedom of action.

Conversely, economic difficulties weaken the position of management by increasing the dissatisfaction of and reducing the costs of displacement by groups and individuals with latent power in the organization. Even in this case, however, managerial control over the flow of information to outside directors and outside financial interests, its influence over board members derived from personal or business relationships, and fears of disruption and open conflict frequently allow managerial survival and continued domination of the succession process under conditions of proven managerial ineptitude.[19]

An important underpinning of any theory of control and its evolution must be the recognition that control is valuable and will be sought and consolidated by those capable of gaining and preserving it. As noted, an exception is that control may be relinquished by entrepreneurial families as a result of a quest for higher profits through superior management. Banker/promoters tend to suffer displacement because of managerial advantages in strategic position and an absence of compelling banker leverage or interest. The top management seeks to enlarge its control in the interest of unobstructed ability to carry out its plans, job security, and other personal and psychological advantages of uncontested power. An obvious threat to secure management control would be a truly independent and strong board of directors. Rational behavior by an inside management group, desirous of maintaining control, therefore, should be to see to it that the complexion of the board becomes friendly and compliant. This is not always possible, or even thought necessary by self-confident insiders, but the mechanics and traditions of board selection processes and practices make a compliant and management-supportive board a dominant tendency in the large corporation of the United States.

I turn now to the question of the role of the board and show how its legal control of corporate policy is reconcilable with de facto dominance by corporate insiders.

The board of directors

Because the legal power to control corporate affairs rests with the board of directors (and ultimately the stockholders),[20] analysis of the dynamics of the board must be a linchpin of any analysis of corporate control. This is especially true in an era of apparently dwindling ownership power, when definitive ownership command over a majority of the board is usually absent and the locus of power is subject to a potentially more complicated set of determinants.[21] The subject is especially important because a great many reform proposals rest on theories of board control and adaptability that may not be realistic.

The role of the board need not be static or uniform, of course, and changes in ownership dispersion and power, in corporate size and diversity, and in the external problems faced by the corporation might plausibly be expected to produce both a change in board character and function and considerable variety among boards. The past decade has seen turmoil in many boardrooms, with scandals that have resulted in adverse publicity, lawsuits and enhanced threat of legal liability for board laxity, pressures for broadening board representation, and antitrust challenges to interlocking directorates. Many commentators claim that these new challenges have already produced major changes and that a boardroom revolution is well under way, with formerly supine directors being replaced by independent, questioning, active individuals.[22] It will be argued subsequently that no boardroom "revolution," actual or incipient, has shown itself or is likely to emerge under present institutional arrangements. A good deal of the emphasis and fervor on board changes arises from an overdramatization of marginal shifts of limited impact, as well as from the fact that much writing on the subject is exhortative, tending to confuse what ought to be with what is and what is likely to be.

Corporate boards exist, in part, to meet the legal requirement of chartering authorities that a board of directors of three or more individuals be constituted who will run the affairs of an incorporated organization. All boards, even those of corporations solely owned by a single individual, must meet this chartering requirement.[23] Because the board is legally responsible for running the corporation, the problem of nominal versus real power is immediately apparent. And it is just as quickly evident that if the Ford Motor Company of 1929 had three directors, including Henry Ford, it would not be sensible to say that all three directors equally dominated the corporation. All the directors would be on the board by grace of Mr. Ford. It is equally well understood, even in corporations where the control group has a minimal stock interest, that outsiders "invited" onto a board are not the power equals of the more permanent top cadres of management. The frequent use of the word "invited" suggests a guestlike and transitory status of the outsider, and because the invitation is very often from top management, board criticism of the corporate leadership violates the laws of hospitality. As observed in a 1975 Conference Board study, "many directors feel a sense of loyalty to the chief executive because they serve on the board at his request, and may even have close personal ties."[24] Criticism also may conflict with business considerations and other forms of reciprocity, as a great many directorships involve director interchanges or business interconnections, discussed in detail later. The transitory status of outside directors may be reinforced by implicit or even explicit agreements that the directorship is terminable at the discretion of the top insider or insiders.[25]

The roles of boards of large companies vary according to the industry and its traditions, the condition and prosperity of the firm, other special circumstances, and the choices of its top management.[26] But it is widely agreed among sophisticated observers of boards that, in the main:

1. Outside directors are not invited to join the boards of major corporations to "run" the firms or to decide on basic policy.
2. Outside directors are usually passive and do what managements want them to do.
3. Managements want boards to carry out certain limited functions, principally advising in areas of competence, solidifying relationships with important external constituencies, assuring the outside world by their presence that the organization is in good hands, and providing a standby facility for emergency use in times of crisis.[27]

Important exceptions to this restricted role can be found where large stockholder interests are still represented on the board or where financial or managerial crises have compelled board activation. More broadly speaking, the board serves as the locus of some of the forces that influence managerial ideology and constrain management power. Nevertheless, the great majority of outside directors of large managerial companies play a limited, dependent, and passive role that has remained essentially unchanged during the course of the twentieth century. In 1905 Jacob Schiff told the Armstrong Committee that, as an outside director:

> I directed as much as under the prevailing usages in corporations was permitted me to direct; in other words, I went to the meetings . . . listened to the reports . . . and gave such advice as was asked of me . . . and if under the prevailing system an executive officer wishes to do wrong or wishes to conceal anything from his directors or commit irregularities such as have been disclosed here, the director is entirely powerless . . . and can only judge of such things as are submitted to him.[28]

Seventy years later Jeremy Bacon and James K. Brown wrote in a Conference Board study that "Unless the chief executive officer wants his directors to become actively involved, it is all but impossible for them to become very effective."[29]

Despite the cyclical return of cries for "directors who will direct," and the claims of lessons learned by the now wiser outside directors, little has happened in the past dozen years to alter the distribution of power or the structure of control of large corporations in the United States. There have been changes in board composition and committee structures, most notably an increase in the relative importance of outside directors and a sharp rise in the use of outsider-dominated audit committees. There has also been an increase in potential liability for carelessness, imprudence, or mere inactivity of board members, more outside pressures on boards and, in recent years, "signs of greater independence and initiative by corporate boards."[30] But offsetting these developments has been the greater complexity of large companies and the enlarged information gap between outside directors and inside management. Stanley Vance has noted that:

> In every recent headlining boardroom scandal, beginning with the classic Texas Gulf Sulphur Company case, there was a preponderance of outsiders on the board at the time of the scandal. For example, the inside/outside balance was 2 to 10 at Texas Gulf, 5 to 12 at Lockheed, 4 to 18 at Penn Central, 3 to 6 at Northrop and 3 to 9 at Gulf Oil. Even at W. T. Grant and Company, where the embarrassment was bankruptcy rather than illegal action, outsiders outnumbered insiders 11 to 6. With scarcely an exception, almost 200 corporations, having confessed to recent illegal domestic political

campaign contributions or to payment of bribes abroad, have all had outsider-dominated boards.[31]

Inside management's incentive to obtain and consolidate control is obviously unchanged by recent developments. Furthermore, the board selection process was traditionally, and still is, dominated by the inside managers in the vast majority of management-controlled firms. E. Everett Smith concluded from his studies in 1958 that "For all practical purposes the board is a creature of the chief executive."[32] A major Conference Board study made the same point in 1975: "It is clear from discussions with directors and chief executives alike that, by and large, the chief executive controls who will come onto the board while he is in power."[33] This is one of the comforts of the CEO position, as Ernest Breech observed when considering whether to move from CEO at Bendix to Number Two Man at Ford: "I liked my job at Bendix. I named my own board of directors. I was having a good time."[34] In many cases the majority of new board nominees and proposed officer realignments are initially put forward by the management itself. In other cases the outside directors are allowed, or even encouraged, to submit names of proposed new directors, but the top management usually retains the power to accept or reject such nominees. The insiders will usually want to meet with and talk to any new directors as well as to make a close study of their backgrounds and qualifications. It is a widely held view by students of the corporate board, including those in favor of substantial board reform, that divisiveness, factionalism, and serious conflict are not desirable board characteristics.[35] For this reason, as well as because of the powerful position of the top management vis-à-vis outside directors, inside recommendations are (in the words of Courtney C. Brown) "seldom contested," and the imposition of new directors unacceptable to the top officers is "usually unthinkable."[36]

Increasing numbers of sizable corporations have nominating committees that bring prospective nominee names to the board for its consideration. In the early 1970s the nomination process in most large companies was handled directly by management and the board; a 1973 Conference Board study found only 58 out of some 853 companies (under 7 percent) with official nominating committees.[37] By the late 1970s, however, the proportion of large companies with nominating committees had increased markedly: to 23 percent in a Conference Board sample, 37 percent of a Korn/Ferry sample, and an even higher percentage according to other estimates.[38] In a number of cases, board nominating committees

are comprised of outside directors only, and in others, the outsiders constitute a majority. But this is hardly indicative of a loss
of nominee control by the inside management. The nominating
committee will be a known and responsible group, and a tacit
acceptance of the convention of management input and of ultimate
clearance is an almost invariable part of the committee framework. General Motors Corporation (GM), for example, has a
board-nominating committee composed entirely of outside directors but that committee's list preparation and review process is
carried out in close coordination with the inside management.[39]
The selection of the Reverend Leon Sullivan to the GM board in
1971 followed a very intensive management/board investigation
and discussion of GM strategies, as well as discussions between
top GM management and Sullivan himself, after which "G. M.
Chairman, James Roche, personally made a trip to Philadelphia to
offer him the job."[40] An outside-director nominating committee
is not a serious obstacle to inside domination of the board selection
process.

   Also bearing on the role of the board in corporate control is the
size of boards of directors. Large boards make for weak boards.[41]
A large board is incompatible with the depth of discussion, the
extensive participation of individual board members, and the kind
of interaction and division of labor characteristic of so-called
"working boards."[42] Large size also makes for diversity and fragmentation, which reduce the likelihood of a board threat to management domination. Board size is directly related to company
size, particularly in manufacturing. Thus in the 1973 Conference
Board survey the median-sized manufacturing company board
was 11, but the median board size for the 83 companies with assets
over $1 billion was 15.[43] Table 2.1 shows that in 1975 the median-
sized board among the 100 largest industrial companies was 14
and that 44 of these companies had boards with 15 or more members. A Conference Board survey of 1976 shows median board
sizes for large companies as follows: manufacturing, 13; retail
merchandising, 5; transportation, 15; utilities, 13; and bank holding companies, 22. Banks and, to a slightly lesser extent, insurance
companies, usually have very large boards, whose roles appear
principally to be strengthening customer relationships and enhancing institutional prestige. In 1975 the median number of directors for the 50 largest financial corporations was 21.5 (versus
14 for the largest industrials), and 13 of the 50 (26 percent) had 25

Table 2.1. *Size of board of directors of the 100 largest industrials, 1975*

Size of board	Number and percentage of firms	
Under 10	3	
10	8	
11	9	
12	10	
13	15	
14	11	Median = 14
15	15	
16	6	
17	11	
18	5	
Over 18	7	
	100	

Source: Compiled from proxy statements for spring 1975.

or more directors. The substantive functions of these large boards of financial corporations do not impinge on managerial control; the same may be said of the larger boards (15 or more members) in other sectors.

Those who feel that there is promise in board reform usually focus on the outside directors as the vehicle for discipline, monitoring, and, if necessary, displacement of operating management. If insiders are numerically predominant, however, or even comprise a very strong minority, outside directors may be able to do little of substance, even if they are truly independent. In the Conference Board surveys the proportion of manufacturing companies with a majority of outside directors has risen steadily over the years, from 50 percent in 1938, to 61 percent in 1961, to 71 percent in 1972, to 83 percent in 1976.[44] But this still leaves room for a great many insiders on the board. The median percentage of insiders on boards of large manufacturing companies in the 1973 Conference Board survey was 39.5 percent, down moderately from 1961. In 1975 almost a third of the 100 largest industrials had a full majority of insiders on their boards, and over two thirds of the 100 largest had boards on which insiders comprised 34 percent or more of the total number of directors (see Table 2.2). The median

Table 2.2. *Insiders as a percentage of total directors of boards of the 100 largest industrial corporations, 1975*

Percentage of insider to total board members[a]	Number and percentage of firms	
75.0+	7	
51.0–74.9	24	
50.0–50.9	4	
34.0–49.9	33	Median = 40 percent
25.0–33.9	24	
10.0–24.9	8	
	100	

[a] Includes narrow insiders only, defined as employees of the company or one of its subsidiaries, earning $40,000 or more per year.
Source: Compiled from proxy statements for spring 1975.

Table 2.3. *Percentage of inside directors among 200 largest nonfinancial corporations, 1975*

Percentage	Number of corporations	Relative frequency (%)	Cumulative frequency (%)
Under 10.0	3	1.5	1.5
10.0–24.9	43	21.5	23.0
25.0–33.9	55	27.5	50.5
34.0–49.9	46	23.0	73.5
50.0–50.9	14	7.0	80.5
51.0–74.9	32	16.0	96.5
75.0+	7	3.5	100
Total	200	100	

percentage of insiders on these boards was 40 percent. Table 2.3 shows that for the 200 largest nonfinancials in 1975 the median proportion of insiders was one third and that half the companies had boards on which inside directors accounted for over one third of the total number of directors. Korn/Ferry's 1979 survey of large company boards shows that the average proportion of insiders was still almost one third.[45] Table 2.4 shows the sharply different picture for the 50 largest financials, where for three quarters of the companies the insiders comprised under a quarter of the board.

Table 2.4. *Percentage of inside directors among 50 largest financial companies, 1975*

Percentage	Number of companies	Relative frequency (%)	Cumulative frequency (%)
Under 10.0	5	10.0	10.0
10.0–24.9	33	66.0	76.0
25–33.9	6	12.0	88.0
34.0–49.9	4	8.0	96.0
50.0–50.9	1	2.0	98.0
75.0+	1	2.0	100
Total	50	100	

Because inside directors normally vote as a solid, unified block under the direction of top management,[46] their sheer numbers make them a formidable factor in establishing management predominance in board affairs. Their power is greatly strengthened by the fact that insiders, working full time on corporate affairs, have a depth of knowledge of the organization, its technology, and business problems that outside directors are not in a position to challenge.

The power of the outside directors depends on a variety of factors – including, among others, their relative number, homogeneity, knowledge, power base in relation to the corporation, and relations with the insiders. Large owners and creditors who serve as outside directors on boards clearly have the most significant independent power base and potential weight. For the most part, however, outside directors do not have substantial power in the corporation and a large proportion of them (including creditors) have some sort of dependency on or reciprocity linkage to the corporation and its active management. The nature of the relationship between inside and outside directors is clearly important in assessing the locus of power in the board. Just how "outside" are "outside directors" and how "independent" are they from the top insiders? If top managers can successfully propose new directors and retain de facto veto power over proposed selections from outside directors, the board should gradually assume a character satisfactory (and subordinate) to the management. A friendly, helpful but definitely unthreatening, and perhaps really compliant and passive, board may be the norm.

Such a possible outcome raises questions about the outside directors' capacity to deal with top managers, at arms length, as fiduciaries of the owners.[47] This issue has been addressed with increasing frequency in recent years; the New York Stock Exchange itself, for example, in its new listing requirement of 1978, calls for "an Audit Committee comprised solely of directors independent of management" and directs specific attention to a number of possible linkages that might compromise such independence.[48] Given the board selection processes, we would expect a great many outside directors to have links to insiders as potent as nominal insiders. An examination of outside directors from this perspective shows an impressive array of linkages that suggest limited "outsideness."

The bases of director selection that may involve significant connections with top management can be classified as follows: (1) former insiders, now retired; (2) relatives and personal friends of insiders; (3) those deriving economic benefits from the existing control group, or having other important business relationships with its members; and (4) those whose institutional roles and dependency on the business community promise limited or minimal demands on the control group.

Table 2.5 classifies directors of the 100 largest industrials in 1975 according to degrees of "outsideness," based on information assembled from a wide variety of sources, but mainly on company proxy statements and directories showing further affiliations of individuals. In 1975 the hundred largest industrials had 1,438 directors, of whom 633, or 44 percent, were inside directors in the narrow sense, that is, employees of the company or one of its subsidiaries receiving at least $40,000 per year. Most of these employees were full timers; a handful were consultants. Correspondingly, in the broadest sense, 805, or 56 percent, of these 1,438 directors were "outside" directors. Row 1 shows that 80 (5.6 percent) of the 1,438 directors were former employees of the company, a surprisingly small number, substantially below that given by the Conference Board, whose studies have shown 15 to 20 percent of the total number of directors as "former employees" of the company. The Conference Board, however, has included many companies smaller than those in our sample.

Until very recently, the Conference Board surveys of director composition defined an inside director as one who was an employee of the company at the time of the survey. The 1973 edition of *Corporate Directorship Practices: Membership and Committees of the*

Table 2.5. *Director characteristics of the 100 largest industrials, 1975*

Director category	(1) Number (gross)	(2) Percentage of all directors	(3) (4) Outside directors in each category[a]		(5) (6) Outside directors (subtracting previous row from total)	
			No.	%	No.	%
Total directors	1,438	100.0				
Inside directors[b]	633	44.0				
Outside directors	805	56.0				
1. Former employee	80	5.6	79	5.5	726	50.5
2. Relative of key insider	5	0.3	3	0.2	723	50.3
3. Affiliated with another company doing substantial business with this company	157	10.9	154	10.7	569	39.6
4. Affiliated with another company doing small or uncertain volume of business with this company	150	10.4	130	9.0	439	30.5
5. Director on outside board with key insider or with outside business ties	274	19.1	93	6.5	346	24.1
6. Director socially linked to key insider	335	23.3	100	7.0	246	17.1
7. Director a substantial stockholder of company (100,000 shares or more)	63	4.4	24	1.7	222	15.4
8. Director on board at least 10 years	235	16.3	60	4.2	162	11.3
9. Director on over six boards	240	16.7	46	3.2	116	8.1

Table 2.5. (*cont.*)

Director category	(1) Number (gross)	(2) Percentage of all directors	(3) (4) Outside directors in each category[a]		(5) (6) Outside directors (subtracting previous row from total)	
			No.	%	No.	%
10. Director is representative of charitable or educational institution	69	4.8	21	1.5	95	6.6

[a]Many outside directors appear in the various rows more than once – they may be officers of a company doing business (rows 3 and 4) *and* on another board in common with a key insider (row 5) *and* otherwise socially linked to a key insider (row 6). This column adds directors in each category as we proceed downward only where the director was not already counted in another row. Thus the sum of column 3 – 710 – indicates that many of the 805 outside directors fall into at least one of the categories shown on rows 1 to 10 and that only 95 of the 805 (as shown in the last row of column 5) do not appear on any row at least once.
[b] Includes narrow insiders only, defined as employees of the company or one of its subsidiaries, earning $40,000 or more per year.

Board, "in response to comments by users of the reports that former employees are really insiders for all practical purposes," finally treats former employees as insiders, although still retaining the old classification system for purposes of comparing inside–outside trends from 1967–1973.[49] Former employees are plausibly still insiders, with close links to the successor management; in a majority of cases, former employees are reliable supporters of management. In a significant minority of cases, however, the former top officers either retain their previous dominance or become an independent power force, operating with a knowledge and prestige base that make them, if not effective "outsiders," formidable independent insiders capable of asserting alternative courses of action. Nonetheless, for the most part, retired officers remaining on the board are tied to the new management and serve as reliable allies.

Relatives and (especially) personal friends of insiders are hard to identify on the basis of publicly available information. Table 2.5 lists only five directors (0.3 percent) as relatives of key insiders (row 2), surely an understatement. Friendships might be associated with social linkages through common membership in clubs, and almost a quarter of the directors were so connected with the insiders, as shown on row 6. A personal relationship might also arise out of the many cases where an insider was also on at least one other outside board with an outside director, as was true for 274 directors of the 100 largest industrials in 1975 (row 5). These are "iffy" matters, however – club memberships may not be used or may involve very limited contact with other members, and multiple common board memberships, although suggesting a greater likelihood of personal relationship, do not inevitably lead to a comradely feeling. But these, and many other bases of personal contact between insiders and outside directors – including doing business (rows 3 and 4) and long tenure on the board (row 8) – make for unquantifiable but certainly numerous friendships and personal loyalties that tie outside board members to corporate insiders.[50]

A great many outside directors of business corporations do business with the companies on which they serve as an outside director. Securities and Exchange Commission (SEC) proxy rules require disclosure in annual proxy statements of "any transactions [in which directors or officers] have a direct or indirect material interest," so that the proxy statement provides a valuable though seriously incomplete source of information on this matter.[51] Proxy statements show, for example, that George Jenkins, an outside director of Bethlehem Steel, was the CEO of Metropolitan Life when it sold approximately $20 million of insurance to Bethlehem in 1974. American Cyanamid outside director, Ian McGregor, was CEO of Amax when it sold $2 million of its products to Cyanamid in 1974. Outside director of Alcoa, Edmund E. Carlson, was CEO of United Airlines when it participated in a joint venture hotel-ownership arrangement with Alcoa, and received, in addition, $5 million in 1974 in lease rentals from a subsidiary of Alcoa. An outside director of American Airlines, William O. Beers, was CEO of Kraftco, which the American Airlines proxy statement says supplied American with packaged goods of unspecified volume in 1975. Beers was also an outside director on the board of Manufacturers Hanover Trust of New York, an important bank to Kraftco, which received $312,796 in interest and fees from the bank in 1974. At the same time, John McGillicuddy, president of Manufacturers Hanover, was an outside director on the board of Kraftco.

The number of these business relationships as shown by proxy statements alone is quite impressive and would radically alter the proportion of inside to outside directors if customer/supplier outsiders were reclassified as inside directors. In the case of Cleveland Electric Illuminating Company, for example, the ratio would change from three inside to eight outside, to seven inside to four outside. Overall, Table 2.5 shows that at least 157, or 10.9 percent, of the directors of the 100 largest industrials were affiliated with a firm doing a substantial volume of business with the company on which they served as a director.[52] Another 150 directors (10.4 percent) were associated with companies doing a small or uncertain volume of business. Thus 21.3 percent of the sampled directors were customers or suppliers of the company on which they were directors, a figure surely understating the actual number. The independence of customer/supplier directors is often constrained by several factors: (1) They may have come on the board following the development of a personal tie with members of the inside management; (2) They are in a commercial nexus with the existing management that makes the decisions to buy and sell, and the maintenance and expansion of this business relationship, potentially sensitive to behavior (support and reliability) at board meetings; (3) Board directorships may be reciprocal (as in the Kraftco–Manufacturers Hanover case previously noted), which implies a further degree of connection and interest that enhances the probability of mutual understanding and support.

An important reason that bankers and other businesspeople go on boards is to protect, enhance, or bring into existence a business relationship. Two high officers of two different top banks explained to this writer that, after repeated solicitation, they had recently joined the boards of major corporations with great reluctance – the work was onerous, the personal advantages were minimal – but the bankers both gave way for fear of offending the customer and thus adversely affecting customer relationships. A director going on to a board for such an accommodating and business-protective purpose is not going to be a "boat rocker" or very independent. But at a certain point, managerial nonperformance may cause the banker's interest in solvency to outweigh the ties of reciprocity and the tacit agreement that the inside management has final authority. Under such circumstances, the banker may have a capacity to act and a degree of influence not available to the many still more dependent outside directors on the board.

Table 2.6. *Principal occupations of outside directors of 511 manufacturing companies, 1972*

Position	Excluding former employee			Including former employee		
	Number	%	Cumulative %	Number	%	Cumulative %
Corporate executive [a]	1729	63.9	63.9	1729	53.3	53.3
Consultants	145	5.4	69.3	145	4.5	57.8
Lawyers	145	5.4	74.7	145	4.5	62.3
Retirees [b]	325	12.0	86.7	315	9.7	72.0
Former employees [c]	—	—	86.7	552	17.0	89.0
All other	358	13.3	100.0	358	11.0	100.0

[a] Sum of following principal occupations: president; managing partner; board chairman; vice-president, executive/senior vice-president; chairman of a board committee; vice-chairman or honorary chairman; senior managing director; corporate officer (other than president, etc.).
[b] Exclusive of former employee. The great majority of them are retired businesspeople.
[c] Number here based on a sample of 508 rather than 511 manufacturing companies.
Source: Compiled from Jeremy Bacon, *Corporate Directorship Practices: Membership and Committees of the Board* (New York: The Conference Board, 1973), pp. 28–29.

A large number of outside directors of companies are jointly on the boards of still other companies with insiders, and in many cases they are on the insider's board as a *result* of their getting to know, like, and trust one another in this outside connection. For example, in 1970, J. F. Forster, CEO of Sperry Rand, joined the board of Borden, whose board included J. D. Finley and Shelton Fisher. In 1971 J. D. Finley became a member of the board of Sperry Rand. In 1972 Shelton Fisher became a board member of Sperry Rand. This sequence is found time and again and suggests a selection process based at least in part on personal relationships reminiscent of the enlargement of the membership of a club.

The "club" in this instance is the community of like-minded and mutually sympathetic businesspeople and selected friends and allies among the nonbusiness elite. Despite the changes in board composition in recent decades, business executives still comprise the great bulk of outside directors. Table 2.6 shows that a majority of outside directors in the early 1970s were active corporate executives. Retired corporate officers, former employees, consultants, and lawyers, who often provide special and personalized services to these companies, comprised another 35.7 percent (including former employees) or 22.8 percent (excluding former employees) of outside directors. The residual proportion of outside directors is under 15 percent of the total. The interconnections between directors *among* boards and in other external linkages add force to the "club" concept of corporate boards, in which a community of ideological and material interests combine to make for a passive group of outside directors.[53]

Table 2.5, also shows the number of directors who are substantial stockholders (row 7), who have been on the board 10 years or more (row 8), who are on more than six separate boards (row 9), and who are primarily affiliated with charitable or educational institutions (row 10). Substantial stockholders with a large stake in the company's well-being and often close to the management group may be considered insiders in some cases, but they are often there to protect their interests and their expertise, wealth, and status may give them more independence of management than many other directors.[54] Long tenure as director also works both ways, tending to cement relationships with management, but, too (sometimes), to add prestige and power based on knowledge and closer links with other outside and inside directors. A director who holds numerous multiple directorships may have greater knowledge and experience as a director but may also have limited time and a vested interest in avoiding a reputation as a trouble-maker.

Professional directors sell their services to buyers. If the buyers are predominantly the top managements of major corporations, a reputation for intrusiveness, unseemly pressure, and boat rocking will spoil what has become a remunerative sellers market.[55] The sheer number of directorships of professional directors also suggests a limited capacity for extended effort in connection with any single company. At a 1976 annual meeting of Eastman Kodak, a stockholder noted from the floor that then director Juanita Kreps, a vice-president of Duke University, was on 13 boards of directors (six corporate, the others nonprofit), and question was raised concerning her ability to contribute much as an Eastman Kodak director.[56] Professional director Don Mitchell, on 12 boards in 1970, was still able to devote half time to serving as CEO of the American Management Association.[57] Joseph Needham, former chairman of the New York Stock Exchange, and subsequently a professional director, was quoted in late 1979 as saying that "the classic clubroom type of board is not the way it works anymore," the accompanying news report noting that Needham devotes "much of his time to his dozen directorships."[58]

Representatives of charitable and educational institutions (row 10) are among the more independent outside directors, but they suffer from lack of expertise and their independence is somewhat compromised by the fact that they are in constant search for sustenance from the business community. They do not have a strong power base and are seldom boat rockers.

Thus a very large proportion of "outside directors" have ties and obligations to insiders that are likely subtly to compromise their independence. In an uncorrected view of the distribution of directors, Table 2.5 shows that 56 percent of the directors of the 100 largest industrials are "outside directors" in the broadest sense of the term. If former employees, relatives of key insiders, and directors doing a great deal of business with the company (rows 1 to 3) are subtracted from the total for reasons of possible lack of independence, we can see in column 6 that the proportion of outside directors has fallen to 39.6 percent. If we move two rows farther down, removing from outside directors those who do some business with the company and those who are on other boards in common with inside directors, the proportion of outside directors falls to a quarter (24.1 percent). Depending on our assessment of the independence of the remaining categories of Table 2.5, it is evident that the outsideness of outside directors can be reduced to levels well below a quarter of the total.

The board selection choices that have produced this result are based in part on the tendency to select and associate with people with whom one is familiar and with whom the selectors are comfortable. It is also almost certainly a result of the interest of the power core of the corporations in establishing and consolidating their control – which calls for outside directors who are *not* very independent of the company, its dominant personalities, and its lines of influence.

When for some corporate purpose outside directors *are* selected who are not entirely known and reliable, and who represent outside constituencies that pose some threat to company autonomy – as in the case of Leon Sullivan and GM – the selection is usually made after the most careful evaluation of costs and benefits, a close consideration of whether the outsider will be satisfied with concessions the company is prepared to make in his area of interest, and an estimate of the extent to which the prospective director will abide by the rules of the director game or go over the heads of the management and board to the general public.

In the mid- and late 1970s the number of representatives of non-business constituencies on the boards of the large companies under special study here was remarkably small. A distinction must be made between the number of companies with *a* constituency representative and the relative importance of constituency representatives in the aggregate of directorships. Constituency representation was and is fairly impressive on the first basis, small on the second. In a mid-1970s universe consisting of the 200 largest non-financial corporations and the 50 largest financials, 112 of the 250 giants (44.8 percent) had at least one educator on their boards, 67 (26.8 percent) had a woman director, 42 (16.8 percent) had a foundation/nonprofit organization representative, and 42 (16.8 percent) had a black director. As a proportion of all directors, however, these nonbusiness constituency representatives added up to unimpressive totals. The largest category, educators, numbered only 108 out of a grand total of 3,060 directors[59] of the 250 largest companies, or 3.5 percent of the aggregate; and of 4,010 total directorships, 141 were held by educators, also 3.5 percent. Those primarily affiliated with foundations and other nonprofit organizations numbered 37, with 55 directorships, or 1.2 percent of directors and 1.4 percent of directorships. There were 56 women directors in 1975, with 80 directorships, accounting for 1.8 percent of directors and 2 percent of directorships. And only 23 of 3,060 (0.8 percent of the total) were black, with 44 directorships, or 1.1 percent of total directorships.[60] The higher ratio of black and women directorships to black directors and women directors reflects the above average duplication of directors in this category. One black director (Jerome Holland) had seven directorships, the most of any director among the 250, and two others had four directorships each. There is some overlap between these constituencies, Patricia Harris, for example, adding one director and four directorships to both the women and black categories. But even disregarding the overlaps, these four large classes together accounted for only 7.3 percent of large corporation outside directors and 8.0 percent of their directorships.

These numbers and proportions have increased since 1975. Korn/Ferry's sample, covering a wider range of companies than the very large company sample used here, shows a more than two-fold increase in the number of companies with a woman director between 1974 and 1978 (from 11.4 percent to 28 percent), and an almost 50 percent increase in the number of companies with "ethnic minority" representatives (from 10.7 percent to 15.1 percent).[61] The 250 largest companies have undoubtedly also moved further in the same direction.

Outside director power is constrained not only by the relationships that compromise director independence and the sparseness and relative weakness of nonbusiness and constituency directors, but it is also limited by an information gap. The imbalance of expertise and detailed knowledge between inside and outside directors greatly weakens the powers of outsiders to initiate and even to react effectively. As noted by one outside director, "The reason I don't get involved . . . is that I don't have time to get the facts, and I prefer not to look stupid."[62] In recent years there has been an enlargement of information provided outside directors, and a greater willingness on their part to ask serious questions, but, at the same time, the continued growth in size, diversification, and foreign expansion has enlarged the volume of relevant knowledge. It is not clear, therefore, that the knowledge imbalance has been affected at all. The problem is also made intractable by the fact that a large proportion of outside directors are full-time occupants of important positions elsewhere and, in the words of one such director, "barely have time to brush their teeth."[63]

The position of the potential boat rocker is further constrained by traditional rules and conventions of board behavior. A first rule of board behavior is that issues must be discussed within the group, without appeal over the head of the board to public opinion.[64] This reduces the power of spokespeople for a larger public constituency to bring pressure from the outside on other board members. That threat may still exist, but it is minimized by careful selection of any outside constituency representative, as previously discussed. In the small group setting of a board meeting, top management normally dominates the drift by virtue of its usually accepted leadership/executive role, responsibility for putting up the agenda and leading the discussion, full-time responsibilities for plans and initiatives, and superior knowledge of company affairs. The top management also benefits from other features of small group interaction processes. People do not like to look foolish, and it is difficult for outsiders to pose questions of a challenging nature to knowledgeable persons without appearing superficial or incompetent. It is also considered bad form to ask questions that imply doubt about motives, competence, and honesty; or to ask serious questions and make challenges out of the blue, without discussing the matter beforehand with the top officers;[65] or to go behind the backs of management and organize cliques in opposition to management. When outside directors behave in this way, they may be ostracized, made uncomfortable, and in the end asked to resign, perhaps because of a newly recognized conflict of interest.[66]

In sum, directors in large mainstream corporations normally tend to play a passive role, as invited guests, characteristically tied to the inside hosts by some sort of personal or business relationship. Outside director power is, in consequence, typically latent at best, activated mainly in response to serious economic or political setbacks to the company, which demonstrate serious management ineptitude or malfeasance that leave management in great disarray and threaten corporate financial integrity and survival. Where a number of prestigious outsiders are brought on to the board, however, there is usually a tacit assumption that the management will adhere to the established rules of the game and will perform acceptably, thus justifying continued support. Outside directors often have money at stake as lenders or owners or represent lenders or owners as fiduciaries, and as directors they accept a fiduciary responsibility to the company and its shareholders. This does not ordinarily cause outsiders to encroach seriously on management discretion, but in a number of ways and in varying degrees, the outsiders are the focal point of constraints on management. In presenting their plans and results to the directors, the dominant insiders must appeal to the outside directors in terms of commonly accepted purposes and standards of evaluation. The outsiders' standards of propriety and their expectations concerning performance must be met if their goodwill and respect are to be maintained.[67] The outsiders are thus one of many constraints, ideological and material, direct and indirect, that greatly influence managerial ends and behavior.

Stability and instability of control via strategic position

Where controlling blocks of stock have been dissipated and a management/board collective has established effective control, the earlier legal solidity of power would appear to have given way to a less stable basis of control. A Robert Sarnoff (RCA) or a D. F. Kircher (Singer), lacking any substantial stock-ownership base, can be abruptly ousted from power in coups that could not easily be brought against a Henry Ford II or a John Paul Getty. But the publicity given to management ousters in corporate upheavals of the RCA–Singer variety makes the control of a mainstream large corporation appear more "up for grabs" than is really the case. Some of the conditions making for instability of control in a managerial enterprise – especially business decline and credit stringency – can also disrupt control of an owner-dominated company, even one subject to majority-ownership control.[68] It seems plausible, however, that the more stock owned by the control group, and the more diffused the ownership of the balance of the stock, the easier it will be to maintain control. Where ownership control in the form of direct involvement in management has given way but the ownership interest remains substantial, and the top insiders are, in effect, hired managers – or at least not yet free of the latent power of large owners (e.g., Gulf) – management tenure should be more precarious than in cases of pure management control (e.g., GM) or of direct owner/management control (Ford before 1979). The hired manager can be fired, whereas under pure management control or direct ownership management the top managers must fire themselves, or more potent forces must be mobilized to bring about their ouster.

Stability of tenure is hard to measure. "Involuntary" ousters are difficult to distinguish from normal turnovers – the basis and power source of a change are not always identifiable, and there is no generally accepted valid measurement to correct for differences in actual versus potential performance. Robert Sorenson tried to standardize for performance in measuring stability of tenure by examining turnover rates of firms that experienced extended periods of profit decline. He found that the turnover rate of top managers was significantly higher under management control than under owner control.[69] William A. McEachern points out that Sorenson does not distinguish between ownership-control cases where the dominant owner is also the top manager (and is thus not easily displaced) and where dominant ownership operates through a hired manager.[70] This is a valid point – that managers hired by large, dominant owners may have greater insecurity of tenure than controlling managers – but it fails to dislodge the finding. Averaging together dominant owners (who *could* replace themselves) and hired managers, as Sorenson does, tenure under management control appears to be less stable.[71]

Great size is clearly an important control-stabilizing factor. The rate of involuntary ouster appears to be inversely related to size. By virtue of their size, giants such as AT&T, General Electric, and Mobil Oil are almost out of reach of the takeover process, which would require enormous resources and the overcoming of considerable powers of resistance. At the turn of the century a company as large as Union Pacific could be seriously concerned about takeovers via stock market raids, despite substantial insider holdings.[72] This is still a matter of concern for large companies, but not for the largest. Only four of the 200 largest were subject to takeover bids in the years 1965–1975, and not one of the 100 largest companies as measured by asset size was subject to an actual takeover offer. One of the four bids among the second 100 was successful – Marcor was taken over by Mobil Oil in 1974–1975. The tender offer by Mobil was supported by the Marcor management, so the transaction was more like a merger than an involuntary ouster from the outside. The Crane assault on Anaconda was opposed and defeated, but at the cost of Anaconda's eventual absorption in 1976 by the "white knight" Arco. Two other takeover efforts, one of Goodrich by Northwest Industries and one of Signal by the Bronfman (Seagram) interests, were defeated. Occidental Oil was threatened with a takeover by Standard of Indiana, but the threat never materialized into an actual bid. The takeover threat has extended pretty far upward in the list of the largest companies, reaching Babcock & Wilcox, CNA, and Anaconda, and threatening Occidental, but it is still mainly a problem of the smaller fry.[73]

Business performance is clearly a major factor affecting the stability of control via strategic position. Rapid or at least respectable growth in earnings per share, a high rate of return on owners' equity and assets, and a minimum of liquid low-yield assets redeployable by an aggressive conglomerator enhance management power and stability, as they reduce the likelihood of an external raid and strengthen inside management's bargaining position vis-à-vis large and small stockholders, creditors, employees, and the board of directors.

The stability of control by strategic position can also be undermined by the occurrence of corporate traumas that are unconnected with declining performance. Revelations of illegal acts, serious conflicts of interest brought to light, major antitrust actions – reduce the prestige of management, threaten it with legal action and negative publicity, and adversely affect organizational unity and morale. They provide the vehicles through which opponents of the management may organize attacks against it. The Dorsey management of Gulf Oil was ousted following a corporate trauma that unleashed latent antimanagement forces that were not only disturbed by the adverse publicity but were also disenchanted by Gulf's economic performance over the prior several years.[74]

Length of tenure of the top inside management also affects stability of control. Rule by strong and dominant personalities makes for stable control. But the unexpected death or retirement of a dominant manager may create a power vacuum. Sometimes the "retired" executive retains power and attempts to maintain partial or complete rule. This can further destabilize control, as consolidation of managerial control may be impeded and displacement may more readily occur as a result of independent board action.[75] With new or weakened managerial control there may be an extended period of maneuvering among the members of the board, shifting coalitions, hirings and firings of new high-level officers, and general instability, as in the case of United Brands following the suicide of Eli Black.[76] The unexpected death of a top manager or ouster based on unsatisfactory business performance suddenly puts a great deal of power into the hands of the board of directors, and control sometimes becomes fluid. It is in periods of transition, when the old top management team has been dislodged and the new one has not yet established a reliable board/employee/external constituency base,[77] that the locus of control is relatively uncertain and hence unstable. Such instability may be prolonged if the new management group is unable to build strength on the basis of renewed company prosperity.

In the typical mainstream managerial giant, the size, diversification, infrequency of sustained and control-threatening losses, and the strategic position of the top management make for a generally high degree of stability of control. A coalition of top insiders – with varying distributions of power between the CEO and other high officers – normally manages the succession process of such companies with a minimum of trauma or necessity for any outside director intervention. This is usually true for the mainstream giants even in times of trouble – as in the case of Westinghouse in the early 1960s and 1970s and the Chrysler Corporation in 1970 and 1974. Instability is the exception, often associated with unusual financial distress, or, more frequently, the termination of one-man rule.

Concluding note

Strategic position is the crucial underpinning of management control of the large corporation. It rests on daily and direct management command over personnel and resources, knowledge, the importance of managerial and organizational skills, and the structural and social relationships that develop on the basis of proximate command. The power lacunae left by the diffusion of ownership is gradually occupied by those who exercise power on a daily basis and who are thereby well positioned to consolidate it more firmly over time. Management's control is facilitated by its domination of the board selection processes and the resultant capacity of top officials to mold boards into friendly and compliant bodies. The recent increase in number and proportion of outside directors, and the shift in director composition, has not altered this pattern to any significant degree.

Management's domination is not total, however – the owners do not disappear, nor do the lenders. In the three chapters that follow I examine the major external sources of influence on corporate managers – owners, bankers, and government – and assess the extent to which they shape and constrain corporate goals.

3

Control of the Large Corporation: Evolution and Present Status

As pointed out earlier, where a former solid ownership control position becomes attenuated by divestment, estate subdivision, and rapid corporate growth, the stock may cease to be important as the mechanism of continued family control. Family control may persist, based essentially on strategic position; or it may disappear altogether. Because Brooks McCormick was the top officer of International Harvester while holding about 0.5 of the voting stock in 1975,[1] it may seem plausible that despite the fall in McCormick family holdings over the years, the 0.5 was still sufficient to maintain control, evidenced by the fact of continued control. This is a *non sequitur;* but it is a convenient one where there is a reluctance to acknowledge the diminution in importance of ownership control.[2] This *non sequitur* is sometimes bolstered by another: namely, that if the stock of a large corporation is widely diffused, small blocks in the order of 1 or 2 percent become capable of exercising domination. Again, support for this comes from the fact that small block holders do dominate, but there is the issue of cause and effect. In some cases stock ownership came *after* control[3] was established, and in a number of cases, control today continues a pattern established in the past when the control group had a much larger proportion of stock. As discussed in the previous chapter, wide diffusion does not increase the power of holders of small blocks of stock; it enhances the power of whoever controls the proxy machinery.

The small percentage block of stock, although not very important for establishing or maintaining control, may, nevertheless, be worth a lot of money and may constitute an important part of the personal wealth of the owner. Small percentage holdings may not be especially relevant to the *how* of control but may be pertinent to the question of *who* – that is, to the issue of the extent to which the controlling individuals have a significant personal stake in the company, or whether they are merely managerial technocrats without a substantial ownership interest. Management ownership, of course, is only one route through which ownership can make its presence felt in fixing or constraining corporate policy.

In this chapter I describe in more detail the control status of the large corporations in the United States in the mid- and late 1970s, the evolution of control during the first three-quarters of the twentieth century, and some of the factors that have affected this process – particularly those influencing the decline in concentrated individual and family ownership blocks. Attention is then directed to the forces shaping corporate decision making in a system of constrained managerial control, stressing the persistence of pressures from ownership interests and toward profitable growth.

Classification of control of the largest nonfinancial corporations

Tables 3.1 through 3.5 describe the control characteristics of large corporations, both in the mid-1970s and as they have evolved since the turn of the century. Tables 3.1 and 3.2 focus on the 200 largest nonfinancial corporations in 1974–1975; Table 3.3 examines the 100 largest industrials in the same time frame. Tables 3.4 and 3.5 show the control pattern for 1900–1901 and 1929–1930, respectively. The tables distinguish between Management Control, Majority Ownership Control, Minority Ownership Control, Intercorporate Ownership Control, Government Control, Financial Control, and Companies in Receivership (along with subdivisions of major categories, as described subsequently).

Management Control, as discussed in Chapter 2, designates cases where the power over key decisions is held by an insider group with a relatively small ownership stake, which has no primary outside affiliations and dominates through strategic position. The question of exactly *how* small an ownership stake is required to justify calling the control *managerial* is discussed under Minority Ownership Control. The more basic question of establishing who has power over the key decisions, as a practical matter, revolves ultimately on determining who has the power to name and displace the top executives of the corporation. This is often reasonably clear from basic structural facts, such as ownership concentration and board composition, supplemented by the recent history of the board and evidence of participation by large owners and creditors. Even if large owners or creditors do not have the power to name or replace top officers, or to dictate corporate policy on major decisions, they may still have to be consulted for certain key decisions and be able to exercise a veto power in these areas. They may be said to share power and to exercise partial control in such cases. Management control is often a constrained control. The specific criteria employed in fixing the locus of control, and in deciding whether the external constraints warrant explicit identification, are discussed in detail later in this chapter, in Chapters 4 and 5, and in Appendix A (which also gives in tabular form the specific classification for each of the 200 largest nonfinancial corporations in the mid-1970s).

Majority Ownership Control, as shown in the accompanying tables, includes all cases of ownership by an individual, family, or small group in excess of 50 percent of the voting shares. It does not include cases where one corporation owns over 50 percent of another, as the controlled firm is no longer considered a separate entity and is subsumed under the name of the parent. The category Intercorporate Control is confined to cases of control by means of a corporate *minority* interest (in the mid-1970s, British Petroleum's 25 percent interest in Standard Oil of Ohio; Kaiser Industries' 38.3 percent in Kaiser Aluminum).[4] I distinguish between "proximate" (direct) control, shown in Table 3.1, and "ultimate" control, shown in Table 3.2 – "ultimate" control designating the control form of the controlling entity. Thus a company subject to minority ownership control by another company is directly controlled by ownership, but "ultimately" controlled by whatever control form characterizes the controlling company. Using the "ultimate" control classification, control of Shell by Royal Dutch/Shell changes from intercorporate ownership to management control;[5] control of Du Pont by Christiana changes to minority ownership by the Du Pont family; control of Duke Power by the Duke Endowment changes to management control.

Proximate control, neglected by Berle and Means, is commonly underrated in importance. Proximate control may be more relevant than ultimate control from the standpoint of firm behavior and performance. A management-dominated firm that is in control of another firm would hardly encourage "expense preference" by the controlled management, even if the management of the parent engages in such behavior itself, and it might plausibly be expected to fix maximization rules such as large firms impose on

Table 3.1. *Control of the 200 largest, publicly owned, nonfinancial corporations in the United States, December 31, 1974 (proximate control)*

Type of control	Number of corporations	Percent of corporations	Assets ($ millions)	Percent of assets	Sales ($ millions)	Percent of sales
A. Inside management						
1. Significant ownership interest (1% or more)[a]	23	12.0	46,106	6.4	58,956	8.4
2. Financial representation or constraint	20	10.0	58,649	8.1	45,331	6.4
3. Regulatory constraint	57	29.0	239,829	33.2	108,005	15.4
4. Unconstrained[b]	46	23.0	241,802	33.5	322,648	45.9
Total[c]	146 − 18 = 128	64.0	532,734	73.8	503,477	71.6
B. Inside management and outside board						
1. Significant ownership interest (1% or more)	15	7.5	32,296	4.5	41,615	5.9
2. Financial representation or constraint	18	9.0	40,551	5.6	32,253	4.6
3. Regulatory constraint	16	8.0	35,994	5.0	23,651	3.4
4. Unconstrained	3	1.5	7,684	1.1	9,202	1.3
Total[c]	52 − 18 = 34	17.0	72,800	10.1	71,447	10.2
Total management (A + B)	162	81.0	605,534	83.9	574,923	81.8
C. Majority ownership	3	1.5	5,978	0.8	7,062	1.0
D. Minority ownership[a]						
1. a. On board and significant committees (10 or more %)	1	0.5	1,768	0.2	1,163	0.2
b. Active officers (10 or more %)	12	6.0	35,259	4.9	47,281	6.7

2. a. Present on board (10 or more %)	6	3.0	25,641	3.6	30,739	4.4
b. Not represented on board (10 or more %)	0	0.0	0	0.0	0	0.0
3. Small stock interest (5 and under 10%) active in management	5	2.5	13,309	1.8	11,384	1.6
4. Small stock interest (5 and under 10%) more than residual power	1	0.5	1,532	0.2	520	0.1
Total	25	12.5	77,509	10.7	91,087	13.0
E. Intercorporate ownership						
1. Majority	1	0.5	6,129	0.8	7,633	1.1
2. Large minority	6	3.0	17,011	2.4	16,094	2.3
3. Small minority	1	0.5	2,288	0.3	2,728	0.4
Total	8	4.0	25,428	3.5	26,455	3.8
F. Government	0	0.0	0	0.0	0	0.0
G. Financial	1	0.5	3,028	0.4	1,599	0.2
H. Receivership	1	0.5	4,271	0.6	2,247	0.3
Grand total	200	100.0	721,748	100.0	703,373	100.0

See Appendix A for a list of individual companies included in the table and a discussion of some of the problems of classification and how they were met here.

[a] These subcategories designate interests capable of influencing some key decisions but falling short of power to control.

[b] Unconstrained means not subject to the level of constraints indicated in subcategories 1, 2, and 3.

[c] Some companies fall into more than one subdivision. Subtotals are calculated net of these duplications.

[d] Five companies in this category are subject to regulatory constraint, and two are under financial constraint as those categories are used in A and B.

Table 3.2. Control of the 200 largest, publicly owned, nonfinancial corporations in the United States, December 31, 1974 (ultimate control)

Type of control	Number of corporations	Percent of corporations	Assets ($ millions)	Percent of assets	Sales ($ millions)	Percent of sales
A. Inside management						
1. Significant ownership interest (1% or more)[a]	26	13.0	52,519	7.3	62,606	8.9
2. Financial representation or constraint	20	10.0	61,161	8.5	45,331	6.4
3. Regulatory constraint	58	29.0	243,641	33.8	108,828	15.5
4. Unconstrained[b]	47	23.5	247,395	34.3	330,281	47.0
Total[c]	151 − 20 = 131	65.5	543,645	75.3	513,870	73.1
B. Inside management and outside board						
1. Significant ownership interest (1% or more)	15	7.5	32,296	4.5	41,615	5.9
2. Financial representation or constraint	18	9.0	40,551	5.6	32,253	4.6
3. Regulatory constraint	16	8.0	35,994	5.0	23,651	3.4
4. Unconstrained	3	1.5	7,684	1.1	9,202	10.2
Total[c]	52 − 18 = 34	17.0	72,800	10.1	71,446	10.2
Total management (A + B)	165	82.5	616,445	85.4	585,316	83.3
C. Majority ownership	3	1.5	5,978	0.8	7,062	1.0
D. Minority ownership[a]						
1. a. On board and significant committees (10 or more %)	3	1.5	9,805	1.4	9,809	1.4
b. Active officer(s) (10 or more %)	12	6.0	35,259	4.9	47,281	6.7

2. a. Present on board	6	3.0	25,641	3.6	30,739	4.4
b. Not represented on board (10 or more %)	0	0.0	0	0.0	0	0.0
3. Small stock interest (5 and under 10%) active in management.	6	3.0	15,597	2.2	14,112	2.0
4. Small stock interest (5 and under 10%) more than residual power	2	1.0	3,123	0.4	3,042	0.4
Total	29	14.5	89,425	12.5	104,983	14.9
E. Intercorporate ownership	—	—	—	—	—	—
F. Government	1	0.5	2,621	0.4	2,166	0.3
G. Financial	1	0.5	3,028	0.4	1,599	0.2
H. Receivership	1	0.5	4,271	0.6	2,247	0.3
Grand total	200	100.0	721,748	100.0	703,373	100.0

See Appendix A for a list of individual companies included in the table and a discussion of some of the problems of classification and how they were met here.

a These subcategories designate interests capable of influencing some key decisions but falling short of power to control.
b Unconstrained means not subject to the level of constraints indicated in subcategories 1, 2, and 3.
c Subtotals are calculated net of these duplications.
c Some companies fall into more than one subdivision. Subtotals are calculated net of these duplications.
d Five companies in this category are subject to regulatory constraint, and two are under financial constraint as those categories are used in A and B.

59

Table 3.3. *Control of the 100 largest industrial corporations in the United States, December 31, 1974 (ultimate control)*

Type of control	Number of corporations	Percent of corporations	Assets ($ millions)	Percent of assets	Sales ($ millions)	Percent of sales
A. Inside management						
1. Significant ownership interest (1% or more)[a]	13	13.0	28,823	7.0	36,822	7.1
2. Financial representation or constraint	8	8.0	17,464	4.3	25,368	4.9
3. Regulatory constraint	6	6.0	24,573	6.0	26,375	5.1
4. Unconstrained[b]	41	41.0	232,569	56.6	307,563	59.5
Total[c]	68−4=64	64.0	296,179	72.0	382,884	74.1
B. Inside management and outside board						
1. Significant ownership interest (1% or more)	8	8.0	19,493	4.7	21,307	4.1
2. Financial representation or constraint	7	7.0	17,848	4.3	19,382	3.8
3. Regulatory constraint	2	2.0	5,413	1.3	5,355	1.0
4. Unconstrained	3	3.0	7,684	1.9	9,202	1.8
Total[c]	20−6=14	14.0	33,067	8.0	37,136	7.2
Total management (A + B)	78	78.0	329,246	80.5	420,020	81.3
C. Majority ownership[a]	1	1.0	3,004	0.7	2,742	0.5
D. Minority ownership						
1. a. On board and significant committees (10 or more %)	3	3.0	9,805	2.4	9,809	1.9
b. Active officer(s) (10 or more %)	8	8.0	29,352	7.1	41,702	8.1

2. a. Present on board (10 or more %)	5	5.0	24,291	5.9	27,666	5.4
b. Not represented on board (10 or more %)	0	0.0	0	0.0	0	0.0
3. Small stock interest (5 and under 10%) active in management.	4	4.0	12,964	3.2	12,491	2.4
4. Small stock interest (5 and under 10%) more than residual power	0	0.0	0	0.0	0	0.0
Total	20	20.0	76,412	18.6	91,668	17.8
E. Intercorporate ownership	—	—	—	—	—	—
F. Government	1	1.0	2,261	0.6	2,166	0.4
G. Financial	0	0.0	0	0.0	0	0.0
H. Receivership	0	0.0	0	0.0	0	0.0
Grand total	100	100.0	411,283	100.0	516,596	100.0

See Appendix A for a list of individual companies included in the table and a discussion of the problems of classification met here.

[a] These subcategories designate interests capable of influencing some key decisions but falling short of power to control.

[b] Unconstrained means not subject to the level of constraints indicated in subcategories 1, 2, and 3.

[c] Some companies fall into more than one subdivision. Subtotals are calculated net of these duplications.

[d] Five companies in this category are subject to regulatory constraint, and two are under financial constraint as those categories are used in A and B.

Table 3.4. *Control of the large corporation in the United States,*
1900–1901

	Proximate control		Ultimate control	
Type of control	Number of companies	Percent of companies	Number of companies	Percent of companies
A & B. Management	7.5	18.75	9.5	23.75
C. Majority ownership	5	12.5	5	12.5
D. Minority ownership (in all cases in excess of 10%)	12	30.0	13	32.5
E. Intercorporate	3	7.5	—	—
F. Financial	12.5	31.25	12.5	31.25
1. Banker	(5.5)	(13.75)	(5.5)	(13.75)
2. Speculator	(7)	(17.5)	(7)	(17.5)
Total	40.0	100.0	40.0	100.0

Based on a sample of 15 large railroad corporations, 17 large industrials, and two companies each from the fields of traction, electric power, gas, and telecommunications. The fractional values result from the fact that in five cases control was classed as shared between owners or managers and bankers. For further discussion, and a list of these 40 companies and their control classification, see Appendix B.

their divisions and profit centers. In short, intercorporate ownership control may elicit behavior similar to that sought by owners, whatever the form of ultimate control.

Minority Ownership Control comprises cases where the control group owns 5 percent or more of the voting stock, irrespective of the importance of the holding as a vehicle of control. Tables 3.1 through 3.3 subdivide minority ownership control according to the size of the holding (5 and under 10 percent, 10 percent or more) and the nature of representation or management participation by the control group. This category straddles a fence, because by drawing a line at 5 percent (instead of 3 or 6 percent), I am saying that 5 percent is a plausible (though arbitrary) number from the standpoint of both who controls and how. The market value of 5 percent of the voting stock of one of the 200 largest corporations is highly variable among the companies, but it tends to be a sizable figure – in early 1975 the market value of the median-sized 5 percent holding of the 200 largest amounted to about $38 million. The 8.4 percent of Gulf & Western stock owned by its officers and directors (6.7 held by Charles Bludhorn) was worth over $58 million; the 6.35 percent owned by the control group of Weyerhaeuser was worth over $210 million; the 4.2 percent owned by the officers and directors of R. J. Reynolds Industries was worth $180 million. Thus 5 percent is likely to signify a sizable investment stake in a large company, although it is a very imperfect measure of the absolute size of that stake or its relative importance in the personal assets of the controlling individuals. At the same time, a holding as large as 5 percent of the total begins to approach nonnegligibility from the standpoint of corporate power. The power significance of a 5 to 10 percent holding will vary with circumstances and with the motives and freedom of action of the holder. It is not likely to give its possessor control of a major corporation but might allow the selection of an outside director or two and the establishment of a weak power position capable of being strengthened; and it may strengthen the control by an existing control group. The same points may be made regarding a holding of 10 to 15 percent, although the investment stake is greater and the holding more likely to allow a voice in corporate affairs.

Thus a 5 percent standard for minority ownership control gives a plausible basis for assuming a substantial investment stake on the part of the control group and a holding that has potential significance as a power factor. Where there is a stockholding of 5 percent or more that is found to be devoid of control significance, as tends to be the case with institutional investor stockholdings, the company is not classified as subject to minority ownership control, despite the large holding. The category Minority Ownership Control is thus restricted to cases where holders of 5 percent or more of the voting stock actually *do* control. Where control is held by an individual or control group with less than 5 percent of the voting stock but with a significant ownership interest – defined here as from 1 percent to under 5 percent – or where noncontrolling outside directors own more than 1 percent of the voting stock, I have placed these cases as subcategory 1 under Management Control. Thus substantial ownership interests, either controlling or held by noncontrolling board members, can be derived by adding rows A-1, B-1, C, D, and E.

Financial Control as used here means control by commercial or investment bankers, other creditors, or financial speculators.

Table 3.5. *Control of the 200 largest nonfinancial corporations, 1929, original and corrected versions*

Type of control	Original number of corporations	Percent of corporations	Adjusted number of corporations	Percent of corporations	Original assets of corporations ($ millions)	Percent of corporations	Adjusted assets of corporations ($ millions)	Percent of corporations
Private	12	6.0	10	5.0	3,366	4.1	3,145	3.9
Majority	10	5.0	9	4.5	1,542	1.9	1,258	1.6
Minority	46.5	23.3	65	32.5	11,223	13.8	18,480	22.8
Legal device	41	20.5	9.5	4.8	17,565	21.7	2,127	2.6
Management	88.5	44.3	81	40.5	47,108	58.1	44,341	54.7
Receivership	2	1.0	2	1.0	269	0.3	269	0.3
Financial	—	—	23.5	11.8	—	—	11,453	14.1
Total	200.0	100.0	200.0	100.0	81,073	100.0	81,073	100.0

Source: Adapted from A. A. Berle, Jr., and Gardiner C. Means, *The Modern Corporation and Private Property* (New York: The Macmillan Company, 1932), p. 115, with changes to correct errors and to accommodate the new "financial control" category.

There has been a great deal of concern and discussion about financial control in recent years. It is a curiosity that Berle and Means never employed such a category, for the potential conflict of interest between owners and controlling bankers or speculators in the late 1920s would seem important enough to have warranted special attention. Instead, they relied on the category Control by a Legal Device, which focused on a *means* of control rather than the distinguishing characteristics of the controlling parties. In a large proportion of the Berle and Means "legal device" cases, investment bankers and speculators were utilizing these legal instruments in 1929, as can be seen in the reclassification of the Berle and Means 1929–1930 data in Table 3.5. In cases where financial interests are in a position of influence but short of full control, they have been included as subcategory 2 (financial constraints) under Management Control. The evolution of financial control, the various mechanisms by which financial institutions exercise power over nonfinancial corporations, the criteria used for measuring full and partial control, and the present status of financial control and influence over the large corporation are discussed in Chapter 4.

A similar classification and subclassification is used for government control. Government Control as a major category is ruled out of these tables by confining the 200 largest nonfinancial corporations to privately owned entities.[6] (The one company included as "government controlled" in Tables 3.2 and 3.3 is Standard Oil Company of Ohio (Sohio), which was 25 percent owned in the mid-1970s by British Petroleum, which was itself majority owned by the British government.) Private corporations are *regulated* to a greater or lesser degree by government, however, and subcategory 3 designates companies that are subject to major price and entry controls, usually by special governmental commissions. Such companies can be considered to be at least partially controlled by government. In Chapter 5 I take up the questions of large government corporations, and examine in greater detail government regulations and their changing importance over time.

The evolution of control of the large corporation: 1900–1975

Tables 3.1 through 3.5 describe the evolution of corporate control from 1900 through the mid-1970s. The principal fact made evident by these tables is the steady increase in management control, as opposed to the two other major potential bases of control – ownership and credit. As can be seen in Tables 3.2 and 3.3, ultimate management control accounted for 82.5 percent of the number and 85.4 percent of the assets of the 200 largest nonfinancials and 78 percent of the number and 80 percent of the assets of the 100 largest industrials in the mid-1970s. That this has been a fundamental *trend* is indicated by Tables 3.4 and 3.5, which show that in 1900–1901, ultimate management control accounted for 23.8 percent by number of a sample of very large companies, rising to 40.5 percent in 1929. It also appears that the shift toward management control *since 1929* has been as dramatic as the shift between 1900 and 1929.

These tables also show a sharp decline in direct ownership control, which changed little between 1900 and 1929 – from 45 to 42 percent – but fell markedly between 1929 and 1975. In 1929 the owner-controlled companies accounted for 42 percent of the number and 28.3 percent of the assets of the 200 largest (on my adjusted basis); whereas in 1974–1975 the owner-controlled companies accounted for only 16 percent of the number and 13.2 percent of the assets of the 200 largest. Direct ownership control is more significant for the 100 largest industrials (Table 3.3), accounting for 21 percent of company numbers and 19.3 percent of assets. These figures understate the influence of ownership interests on corporate behavior, as I will soon discuss. However, if this is true, it is because ownership is exercising its influence through constraints and pressures on control groups that typically have limited direct ownership interests.

These tables also reveal the decline of financial control over the large corporation. Financial control as used here encompasses both domination by financial institutions (mainly commercial and investment banks) and control by speculative interests whose primary orientation is short-term capital gains, stock manipulation, and more direct gain via personal and service-contract overpayment and privileged access to corporate opportunities. A huge 31.3 percent of the 1900–1901 sample was banker/speculator controlled, 11.8 percent in 1929, and only 0.5 percent in 1975. This refers to control in a narrow and strict sense as opposed to capacity to exercise broad influence and to impose significant constraints on policy. It can be seen from Table 3.2 that of the 165 cases of management control, 38 companies are subclassified as subject to significant financial constraint, often a result of financial difficulties that caused the company to press close to indenture limits or that otherwise increased the bargaining power of financial interests.

The decline in financial control is, in part, a reflection of the fact that both 1900–1901 and 1929 were years of booming stock markets and great speculative and merger activity. They were also years of greater economic instability; in 1900–1901 there was residual banker control stemming from the numerous railroad failures and reorganizations of the 1890s depression. Thus 1900–1901 and 1929 may be relatively high points, perhaps even close to peak years, of financial control. But this does not alter the strong likelihood that these were peaks on a downward trend.

Another point to be noted is the rise and decline of intercorporate control of the large corporation. No proximate control figures are given for 1929–1930 in Table 3.5, but if they were, by my count at least 53 of the Berle and Means 200 largest would be shown as controlled by other corporations. A large proportion of this group were parts of utility company and railroad systems, but a number were controlled by investment companies and a variety of other financial and industrial concerns. The TNEC Monograph No. 29, which examined 200 largest corporations in 1937–1938, showed a similarly large number subject to intercorporate control. In contrast, the 1900–1901 figures show only 3 out of 40 companies controlled by other corporations, and the 1974–1975 tabulation shows only 8 out of 200 to be subject to intercorporate control. The late 1920s was a period of extensive intercorporate control among large companies. Many of the intercorporate control cases during that time were based on speculative holdings, soon to be liquidated. The decline of the railroad, which removed many railroad systems from the largest size class, reduced the number of intercorporate holdings, and the dismantling of utility holding companies under the Public Utility Holding Company Act of 1935 accounted for the disappearance of a great many others.

These tables also show that the separation of ownership and control of the large corporation was already well advanced by the turn of the century. Majority ownership control even then was of relatively modest importance (under a fifth of the companies by number); in all other cases the control groups had at best a minority of the voting stock. By my calculations, over half of the companies controlled by financial interests in 1900–1901 were dominated by speculators with large minority interests (often over 20 percent of the voting stock). It is important to recognize that where separation of ownership and control prevails, conflicts of interest and potential abuses are only slightly less acute between minority controlling interests and other stockholders (and creditors) than they are between pure manager and stockholder (and creditor) interests. To make a speculative killing on a stock that one intends to manipulate, one must own a good deal of the stock. Some of the great plunderers in U.S. industrial history were large minority holders,[7] at least temporarily. And despite the greater ownership interest on the part of control groups in earlier years, the cruder abuses of stockholders and creditors were much more prevalent in 1900 and 1929 than in 1975.

Factors underlying the evolving pattern of control

During the present century the turnover rate of the largest companies (i.e., the rate of displacement of companies by new entrants into the top-size class) has been gradually slowing up. Substantial ownership control, with a major proportion of stock in the hands of entrepreneurial families, has diminished because the gradual dispersion of ownership of older and mature giants is not being offset by a sufficiently high rate of entry into the giant class by new entrepreneurial firms. This long-term factor has been periodically accelerated by waves of mergers in which entrepreneurial firms have been combined or swallowed up, with immediate reductions in large holdings and frequent complete divestments by former dominant families.

Diminishing Turnover of Largest Firms

The turnover rate of the largest firms was very much higher in the pre-World War I period than thereafter. Norman Collins and Lee Preston found a fairly steady decline in size mobility of industrial firms from a "high" level in 1909–1935 to "low" thereafter.[8] Using 1919 as a breakpoint, A. D. H. Kaplan, Collins and Preston, and Richard Edwards all found a better than two-thirds reduction in the rate of exit of large industrial firms in the decades after 1919, compared with the preceding 10 to 15 years.[9] Edwards found that the rate of exit per year per 100 firms fell from 3.4 between 1903–1919 to 1.0 between 1919–1969. Edwards makes a persuasive case that "by the early twenties – certainly by 1923 – the system had 'stabilized' and relatively little change has occurred since then."[10] According to Edwards's calculations, by 1969 only 8 of 110 large industrials identifiable in 1919 had been liquidated; 2 had failed to grow; 30 had disappeared in mergers; and of the 70 survivors, 63 were still among the leaders in their fields. Similarly, by 1975 only 3 of the 99 industrials on the Berle and Means list of 200 largest companies in 1929–1930 had been liquidated; only 1 had failed to grow; 28 had exited by merger; and of the 67 survivors, 55 were still among the 200 largest, while the other 12 were still on the Fortune 500 list.

The concept of "exit by merger" is a bit misleading. Edwards, who I am following here, classes a merging company as a "survivor" if it brings 50 percent or more of the assets to a combination but considers the move an "exit" if the company brings in less than 50 percent. Thus when Armour merged with Greyhound, and Armour accounted for only 46 percent of the assets of the merged company, this was counted as an "exit"; when United Fruit accounted for only 45 percent of the assets of the postmerger AMK (now United Brands), it thereby "exited." Of the 28 "exits" by merger of the 99 industrials on Berle and Means's list of 1929–1930, fully 13 were absorbed by one of the other 99 that survived and remained in the ranks of the 200 largest in 1975; and 7 more are constituents of one of the de novo members of the 200 largest in 1975. Another 6 of the 28 merged into companies that were large enough to be on the Fortune 500 list in 1975. Only 2 of the 28 merged into companies that are not even on the Fortune 500 list. Thus the "exits" involved are of a special sort, with the absorbed companies often key constituents of companies whose presence among the largest was dependent on the merger. It is also evident that absorption of very large firms by other very large firms must have been an important influence on aggregate concentration and the retention of position of the acquiring firm.

The reasons for the declining turnover rate of the largest firms are still in dispute, but the advantages of great size, diversification, and enhanced market power have been important parts of the picture. Alfred D. Chandler stresses that the vertical integration – backward into raw materials and forward into the development of a national and international marketing apparatus – that emerged out of a maturing machine technology of the pre-World War I period was important in pushing out many smaller firms and consolidating the market positions of many of the remaining large firms.[11] The post-World War I advances in technology, increased market scope, and institutionalization of a diversification growth strategy[12] further contributed to stabilization of the positions of the largest firms. In many cases, scale factors created serious obstacles to entry, sometimes in conjunction with problems of raw materials access, product differentiation advantages, or marketing costs and risks. The extensive diversification of many of the giants gave them a degree of insulation from the vagaries of particular markets and allowed them to shift resources into the most promising growth areas, which added to the stability of their positions. It is possible for small companies to diversify rapidly and for large diversified companies to decline by virtue of misjudgments and ineffective integration. But successful integration that is developed both internally and by acquisitions is not an overnight process and creates institutions with interests and advantages that, although not invulnerable, give them great power to protect and enlarge their positions.[13]

Diffusion of Ownership

As firms grow to large size over an extended period, individual ownership tends to become more diffused, family-dominated blocks in particular diminish in importance, and institutions tend to displace individuals as the holders of the largest blocks of stock. The process is neither uniform nor invariable, but the trend is clear enough.

Number and Concentration of Shareholders. Size is closely associated with number of shareholders. Firms able to maintain their position among the largest corporations have generally grown enormously in size, and substantial increases in the number of shareholders have come with this growth. Of the 60 giants of 1929 that survived to make the list of the 200 largest in 1975 (and for which data are available on shareholder numbers), only 2 had fewer shareholders in 1975, and the median change in shareholder numbers was a fivefold increase. Table 3.6 shows that 57 percent of the 165 largest companies of 1929 for which Berle and Means provided usable information had under 20,000 shareholders, whereas only 4.5 percent of the largest companies in 1975 had so few shareholders. It is clear that there has been a major upward drift in shareholder numbers for the largest corporations.

There is a strong inverse correlation between the number of shareholders and the concentration of shareholdings at a point in

Table 3.6. *Number of shareholders of the 200 largest nonfinancial corporations, December 1929 and December 1974*

	1929		1974	
Number of shareholders [a]	Number of companies	% [b]	Number of companies	%
Under 5,000	41	24.9	1	0.5
5,000–19,999	53	32.1	8	4.0
20,000–49,999	39	23.6	52	26.0
50,000–99,999	22	13.3	69	34.5
100,000–199,999	7	4.3	43	21.5
200,000–499,999	3	1.8	21	10.5
500,000–999,999	—	—	4	2.0
1 million and over	—	—	2	1.0
Voting trust or unknown	35	—	—	—
Total	200	100.0	200	100.0

[a] The range of number of shareholders in 1929 was as follows: smallest = 1; largest = 469,801 (AT&T). The range of number of shareholders in 1974 was as follows: smallest = 6,447 (The Williams Companies); largest = 2,929,615 (AT&T).
[b] Percent of cases (165 out of the 200 companies) for which data are available for 1929.

time. But the relationship is imperfect, and it is clearly possible for the number of shareholders to rise while concentration at the upper end increases for a single firm or for many firms over time. Historic data on ownership concentration are sparse. The great increase in the number of shareholders almost certainly reflects and parallels a substantial deconcentration of *individual* shareholdings, but the rise of large institutional holdings makes it difficult to generalize about changes in overall shareholder concentration.

Some direct evidence of the secular deconcentration of the shareholdings among the largest firms can be derived from Tables 3.2 and 3.5 and the data underlying them. Of the 200 largest nonfinancial corporations listed by Berle and Means in 1929, 10 were privately controlled and an additional 9 were majority owned, whereas in 1975, there was only a single case of private ownership (Cargill) and a grand total of 3 private-plus-majority-owned cases among the 200 largest (compared with 19 in Berle and Means's listing). The Berle and Means 1929 data disclose 65 minority ownership cases, most with control group holdings in excess of 10 percent, whereas the 1975 data show 29 minority ownership cases, of which only 21 have holdings of 10 percent or more. TNEC Monograph No. 29 gives an ownership control designation to 139 of the 200 largest for 1937–1938, in contrast with Berle and Means's listing of 84 for the years 1929–1930. But the TNEC classification includes intercorporate ownership control, whereas Berle and Means use an ultimate control basis of classification. The intercorporate ownership control cases in the TNEC study number 56, with an additional 6 designated as joint family and intercorporate. Excluding this group of 62 cases, there remain 15 instances of noncorporate majority control (compared with 19 in Berle and Means's listing) and 52 cases of minority ownership control (compared with 65 in Berle and Means's listing). The two sets of figures are thus not at all inconsistent when adjusted for intercorporate ownership, showing, in fact, a possible slight decline in ownership control between 1929–1930 and 1937–1938.

The Decline of Family Control. The ownership deconcentration process is also evident in an examination of the holdings of major family groups who have dominated many of the largest corporations for quite a few decades. Table 3.7 shows changes in the holdings of 35 families or family groups in 43 companies that are still among the 200 largest where family interests and power were considerable in the late 1920s or 1930s. The data presented are spotty because there are no regular and reliable sources of information on ownership by individuals or family groups. The diffusion of family ownership among larger numbers over time and the fact that official reporting requirements apply only to directors and concentrated holdings are factors making for a downward bias in estimates of family holdings. On the other hand, the post-1933 enlargement of corporate, institutional, and foundation disclosure requirements, some decline in corporate secretiveness, and greater public interest in ownership have made information more readily accessible, which has partially offset this bias. The data for family stockholdings in the 1970s, shown in Table 3.7, includes not only direct and trust holdings but also the holdings of family-created foundations (where ascertainable) and additional holdings of closely affiliated banks.

It is evident from Table 3.7 that there has been a consistent and substantial decline in family holdings over the 1929–1976 period. A summary picture is provided in Table 3.8, which shows the

Table 3.7. *Changes in the common stock holdings of families dominant in the large corporations of the United States,* 1929–1976

Family	Company	Estimated percentage holdings[b] as of:				
		1929–1930	1937–1938	1972	1974–1975[c]	1976
Armour–Prince	Greyhound (Armour)[a]	Mgmt. (no ownership data)	3.0	—	under 2.0	—
Bell, Darby & Duke	American Cyanamid[a]	—	41.6	—	Prob. under 2.0	—
Clark & Singer	Singer Co.[a]	50+	31.0	—	Prob. under 2.0	—
Colgate	Colgate–Palmolive[a]	—	15.3	—	1.4[p]	—
Davies–Post, Woodward & Iglehart	General Foods[a]	—	12.3	—	Prob. under 2.0	—
Deere	John Deere	50+	37.2	—	13.7[p]	—
Dow	Dow Chemical Co.	(circa) c. 25[d]	—	8.03	c. 10.0	—
Duke	Duke Power	43.7+	43.0	—	28.0[e]	25.5
Duke–Widener	American Brands	Legal device (no ownership data)	6.4	—	Prob. under 2.0	—
Du Pont	E. I. Du Pont	30.5	43.0	28.2 (Christiana alone)	28.7[p]	28.2
	Uniroyal[a]	c. 17	13	—	c. 2	—
	General Motors[a]	32.6	23.3	—	Prob. under 8.0[f]	—
Firestone	Firestone Tire	Mgmt. (no ownership data)	35.5	—	28.7[pf]	—

73

Table 3.7. (cont.)

Family	Company	Estimated percentage holdings[b] as of:				
		1929-1930	1937-1938	1972	1974-1975[c]	1976
Ford	Ford Motor Co.	100	100	40	40.4[p]	40.3
Guggenheim	Kennecott[a]	Mgmt. (no ownership data)	1.2	—	Prob. under 2.0	—
Harriman	Union Pacific	1.9	0.8	—	0.6[p][g]	0.6
Hochschilds	Amax	—	11.9 American Metals / 10.2 Climax Molybdenum	—	3.7[p]	—
James & Dodge	Phelps Dodge[a]	50+	15.3	—	Prob. under 2.0	—
Jones & Laughlin	LTV (Jones & Laughlin)[a]	80+	38.8	—	Prob. under 2.0	—
Kirby & Woolworth	Woolworths	Mgmt. (no ownership data)	6.4	—	0.3[p]	1.8
Kresge	Kresge[a]	Prob. 20+	44.2	9.3	9.1	4.0
Lasater, Reynolds & Gray	R. J. Reynolds Industries	Legal device (no ownership data)	27.4	2.2	Prob. under 2.0[h]	(5.3)[i]
Levis	Owens-Illinois[a]	—	16.8	—	Prob. under 2.0[j]	—
McCormick	International Harvester	Mgmt. (no ownership data)	32.2	—	0.5[p]	0.5
Mellon	Alcoa	80+	35.2	—	c. 22 (c. 30)	—
	Gulf	90+	70.2	—	10.2 (14.4)	7.6 (14.6)
Milbank-Borden	Borden[a]	Mgmt. (no ownership data)	6.4	—	under 1.0	—

Family	Company					
Moore	Southern Railway[a]	1.9	4.1	—	under 2.0	under 0.1
	American Can[a]	Mgmt. (no ownership data)	9.8	—	under 2.0[k]	—
Pew	Sun Oil Co.	—	69.4	—	36.5[pf]	36.5
Phipps	International Paper[a]	Mgmt. (no ownership data)	14.4[l]	—	4.5[l]	—
Pitcairn	PPG Industries	Prob. 20+	35.3	—	15.7 (2.76)	—
Rockefeller	Standard Oil (Indiana)[a]	14.5	11.4	—	1.2 (2.3)	0.9 (1.4)
	Exxon[a]	c. 20 Standard Vacuum	13.5	—	2.0 (3.6)	0.8 (2.1)
	Mobil[a]	c. 20 Standard of NY	16.3	(5.2)	2.2 (4.1)	0.4 (1.9)
	Standard Oil (California)[a]	Prob. 20+	12.3	—	2.2 (3.1)	— (1.6)
	Standard Oil (Ohio)[a]	Prob. 20+	14.8	—	under 1.0 (0.5)	—
Rosenwald–Levy–Stern	Sears[a]	Mgmt. (no ownership data)	12.8	—	0.3[p]	0.3
Solvay	Allied Chemical	18.1	20.3	—	9.7[p]	—
Walters, Jenkins & Newcomer	Seaboard Coastline Inds.[a]	38.9	36.9	(5.4)[m]	under 2.0[n]	under 2.0
Weyerhaeuser	Weyerhaeuser	—	15.7	—	2.2[p]	—
Woodruff	Coca-Cola	—	7.8	—	7.3[pf]	1.6
Zellerbach	Crown Zellerbach[a]	Legal device (no ownership data)	8.5	—	1.1[pf]	—

Notes to Table 3.7 (cont.)

Includes virtually all cases where data are available for at least two of the following three time periods: 1929–1930, 1937–1938, 1972–1976.

[a] Indicates that family control of the company was lost during the period 1929–1976.

[b] Holdings include beneficially owned stock (directly owned or through trust accounts) and stock of controlled foundations. Discretionary holdings of a controlled bank are shown by a parenthetical figure, which includes both the family holding plus the additional bank holding. (See Mellon – Alcoa, which shows a 1974–1975 Mellon family holding of approximately 22 percent, then a larger figure of about 30 percent, which adds in the Mellon Bank's discretionary ownership of Alcoa.) Where several families were collectively important in control, the numbers for the several families are treated as a unit.

The years chosen were based on data availability and derive from the following sources: (1) 1929–1930 are the years used by Berle and Means, and the numbers given are theirs; (2) 1937–1938 are the years for which data were assembled for TNEC Monograph No. 29, the most exhaustive study ever made of ownership of large U.S. corporations; (3) 1972 data for some 163 companies were collected in the Metcalf Committee's study *Disclosure of Corporate Ownership*; (4) 1974–1975 are the years for which data were collected for the 200 largest for the present study; (5) 1976 data for 122 large corporations were put together by Corporate Data Exchange and published by the Metcalf Committee in 1978 under the title *Voting Rights in American Corporations*.

[c] Proxy based data are indicated by a subscript "p"; data taken from foundation reports are shown by a subscript "f." Many divestments were traced through an examination of past proxies, SEC Monthly Transactions data for corporate insiders, newspaper reports of secondary offerings, and articles on companies and families in major newspaper and periodical articles. In a number of cases where information was exceptionally sparse, company officials were willing to provide order-of-magnitude figures for family holdings.

[d] Don Whitehead, *The Dow Story* (New York: McGraw-Hill, 1968), p. 271.

[e] This is a combined figure for the Duke Endowment (24 percent) and the Doris Duke Trust (4 percent). As described in the text, control of the stock of Duke Endowment is not held by the Duke family but, rather, by a group closely affiliated with the Duke Power Company. If there is a focal point of control, it is the management of the power company.

[f] The approximately 8 percent figure is computed from an estimate of the value of Du Pont-held GM stock in 1978–1979, given by Dan Machalaba in "Founding Families, Few Du Ponts Remain in the Company Today, but Few Are in Need," the *Wall Street Journal*, May 24, 1979, p. 39. Several informed insiders consider this estimate to be on the high side.

[g] This may be an underestimate; an Interstate Commerce Commission (ICC) report of 1974 listed Brown Brothers Harriman and the Harriman family as having some 3 percent of Union Pacific. The Corporate Data Exchange's *CDE Stock Ownership Directory, Transportation Industry* (New York: Corporate Data Exchange, Inc., 1977), p. 319, however, shows only 0.6 percent for the Harriman family in its tabulation of the holdings of the 20 largest Union Pacific shareholdings at the end of 1974.

76

[h]Proxy statement shows only 1.0 percent family holdings, but they are known to be substantially larger.

[i]This is a holding of the Wachovia Bank, closely affiliated with R. J. Reynolds Industries.

[j]In 1975 only Robert Levis, with 35,310 shares, 0.2 percent of the total, remained on the Owens–Illinois board.

[k]The 1974 proxy statement of American Can showed both William H. Moore and his mother holding only 28,073 shares, or about 0.2 percent of the total.

[l]The numbers are for holdings of Bessemer Securities Company, a Phipps family–dominated holding company, although with a greatly reduced Phipps interest by 1975.

[m]This is a holding of Mercantile Trust of Baltimore, which was controlled in earlier years by Henry Walters and associates; the bank was long the holder of Walters's (and associates') stock in Seaboard and its predecessor.

[n]See Corporate Data Exchange, Inc., *CDE Stock Ownership Directory, Transportation Industry* (New York: Corporate Data Exchange, Inc., 1977), p. 279.

Table 3.8. *Percentage declines in ownership by family groups in 43 large corporations from peak holding to trough, 1929–1976*

Percentage decline	Number of companies	Percentage of companies
75% or more	25	58.1
50–74%	12	27.9
25–49%	3	7.0
Under 25%	3	7.0
Total	43	100.0

percentage decline of family holdings in the 43 companies shown in Table 3.7 from peak to trough. In more than half the cases the family holding fell by 75 percent or more, and in more than four-fifths of the cases the percentage decline was 50 percent or more. By my estimate, control passed out of the hands of the entrepreneurial family (families) during this era in 26 of the 43 companies, and in several other instances it weakened markedly. Among the cases of lost control are the five Standard Oil companies, subject to a diminishing and tenuous Rockefeller control or influence in 1929–1938, but clearly outside the orbit of Rockefeller family control by 1975.[14]

The major declines in family control of the largest corporations described in Tables 3.7 and 3.8 have not been offset by any comparable replacements. The John Paul Getty type of ownership and control – with one or a few family members owning a clear majority of stock – has been rare. Although powerful industrial empires have been created by individuals like J. Peter Grace and George Brown[15] – these fiefdoms have not been based on large stock interests, have not provided family successor management, and have been inherently transitory. Thus they are hardly qualifications to the conclusion that family control of the large corporation has dwindled markedly. The "interest groups" identifiable at the time of the Pujo report, often based on the economic power of family groups, also have tended to lose whatever significance they had as *control* groups (as described in greater length in Chapter 6).

A number of analysts have contested the erosion of family domination of the largest corporations, sometimes out of an apparent unwillingness to concede an ideologically unpalatable point.[16] But the decline appears to be an unassailable historical fact, if family control is interpreted to mean durable control based on a combination of very substantial ownership and a special historic role of a family in the origination and/or management of a company. One mode of denial is by simply redefining "family control" to mean mere ownership control, which, if combined with a liberal enough criterion of control, can prove a great deal of family control without either family *or* control.[17]

Growth, Family Divestment, and Deconcentration of Ownership. The trend toward deconcentration of individual and family ownership has been based on several factors. One is that if a firm grows rapidly and has to tap public equity markets, dominant large stockholders may not want (or be able) to put in additional capital sufficient to maintain their proportionate share. Corporate success and growing prestige increase public and institutional interest in the company and facilitate a widening of the ownership base. Entrepreneurial families with large initial holdings may not only not want to add new capital, but may also further contribute to deconcentration by within-family diffusion and divestment. By the third generation the holdings of a single individual like John D. Rockefeller may be distributed among scores of individuals, trusts, and foundations. In his testimony at the Nelson Rockefeller confirmation hearings, J. Richardson Dilworth described the 1974 Rockefeller family assets as divided among 84 individuals in personal and trusteed holdings, with additional large sums in foundations.[18] Intrafamily diffusion is often ignored by analysts on the assumption that there is a high degree of family agreement, loyalty, and coordinated behavior. This assumption is often, but not invariably, correct. Family squabbles have sharply divided the du Ponts,[19] Hartfords,[20] and Guggenheims,[21] among others. The curious twists and turns that family struggles take can be seen in the alliance of the president of Doubleday and Company, John Sargent, with his former brother-in-law and fellow board member, Nelson Doubleday, Jr., and his former mother-in-law, in opposition to his former wife, Neltje Doubleday Sargent Kings, the leader of Doubleday dissidents who are seeking independent outside directors, greater disclosure, and creation of a public market for Doubleday stock.[22] It is true that, generally speaking, family blocks can be mobilized by key family members and tend to be regarded as unified (or potentially so) by outsiders, but greater dispersion tends to weaken collective interest and power.

Another significant factor in dispersion (and sometimes de facto reduction) of family holdings is the placement of family resources in foundations. Foundations were designed and long used for a variety of ends – mainly to avoid estate taxes, to preserve a family control holding, and to maintain family control and influence over the future disposition of donated assets. Legislation in 1969 greatly reduced the serviceability of foundations for control purposes and forced important adjustments, including divestments of large blocks of stock placed in foundations by entrepreneurial families.[23] Foundations usually have been sufficiently tied to the founding family to make it reasonable to class their company stock as part of the family holding. Of 13 large (2 percent or more) foundation holdings of voting stock in the 200 largest nonfinancial corporations, 8 were classed in this study as under family control in the mid-1970s,[24] but their loyalty is rarely put to the test and several of the 8 were on the verge of complete independence. The important exceptions to family/foundation control have arisen out of a founder's primary interest in preserving a unified holding in responsible hands, family disputes, the attrition of family interest and participation in foundation affairs, and the company management's interest in influencing the foundation. This last point is important but has been neglected in the preoccupation with family power. However, a management struggling for autonomy and control through strategic position has a clear interest in dominating, or at least neutralizing, a foundation with a large block of company stock, in which case the large foundation holding becomes a vehicle of *management control.* The management consolidates its strategic position in the company by obtaining strategic position in the foundation.

One illustrative case is the Duke Endowment Trust in its relation to the Duke Power Company. The trust was a majority owner of Duke Power until 1970 and still held 24 percent of Duke Power Company stock[25] in December 1975. There were two Duke family members among the 15 trustees of the trust, but 7, including the chairman of the board, were officers of the Duke Power Company. The Duke family has not been active in Duke Power for a long time; and the interpenetration of company and trust officers suggests that if the Duke Power Company management does not dominate the trust – at a minimum the trust is a friendly affiliate, not a wholly separate entity that controls the power company.

In the case of the Johnson Foundation and Johnson & Johnson Company a similar conclusion seems appropriate. The foundation held about 16.6 percent of the stock of Johnson & Johnson in 1975 – probably considerably more than the Johnson family at that time.[26] Members of the family were not active in or directly represented on the foundation or company boards in 1975. Johnson & Johnson's board was not directly represented on the foundation board, but three of the nine trustees of the foundation were former high officers of the company, and another was a longtime consultant to the company. The foundation had significant links to the company, but there was no obvious basis of family control through the foundation.

The Hartford Foundation's relationship to A&P is a more complex variant of the same trend. One of the main purposes of the foundation was the maintenance of unified control of A&P. With the death of John Hartford in 1951, control of the foundation, and thus the company, quickly passed into the hands of a nonfamily management-affiliated group. This group selected foundation trustees from company management and friendly family members, and was at constant odds with more numerous unsympathetic family members. The weakening condition of A&P in the late 1960s and early 1970s led to many law suits by large stockholders and to an enlargement of the foundation board in 1973 to include independent outsiders.[27] The Hartford Foundation thus shifted from family control to management control (with some family allied with management), and then, as a result of poor company performance and pressures from family and other large stockholders, to an even more independent status. In 1979 and 1980 all the Foundation's shares were sold to the West German Tengelmann Group, which then assumed control of A&P.

In sum, in a number of cases, family control over a company has been preserved through control of a foundation. But some foundations have gravitated into the power orbit of the managements of the controlled companies, and many others have become diversified and independent or quasi-independent. This mechanism of corporate control has been critically weakened in recent years by legislative limits on foundation holdings in single companies and the requirement of a high payout rate on foundation assets.

When family holdings are large, their control advantages must be weighed against the disadvantages of an undiversified family asset portfolio. Once entrepreneurial and managerial capacity of a high order is no longer present, the advantages of family control of a corporation are not obvious.[28] The less significant the control objective becomes to the family members, the greater the incentive to divest for purposes of diversification. The family could continue to try to hire first-rate managers, but movement to a fully diversified portfolio would seem even more sensible. From this perspective, divestment plus diversification is the economically rational course. The second and third generations of Rockefellers, for example, have not been interested in control of the former Rockefeller-dominated oil companies, and their diversification out of oils was probably hastened by a desire to avoid the very appearance of control.

There are other reasons for divestment of large family holdings – among them, the need for money for other purposes, a pessimistic assessment of the company's future, estate tax liabilities, and the serviceability of stock for charitable donations. Charitable contributions in the form of stock acquired earlier at low prices has long had the dual advantage of being tax deductible at market value of assets and of allowing the avoidance of tax payments on substantial capital gains. The skillful use of durable trusts, marital deductions, gifts, charitable contributions, and placement of family resources in foundations still allows wealthy families to pay nominal estate taxes. George Cooper, in reviewing the various sizable escape routes that still prevail, concludes that the estate/gift tax system "serves no purpose other than to give reassurance to the millions of unwealthy that entrenched wealth is being attacked. The attack is, however, more cosmetic than real . . ."[29] However, although the very wealthy have been able to escape estate taxes to a considerable degree, some have voluntarily given away a great deal of money for public purposes. Although the Mellon family "does not appear to be dissipating its fortune in riotous charity,"[30] Andrew Carnegie so dissipated his fortune, and a significant proportion of the Rockefeller fortune has been allocated to good works.[31] If estate taxes have been nominal, diversification, charitable contributions, sales of stock for personal expenditures, and intrafamily diffusion all have had a significant deconcentration effect on entrepreneurial family holdings in the largest companies.

Mergers and the Deconcentration of Ownership. Mergers have been extremely important in the growth of many large corporations and have had major effects on the distribution of stock ownership. They tend to increase market and aggregate concentration, but at the same time they tend to *reduce* the concentration of ownership. Between 1890 and 1905 a public market for industrial securities came into existence and a great many mergers occurred among formerly closely held companies. Typically, quite a few companies were combined to form the new entity – the mean number of combined companies in turn-of-the-century mergers was nine, the median number, 5.2.[32] If the original constituent owners held on to their new voting stock, at most a collective majority or substantial minority control would prevail. But the owners often quickly sold out their minority holdings to take advantage of merger-created high stock prices, and very often additional merger activity ensued. One of the main purposes of these mergers was precisely to allow formerly locked-in owner/managers to take advantage of the new public interest in stocks, the market's optimistic capitalization of expected monopoly profits, and the opportunities for diversification of personal wealth. The trade-off was greater wealth and security at the cost of reduced or lost control.

When the U.S. Rubber Company was formed in 1892, for example, 12 companies were initially absorbed (encompassing over 50 percent of national rubber footwear capacity), and acquisitions continued over the next decade.[33] Concentration in footwear manufacturing was clearly increased, but only one large firm with relatively dispersed ownership came out of the score of mainly closely held companies. The formation of the U.S. Steel Corporation in 1901 obviously increased concentration in the iron and steel industry, but the combination of eight separate companies (several themselves products of extensive merger activity) greatly dispersed ownership in the steel industry. Andrew Carnegie had had majority ownership control of the most important constituent of U.S. Steel, the Carnegie Steel Company, whereas no individual, family, or corporation appears to have held as much as 5 percent of the voting stock of the newly formed U.S. Steel Corporation by 1902.[34]

More recent combinations of large firms also illustrate the same phenomenon. The merger of Champion Paper and U.S. Plywood in 1967, with further divestments thereafter, converted two family-dominated firms into a managerial firm, with the only large holdings in the hands of institutional investors. The 1954 merger of Philip Morris and Benson & Hedges, reduced the Cullman's substantial minority interest in Benson & Hedges (about 25 percent) to a 5 percent interest in the combined entity (down to 0.6 percent in 1975, following additional absorptions). A more common sequence for the modern giants is a gradual reduction in family ownership by a succession of mergers over an extended period of time, with the acquisitions often made by an exchange of stock. Between 1967 and 1972, for example, City Investing increased its voting shares from 2.1 million to 30.7 million, in a major acquisition binge. R. W. Dowling, who had dominated the firm before 1966, and probably had majority ownership control in 1959, had 10 percent of the voting shares in 1967, 2.5 percent in 1969, and left the board in 1972 with under 2 percent. In companies like Borden, American Cyanamid, Colgate–Palmolive, General Foods, Singer, and many others, merger activity has continued over decades, with consequent attrition of major family holdings (in each of these cases, family ownership has fallen over 75 percent since the late 1930s).

Merger activity can also have exactly the opposite effect on ownership concentration. When majors like Colgate–Palmolive, Pepsico, or R. J. Reynolds Industries acquire large, closely held companies via an exchange of stock, the selling principals often become substantial owners and frequently join the board of the acquiring company. Such transactions rarely result in a concentrated block as large as 5 percent of the acquiring company, but they are nonetheless significant in size (usually much more substantial than management holdings). Thus the Colgate–Palmolive acquisition of the Kendall Company in 1972 gave John Kendall close to two million shares (2.8 percent, as compared to John Colgate's 1.3 percent of voting shares and the inside officers' 0.1 percent). The Pepsico acquisition of Frito-Lay in 1965, made Herman Lay the largest individual owner and board member with 1.7 percent of the voting shares. The acquisition by R. J. Reynolds Industries of McLean Industries in 1969 gave Malcolm McLean an exceptionally large position in the acquiring company – 3.5 percent of the voting stock, including over three million shares of a convertible preferred, which, if converted into common, would have given McLean 10.1 percent of the vote.

These absolutely large but proportionately moderate-sized blocks obtained via merger very rarely affect the control position of the acquiring management in the short run, but they are quite important. They usually involve new board membership by individuals who are both successful businesspeople and possessors of a very substantial stake in the management's effective performance in the shareholder interest. A management that fails in the pursuit of that interest would face a more formidable challenge than one having a set of nonowning outside directors connected by friendly and business links.[35] Such merger-based minority blocks with an associated directorship have been quite common and account for a significant number of the minority holdings classified in Tables 3.1, 3.2 and 3.3 under Management Control, but with a residual ownership constraint. In 11 of those companies there was at least one board member in 1975 who held 1 percent or more of the stock acquired in a merger exchange; and there were as many more where the holding was between 0.2 percent and 0.9 percent (usually the largest holding on the board and a substantial asset in value terms).

The persistence of ownership influence and the profit incentive

The decline of direct ownership control in the largest corporations suggests the possibility of an autonomous management group that is free of ownership influence. This development, in consequence, has given birth to a large progeny of managerial theories, built on assumptions of management objectives and policies that deviate more or less materially from owner interest and the traditional assumption of profit maximization.

There is no doubt that the top managers of large corporations have considerable discretionary authority (as described in the previous chapter). But there is a question not only of the outer limits of that discretion, but also, and even more significantly, what it is that determines the range of choices over which discretion is *normally* exercised. If managers are free to make decisions on new product lines to be pursued in order to yield the highest net return on investment, the discretion is of a different order than one that allows them either to invest for profit *or* to give away corporate assets to worthy causes. The authority to choose among investment proposals whose returns are uncertain, but where profitability is the acknowledged criterion, involves limited discretion, where the standards of choice and evaluation are already determined. The manager is "free" to pursue profits within the framework of certain rules of the game.

Besides the question of the extent of managerial discretion, there is also the major issue of the degree of overlap or conflict of interest between owners and managers. Owners might want to compensate managers generously, as a means to elicit dedicated effort or even as a matter of justice, but managers might want to enlarge their own salaries and expense perquisites even further. This conflict is fairly obvious. Less obvious, and more debatable, is the potential conflict between managerial (and organizational) interest in growth per se and the owners' interest in maximizing the present value of ownership claims. This is a difficult question (addressed further later), because growth and profits are clearly not mutually exclusive objectives. In a dynamic system a linkage between the two is often plausible. Growth and profits are sometimes not only compatible but even inseparable goals. Furthermore, even the top managers of large firms that appear to be very growth oriented always *claim* that their ultimate end is enlarged profits. Perhaps the corporate claim of a profit end underlying the growth drive is sometimes untrue, with growth the real objective and profits of secondary interest, serving merely as a constraint required for managerial survival. But this may still be only a deviation from a norm. In addition, policies suggesting a bias toward growth per se are also found in owner-dominated and even closely held firms,[36] so that establishing their presence in large managerial firms proves little about changes in the motives associated with a decline in direct ownership control.

Management control as seen from this author's vantage point, however, exists within a system of powerful pressures and constraints that still have ownership interests as their taproot. The view here is that *profitable growth*[37] is a reasonable summary of the primary objective of the large managerial corporation today, as well as of the large firms of 50 or 75 years ago. The profitable growth objective has come about through complex channels – ownership interests represented on the board, market-based and social pressures, and structural/organizational changes – grounded ultimately in the interests and power of ownership. A closer examination of these channels follows.

Ownership Interests Represented on the Board of Directors

There are three distinguishable levels of ownership representation on boards – the direct and family ownership of the top officers who are also board members, the direct and family ownership of

Table 3.9. *Ownership of voting stock of the directors of the 200 largest nonfinancial corporations, 1975*

Percentage of voting stock	Companies		Market value of the owned stock (millions of dollars)	Companies	
	No.	%		No.	%
20 and over	17	8.5	250 and over	9	4.5
10 and under 20	3	1.5	100 and under 250	8	4.0
5 and under 10	8	4.0	50 and under 100	9	4.5
2 and under 5	25	12.5	25 and under 50	17	8.5
1 and under 2	15	7.5	10 and under 25	23	11.5
0.5 and under 1	23	11.5	5 and under 10	16	8.0
Under 0.5	109	54.5	1 and under 5	57	28.5
Total	200	100.0	0.5 and under 1	24	12.0
			0.1 and under 0.5	35	17.5
			Under 0.1 (=$100,000)	2	1.0
			Total	200	100.0

Includes ownership reported in proxy statements for directors and their associated family and family-dominated holdings. Where information was available concerning extended family holdings not reported in proxy statements, as with du Pont and Alcoa, these were also included.

all board members (inside and outside directors), and direct board ownership plus ownership represented on the board by agents of institutions owning stock directly or holding it in a fiduciary capacity. (The last case would be illustrated by an officer of an insurance company on the board of an electronics firm whose stock was owned by the insurance company for its own account or as a trustee-manager of a pension fund account.)

Board Direct and Family Ownership. Tables 3.9 and 3.10 describe the ownership holdings of the board as a whole for the 200 largest nonfinancials and the 100 largest industrials in the mid-1970s, largely as reported in proxy statements. These tables show quite a skewed distribution that supports the view that there is a high degree of separation of ownership from control of the large corporation. In 28 out of the 200 largest nonfinancials (14 percent) the board owned 5 percent or more of the voting stock, and in 68 out of the 200 (34 percent) the board owned 1 percent or more. In 26 out of 200 cases (13 percent) board ownership was worth $50 mil-

Table 3.10. *Ownership of voting stock of the directors of the 100 largest industrials, 1975*

Percentage of voting stock	Companies		Market value of the owned stock (millions of dollars)	Companies	
	No.	%		No.	%
20 and over	10	10	250 and over	7	7
10 and under 20	3	3	100 and under 250	5	5
5 and under 10	6	6	50 and under 100	7	7
2 and under 5	15	15	25 and under 50	12	12
1 and under 2	6	6	10 and under 25	11	11
0.5 and under 1	14	14	5 and under 10	10	10
Under 0.5	46	46	1 and under 5	37	37
Total	100	100	0.5 and under 1	4	4
			0.1 and under 0.5	7	7
			Under 0.1 (=$100,000)	—	—
			Total	100	100

Includes ownership reported in proxy statements for directors and their associated family and family-dominated holdings. Where information was available concerning extended family holdings not reported in proxy statements, as with du Pont and Alcoa, these were also included.

lion or more, and in 66 cases (33 percent) it was worth $10 million or more. For the 100 largest industrials, the proportions are higher: 19 boards held 5 percent or more of the voting stock, 40 boards held 1 percent or more; 19 held stock worth $50 million or more, 42 held stock worth $10 million or more. But at the other (larger) end of the distribution, in 109, or 54.5 percent, of the 200 largest nonfinancials and 46 of the 100 largest industrials, the directors owned less than 0.5 percent of the voting stock; and in 118 (59 percent) of the 200 and 48 of the 100, directors owned under $5 million worth of company stock. These data underrate direct family ownership interests, given the limited reporting requirements of family holdings beyond those of the director and his or her immediate family; on the other hand, they include family-created foundations, whose control via family may be tenuous and whose economic well-being may be of less urgent concern to families than their direct and trusteed holdings.

Direct and Represented Ownership on Board. Tables 3.11 and 3.12 supplement the preceding two tables by adding to direct board

Table 3.11. *Ownership of voting stock by directors and interests represented on the board of directors of the 200 largest nonfinancial corporations, 1975*

Percentage of voting stock	Companies		Market value of owned stock (millions of dollars)	Companies	
	No.	%		No.	%
20 and over	21	10.5	250 and over	19	9.5
10 and under 20	11	5.5	100 and under 250	14	7.0
5 and under 10	20	10.0	50 and under 100	16	8.0
2 and under 5	40	20.0	25 and under 50	20	10.0
1 and under 2	16	8.0	10 and under 25	33	16.5
0.5 and under 1	33	16.5	5 and under 10	20	10.0
Under 0.5	59	29.5	1 and under 5	49	24.5
			0.5 and under 1	10	5.0
Total	200	100.0	0.1 and under 0.5	18	9.0
			Under 0.1 (=$100,000)	1	0.5
			Total	200	100.0

Represented holdings include all identifiable ownership interests in the companies by institutions represented on the board, with sole voting power held by the institution. The main institutions involved are commercial banks, insurance companies, and investment companies.

holdings the major intercorporate and institutional holdings represented on the board – the latter, usually by officers of banks, insurance companies, or investment companies. "Represented" may be too strong a word in some cases, as the large banks usually claim that their officer/directorships in a company are rarely or never based on the fact that their trust departments hold stock in that company but, rather, that they are based on their commercial relationships and general prestige. Because a banker/director is usually on a board in connection with the commercial function of the bank, and because the director is barred by inside information rules from transmitting commercial information to the trust department, it is understandable why banks would disclaim *any* relationship of a director to trust holdings. The banker/ director does have a fiduciary obligation to the trust accounts, however, and his total disinterest in the company's performance as it would bear on bank trustee stock is hard to swallow. When insurance and (especially) investment company representatives serve on boards of companies whose securities are held by their home firms, they

Table 3.12. *Ownership of voting stock by directors and interests represented on the board of directors of the 100 largest industrial corporations, 1975*

Percentage of voting stock	Companies		Market value of owned stock (millions of dollars)	Companies	
	No.	%		No.	%
20 and over	11	11	250 and over	10	10
10 and under 20	8	8	100 and under 250	10	10
5 and under 10	13	13	50 and under 100	11	11
2 and under 5	19	19	25 and under 50	12	21
1 and under 2	7	7	10 and under 25	18	18
0.5 and under 1	21	21	5 and under 10	9	9
Under 0.5	21	21	1 and under 5	23	23
Total	100	100	0.5 and under 1	3	3
			0.1 and under 0.5	4	4
			Under 0.1 (=$100,000)	—	—
			Total	100	100

Represented holdings include all identifiable ownership interests in the companies by institutions represented on the board, with sole voting power held by the institution. The main institutions involved are commercial banks, insurance companies, and investment companies.

often acknowledge that their purpose is to follow and protect their investment. The same is true of representatives of other companies that have a substantial stock interest in the company in question (British Petroleum in Sohio, Royal Dutch/Shell in Shell Oil, Hanna Mining in National Steel).

It is evident from Tables 3.11 and 3.12 that with these interests taken into account, *ownership* representation on the boards of large corporations is fairly impressive. For 32 companies out of the 200 largest nonfinancials (16 percent) and 19 out of the 100 largest industrials, the stock representation exceeds 10 percent; for 52 out of the 200 nonfinancials (26 percent) and 32 out of the 100 industrials, it exceeds 5 percent. For 49 out of the 200 nonfinancials (24.5 percent) and 31 out of the 100 industrials the stock represented on the board was worth $50 million or more. At the other end of the spectrum, in 92 out of the 200 largest nonfinancials (46 percent) and 42 of the 100 largest industrials, the voting stock represented on the board was under 1 percent; and in 78 out of the

200 largest nonfinancials (39 percent) and 30 out of the 100 largest industrials, the value of the stock represented on the board was under $5 million.

These data show a great deal of separation of ownership and control, but they also indicate that in a large minority of cases, ownership representation on boards of directors is quantitatively significant. Whether, and to what degree, these representatives will press very hard for an owner-interest orientation is less clear. In contrast with a director who personally holds a large block of stock, a representative of British Petroleum on the board of Sohio, for example, has only a second-order owner interest, although given British Petroleum's large ownership stake in Sohio and the probable role assignment of the BP representative, we would expect strong and well-informed owner representation in this case. Institutional investor representatives are usually associated with lesser holdings, plus a weaker, second-order interest and role.

In the case of bank trust department ownership there is an even more remote interest in stock performance, because the stock is owned for the account of others and the director usually disclaims representation of the stock interest. There are other complexities as well, such as the possible reciprocity relationship between the portfolio company management and the commercial department of the bank, offset in part by the bank's direct and indirect profit stake in performing well for its fiduciary customers.[38] Reciprocity relationships may compromise the "outsideness" of other institutional-owner/directors and may also make the outsiders more tolerant of an emphasis on growth.

For a variety of reasons, therefore, institutional representatives may be less intense and single-minded in pursuit of the owner interest than direct owners, but their institutions do have a stake in the company's performance and in the investments that these representatives seek to protect and advance with varying degrees of zealousness. Their presence, prestige, and definite connection with ownership (and creditor) claims help create a system of expectations, rules, and criteria of evaluation that are owner oriented.

Managerial Ownership Interests. The direct ownership interests of managers who are also on the board of directors is shown in Tables 3.13 and 3.14. These tabulations do not include all senior officers, and there is much variation among companies in the number of officers on boards. But really sizable officer holdings are usually

Table 3.13. *Ownership of voting stock of the top officers on the boards of the 200 largest nonfinancial corporations, 1975*

Percentage of voting stock	Companies No.	%	Market value of the owned stock (millions of dollars)	Companies No.	%
20 and over	11	5.5	250 and over	3	1.5
10 and under 20	3	1.5	100 and under 250	5	2.5
5 and under 10	3	1.5	50 and under 100	4	2.0
2 and under 5	13	6.5	25 and under 50	13	6.5
1 and under 2	8	4.0	10 and under 25	13	6.5
0.5 and under 1	15	7.5	5 and under 10	18	9.0
Under 0.5	147	73.5	1 and under 5	55	27.5
Total	200	100.0	0.5 and under 1	21	10.5
			0.1 and under 0.5	53	26.5
			Under 0.1 (=$100,000)	15	7.5
			Total	200	100.0

Includes ownership reported in proxy statements for officers on boards of directors and their associated family and family-dominated holdings. Where information was available concerning extended family holdings not reported in proxy statements, as with Du Pont and Alcoa, these were also included.

concentrated in the few top officers (and their families), and other officers with large holdings often obtain board representation. As in the case of Tables 3.9 and 3.10 previously discussed, these tables also suffer from underreporting. Family holdings beyond the officer and family members residing in the same house do not have to be provided in proxy statements. Trust holdings and those held under special plans (profit sharing, stock options, phantom stock)[39] are often not included in proxy statements. Thus the data tabulated here is an understatement of both personal and familial ownership stakes.

These distributions also are highly skewed, with the vast bulk of companies showing officer holdings under 0.5 percent of the total (73.5 percent for the 200 largest nonfinancials, 65 percent for the 100 largest industrials) and worth less than $5 million (72 percent for the 200 largest nonfinancials, 62 percent for the 100 largest industrials). At the upper end of the distribution, however, in 25 out of the 100 largest industrials, top officer holdings were 1 percent or more of the total, and in 38 cases they were worth $5

Table 3.14. *Ownership of voting stock of the top officers on the boards of the 100 largest industrials, 1975*

Percentage of voting stock	Companies		Market value of the owned stock (millions of dollars)	Companies	
	No.	%		No.	%
20 and over	6	6	250 and over	2	2
10 and under 20	2	2	100 and under 250	2	2
5 and under 10	2	2	50 and under 100	3	3
2 and under 5	9	9	25 and under 50	11	11
1 and under 2	6	6	10 and under 25	8	8
0.5 and under 1	10	10	5 and under 10	12	12
Under 0.5	65	65	1 and under 5	40	40
			0.5 and under 1	9	9
Total	100	100	0.1 and under 0.5	11	11
			Under 0.1 (=$100,000)	2	2
			Total	100	100

Includes ownership reported in proxy statements for officers on boards of directors and their associated family and family-dominated holdings. Where information was available concerning extended family holdings not reported in proxy statements, as with Du Pont and Alcoa, these were also included.

million or more. It should be kept in mind that small percentages of ownership in very large companies can amount to large absolute values and possibly large fractions of the personal wealth of the officers. Wilbur G. Lewellen found that although the fractional share held by the top five executives in a sample of large manufacturing firms declined from 1.06 percent in 1940 to 0.59 percent in 1963, the mean value of their holdings rose from $574,743 to $2,365.847.[40] On average, Lewellen found senior executives to own between $1 million and $2 million of their company's stock. The median-sized holding of company stock by individual officer/directors of the 100 largest industrials in December 1974, a period of depressed stock prices, was $920,000.

In addition to this fairly substantial direct ownership, officers of the largest corporations very often have stock options and participate in a variety of other plans that tie executive income to stock and earnings performance. It has been suggested, therefore, that despite the substantial separation of ownership and control, and small proportional holdings of top officers, managements' ownership and ownership-based income is absolutely so large as to gear manager and owner interests together.

The issue of the importance of the ownership interests of managers has been addressed in several different ways. One is simply to look at the size of management ownership in its various forms; a second is to see just how important owner-related income is in the total income package received by managers; and the third approach has been to study the overall determinants of management compensation, testing the "fit" of independent variables, such as volume of sales, profits, and earnings per share (as well as changes in these variables) in explaining changes in compensation levels.

As regards the size of management ownership interests, it should be reiterated that available data understate these, for they exclude the holdings of a manager's children who are not living in the household and sometimes exclude trusted holdings. Holdings under stock option plans are also usually not included under direct ownership, nor are "stock appreciation rights" and other arrangements that give managers a claim on or direct interest in company stock value. A small sample analysis by this writer suggests that inclusion of these other sources might easily double the direct ownership stake of managers in company stock. Thus these management interests are fairly substantial in terms of absolute values, but they are still not especially meaningful without a relationship to some base, like total personal assets of the officers or proportionate contribution to their income. Data are lacking on personal assets other than company stock, but Lewellen surmises that with company stockholdings as large as $1 million to $2 million, "It is hard to see how these men could have funds left for alternative portfolio commitments."[41] My finding of officer/director holdings worth only $920,000 in 1974–1975 suggests a more modest conclusion, but unreported ownership claims under option and other plans as noted, would push these values higher. Table 3.14 shows, furthermore, that for more than a quarter of the largest industrials, the officers on the board together owned $10 million or more in company stock. Robin Marris, in contrast with Lewellen, has claimed that company stock accounts for a small percentage of the total wealth of corporate managers, but he presented no supporting evidence for this conclusion.[42]

An experiment was conducted by this writer, based on the evidence provided in confirmation hearings of high-level government officials who were drawn from senior executive positions in business, because the question of potential conflict of interest is regularly brought up and the size and distribution of the nominee's assets is therefore at issue. In the case of the 1976 appointment of G. William Miller to the chairmanship of the Federal Reserve, for example, the details of his portfolio were made public and showed that of personal assets of approximately $2.8 million, about $2.3 million (82 percent) was in shares of Textron, the company of which he had been chief executive.[43] Unfortunately, in many cases, especially in earlier years, portfolio information was provided on a confidential basis if at all. Nevertheless, in 11 of the 16 cases examined, a reasonable probability was established that company stock accounted for over half of the individual's personal assets.[44] I suspect, but cannot prove, that this proportion would hold rather widely for top executives in the 100 largest industrials. Even if it did, however, although this would be suggestive, it would not prove an integration of top officer and shareholder interests. Left open is the question of whether the factors determining large salaries, bonuses, and deferred payments and pensions might have more impact on management than stockholdings; managers may be income and pension "rich" and asset "poor."

The second approach to evaluating the significance of management ownership interests focuses on the importance of ownership-based income in management's total compensation package. This approach was very effectively explored by Lewellen, who found that in 1940–1963 the ownership-based income of senior managers grew relative to fixed-payment income and that, by the end of the period, ownership-based income on an after-tax basis surpassed by "three to five times the value of the corresponding fixed-dollar rewards from salaries, cash bonuses, pensions, and similar items."[45] The period examined was one of great stock market euphoria, however, and stock options and capital gains were major factors affecting the results. In a more recent survey, following the end of the stock market boom and the tax legislation of 1969, Lewellen noted the sharp deline in stock options from 36 percent of the compensation package in 1955–1963 to only 12 percent in 1970–1973 and a decline in stock-related compensation from 44 percent to 23 percent of the compensation total.[46] Lewellen himself points to the apparent weakening of the link between management and shareholder between the two periods, and it is evident that much of the increase in importance of management/ ownership income in the earlier period was a result of special stock market conditions.[47]

Lewellen also noted the fact that with the fading of stock mar-

ket-based management earnings in 1969–1973 there was no slack-
ening in the growth of management earnings, merely a replace-
ment of ownership-based income with other forms of payment.
This suggests an important point regarding the significance of *form*
of management income; it is possible that the "incentive" effects
of different kinds of income may be overrated if the determinants
of income are under management control and management can
rearrange them to achieve a predetermined result. In recent years
there has been a large outcropping of supplementary bonus plans
that tie executive bonuses to market prices or company performance goals "most often stated in terms of earnings per share
growth."[48] Sometimes a pool of resources is set aside, to be distributed to executives at the discretion of a top-level committee,
at a rate, say, of 10 percent of the excess of net earnings over a 5
percent or 10 percent return on capital.[49] These plans formally tie
management income to share price and profit performance, but
they are fixed by the management or the board at levels of their
own choosing.[50] Because most of the factors that will determine
the size of the pool are outside the control of the individual officer
and many are largely uncontrollable in the short run, even by the
management as a whole, the size of windfalls to management
groups would seem to depend very much on managerial choices
of limits and random factors. Incentive systems, such as supplementary bonus plans, based on performance goals, may be one
method of reaching managerial income targets in a way acceptable
to shareholders. This is not to deny that performance standards
may be effective, especially when rewards are tied, as they often
are for lower-level personnel, to specific subunit profit goals, but
it should give pause in thinking about both the equitable basis and
incentive impacts of compensation systems.

A third approach to evaluating the impact of the separation of
ownership and control on management incentives is by examination of the factors influencing compensation. The main hypotheses that have been tested are (1) that management compensation is related primarily to company size, and growth in size,
independent of profitability *or* (2) that management compensation
is related primarily to growth of earnings and profitability, with
size per se, or growth in size, secondary. These hypotheses suffer
from the fact that causal relationships remain uncertain. Are compensation systems established to allow management to capture a
larger fraction of the income flow in an acceptable way or are they
designed to induce properly directed effort? And, more basic yet,

are these sometimes elaborate compensation systems of fundamental importance in motivating highly paid executives nurtured to be "achievers" in any case?[51]

Among the numerous technical problems involved in testing these hypotheses are the definition of management compensation and the static and dynamic interrelationships between size and profitability and their growth. Lewellen included dividend and capital gains income from owned stock as part of management compensation, obviously pertinent for the study of the degree of integration of management incentives and shareholder interests. Ordinarily, however, in studies of these relationships, management compensation is confined to salary and bonus and does not even include option profits, the discounted value of deferred payments and future pension receipts, or other forms of deferred credits, let alone dividends and capital gains from owned stock. It is possible that compensation narrowly defined is primarily related to size, or growth in size, whereas compensation extended to include the owner-based income of management is primarily related to profitability. In fact, this is part of the reason for the dichotomy in existing studies. Blaine Huntsman and Lewellen[52] and Robert T. Masson[53] use a somewhat broader definition of managerial income than J. W. McGuire et al., Arch Patton, and David R. Roberts,[54] along with more sophisticated methods, and found profits or stock prices key variables for managerial compensation, whereas the others all found sales predominant, with profits secondary or insignificant.[55]

Insofar as management compensation *is* related to size variables, such as sales or assets, it is not clear that any important behavioral consequences follow. A recurrent theme has been that if compensation is tied to size, managers will strive for growth per se rather than for profits. As noted, however, this theory rests on unproved assumptions about causality and the true sources and direction of managerial drives. Furthermore, the relationship between management compensation and size is partly a function of the scope of responsibilities associated with the position, the workings of a quasi-competitive market for executive talent, and managerial preference for incomes based on some relatively stable underlying variable. Firms have to pay the going rate for executives to keep them or to bid them away from others,[56] and the scope of the job is a factor in fixing the price. If there is an active external market for executive talent, higher salaries may be obtained by proving real managerial skill, that is, achieving an outstanding rate of return on resources employed and then moving on to larger responsibilities in a bigger company at higher pay. But even within the organization, superior profit performance is encouraged as the road to advancement, so that although there may be an overall bias toward growth in the collective interest, it runs counter to a market performance morality cultivated for underlings and in the executive market.

The issue is also complicated by the existence of strong but complex relationships between size and profitability and between growth in size and growth in profitability. Most studies have tried to correct for these intercorrelations by the use of multiple regression techniques, but the problems have been severe and perhaps even intractable.[57] A management wanting to grow will need profits to allow this, so that "growth and profits become equivalent as the criteria for the selection of investment programs."[58] Other possible preferences such as prestige and power are also closely tied in with profits. A management may want to achieve size because managerial wages will go up thereby, but growth without a profit payoff is quite generally regarded in the business community as unsuccessful growth. It is profitable growth that marks the successful business and manager.[59] And the managerial payoff in profitable growth goes well beyond growth per se.

The ultimate proof of the impact of control form on managerial incentives and pressures is in performance differences. The somewhat Delphic wisdom that can be distilled from that evidence, reviewed later in this chapter, suggests limited performance effects.

Other Market and Owner-Related Forces

If in many large firms management ownership is slight and large ownership blocks either do not exist, are not represented on the board, or are not normally used to influence corporate behavior by direct intervention,[60] what forces can press managers – who control by strategic position – toward efficiency and profit growth? This has been an area of great controversy. Clearly, at one extreme, there are limits beyond which mismanagement and stockholder abuse do result in managerial ouster. Yet it is also clear that managers sometimes survive despite singularly poor performance and serious abuse.[61] Depending on the moral one wishes to draw, emphasis may be placed on the discretion, periodic abuses, and the cooptative selection and succession processes, or on the boundaries to that discretion, and the pressures – external, internal, and internalized – that push managers toward a profit objective.

Other than compensation and direct ownership, the factors that have been stressed as fixing managerial boundaries and pressing managers toward the pursuit of owner-consistent objectives may be broken down into the following categories: (1) financing constraints; (2) threat of displacement by takeover; (3) ideological and socioeconomic pressures generated from within the organization and by peer groups and ownership interests on the outside; and (4) organizational role and control requirements. These factors are interrelated and are linked to the managerial, board, and represented ownership considerations previously discussed. There is little disagreement that these factors are operative; there is much dispute over their strength in keeping managements within bounds that are assumed to be imposed on owner/managers or hired managers by direct ownership interests. That owner/controllers actually engage in or compel an undeviating pursuit of profits is a common assumption, however, not a demonstrated fact.[62]

A company that performs badly in terms of its opportunities will suffer market penalties; credit will tend to be less available and more costly, stock prices will be lower, and thus external financing plans may be constrained. This may not be a very serious threat to the control position of managers of large firms, however, if internal financing suffices or comes close to it[63] and if its credit standing, although not first class, is still respectable. Barring a corporate disaster, a decline in company stock price and credit standing is not a direct challenge to managerial autonomy;[64] its discipline works through its contribution to a takeover threat and in the damage involved in loss of peer group, creditor, stockholder, and intraorganization prestige and support. Looked at another way, however, because market success reflected in excellent profit performance, high stock prices, and high credit rating add to company strength and managerial power and discretion (as well as to owner/creditor welfare), they serve managerial interests, and thus tend to be regarded with favor.

The threat of a takeover of a badly managed firm has been given the greatest attention as a reconciler of management control and market efficiency.[65] In recent decades the corporate takeover bid has become a more important mechanism of ownership transfer, reflecting the rise of new and more independent power entities in the market, the continued expansion of large firm diversification, organizational changes that have made it easier to absorb new entities painlessly, and the inflationary conditions and depressed stock prices of the late 1970s. Takeover bids allow outsiders to appeal to stockholders in a very material and practical fashion, circumventing the cumbersome and ineffectual internal machinery of voting and proxy fights. Barring failure and bankruptcy, it is the only direct route for market displacement of a management that is controlling by strategic position.

That profit maximizers will displace nonmaximizers by simply buying control of an undervalued stock makes an attractive theory. Also, it describes an important facet of reality, even if it overrates market efficiency and the effectiveness of the takeover threat and underplays the complexity of the results of this process.[66] Although there appears to be a tendency for undervalued companies to be taken over more frequently than others, the exceptions are numerous; in 19 of 41 British cases studied by Agit Singh, the acquired firm was more profitable than the acquiring firm,[67] and U.S. experience is comparable.[68] In the 1970s there has been an even more marked tendency for large, cash-rich firms to seek out well-managed and profitable smaller companies in areas of potential growth.[69] Thus the most conspicuous characteristics observed in recent takeover experience are the vulnerability of small companies, the dominance of large companies as purchasers, and the lack of evidence of profitability enhancement as a consequence of acquisitions.[70] Most important from the standpoint of impact on managerial incentives, the probability of takeover declines as company size increases,[71] with the result that for large but unprofitable firms further growth in size may be the preferred alternative survival strategy to the more onerous option of increasing profitability by internal renovation. Ironically, therefore, the rise of the "market for corporate control" via takeovers may increase inducements to grow large and merge at the expense of small- and medium-sized companies, perhaps also at the expense of more competitive and progressive market structures.[72]

Another irony is that managers impelled to pay close attention to the concerns of stockholders[73] may be *too* profit oriented – insofar as owners stress short-run stock prices, managers may be pressed toward a focus on quick gains at the expense of risk-taking and longer-term investment that more stable tenure might allow. Thus managerial capitalism may yield social inefficiencies by its better integration into an efficient capital market that heavily discounts large but uncertain long-term profits (and disregards the positive social externalities of the longer view and risk taking). This may be a real social cost of the American Way as it has evolved in an environment of performance-oriented institutional investors, widespread preoccupation with the stock market, the takeover threat, and insecure managers.[74]

Managers may try to prevent takeovers by protective strategies, such as the requirement that merger offers be approved by 80 percent of the shareholders, staggered-year directorships, and, on a longer-term basis, growth to a size virtually precluding takeover. But takeover-free size is now quite large. Although not yet reaching up to the 100 largest companies, there have been takeover attempts of giants the size of Anaconda, Babcock & Wilcox, CNA, and Marcor. And short-term protective strategies – along with outright rejection of high premium takeover bids – are the expedients of weakness that bring managements into some disrepute (and potential legal liability) for protecting their own interests at the expense of the shareholders.[75] In sum, then, the takeover phenomenon is a factor that adds its bit to others also pushing managers toward a focus on share price and earnings enhancement, but it pushes them also toward growth to takeover-free size, and its disciplinary effect on the largest firms may be slight.

Ownership has what might be termed an "omnipresence effect" on managerial purpose and behavior, affecting them at many levels and through a variety of channels. It is impressively important in quantitative dimension – in early 1978 the stock of the 200 largest corporations had a market value of $530 billion.[76] The ownership interest in most large firms, however, is diffused, with few if any holdings large enough to pose a control threat in themselves. (As shown in Table 3.15, the median value for the 20 largest holdings of voting stock in 122 large corporations in 1976 was 18.15 percent.) Nevertheless, several score institutions and several thousand wealthy individual investors account for a great deal of stock ownership,[77] and this group is informed and powerful. Many top officers and outside directors are members of this wealthy investor community, and its interests filter into corporate attitudes, ideology, and standards in a variety of ways – directly through substantial representation on boards and in some cases by outright control; indirectly through transactions with financial interests and continuous inquiries and suggestions from owners and creditors and their representatives (brokers, security analysts). If all these downgrade a management, there is not merely a loss in

Table 3.15. *Percentage of voting stock held by the 20 largest owners in 122 large corporations, December 31, 1976*

Percentage of stock	Number of corporations	Percentage of corporations
50 and over	7	5.7
40 and under 50	4	3.3
30 and under 40	9	7.4
20 and under 30	31	25.4
10 and under 20	47[a]	38.5
5 and under 10	11	9.0
1 and under 5	12	9.8
Under 1	1	0.8
Total	122	100.0

[a] Median value = 18.15 percent.
Source: Compiled from U.S., Congress, Senate, Committee on Governmental Affairs, Subcommittee on Reports, Accounting and Management, *Voting Rights in Major Corporations,* 95th Cong., 1st sess. (Washington, D.C.: Government Printing Office, January 1978), pp. 8–10.

status but also a slippage of support from important constituencies that is costly to the company and may be threatening to the management. Normally passive outside directors become more restive, bankers less cooperative, institutional investors more interested in selling, and the investor community in general critical and inclined to support demands for a housecleaning. The criteria of evaluation of market analysts and investors are thus of substantial practical as well as of social importance to managerial firms, even when stock ownership is diffused.[78]

But ownership also has a more subtle ideological impact. Because ownership and its interests are omnipresent, discourse in boardrooms, in executive committee planning sessions, and in portfolio-investment manager evaluations centers on return-risk trade-offs. The power of ownership is such that the application of criteria other than profit as a basis of systematic valuation has been ruled off the agenda. This profit-oriented value system may have greater applicability to nonowners as managers than to owner/managers, "since there is considerable uncertainty about the institutional role of the manager, [and] there will be a greater tendency for him – then, say, for the professional – to concentrate on pecuniary gain; i.e., to concentrate on that aspect of his self-interest which has least dependence upon meeting the expectations implicit in a normative code."[79] To which I would add that any other emphasis might also bring the manager into conflict with representatives of the investor community,[80] and by the time a manager rises to the top, he or she is both well-to-do and well socialized to the expectations of that community.

If profitability is the very premise of a corporation's evaluation of its plans and personnel, this suggests internalization of profit-centered criteria in the form of rules and self-appraisals. Nevertheless, there may be room for important deviations from the profitability norm, including excessive preoccupation with growth, overcompensation of executives, nepotism, bureaucratic excesses in staffing, and so forth. But these are not new or unique to management-dominated corporations. The organizational changes that have brought a sharper focus on profitability are also not confined to managerial corporations, although managerialism has grown *pari passu* with these important structural changes.

Structural Change and Managerial Motives

There has been a long-term organizational transformation of the large firm in the United States – traceable back into the nineteenth century, but with important developments in the 1920s and thereafter – that has significantly affected corporate goal setting and behavior. Increasing size and complexity, need for better and more readily available knowledge, and improved control and coordination, all led to the gradual displacement of personalized ad hoc management by more bureaucratized, rule-dominated, and impersonal structures. According to Alfred D. Chandler's pioneering analysis, organizational change followed the evolving strategic plans of the corporate leadership, allowing it to cope with new problems while maintaining and improving control and efficiency.[81] With wider geographic scope and vertical integration, large firms found it necessary to replace single, general administrative offices with a central office plus subdivisions – the latter broken down by area served and function performed (buying, sales, finance, and so forth). With even further geographic expansion and diversification into new product lines, new organizational needs arose again.

Organization along functional lines proved cumbersome, as it was difficult to fix goals and measure performance of the many interlocking and incommensurable subunits. The resultant inefficiencies led to the gradual emergence (initially by internal reorganization) of a new arrangement, with a general office at the top, overseeing various subdivisions, each of which performed all major administrative functions (planning, operations, purchasing, finance, marketing). This new arrangement reduced interdependence (confining it largely to the self-contained divisions) and, by establishing each division as a profit center, enlarged the possibilities for centralized evaluation and control. The top office, with its expert staff, now free of responsibility for coordinating functions and no longer finding it necessary to seek methods of avoiding control loss, could focus on strategic planning, development of new administrative and operational methods, and evaluation of the performance of the divisions. The tendencies of the subdivisions to build up expenses and staff empires were constrained by their narrow role and by the new systems of standardized and systematic profit-center evaluation.

Because coordination was improved by this new organizational form, control and evaluation were also more efficient, which compelled reorganization for survival in some industries – real laggards failed, or became subject to takeovers by divisionalized companies.[82] Some reorganizations, however, were necessary to avoid utter chaos in companies put together in helter-skelter fashion; in other cases, mergers to great size, and the resultant enhancement of monopoly power, allowed a postponement of needed organizational changes.[83] Some large companies retained a more traditional, functional structure with no evident distress. But the transformation was a major one, and occurred on a dramatic scale in the post-World War II era. In Richard Rumelt's estimate, between 1949 and 1969 the percentage of the Fortune 500 industrials, organized on product division lines, increased from 20.3 percent to 75.9 percent; those with strictly functional organization declined from 62.2 percent to only 11.2 percent of the total.[84] The latter group has also gradually developed more effective systems of coordination and internal control, despite wide geographic dispersion and a multiplicity of products.

There is no simple dichotomy, actually, between functional and divisional organization but, rather, "a continuous range of distribution of influence between product and functional orientation."[85] Some companies seem to shift between the two types of organization as they change their organizational format from time to time, and many have at least partial overlaps between the two broad structural forms.[86]

From the standpoint of owner versus manager control, and corporate objectives, the organizational changes implemented within many of the modern managerial giants have several important implications. First, the divisional structure made possible the imposition of standardized financial goals on the various divisions, in place of ad hoc evaluations of the performance of noncomparable functional parts. The very formalization of goals tended to enhance the importance of profits and rate-of-return considerations, as it is hardly possible to impose "profitless growth" as a formal divisional goal. Profitable growth is thus the focal point of these formalized systems, with great emphasis on rate of return on committed resources. The great expansion of divisional organization in the 1950s and 1960s was paralleled by a proliferation of the use of decentralized profit-responsibility centers, with systematic calculation of return on the investment allocated to each division.[87] With these arrangements, a profit-maximization goal is imposed on division managers, whose compensation and promotion opportunities are heavily dependent on profit performance.[88] These control and reward systems also "allow a top management to create great pressure for profit maximization. Pressure so created can, in fact, be greater than that caused by the competitive struggle among firms."[89] J. K. Galbraith contends that with the rise of the technostructure, "power passes down into the organization," and the link between management and stockholder objectives "dissolves entirely,"[90] but this interpretation disregards the retention of control from the top and the profit-oriented nature of that control.

A second important consideration is that under the divisional structure one of the core functions of the top management is the allocation of capital. As part of this process, great attention is given to the profit performance and plans of the divisions, as well as to criteria for best overall use of corporate resources. Those divisions with promisingly high rates of return will get the bulk of corporate funds; those with shrinking opportunities will get little or none and may be closed out entirely if their overall expected returns do not justify further needed investment.[91] The existence of this internalized capital market produces a bias *toward* rate-of-return considerations and away from growth in sales or market share per se, because the latter do not provide a basis for deciding between interdivisional claims on scarce corporate capital. Of course, a growth-oriented management could still retain too high a share of earnings at the expense of the shareholders, whatever the rationality imposed on the division in the use of the retained share.

Capitalism is a system in which the search for rational means to achieve business ends is continuous and powerful; and just as the development of business accounting facilitated a more systematic pursuit of profits, so divisionalization, with its increased capacity to ensure adherence to rules of rational calculation, has led to further refinement in the pursuit of profits in the large diversified corporation. Oliver Williamson notes the irony of the almost simultaneous appearance in the 1930s of concern with separation of ownership and control and potentially large managerial discretion and the rapid spread of divisionalization with its "effect of restoring integrity to the goal-specification and policing processes."[92] Technically, it is possible for goal specification not to be profit maximizing, even under this new organizational format, but much nonprofit-maximizing behavior (allowing slack, inflating other expenses) has been ad hoc and based on a lack of control and inadequate goal specification. With goal specification and capital allocation procedures formalized, with rational criteria of performance imposed on the profit centers, all of this "educes a profit preference at the top as well."[93] With a formalization of corporate objectives, the continued power and ideological dominance of ownership must prevail, as it defines the only generally acceptable criteria of performance within the business community. The pursuit of subgoals may persist, but on an ad hoc basis or by secretly pursuing *real* objectives (such as sales, expense preference) different from those explicitly proclaimed and bureaucratically imposed within a complex organization.

Control form and performance

The impact of the "managerial revolution" on economic performance is difficult to assess because the rise of management control occurred simultaneously with many other changes likely to have had powerful effects – especially the growth in absolute company size and diversification, the reorganization of the structure and internal control processes of large firms, and a changed legal environment. When organization theory, for example, is used to analyze large firm behavior, it is logically applicable to both owner- and manager-dominated firms, as organization is presumed to be a function of size, not of control. Nonetheless, there has been a tendency to identify bureaucratic structure and the limits it imposes – alleged to have led to "satisficing" and other forms of suboptimization – with managerialism; and although there is some relationship between them, this is obviously a basis for major confusion as well as serious statistical problems.

There are other factors that have also made evaluation of the "managerial revolution" problematical. Very large companies are usually diversified and oligopolistic and meet their large company rivals in numerous markets. Large owner-controlled firms are not isolated from their managerial rivals; both sets of firms are subject to a competitive, emulative, and interactive process that leads to standardization on matters extending from management compensation, organization, and control systems to responses to external pressures.

Even more serious are the problems of bias. Owner-dominated firms in the large company universe have sometimes been found to have better than average performance. One possible reason for this is that dominant owners, likely to be especially well informed, may gradually divest themselves of stock in firms lacking promise; whereas nonowning managers and other insiders (including some dominant owners) will maintain and build up their holdings in firms showing great promise.[94] Such "insider" behavior reverses the usual assumption about causality: Performance is not a result of the presence and effects of large ownership blocks; rather, large ownership blocks exist (or disappear) because of rational investment (and divestment) by informed and wealthy insiders in *anticipation* of performance. Thus, in part because of this divestment, which will leave the ownership of large "has-beens" diffused in the hands of the mass of uninformed investors, companies in stagnation and decline will tend to be subject to management control. An example of this phenomenon may be seen in the growth, in the 1920s, of the Van Sweringen railroad empire. The Van Sweringen brothers were encouraged and supported by eastern financial interests in recognition of their flair for selling securities and their consequent role in the bailing out of large old family holdings at the expense of the small investor. "Someone was needed to popularize railroad securities and make possible the transfer of these obsolescent investments to the public at large."[95]

It is a notable fact that in 1975, among the 200 largest nonfinancial corporations, management holdings in public utilities and in the railroads were generally negligible, in contrast with managerial ownership in manufacturing.

Another source of bias arises from the fact that the large company universe does not comprise randomly chosen firms that happen to be owner or manager dominated and which are also large. The general trend is toward gradual divestment of large blocks of family-owned stock and the eventual emergence of managerial control. Companies that make it into the large company universe while preserving owner domination are exceptions and may have special performance characteristics, such as unusually fast growth and exceptional profitability that allowed them to reach large size without heavy external financing – and dilution of family ownership and control.[96] This point is supported by the fact that of the 72 large companies analyzed for the years 1967–1976 in Appendix C, only 27.6 percent of the owner-dominated companies (8 out of 29) were members of the large company universe in 1919, whereas 46.5 percent of the management-dominated companies (20 out of 42) were large companies in 1919.

Traditional explanations of why there should be performance differences between owner- and management-dominated firms have tended to portray managers as purely economic individuals, trying to maximize their "lifetime income" in a situation where they have de facto but not unlimited control and a negligible stake in ownership.[97] Their "problems" are to design policies that will simultaneously protect their security and enlarge their income as much as possible without violating the law or causing a stockholder revolt. Owner-controlled companies, on the other hand, are posited as profit maximizers. With this simple, dichotomous set of motives, performance differences by control type should be discernible: In the most common formulations, managers seeking security and job protection will tend to be risk averse; because they want the increased compensation associated with larger size, they will push toward faster growth, higher rates of retained earnings, and lower rates of return on equity; and because they prefer expenses to increases in income payable to owners, they will inflate administrative costs. Owner/controllers, on the other hand, will be more willing to take risks in the interest of higher average returns on equity, will not be interested in growth per se, and will try to minimize expenses in the pursuit of maximum present value of the firm's net worth.

Problems arise quickly, however, on two fronts. One is that

owners have varied interests even as profit maximizers – small owners may prefer relatively stable, moderately growing dividends and stock prices, whereas large owners may prefer greater risk taking and lower payout rates in exchange for more rapid growth in stock prices. Thus only if specific assumptions are made about the composition of ownership can payout rates and rates of growth be expected to vary by control form. Proof that managerial corporations show risk-averse behavior and relatively high payout rate could be evidence that they are responding to the desires of small owners; and, conversely, low payout rates might be evidence of managerial responsiveness to large owner interests. Differences in payout rate might also reflect actual or expected rates of return (which may in turn influence stockholder composition and objectives). With great profit opportunities, maximization of growth and high retention rates might be the best profit-maximizing policy from the shareholders' viewpoint, whereas with slackened opportunities short-run profit-maximizing policies and high dividend rates may be better attuned to shareholder interests.[98]

Difficulties also arise when an attempt is made to correlate managerial interests with performance results. If managers seek both security and high income, weighting the two presents a problem: Security calls for cautious expansion and high rates of return on capital, whereas high managerial income is alleged to demand high rates of growth in assets or sales, which may threaten security. Growth models usually shunt the security motive into the background as a constraint and make income enlargement (or one of its proxies) the primary objective. But why should managers be assumed to push growth to the very limit of security? Why not grow only to the limit of profit advantage, thus achieving a relatively high degree of security along with reasonable growth? Risk-averse managers may grow moderately and "satisfice" as regards growth as well as (or rather than) profits.

In more sophisticated theoretical models, such as those of W. J. Baumol and Robin Marris, little is said of how owner-dominated companies operate. The discussion focuses on the managerial firm, which is said to put growth of sales and/or assets first, profits second. Evidence for this ordering of priorities is sparse. The empirical foundations in Baumol and Marris are small management stockholdings, compensation systems that appear to be tied to size, low managerial mobility, a reluctance to divest, and impressions that firms put great weight on growth per se.[99] The motivation of managers is cast in a narrow individual-maximizing framework: The manager's personal advantage is identified with financial return and security, and these (and other benefits mentioned in passing, like power, prestige, organizational esprit) are viewed as a function of size and growth, not profits. In these models, owner-creditor interests, pressures, threats, ideological influences, and market impacts affect managers strictly as constraints, not as factors directly affecting managerial objectives. Managers can cause firms to grow only so fast, reduce payout rates so much, and allow the rate of return and market value of the stock to fall only so low, or they will be threatened by latent owner-creditor forces.

These assumptions concerning managerial motivation neglect a number of economic, organizational, and sociological considerations (previously discussed) that yield simplicity at the cost of realism and relevance. Even in a narrow economic framework, a serious analytic problem arises from the number of ways in which growth and profits interact. This is implicit in the analyses of both Baumol and Marris. Baumol suggests that growth brings continuous economies of size, that increased size may bring the advantages of monopoly power, and that growth is advantageous to a company in its relations with employees, distributors, suppliers, and lenders. Marris stresses the need to take advantage of corporate opportunities and to maintain a sufficiently high rate of profits and value of equity to satisfy stockholders and to preclude a takeover bid.[100] Ownership interest would call for growth if it yields economies of size, higher institutional morale (and thus productivity), advantageous positions with respect to suppliers and lenders, and an intelligent pursuit of corporate opportunities. Well-conceived growth is a condition of survival in a dynamic economic environment, and the great weight given by managers and analysts to size of market share as a critical determinant of profitability[101] makes it difficult to say that a firm seeking growth is not really seeking profits. If growth is essential to profits, and profits to growth, from the standpoint of motivation, how do we establish which came first? Some of the greatest theorists of capitalism such as Marx and Schumpeter have stressed the growth dynamic of the capitalist enterprise as one of its essential qualities, and both were speaking primarily of the owner/entrepreneur. Schumpeter emphasized the desire of the entrepreneur to build a monument;[102] Marx, the constant search of capital for profit opportunities and the pressure of competition and technical change forcing aggressive and defensive investment of capital.[103]

Marris acknowledges that dominant owner/managers have

tended to identify with their corporate "babies" and have pressed for their growth, sometimes in apparent disregard for profit considerations.[104] Marris makes a good case for managers desiring growth, but none whatsoever for their wanting to *maximize* the rate of growth in firm size. It is not at all evident that managers will pursue growth faster than dominant owners attached to their corporate progeny (and subject to high marginal tax rates on dividends); furthermore, there is a greater takeover threat facing non-performing managers (as compared with owner-managers) and pressures from profit-minded large investors that managers can less afford to ignore. There are other factors pressing managers toward a concern for profits that I have previously discussed, all leading to the conclusion that profitable growth is a closer approximation to the primary managerial objective than maximizing the rate of asset or sales growth.[105] Robert Solow has also shown that the Marris managerial model yields performance results very similar to those of a neoclassical profit-maximizing model – especially on the realistic assumptions of high personal tax rates and preferential capital gains treatment that enhance owner interest in retention of earnings and firm growth.[106]

Marris, Baumol, and others who claim a deemphasis on profitability by managerial firms, have also given little or no attention to the major organizational changes that have affected big business – particularly the development of profit and investment centers, and evaluations based on performance in the use of capital. One advantage of the modern divisionalized giant is that it can grow in those directions that promise large returns and neglect or liquidate those divisions in decline, without sacrificing rate of return.[107] Also, contrary to the opinion of Baumol, large companies divest nonperforming operations almost as freely as they acquire them.[108] There are exceptions, where acquisitions have led to major losses – mistakes no doubt encouraged by the very ease in dealing in companies and the capacity of large businesses to absorb losses that would be fatal to smaller or less-diversified firms. The external social costs of the associated transformations in size and market structure are hard to assess and may be serious,[109] but the processes of growth involved seem usually to be based on a rational, profit-based calculation.

There have been many statistical efforts to show the impact of management control on performance. Of 14 such studies of varying inclusiveness, methodology, and quality, 9 have found superior performance on the part of owner-dominated companies as regards rate of return on equity investment (ROE) and 5 have found no such superiority.[110] William McEachern reviews 8 of these studies and adds his own formidable assent to the group that claims a superior profit performance on the part of owner-dominated firms.[111] Most of these studies use data from the 1950s and early 1960s and deal with firms covering a fairly wide size range. The facts on alleged control also are often debatable,[112] as are the statistical methods employed and the basis of company selection.

In connection with the present study, a further analysis of control-performance relationships was carried out, based on more up-to-date data, covering 72 very large firms for the years 1967–1976. The effect of differences in control form was related to ROE, growth of earnings per share, rate of return on investment, risk, sales growth, and payout rate, adjusting for company asset size and industry class.[113]

The most important finding from this analysis, shown in statistical summary form in Appendix C, is the absence of any significant relationship between any measure of earnings rate – or earnings growth – and the form of control. As regards rate of sales growth, also, there is no significant relationship to control form; payout rate is shown to be positively related to management control (significant at a 10 percent level). The latter finding is not incompatible with the more sophisticated analyses that take the variety of stockholder interests into account, but it is incompatible with those models in which management control is seen to indicate a unique preoccupation with growth per se.

The finding that there is no relationship between the control variable and ROE may be a result, in part, of data characteristics. The firms included in this analysis are all very large (67 from the top 100 industrials, the other five from among the top 150), whereas many of the earlier studies selected firms of greater size variety from among the 500 largest industrials. And the time frame for this analysis is relatively recent. I argued earlier that the forces making for a convergence in performance of large managerial and owner-dominated companies have gradually strengthened, so that any real performance differences might be expected to diminish over time. The empirical findings of this study are consistent with this expectation.

Concluding note

In sum, the triumph of management control in many large corporations has not left them in the hands of neutral technocrats.

The control groups of these organizations seem as devoted to profitable growth as are the leaders of entrepreneurial and owner-dominated companies, past and present. The frequently assumed decline in managerial interest in profits, which supposedly should result from the decreased importance of direct owner control, has not, in fact, been proved. The empirical evidence has been shown here to be inconclusive. This should not be surprising, given the weakness of the case that has been made for a transformation in corporate objectives – a case that has rested on the comparison of an unswervingly profit-oriented entrepreneurial corporation which never existed, to a vision of a managerial corporation that is equally removed from reality by different oversimplifying assumptions. In fact, organizational changes, continued technical progress and competitive pressures, and the "brooding omnipresence" of ownership interests, operating through both market and nonmarket forces, have led to an internalization of profitable growth criteria in corporate psyches and in the rules of large managerial corporations. There are expense preference tendencies and other substantial deviations from profitability criteria in their operations, but such deviations existed, and still exist, under owner control.

The main exceptions to this conclusion are to be found in the public utility sector, where a combination of extreme diffusion of stock ownership; minimal managerial holdings of stock; a deteriorated economic environment; heavy debt obligations and financing requirements; and government control over investment, service, and rates of return together have made for a downgrading of an owner-profit orientation. Under the conditions of financial stress that many utilities have faced during the past decade or so, they have been pressed to meet basic service and financial obligations. A profit constraint must be met as part of this system of financial obligations, and some of the more prosperous utilities give profit more enthusiastic attention, but many of them have been driven to ruthless stock dilution and conversion of the owners' status to that of de facto fixed-income claimants. The sorry state of the industry has even precluded much expense preference, and the purer form of management control found there has been subject to relatively severe external constraints from banks and government.

4

Financial Control of the Large Corporation

The idea of financial (or banker) control of business enterprise has a long history and sometimes has been based on solid fact. In this chapter I will examine the nature and evolution of financial control in the United States, giving particular attention to the main sources of financial power – underwriting and promoting new companies, lending, stock ownership, and directorships – and their relevance to control and influence over corporate decision making. Also specifically discussed is the question of the nature of the threat of financial control and the extent to which that threat has materialized. The chapter concludes with an assessment of the extent of financial control and the nature of the impact of financial power on the large corporation today.

Financial and industrial control

Prior to the 1880s ownership and financial control in the United States were not easy to distinguish. The important financiers of new and expanding large businesses were mainly wealthy capitalists looking for more promising profit horizons.[1] Even a major speculative financier like Jay Gould used personal resources, derived mainly from his own financial operations. It was in the late 1880s and thereafter, when capital demands continued to grow,[2] that investment banking institutions, such as Drexel Morgan and Kidder Peabody, with networks of outlets to investors, began to assume a major role. The importance of these institutions was accelerated by the railroad failures and reorganization of the 1890s and the great merger movement around the turn of the century. In fact, between 1890 and 1910, banker power reached new heights in the United States, as half a dozen groups of financial and nonfinancial companies emerged, which included some of the largest U.S. railroads and industrials, that were dominated by one or more commercial or investment banks.

This development led to a great deal of theorizing and speculation on the causes, consequences, and possible future extension of financial power. Writings like Louis D. Brandeis's *Other People's Money and How the Bankers Use It,*[3] and the 1913 Pujo Committee report on the "money trust,"[4] focused heavily on financial concentration and the stimulus of finance to collective action and unwarranted bigness. Warnings were put forward that these tendencies fed on themselves and that banker dominance could be expected to spread, barring government intervention.[5] The rise of banker control led to the emergence of the Marxist concept of "finance capitalism" as a final stage of capitalist development.[6] Subsequent developments culminating in the sharp decline in the banks' prestige and power during the Great Depression were not easily accommodated to this concept. In the early 1940s the noted U.S. Marxist Paul M. Sweezy rejected the idea of "finance capitalism" as a last stage of capitalist development, arguing that the pre-World War I theorists had been misled by a temporary efflorescence of investment banker power that was transitory in character.[7] Although Sweezy stood by this view in the 1970s,[8] there has been a resurgence of financial control theorizing in the past decade based on commercial bank power – power allegedly arising in part out of the credit function, but even more from trust department stock ownership.[9]

Financial control as used here means that key decision-making power is held by individuals, groups, or organizations whose primary interest is the performance of external financial functions – either raising and supplying funds, buying and selling securities, or both. In a modified Veblenian dichotomy,[10] financial control may be contrasted with *industrial control,* where the primary role of the people in charge is to perform the functions of the controlled entity. They may have an abiding interest in the company's stock price and in raising capital, but their main institutional role is not in those areas. The control group of the Ford Motor Company, for example, concentrates almost exclusively on the production and sale of motor vehicles.

Although it is easy enough to identify financial or industrial control in cases like the Ford Motor Company, or the United Corporation (organized in 1929 and dominated by two investment banking houses), classification problems occur with empire builders and speculators who have an inordinate interest in selling securities, obtaining short-term personal gains, and manipulating securities and the underlying industrial properties for strategic ends. The problem is in differentiating "financial" control from that of managers whose primary relationship is to the organization and its work, but who have an above-normal "expense preference" or securities market orientation. In the nineteenth century, and to a gradually diminishing extent up to the Great Depression, it was commonplace for corporate leaders to take advantage of inside information at the expense of the company shareholders. A Jay Gould, even when proposing a sound move from the corporate interest, "could not overlook the exploitation of an opportunity for personal gain."[11] After the Civil War, and especially after the depression of the 1870s, "as specific [self-dealing] policies proved to be disadvantageous for the influential stockholders or for the managers themselves, a code of proper policy emerged."[12] But it emerged slowly. Even a corporate leader of the stature of E. H. Harriman at the turn of the century would make large purchases and sales based on inside knowledge of a change in dividend rate, although he also bought heavily in times of cyclical lows and undervaluation and in anticipation of his own renovations of the Union Pacific.[13]

With manipulative practices, speculative purchases and sales, and insider utilization of privileged information a conventional practice, it is not always easy to differentiate financial and industrial control in earlier years.[14] The classification problem is alleviated by the fact that many of the speculators controlling large corporations have been closely connected with brokerage and investment banking houses. Others have been put under the rubric of financial control only when the transitory and exploitative character of their relationship to the controlled organization was indubitable (as with W. H. Moore and D. G. Reid's control of the Rock Island Railroad and Elkins–Widener domination of the Philadelphia Rapid Transit Company at the turn of the century).[15] In the 1920s public support was once again easily obtained for "a well-dressed speculation"[16] and financial control was quite significant among large corporations. Most large corporations so classified in Table 3.5 were organized and/or otherwise controlled by investment banks or brokerage houses; those that were not, but which are still classed as financially controlled, had control groups that were in close alliance with security firms, inordinately preoccupied with security issues, and also commonly using their control position to manipulate stock prices and drain income into external organizations.[17]

Sources of financial power and control

In recent decades fears about financial control have centered on *institutional* control, not the seizure of power by isolated speculative interests. And, in fact, most of the important cases of financial control of large nonfinancial corporations in the twentieth century have been rooted in institutional power.

Underwriting, Investment Banking, and Promotional Activities

The underwriting, or investment banking, function involves the selling of new securities by the banker and associates in an underwriting syndicate to a clientele of individual and institutional investors. This function is now performed by so-called investment banks, as opposed to commercial banks, the latter having been prevented by the Banking Act of 1933 from underwriting securities except for state, local, and national governments.

The investment banking function can be a strategic one for promotion and reorganization activities, because these are heavily dependent on the successful sale of new securities. The bankers who were of central importance in the first great promotional era (1890–1904) were primarily investment bankers, although they were either commercial bankers as well or closely linked to major commercial banks in personal and business alliances. In 1900, for example, J. P. Morgan and Company was both an investment bank *and* a major commercial bank. This enhanced its investment banker power, because commercial bank credit is necessary to carry securities, pending sale to final investors.[18] The National Banking Act of 1864 had constrained commercial bank investment banking activity up to the turn of the century, although many commercial banks found means of evasion. After 1900, however, restrictions on bank underwriting were bypassed on an increasing scale by the creation of security affiliates of banks and by the ownership of, and communities of interest with, institutions that could carry out financial functions prohibited to banks. Through the security affiliate, the major commercial banks had joined the top rung of investment bankers proper by the late 1920s,[19] but this fusion of functions was short lived: The Banking Act of 1933 forced a separation of commercial banks from their investment affiliates and pushed the banks out of the private security underwriting business.

The power of investment banks depends on the importance of access to public securities markets and the degree to which that access has been monopolized. Access was especially important for large firms in the 1890–1914 era because of the capital-intensive nature of much of big business (railroads, traction companies, rapidly expanding heavy industries like steel), its dependence on borrowing, and the underdeveloped state of banks and other institutional lenders. Many industrial companies were going public for the first time in the 1890s,[20] and the name and the technical and marketing support of investment bankers were of strategic importance. There were numerous railroad failures and reorganizations at this time. Morgan and Kuhn Loeb, and their partners and allies, were often sought to help rework the structure of securities, to provide outlets for new issues, and to placate contending factions by their prestigious and relatively neutral presence. Very often the railroad reorganizations led to the establishment of voting trusts, with important powers given over to three trustees for some term of years (typically five), partly to assure the security holders that responsible management would be in charge during the period of corporate revival.[21] Investment banker domination of these voting trusts was commonplace, and several major railroads were banker controlled through this vehicle.

In the great merger movement of 1893–1904 the investment banker often played a strategic role and assumed a substantial position of power as the promoter of combinations and as the quasi-monopolistic seller of securities. The rationale of these mergers is still under debate, and the factors involved probably varied by merger, but there is some agreement that two strategic elements were (1) the desire to mitigate competition and (2) the desire to take advantage of a buoyant securities market and public optimism as to the profits of trustification, with corresponding advantages to the promoters of trusts.[22] Investment bankers were well situated to promote trusts. In a number that were Morgan promoted – such as U.S. Steel – Morgan resources and prestige were crucial to implementing these enormous ventures. And out of such strategic roles in promotion came positions of power in the newly formed enterprises.

Access to public securities markets has always been difficult for small and unknown companies, which normally have had to raise long-term capital from special sources (individuals, suppliers, customers, banks) and internal cash flows. For larger firms there has been an easing of access since the turn of the century, especially since the legislation and institutional changes of the 1930s and thereafter. In 1900 investment banking was concentrated in the hands of a small number of institutions that were closely allied with major banks and insurance companies. These groups had great prestige among domestic and foreign investors, and there was a substantial degree of cooperation and collusion among the major groupings. This placed the Morgan–Baker, Kuhn Loeb, and Dillon Read interest groups in positions of power when new securities had to be sold in volume in public securities markets. There *was* a "money trust" in 1900–1905, although it was neither complete nor wholly lacking in competition among the few major interest groupings or from the outside.[23] George Baker himself (head of the First National Bank of New York and close friend of J. P. Morgan) conceded to the Pujo Committee that the concentration of financial control "has gone about far enough. In good hands, I do not see that it would do any harm. If it got into bad hands, it would be very bad."[24]

It is not readily demonstrable quantitatively, but the concentration of financial control that had "gone far enough" in the pre-World War I period was unsustainable, and declined in succeeding decades.[25] This downtrend was interrupted by an upswing of banker control in the 1920s, when a combination of renewed merger activity and a buoyant stock market once again caused the investment banker and other professional sellers of securities to become important as promoters – especially in the rapidly expanding and capital hungry utility field. Many of the utility systems of the 1920s were sponsored and controlled by security business professionals through "super" holding companies, formed by banking interests "for the purpose of again substituting securities of a holding-company organization for those of other holding companies owned by the bankers."[26] The United Corporation, a super holding company controlled by the Morgan and Bonbright investment banking interests, included within its orbit a series of utilities that in 1931 accounted for 27 percent of the national electric utility output.[27]

But investment banker/promoter control once again proved transitory. The stock market crash, Great Depression, New Deal legislation, and subsequent economic developments pushed investment banker control of large enterprise into an apparently permanent minor status. Even in the 1920s a weakening of the investment bankers' position was evident.[28] Important legislative developments that helped further the process were: the Glass Steagall Act, enforcing the separation of commercial and investment banking; the legislative requirement of competitive bidding for important classes of underwritten securities; the disclosure legislation and regulation of the 1930s; and the Public Utility Holding Company Act of 1935, which compelled the breakup of many banker-dominated utility systems and excluded bankers from directorships of registered companies.[29] The publicity given abuses in the securities business of the late 1920s, in the Pecora hearings and elsewhere, also diminished the prestige and power of the investment banking fraternity.[30] The long, drawn out government suit against the investment banking industry for monopolization of that business, although lost by the government, probably had an important constraining effect on industry's behavior. The steadily increasing importance of other financial intermediaries and private placements, and the decline of concentration in the investment banking industry proper, also helped to diminish investment banker power.[31]

During the past three decades some of the conditions favorable to investment banker power have returned: rapid economic growth, inflation, a resultant great increase in the importance of external financing,[32] a buoyant stock market for some periods during the 1950s and 1960s, and substantial merger activity. External financing, which has been done by a wide variety of financial institutions, has mostly bypassed the investment banking industry. Investment banks have made an important comeback in participating in merger and takeover offense and defense, but their role has been much more modest than in the pre-1930 era. The intense, post-1960 merger activity has not been a joining of substantial numbers of firms in great combines but, rather, a series of acquisitions by affluent and solidly entrenched firms. These businesses have needed banker support in financing and packaging takeover offers and transactions, and commercial banks, broker/dealers, investment banks, and other financial institutions have been finders as well as financiers in these activities. Bankers, including investment bankers, have been *instruments* of these firms, not dominating forces in the merger process.[33]

Lazard Frères, for example, has played an important role as a finder and organizer of many important International Telephone and Telegraph (ITT) acquisitions since 1965. But although Lazard's partner Felix Rohatyn has been on the board and executive committee of ITT since 1967, and has helped shape its acquisition policy, his (and Lazard's) position is clearly not one of dominance or even shared power – it is that of a trusted, well-paid[34] advisor to the dominant management. Most broker/investment banker relations to major acquiring firms in the last two decades have been of the Lazard–ITT variety, and the same may be said of commercial banker relations to conglomerators. The Gulf & Western–Chase Manhattan Bank case is especially instructive in that the bank was clearly the more powerful of the two – in 1964 the total assets of Gulf & Western were only $68 million;[35] Chase's assets were $13 billion. Chase was the principal financier of a string of Gulf & Western acquisitions that followed and was clearly important to the small but rapidly growing conglomerate, but there is no suggestion in the Celler Committee hearings of 1969 or the final report of 1971 that the bank dominated Gulf & Western or even shared power with its management. Chase was a provider of services, expecting a generous return, but it neither engineered the expansion nor at any point significantly controlled the lesser entity.

Lending

Financial control or influence over nonfinancial organizations can also stem from the power to grant or withhold credit, to impose conditions in extending credit, and to enforce the terms of credit agreements. This is the principal basis of the power of financial institutions – especially commercial banks and insurance companies – over nonfinancial business in the United States today. Board representation by financial institutions is most commonly related to credit extension, not to stock ownership or the underwriting function.

The dominant institutional lenders to business, by a wide margin, are commercial banks and insurance companies. The *Institutional Investor* magazine's ranking of the 300 largest money managers in 1975 shows the banks leading the parade, with 123 bank trust departments included among the 300, controlling about $301 billion, 44 percent, of a pool of managed assets of $685 billion.[36] Seventy-eight insurance companies were included in the top 300, controlling about $181 billion, 26.4 percent, of the assets of the

300. Banks and insurance companies thus accounted for over two-thirds (70.4 percent) of the 300 company total.

Despite the enormous sums involved, the *Institutional Investor*'s concept of money managing did not include bank lending of its own internal funds (as opposed to fiduciary assets) and thus excluded, among other things, $175 billion of commercial and industrial loans, plus a few hundred billion assorted other lending categories. Commercial banks reign supreme and virtually unchallenged in the area of short-term lending to business. Most businesses have lines of credit with one or more commercial banks, and the ability to get these credits is often of critical importance to business growth and survival. Bank influence here derives in large part from simple market power – credit is scarce, risks may be high and hard to assess, and lenders of short-term credit in particular markets (almost exclusively commercial banks) have often been few and not always willing to compete.[37] Bank influence may be enhanced by personal relationships that the customer may not want to disrupt and by knowledge of confidential information that the borrower may not want to be widely shared. The bank may also strengthen its relationship with the customer by lending for special purposes, such as to finance an acquisition program, or by lending in circumstances where other lenders are not available.

Bank influence is likely to depend on the importance of bank borrowing to customers, their banking options, and their financial condition. Bank power tends to be inversely related to borrower size, because the latter is closely correlated with credit rating and the number of available borrowing options. The largest nonfinancials analyzed in this study each tend to do business, including the maintenance of lines of credit, with many banks, often hundreds of banks. The scope of commercial banking markets and the number of options available to very large borrowers have increased since 1900, particularly since 1929. One reason is the integration of the national market by improved transport, communications, and knowledge, so that a greater number of the large banking institutions do more business at more remote points than in earlier years. And with 139 insured commercial banks having assets of $1 billion or more in 1978, the number of large institutions capable of participating in the national market is substantial. A second reason is the extension of the scope of banking markets for the large multinational borrower beyond national boundaries, which has further increased the effective numbers of lenders in the large borrower market.

A third factor is the greater relative importance of other institutional lenders – insurance companies, pension funds, finance companies – and the parallel relative decline of the commercial bank as an institutional lender. These other lenders compete with banks mainly in the intermediate- and long-term credit markets, but there is an overlap and some degree of substitutability between lending in the short-, intermediate-, and long-term maturity ranges. In the debt structures of many large corporations insurance companies hold the long-term instruments; short-term obligations are held by the banks. But there are encroachments by both into the intermediate-term ranges, and large borrowers can often choose between bank term loans[38] and private placements with insurance companies.[39] Thus if banks are asking for an excessively high rate on short-term loans, large companies may seek longer-term funds, even for working capital purposes. Or they may arrange for the sale of open market paper, which would give them short-term funds outside the orbit of bank control.[40] This may be regarded as another important factor that strengthens the options of large customers vis-à-vis banks. There are others.[41]

Because the largest companies require enormous sums, a great many revolving credits and private placements are provided by a relatively small number of powerful joint venture financial partners – the major New York banks and Metropolitan, Prudential, and Equitable show up often and in large dollar volume.[42] Their power relative to their very large customers is greatly qualified, however, by the mutuality of need, the existence of effective options for the giants, and the traditional and continued reluctance (and frequent inability) of large lenders to intervene in the decision-making processes of large borrowers. The largest bank lenders assiduously cultivate the largest nonfinancial firms for deposits, loans, and the wide variety of other business obtainable from companies of great size and scope. The large lenders and borrowers are in a long-lived, reciprocal relationship in which the power equation is not normally one of financial institution superiority.[43] Bank lines of credit are very handy backup sources of working capital – even more important for some large borrowers – but bank credit is dispensable for some giants, and for all but those in deep financial distress the number of bank options is substantial. The large banks and insurance companies are in no position to impose their will on large borrowers beyond the conventional right to information and consultative and veto powers where indentures are violated.

Lender power does tend to be enhanced when borrowers get into financial difficulties. At that point, two factors come into play: a reduced availability of credit from alternative sources and greater creditor interest in protecting their existing loans. Lenders not already doing business with the ailing firm are less interested in it, and external supplies and potential competition to existing lenders thus dry up. Already committed lenders assume a more strategic and monopolistic position, and their power tends to be enlarged for this reason. But an aggressive stance may be harmful to the lender. Alienation of the borrowing company management may jeopardize relationships and deposits, both at that time and in the future (assuming company and management survival). By calling loans, reducing lines of credit, or refusing to renew loans, lenders could easily push the weakening firm into a liquidity crisis and bankruptcy proceedings, thereby worsening their own position by reducing the prospects of ultimate credit payout. If a firm's normal operations are impaired, income flow is reduced, and an important source of payment of interest and principal withers away. If the company is forced into bankruptcy, existing law allows the bankrupt to continue to function and prevents the immediate seizure of its assets by creditors. Thus bankruptcy tends to result in a loss of creditor control[44] as well as a reduction in the hopes of recouping credits via improved company performance.

The possible range of creditor intervention in distressed companies is exceedingly wide. When Memorex got into deep difficulties in 1973–1974, its lead bank, Bank of America, played an extremely active role in forcing out top management and selected – in fact, underwrote – a new top officer, to whom they seem to have given a relatively free hand.[45] In its time of troubles, and during its recovery period (1975–1977), Memorex could be designated as bank controlled.

Penn Central offers a sharp contrast to Memorex in that increasingly severe financial difficulties did not lead to assertion of banker authority. Command remained firmly in the hands of the inside management until the very last stages of independent corporate life. Much attention has been paid to the availability of inside information to the banker-creditors of Penn Central, but the far more interesting points are how little the bankers *knew* and how little they *did* to extricate themselves from prospective huge credit losses. The Securities and Exchange Commission (SEC) report on the Penn Central failure states that "prior to an attempt to get additional security in early 1970, it appears that the banks, through their agent First National City Bank, never seriously doubted the financial ability of Penn Central to pay off its loans . . ."[46] None of the major banks were represented on the Penn Central Board in 1969–1970, and there is no evidence that they tried to get full details on the financial status of Penn Central or attempted to force any change in management or policies. The reasons for this are not entirely clear, but the intimidating size and fear of loss of business with Penn Central seem to have been important factors. The major banks were also large holders of Penn Central common stock in trust accounts, the value of which would be jeopardized by refusals to lend – as would preexisting bank credits. Thus bank power seems to have been constrained by a mutality of dependence with Penn Central, which gave Penn Central's management protective leverage.[47] Like the fabled two scorpions in the bottle, if one strikes the other a fatal blow, the victim can retaliate before expiring. Lenders may not be able to afford total borrower disclosure and a major borrower managerial upheaval, because its effect on alternate credit sources, stock prices, suppliers, customers, and employee morale could shatter a precarious equilibrium. Because corporate borrowers know this, their power in times of severe financial distress may be greater than theoretical banker rights would suggest.

Nevertheless, when large corporations get into serious financial difficulty, banker power tends to increase markedly and may eventually include veto power over expenditures and influence over management succession that qualifies as full or shared control. Direct bank intervention and virtually unilateral displacement of the management, as in the Memorex case, are rare among very large companies. But management changes under the pressure of creditors – with the creditors, if not choosing a successor, at least insisting on veto power – are not uncommon in cases where the large company is in acute distress. Banker influence over management selection in a weakened Pan Am was evident in the departure of the top officers just prior to the renewal of a large revolving credit in both 1972 and 1976;[48] and the sagging fortunes of Ling–Temco-Vought (LTV) and Grant in the 1970s led to well-authenticated banker influence over management choices and other business decisions.[49] A less clear-cut case is that of Westinghouse in 1974–1975, when the company was barely emerging from a time of troubles in which profits had collapsed and short-term debt had grown from $208 million in December 1972 to $514 million in March 1974. At that time John McGillicuddy and Richard Cooley (high-ranking officers of Manufacturers Hanover Trust and Security Pacific Banks respectively) joined the Westinghouse board and D. C. Burnham retired as chief executive officer. The two commercial bankers joined Jacob Schiff, a long-time Kuhn Loeb representative on the board, and it is reasonable to suppose that this triumvirate had weight in the deliberations on the selection of Fred Kirby as Burnham's successor[50] and on other policy matters confronting Westinghouse. On the other hand, in the case of Chrysler Corporation, another giant in some distress in 1974, the retirement of Lynn Townsend and the succession of John Riccardo and Eugene Cafiero seem to have been based strictly on insider decisions without any external pressures. With the still more acute difficulties of 1979–1980, the threat of failure without banker agreement to stand by the stricken auto giant created a scorpion-in-the-bottle scenario – and, accordingly, the bankers were mobilized, many grudgingly, with Chrysler's management strategy and prerogatives no longer a practical issue.[51]

Restrictive Covenants

In lending under revolving credit agreements, or under straight loans where maturities exceed one year, banks and insurance companies typically extend the credit under the protection of a written agreement with the borrower. This agreement normally contains a list of negative covenants that limit the borrower's freedom of action within a certain agreed upon range. The agreement attempts to protect the lender from actions damaging to its interests that could occur over extended time periods, such as selling off important parts of the business, incurring excessive new debt, issuing obligations with rights senior to those of the lenders in question, paying out excessive cash dividends, and otherwise allowing liquidity to deteriorate. These restrictive covenants also serve as benchmarks to warn the lender of any weakening of the borrower's credit position and of a need for action.

The severity of negative covenants and their actual or potential encroachments on managerial discretion depend mainly on the quality of the credit (the financial stability and expected ability to pay of the borrower), the relative strengths of lender and borrower, and lender policies. For borrowers of the highest credit rating, restrictive covenants may be waived entirely. With lesser but strong borrowers they are ordinarily present but inoperative. For weak borrowers, however, covenants may significantly limit managerial discretion and can involve some degree of financial control. For one thing, in fixing the parameters of an agreement, the negotiations may encroach directly on managerial decision making. The agreement often fixes a dividend ceiling, and in the case of a weak borrower the ceiling is sometimes lower than the management would like. For example, revolving loan agreements in 1972–1973 allowed the financially strong Delta Airlines to pay $11 million in dividends; TWA, more than twice Delta's size in assets and operating revenues, but financially troubled, was allowed to pay only $5 million; and Pan Am, in even deeper financial difficulties, was allowed no dividend payments. It is not certain that the managements of these airlines would have paid more dividends than the allowable even with discretion, but the frequent hard bargaining over dividend limits suggests some degree of encroachment in cases of severe constraints. The agreement often involves specific working capital minima, debt ceilings, and limits on guarantees, lease obligations, asset sales, and acquisitions of other companies.[52] These limitations involve key decisions and could be said to involve some degree of lender control where lender-imposed constraints conflict sharply with management choices.

Restrictive covenants require lender approval of certain actions or waivers of restrictions where violations materialize or are threatened. Sometimes the covenants specifically prohibit mergers into another corporation and, on rare occasions, may require approval of managerial changes by the noteholders.[53] Mergers more commonly require lender approval, either explicitly or because the transaction would carry the debt beyond the fixed ceiling or would bring certain ratios into violation. Some degree of power inheres in the right of the lender to review and approve the merger – a right that might influence the shape of the merger transaction from its inception. Power can be exercised directly by refusal to approve a merger or by refusal to approve without compensating adjustments elsewhere (e.g., more collateral to offset approval of a weakened working capital position). Where the position of the borrower deteriorates seriously, the lender may not only seek direct financial protection of its credits but may also press for management changes or merger as a condition of waiving indenture violations and the continuation of credit extensions. The range of discretion of the management of a troubled borrower may be sharply restricted if lenders are alert and aggressive; if decisions on financing, investment, and expansion or contraction require lender approval, management discretion without banker inputs may be confined increasingly to operations per se.

The actual extent of lender power and control realized under indentures and the lending relationship is not easy to assess. Lenders claim that it is extremely modest – that they are not competent to interfere and do not believe in intruding on managerial prerogatives – and that the restrictive covenants are mainly benchmarks to help guide both parties, commonly waived for borrowers under temporary stress. For companies not presenting special problems to lenders, waivers are commonly made without undue strain or insistence on added protection.[54] The preservation of borrower autonomy even under conditions of financial stress is affected by a tradition of banker nonintervention in managerial prerogatives plus the shortage of lender options in dealing with troubled borrowers. We are back to the scorpions in the bottle previously discussed.

Nevertheless, the fact is inescapable that some power and influence must flow from the fixing of "guideposts" under loan agreements, the right to veto actions like mergers under specific covenants, and the need to waive violations of the agreement. Financial power may be merely latent and "atmospheric," but with weak borrowers it may be active and participative. Weak borrowers not adhering to lender rules may find credit less available and lenders pressing them more actively. They may find the guideposts in a credit agreement constraining them more narrowly than they would like with respect to allowed dividend payments, required liquidity ratios, and rights to issue more debt. The creditors become "active" in the limited sense of fixing certain key decision parameters in negotiated agreements with management and requiring clearance for "exceptions."

This degree of participation would not be applied by lenders to General Electric, Goodyear, or ITT, but it has been applicable in varying degrees to LTV, TWA, Rapid American, Chrysler, and Westinghouse in certain troubled years. This kind of intervention is still of the constraint/parameter-fixing variety. Corporate directors as well as bankers contend that even under conditions of severe financial stress, banker encroachments on managerial prerogatives are not great – mainly a pressure for constraint and conservatism, the maintenance of protective financial ratios, and more collateral supportive of outstanding credits. Even with smaller companies the bankers claim that when things get really tough they do not force mergers or managerial changes, with rare exceptions, although they may suggest and press moderately for the company to do both. Bankers fear the adverse publicity associated with intervention and are often trapped in the boat with the existing management, which frequently is able to preserve its power well into insolvency.

Bank Directorships

Banks and other financial institutions are very well represented on boards of directors and important committees of nonfinancial corporations. In the Conference Board 1973 survey of the affiliations of outside directors of 511 manufacturing companies, banks ran a close second to manufacturing companies as a source of directors (299 companies, 58.5 percent, had a banker as a director); those in the business of "investments" were also well represented (210 companies); insurance companies, less so (58 companies).[55] Out of the aggregate of 2,914 directors, 428 (or 14.7 percent) were bankers, 299 (10.3 percent) were in investments, and 66 (2.3 percent) were in insurance. Table 4.1 shows that representation of financial institutions on the boards of very large nonfinancial corporations in 1975 ran substantially higher than in the Conference Board sample. Two-thirds of the 200 largest nonfinancials, and over three-quarters of the 100 largest industrials, had a commercial bank officer on the board, and financial representation overall is impressive. Investment bankers, listed separately, are also well represented on the boards of large companies and are second only to commercial banks in importance.

Table 4.2 shows the extent to which financial institutions have multiple representation on boards of large nonfinancial corporations. The table describes both representation by institutional type and total financial institution representation. It does not distinguish between multiple interlocks involving several representatives of the same financial institution and representatives of different ones, but there are very few cases of the former (although quite a few cases of an inside and an *outside* director of a financial institution on one of the boards under study). It can be seen from Table 4.2 that 7 percent of the 200 largest nonfinancials had more than one investment banker on the board, 31 percent had more than one commercial banker on the board, and 47 percent had

Table 4.1. *Large corporations with financial officer representation on their boards, 1975*

Types of financial institutions	200 largest nonfinancials		100 largest industrials	
	No.	%	No.	%
Banks				
Board	131	65.5	76	76
Executive committee	56	28.0	30	30
Investment banks				
Board	58	29.0	42	42
Executive committee	13	6.5	8	8
Insurance companies				
Board	42	21.0	27	27
Executive committee	10	5.0	7	7
Investment companies				
Board	8	4.0	3	3
Executive committee	—	—	—	—
All financial institutions				
Board	162[a]	81.0	98[a]	98
Executive committee	64	32.0	35	35

Includes only officers of financial institutions on boards of large companies; outside directors of the financial institutions serving on company boards are ignored here.
[a] This is not a total of officer directors but, rather, of companies with at least one officer of a financial institution on the board of directors.

more than one financial institution represented. The proportions are higher for the 100 largest industrials.

Not included in these tables, but shown in Table 4.13, is a further tabulation that distinguishes between major banks and local banks. (Major banks are defined as those among the 50 largest financial institutions, which includes the 30 largest banks.) In 87 out of the 200 largest corporations, there was at least one major bank represented on the board, and in 85 out of the 200, there was at least one local bank on the board. Similar proportions between major and local institutions prevailed for insurance companies represented on large firm boards, but over 80 percent of the invest-

Table 4.2. *Multiple financial institution representation on the boards of large corporations, 1975*

Types of financial representation	200 largest nonfinancials		100 largest industrials	
	No.	%	No.	%
Commercial bank representation				
1	69	34.5	43	43
2	39	19.5	23	23
3	17	8.5	8	8
4	4	2.0	1	1
5	2	1.0	1	1
Total	131	65.5	76	76
Investment bank representation				
1	44	22.0	33	33
2	10	5.0	7	7
3	2	1.0	1	1
4	2	1.0	1	1
Total	58	29.0	42	42
Insurance company representation				
1	38	19.0	25	25
2	3	1.5	1	1
3	—	—	—	—
4	1	0.5	1	1
Total	42	21.0	27	27
Total financial institution representation				
1	66	33.0	42	42
2	42	21.0	24	24
3	32	16.0	19	19
4	12	6.0	5	5
5	9	4.5	7	7
6	1	0.5	1	1
Total	162	81.0	98	98
Total financial institution representation on executive committee				
1	36	18.0	22	22
2	21	10.5	9	9
3	5	2.5	3	3
4	2	1.0	1	1
Total	64	32.0	35	35

ment banking representation on large corporation boards was from major firms of more than local scope.

Table 4.3 shows the number of board and executive committee members of those financial institutions with three or more officer directorships among the 200 largest nonfinancial corporations in 1975. It is evident that the large commercial banks predominate, with only Lazard Frères and Lehman Brothers among the 10 financials with a half dozen or more directorships (the other eight being commercial banks).

Financial representation on board committees of large corporations is another measure of participation in corporate affairs. Unfortunately, the functions of board committees are highly variable, as is their power, which often depends on the status of particular individuals on the committees, irrespective of committee position. Financial representatives are commonly on finance committees, where their function is usually purely advisory and their weight dependent on factors other than committee role.

The executive committee is usually the most powerful board committee, often small in size, meeting relatively frequently and usually with considerable authority to act in the interim between board meetings. It is easy to overrate the power of its members, however, because in many cases the functions of executive committees are nominal and membership is often based on convenience of location for quick assembly, whereas in other cases membership is structured to assure easy domination by insiders. Nevertheless, because this is the most important of board committees, financial participation is of some possible relevance to financial power. Tables 4.1, 4.2, and 4.3 describe the impressive overall presence of financial institutions on the executive committees of the largest nonfinancials. Almost a third of the 200 largest have at least one financial representative on their executive committees (Table 4.2), and 14 percent have two or more. The commercial banks again predominate, with membership on the executive committees of 56 (28 percent) of the 200 largest companies; investment banks are a distant second, with 13 (6.5 percent) executive committee members.

The significance of this extensive financial presence on boards and executive committees has been subject to varying interpretations. Some analysts infer a parallel degree of bank control on the naïve theory that if boards and executive committees have the legal power to make policy and to hire and fire the insiders, and bankers are on them in significant numbers, bankers share control

Table 4.3. *Financial institutions represented on the boards and executive committees of the 200 largest corporations, 1975, by number of board representations*

Financial institutions	Number of directors	Number of executive committee representations
Citibank	20	5
Morgan Guaranty Trust	14	6
Lehman Brothers	12	1
Mellon Bank	10	2
Manufacturers Hanover Trust	10	2
Chemical Bank	9	6
Chase Manhattan Bank	9	1
Bankers Trust	7	1
Lazard Frères	7	1
National Bank of Detroit	6	2
White Weld	5	2
Kuhn Loeb	5	2
Metropolitan Life	5	1
Wells Fargo Bank	4	3
U.S. Trust	4	2
Security Pacific	4	2
Wachovia Bank	4	1
Eastman Dillon	4	1
Goldman Sachs	4	1
Brown Brothers Harriman	4	1
Irving Trust	4	—
State Street Trust	4	—
Marine Midland	3	2
First Boston Corporation	3	2
Bank of California	3	1
Kidder Peabody	3	1
Crocker	3	1
Aetna	3	1
Equitable	3	1
Massachusetts Investors Trust	3	1
First Chicago Corporation	3	—

Includes only cases with three or more directorships among the 200 largest and only directors who are officers of the financial institution.

by this route alone.[56] But for the great majority of mainstream giants, the top inside management dominates policymaking and board selection, and outside directors, even when prestigious bankers, do not normally share in control.

A distinction should be made between cases where bankers are on boards that fit this mainstream model and exceptions where the power of banker-directors (and perhaps other outside directors) may be more significant. Caterpillar Tractor, General Motors (GM), Texaco, and Union Carbide are illustrations of the mainstream model cases, where eminent bankers serve on the boards but have close to zero control. The bankers on mainstream model boards are almost always invited to be on the boards by the top insiders of the companies; they are not there because they asked to serve. The large and prosperous companies seem to be able to get the most prestigious bank representatives. The banks also seek distinguished members for *their* boards. Often there is an exchange of directorships, which reinforces the mutual enhancement of prestige and strengthens a reciprocal business relationship.

When a bank representative sits on the board of a large company, the business tie between them is usually strong. Caterpillar Tractor, for example, has had a long-standing relationship with the First National Bank of Chicago. In 1975 Gaylord Freeman, chairman of the bank, was a 12-year veteran of the Caterpillar board, and L. L. Morgan, president of Caterpillar, was serving on First National Bank of Chicago's board. First National lends Caterpillar money (a $38 million peak volume in 1974), serves as transfer agent and as trustee on four Caterpillar debenture issues, and manages several of Caterpillar's employee benefit plans. First National Bank of Chicago held 5.6 percent of the voting stock of Caterpillar in 1974, but it had the power to vote less than 1 percent of that total. The relationship is important to the bank, as Caterpillar is the largest employer in Illinois, enormously profitable (far more so than the bank)[57] and a source of valuable banking business. There is hardly more basis for assuming bank control through Freeman than Caterpillar control of First National Bank of Chicago through Morgan.

Several of the largest companies still have banker representatives from banks that did at one time control the company. General Electric Company was Morgan controlled at the turn of the century and still has Morgan representatives on the board.[58] But this is minority representation, devoid of a large ownership base or of a function incapable of duplication by others, with limited sustaining power. In theory, it would have been possible for Morgan to obtain control in 1895 and then to maintain it indefinitely by naming controlled agents to the board and top officers over the years. But without a capacity to select a majority of the board each year, and without an active presence among the top insiders of the organization, it is unlikely that it could have maintained domination. The top insiders of a large company will want to control, and they are well situated to do so, given wide stock diffusion and successful business performance.

Exceptions to management control that are based on financial power involve companies that are suffering, or have suffered in the recent past, from acute financial difficulties, or cases where bankers have played a unique financial role that gave them a strategic position not yet eroded. The promotional activities of bankers gave them strategic position, as did their role in the reorganization of failed companies. These bases of power have not been important since the 1930s, but there are several cases where bankers' earlier positions of domination have not yet been wholly dissipated. A notable case is General Telephone and Electronics (GTE), which went into bankruptcy in 1935 and was then openly dominated by a banker group until a forceful top officer, Donald Power, took over the reins in 1951. Within a decade, using an aggressive merger policy, Power changed GTE from a modest-sized company to a billion dollar giant.[59] Power, and his successor Leslie Warner, who took over in 1966, appear to have brought GTE into the mainstream sequence of managerial control, but the residual position of bankers on the board is impressive. In the late 1970s Paine Webber had two representatives on the GTE board – both on the nominating committee (one its chairman). Paine Webber's relationship with GTE dates back to GTE's inception in 1926. Paine Webber was one of the controlling bankers during GTE's bankruptcy and in the banker-control era of 1936–1951. Paine Webber was long the principal investment banker of GTE and has retained this position up to the present time.[60]

Charter New York Corporation and its main subsidiary, Irving Trust, also have had a long-standing relationship with GTE. The chief executive officer (CEO) of Charter–Irving has long served on the GTE board, along with several Charter outside directors, and as a member of GTE's nominating committee. The CEO of GTE has also been on the boards of Charter and Irving. GTE's stock is widely dispersed. No single holder has as much as 5 percent, and the top 30 combined have only 18 percent. The 1970s' GTE boards consisted of one-third inside directors and two-thirds outsiders, but Power and Warner had 25 years to build a power base, and they seem to have succeeded. The financial interests so heavily represented on the GTE board have derived substantial benefits from their affiliation. Insiders confirm that the top officers are definitely in charge of GTE but that the bankers – knowledge-able and prestigious – are close to the insiders and are also influ-ential for reasons of expertise and long-established status.

When a company has gotten into financial difficulty, a banker may *ask* to go on the board. He or she may then merely observe, but may also attempt to exercise influence. When bankers join boards in times of trouble, it is plausible that their presence will not be nominal and that their counsel will have some weight. But this is not always true – bankers are sometimes urged to join boards by ailing companies for image value or to encourage a greater bank commitment to the company, as well as for counsel (although not always taken). With financial stress, the mutual sup-port aspect of a board relationship tends to weaken, as creditor self-protection and continued borrower needs conflict. A mutual-ity of interest remains, however, as the large creditor has a contin-ued stake in the survival and recovery of the borrower and the two parties remain "in the boat" together.

In the 1970s the board meeting was not where most fundamen-tal decisions were made in large U.S. corporations. Therefore banker presence or absence on boards is a limited and potentially misleading measure of bank power. Banks can and do use other avenues of influence. If bank power is great enough through credit dependence and associated loan agreements, the use of restrictive covenants and the required steady flow of detailed information via reports and telephone may enable the bank to exercise influence by direct communication with top insiders.

Boards *can* act, however, and outside directorships and posi-tions on board committees can provide some increment of knowledge and influence. In the W. T. Grant bankruptcy case the creditor claims of Morgan Guaranty Trust were resisted by the court-appointed trustee on the ground that Morgan had used a directorship to rewrite lending agreements in favor of Morgan (and associated banks), at the expense of unrepresented credi-tors.[61] In principle, such protections could have been insisted on as a condition of credit extension or renewal without director representation, but the contention of the Grant trustee was that the increment of power stemming from a directorship – which he claimed gave Morgan de facto control – reduced the ability of the other directors and management to bargain on behalf of the stockholders and excluded creditors. The trustee's position implied that control resulted from the directorship rather than from the underlying creditor position of Morgan. This case, settled out of court, suggests that it may be in the interest of financial institutions to move away from the more explicit forms of control, such as directorships, and to rely more on contract rights and behind-the-scenes negotiations and pressures. Logically, this kind of vulnerability should cause a reduction in the number of directorships held by financial institutions in situations where they might be in a position to wield power! It is a moot question whether their real power in circumstances like the Grant situation would be reduced thereby. In brief, board and committee presence, or absence, must be looked at with caution as part of a larger power ensemble.

Institutional Stock Ownership

Ownership power may be exercised through a variety of channels. The most direct channel is command over votes in the selection of boards of directors. A less direct channel is the purchase and sale of stock, which influences stock prices, has an impact on the company's financial strength, and affects managerial security. The strength of ownership power clearly depends, in part, on the quantitative importance of the ownership interest, used alone or coordinately.

Quantitative Aspects of Institutional Stock Ownership. Institutional ownership of stock has been growing relative to individual ownership for many years, although the latter regularly tends to be underrated because of its lesser turnover rate. Institutional volume on the New York Stock Exchange (NYSE) was 69 percent in 1974, but institutional ownership in that year was well under 50 percent. Its exact magnitude depends, in part, on whether institutional account holdings in which the institutions have limited discretion in voting and/or buying and selling are included. This factor is especially relevant in evaluating "personal trust funds," the second largest category of institutional investor (see Table 4.4), where the institutions very commonly have only partial, or no, voting power over the stock. In 1974 Chase, Citibank, First National Bank of Chicago, and Morgan Guaranty had sole voting

Table 4.4. *Institutional ownership of assets, stocks, and common stocks, by market value, 1978*

Types of investment	All assets	All stocks	Common stock only
Personal trust funds	167.9	93.1	91.1
Private noninsured pension funds	201.5	107.9	106.7
Investment companies	80.4	36.8	36.3
Life insurance companies	393.4	35.5	24.5
State and local retirement funds	148.5	33.3	33.3
Foundations	38.5	27.0	26.5
Property-liability insurance companies	155.9	19.4	15.2
Educational endowments	16.3	10.2	10.1
Mutual savings banks	158.1	4.8	3.0
Subtotal	1360.5	368.0	346.7
Less: Institutional holdings of investment company shares	—	10.3	—
Total stock ownership of institutional investors	—	357.7	—
Total stock outstanding	—	1041.0	—

Figures taken as of end of year; in billions of dollars.
Source: Securities and Exchange Commission, *Statistical Bulletin* (Washington, D.C., July 1979), pp. 16–20.

rights for about 64 percent of their total discretionary holdings.[62] Bank voting rights and investment discretion are greater in pension funds than in personal trust assets; a figure for personal trusts alone would probably be in the order of 50 percent or less. As shown in Table 4.4, with personal trusts included, the nine major categories of institutional investors held $357.7 billion of stock at the end of 1978, or 34.4 percent of the outstanding. Excluding personal trusts from the institutional investor total would reduce it to $264.6 billion, or 25.4 percent of aggregate stockholdings.

Institutional investors are not a homogeneous and unified power complex, although they all have a stake in the dividend and price performance of securities held. Some of the institutions included in Table 4.4 are mutual organizations (mutual savings banks and some life insurance companies), others are stock companies. There are other types of nonprofit organizations – foundations and educational endowments – along with profit-oriented companies like banks and investment counseling firms (each of which manages a part of "private noninsured pension plans"). Some institutional investors, such as company-managed pension funds, are closely tied to and dominated by nonfinancial companies; others, such as state and local retirement funds, are affiliated with governments. Some are under strong competitive pressure for superior performance (mutual funds, managers of corporate pension funds); others, such as foundations, are under less pressure.

By the end of the 1970s there were 99 separate and independent financial organizations that owned stock worth over a billion dollars.[63] This group held a stock aggregate of $237.3 billion (of an institutional total of $332.6 billion). Of these 99 large stock owners, 43 were banks; 31 were investment companies, advisors, or groups; 10 were insurance companies; 6 were government-sponsored trust funds; 6 were self-managed private pension funds; 1 was a foundation; 1 was a university; and 1 was a private trust company. The 43 banks held stock valued at $119.9 billion, or 50.5 percent of the 99 institutional total. The stock values controlled by these institutional investors are clearly large (this group of 99 accounts for over two-thirds of the institutional total), but the stock aggregates from which this ownership is drawn are *very* large, and it is evident that there are a great many separate institutions with a lot of stock.

Institutions tend to concentrate their stock investments more heavily on very large companies than do individual investors. In 1969 bank pension and trust holdings in the 500 largest New York Stock Exchange (NYSE) stocks were three times as great as their holdings in other NYSE issues, and their preferences were tipped even further toward the top 100. In part, this is a consequence of their need for investment opportunities in which large sums can be absorbed without very large price effects (and without automatic domination via stock ownership). The result is a lesser proportionate interest and control potential than would be the case if investment were oriented toward smaller companies.

Tables 4.5 and 4.6, adapted from the 1971 *Institutional Investor Report,* show the distribution of large holdings of a wide array of institutional investors in 125 very large companies and 111 medium-sized companies, respectively, in 1969. It is evident that in-

stitutional investor holdings were slightly more concentrated in
the very large companies than in companies of lesser size. It can
also be seen that 47 institutional investors held between 5 and under
10 percent of the stock of the 125 largest companies, and in 9 cases
a single institutional investor held 10 percent or more.

The nine cases of holdings of 10 percent or more suggest a real
control potential. But in column 2 of Tables 4.5 and 4.6 it can be
seen that in only four of the nine cases does the institution possess
the sole power to vote. Furthermore, each of the four alleged to
be solely voted by an institution were so included in the *Institutional Investor Report* by error. Two of the four, Sears Roebuck and
Proctor & Gamble, have as their large stockholder a self-adminis-
tered employee stock savings plan, with "passed through" voting
rights to the employee beneficiaries for Sears (therefore never a
unified institutional vote) and a policy of nonvoting of plan-
owned stock on the part of Proctor & Gamble. These two were,
therefore, improperly included as being held by institutions with
sole voting powers. The third case, the Ford Motor Company,
again involves the erroneous crediting of an institution, presumably the Ford Foundation, with sole voting power, because the
stock held by the Foundation had no voting power while in the
Foundation's possession.[64] It is also interesting to note that here,
as with Sears Roebuck, the institution was not independent of the
management of the company and was not an arms-length investor. The fourth case is that of the Gulf Oil Company. The institution is presumably the Mellon Bank, which has held over 10
percent of the voting stock in Gulf for many years, but in 1967
and in 1974 the bank was reported as having sole voting power
over less than 2 percent of their over 10 percent total. Also, the
bank was under common control, along with Gulf, by Mellon
family interests; therefore the institutional holding was not that of
an independent institutional investor but one part of a loosely integrated but commonly controlled set of institutions. With these
corrections, *none* of the 125 largest companies in the 1969 study
was subject to 10 percent ownership with sole voting power by
a single institutional investor.

Table 4.7 shows a distribution of 380 large holdings – defined
here as those of 2 percent or more of the voting stock – in the 200
largest nonfinancial corporations as of December 31, 1974, classed
by size of holding. Of these 380 large holdings, 41 were 10 percent
or larger, whereas 339 were between 2 and under 10 percent. Table
4.8 reveals that the big three institutional stock owners – commer-

Table 4.5. *Concentration of institutional investor ownership of voting stock in 125 companies with market value of $500 million and over, 1969*

Percentage of stock	All holdings		Holdings with sole vote by institution	
	No.	%	No.	%
Concentration in largest holder				
20+	2	1.6	2[a]	1.6
15 to under 20	1	0.8	0	—
10 to under 15	6	4.8	2[a]	1.6
5 to under 10	47	37.6	32	25.6
2.5 to under 5	53	42.4	50	40.0
1 to under 2.5	8	6.4	29	23.2
Under 1	8	6.4	10	8.0
Total	125	100.0	125	100.0
Concentration in largest two holders				
20+	4	3.2	2	1.6
15 to under 20	7	5.6	1	0.8
10 to under 15	31	24.8	14	11.2
5 to under 10	55	44.0	59	47.2
2.5 to under 5	18	14.4	32	25.6
1 to under 2.5	4	3.2	9	7.2
Under 1	6	4.8	8	6.4
Total	125	100.0	125	100.0
Concentration in largest five holders				
20+	20	16.0	8	6.4
15 to under 20	34	27.2	19	15.2
10 to under 15	36	28.8	46	36.8
5 to under 10	23	18.4	36	28.8
2.5 to under 5	5	4.0	7	5.6
1 to under 2.5	3	2.4	3	2.4
Under 1	4	3.2	6	4.8
Total	125	100.0	125	100.0

[a] These cases were erroneously included as involving a single institution's sole vote – see discussion in text.

Source: Adapted from *Institutional Investor Report of the Securities and Exchange Commission,* vol. 5 (Washington, D.C., 1971), Tables XV–4 and XV–17.

Table 4.6. *Concentration of institutional investor ownership of voting stock in 111 companies with market value of $100 million to $249 million, 1969*

Percentage of stock	All holdings		Holdings with sole vote by institution	
	No.	%	No.	%
Concentration in largest holder				
20+	4	3.6	1	0.9
15 to under 20	1	0.9	1	0.9
10 to under 15	8	7.2	5	4.5
5 to under 10	35	31.5	31	27.9
2.5 to under 5	34	30.6	37	33.3
1 to under 2.5	12	10.8	17	15.3
Under 1	17	15.3	19	17.1
Total	111	100.0	111	100.0
Concentration in largest two holders				
20+	5	4.5	1	0.9
15 to under 20	7	6.3	6	5.4
10 to under 15	21	18.9	15	13.5
5 to under 10	43	38.7	43	38.7
2.5 to under 5	15	13.5	25	22.5
1 to under 2.5	4	3.6	3	2.7
Under 1	16	14.4	18	16.2
Total	111	100.0	111	100.0
Concentration in largest five holders				
20+	20	18.0	11	9.9
15 to under 20	19	17.1	16	14.4
10 to under 15	26	23.4	19	17.1
5 to under 10	24	21.6	37	33.3
2.5 to under 5	3	2.7	9	8.1
1 to under 2.5	8	7.2	3	2.7
Under 1	11	9.9	16	14.4
Total	111	100.0	111	100.0

Source: Adapted from *Institutional Investor Report of the Securities and Exchange Commission,* vol. 5 (Washington, D.C., 1971), Tables XV-4 and XV-17.

Table 4.7. *Large holdings (2 percent or more) of voting stock in the 200 largest nonfinancial corporations, by size of holding, December 31, 1974*

Size of holding (%)	Proximate (record) ownership		Ultimate ownership[a]	
	No.	%	No.	%
20 and under	13	3.4	17	4.5
15 and under 20	7	2.4	5	1.3
10 and under 15	21	5.3	22	5.8
5 and under 10	60	15.8	58	15.3
2 and under 5	279	73.1	276	73.0
Total	380	100.0	378	100.0

[a] Consolidating family-controlled foundations and personal holding company ownership.

cial banks, investment companies, and insurance companies – *do not even appear among the holder types for any of the 41 very large holdings in this tabulation.* If we consolidate foundations, personal and family-dominated holding companies, and family-controlled banks (see the last column of Table 4.7), the largest owner group for the 10 percent and over holdings is "Individual or Family," and the only important institutional owner of very large holdings is "Employee Stock Saving or Profit-Sharing Plan" (both hereafter referred to as ESPs).

Most ESPs are given to a bank trustee to manage, and a number of analysts have assumed that banks have real voting and other powers deriving from their handling of these plans.[65] Ordinarily, however, the plan trustee is a custodian/administrator with some investment discretion if the plan calls for diversification beyond the company's own stock, but with very limited voting powers.[66] In 14 of the 16 plans shown in Table 4.8 there is a "pass-through" vote to employees, with the trustee allowed at best (in 9 of the 14 cases) to vote the unvoted stock. In one further plan mentioned earlier, that of Procter & Gamble, the company stock is not voted at all, by fixed rule. In none of the 16 cases does the trustee have the power to vote all plan stock solely at his own discretion.

In general, the ESP is removable, on short notice, by the management of the sponsor company, so that the independence of the

Table 4.8. *Very large holdings of voting stock (10 percent or more) in the 200 largest nonfinancial corporations, by type of holder, December 31, 1974*

Type of holder	Proximate (record) ownership		Ultimate ownership[a]	
	No.	%	No.	%
Employee stock savings or profit-sharing plan	16	39.0	16	39.0
Individual or family	13	31.7	20	48.8
Other companies[b]	9	22.0	3	7.3
Foundations	3	7.3	2	4.9
Total	41	100.0	41	100.0

[a] Consolidating family-controlled foundations and personal holding company ownership under "individual or family."
[b] Includes nonfinancial corporations and closely held investment companies.

trustee's voting power is constrained – if not by an implied gentleman's agreement on appropriate behavior, then by the threat of trustee removal. It is by this line of reasoning that I heavily discount *bank* power arising from the ESP trustee function. Because banks are dependent on management in all aspects of such plans, the ESP strengthens *management* control.[67]

The major institutional investors are extremely important as owners of large blocks of voting stock in the large corporation, but it is clear that the holdings over which they have voting discretion fall almost entirely in the under 10 percent category. Table 4.9 shows that commercial banks, investment companies, and insurance companies together have 226 of the 380 large holdings in the 200 largest companies. Table 4.10 indicates how dominant these institutions are as multiple holders of sizable blocks of stock. Of the 20 institutions that had three or more large holdings (over 2 percent) in the 200 largest nonfinancials at the end of 1974, nine were commercial banks, eight were investment companies, and three were insurance companies. Morgan Guaranty Trust led the parade with large holdings in 29 of the 200 largest; Morgan also had the largest single holding in 11 different large nonfinancials. National Bank of Detroit was next with the largest single holding

Table 4.9. *Large holdings (2 percent or more) of voting stock in the 200 largest nonfinancial corporations, by type of holder, December 31, 1974*

Type of holder	Proximate (record) ownership		Ultimate ownership [a]	
	No.	%	No.	%
Commercial bank	98	25.8	98	26.3
Employee stock savings or profit-sharing plan	75	19.7	75	20.2
Insurance company	30	7.9	30	8.1
Investment company	98	25.8	98	26.3
Other companies [b]	15	3.9	8	2.2
Foundations	13	3.4	5	1.3
Individual or family	50	13.2	57	15.3
Retirement fund	1	0.3	1	0.3
Total	380	100.0	372	100.0

[a] Consolidating family-controlled foundations and personal holding company ownership under "individual or family."
[b] Includes nonfinancial corporations and closely held investment companies.

in eight; and Investors Diversified Services followed with the largest holding in six. Table 4.11 lists the largest holders of voting stock by institutional type. The ESP shows up first, but banks and investment companies account for over a third of the largest holdings.

The overall importance of banks, insurance companies, and investment companies as stockholders of large corporations is shown in Table 4.12, which describes the distribution of their aggregate holdings in the 200 largest nonfinancials at the end of 1974. As seen in the table, 30 percent or more of the voting stock was held by these institutions in 35 (17.5 percent) of the 200 largest nonfinancials, another 64 nonfinancials (32 percent) were owned between 20 and under 30 percent by this group, and 77 percent of the top 200 nonfinancials were owned 10 percent or more by this same investing group. These are important ownership interests, although it is clear from this table that the bulk of ownership of the 200 lies outside this group of institutional investors.

Table 4.10. *The 20 largest owners of big blocks of stock in the 200 largest corporations, by frequency of large holdings, December 31, 1974*

Institution	Number of large holdings[a]	Number of largest holdings[b]
Morgan Guaranty Trust	29	11
Investors Diversified Services	19	6
Prudential Life	16	2
Lord Abbett	15	5
Capital Research & Management	13	4
Citibank	13	4
National Bank of Detroit	13	8
Dreyfus	12	4
Massachusetts Financial Services	11	1
Chase Manhattan Bank	8	3
Fidelity Management	8	3
First National Bank of Boston	8	3
Wellington Management	7	1
Equitable Life	5	2
First National Bank of Chicago	5	2
Wachovia Bank	3	1
Mellon National Bank	3	—
Metropolitan Life	3	2
Delaware Management	3	—
Bankers Trust	3	—

[a] Holdings of 2 percent or more of the voting stock.
[b] The largest block of voting stock in the given corporation.

The picture conveyed by the given data suggests that holdings among the institutional majors that are large enough to have an inherent control significance are sparse, but these institutions' overall large holdings in giant companies are substantial enough so that major shifts would surely have stock price and other implications. If institutions decided collectively how to vote corporate stock, or which ones to favor or disfavor as investments, even greater consequences would ensue.

Institutional Investor Behavior. The institutional investor is generally less interested in obtaining control than an individual or nonfinancial corporation that makes comparably large stock investments. Wealthy individuals and acquiring corporations may

Table 4.11. *Largest holder of voting stock in each of 163 [a] large nonfinancial companies, by type of holder, December 31, 1974*

Type of holder	Proximate (record) ownership		Ultimate ownership [b]	
	No.	%	No.	%
Commercial bank	35	21.4	34	21.4
Employee stock savings or profit-sharing plan	53	32.5	53	33.3
Insurance company	7	4.3	7	4.4
Investment company	27	16.6	27	16.9
Other companies [c]	11	6.8	2	1.3
Foundation	7	4.3	4	2.6
Individual or family	23	14.1	32	20.1
Total	163	100.0	159	100.0

[a] For companies in the 200 largest that had a single owner with 2 percent or more of the voting stock.
[b] Consolidating family-controlled foundations and personal holding company ownership under "individual" or "family."
[c] Includes nonfinancial corporations and closely held investment companies.

actively seek control because they think that they can manage a company better than the incumbents or that the target fits their personal or corporate diversification plans. Institutional investors may feel that companies they own could be managed better, but, with rare exceptions, they do not consider themselves qualified or organized to manage. They are in the business of portfolio management and still generally adhere to the "Wall Street Rule" as their method of coping with managerial ineptitude; that is, they sell off their stock in a company whose management has lost favor.[68] This behavior pattern is rooted, in part, in their functional specification as portfolio managers and their associated lack of management capability and interest. It is also based on their recognition that obtaining control is not easy, so that there would have to be important potential gains to make its pursuit worthwhile.

The theoretical gains of obtaining control for an institutional investor would appear to be: (1) better access to inside informa-

Table 4.12. *Commercial bank, insurance company, and investment company aggregate holdings of voting stock of the 200 largest nonfinancial corporations, December 31, 1974*

Size of aggregate holdings (%)	Companies	
	No.	%
50 and over	1	0.5
40 and under 30	6	3.0
30 and under 40	28	14.0
20 and under 30	64	32.0
10 and under 20	55	27.5
Under 10	46	23.0
Total	200	100.0

Includes holdings of federally insured banks with assets over $75 million, several large state chartered banks that voluntarily submit data to the comptroller, investment companies with assets of $10 million or more, and the holdings of 1,314 insurance companies, as reported in *Best's Market Guide* (Oldwick, N.J.: A. M. Best Company, 1975), vol. 1 (Corporate Stocks). Data on bank and investment company holdings are taken from Computer Directions Advisors, Inc., *Bank Stock Holdings Survey* and *Stock Holdings Survey* (December 31, 1974).

tion; (2) additional business obtainable from a controlled company; and (3) profit advantages of enforced stabilization over many competitive firms and industries. But control is not required to gain inside information, merely some important inside track, and contemporary legal constraints on the use of inside information make this advantage of diminished utility.[69] The additional business advantage is relevant only to diversified institutions like banks and, to a lesser extent, insurance companies. The stabilization gain is potentially applicable only to the largest banks, which might conceivably have the vision and power to stabilize entire industries. These last two advantages might be attractive to banks if they were free to pursue them without constraint. But the constraints, and associated costs of seeking control, have been severe and have increased over time. Consequently, the banks have not established positions of dominance over large nonfinancial corporations by deliberate pursuit of ownership control.

It is sometimes contended that banks and other institutional investors have control "thrust upon them" by the size of their holdings and the need to intervene to protect a stock under condition of virtual unsalability. There is some truth to this claim, but its significance is greatly overrated. The point applies with much greater force to credit extensions, where the lender is locked in by virtue of the fact that attempted withdrawal could precipitate failure and a resultant partial or complete loss of the lender's original investment, and where the creditor has legal rights to intervene that are not available to the owner of 6 percent of the common stock. The creditor can also try to salvage a credit through limited intervention – such as obtaining more collateral or forcing the sale of parts of the company[70] – which would hardly help the owner of an equity interest. The sale of a stock interest, even a large one, will not critically damage the portfolio company, and the power of an equity owner to protect his or her interest is not so great as that of a creditor. It is true that the equity owner may have trouble selling off a very large block of stock quickly without a substantial price concession, but liquidation programs by institutional investors have been successfully carried out on a large scale and the big block traders that have emerged in recent decades in response to the demands of institutional investors can move large blocks of stock fast and with modest price effect.[71] There are, no doubt, many cases in which a sudden change in conditions leaves a major institutional holder with a large position difficult to dispose of quickly, which occasionally provokes an interest in internal reform and greater intervention. But institutions usually still struggle to get out as best they can. The constraints on efforts to control are potent, and the cases of serious intervention efforts based on locked-in stock holdings in large corporations are hard to find.

One constraint on the institutional investor is legal restriction on portfolios. Insurance companies are subject to sharp limits on stock ownership and concentrations of holdings in single issuers. Open-end investment companies (mutual funds) are required to adhere to a 5- and 10-percent rule for 75 percent of their assets,[72] mainly in the interests of diversification and marketability. Bank trust departments are subject to the limits of trust agreements, legal lists for investment portfolios,[73] and, most importantly, "a prudent man" rule and a trust law, which stress safety, the avoidance of speculation, and the obligation of the trustee to undeviating pursuit of the interest of the trust. If banks were to seek control via trust investment for the advantage of other parts of the bank (e.g., to bring controlled entities into commercial relation with the bank), this would be a blatant violation of the banks fiduciary obligations to their trust customers, and the banks would be subject to lawsuits for damages and removals of trust and pension accounts, besides a great deal of adverse publicity. The antitrust laws are also an important legal constraint on bank pursuit of control. If control were used to bring in other banking business, this would eliminate competition by means of a form of vertical integration and would be prohibited by the Clayton Act. An attempt to stabilize by acquiring control over a number of competitors in the same industry would violate both the Sherman and Clayton Acts.[74] This hardly precludes the possibility of an attempt at such restraints. But the banks are image sensitive, and the real possibility of antitrust action is, at a minimum, a genuine constraint.

Another important constraint arises out of competition and customer pressure. Many customers of institutional investors are powerful and sophisticated – especially corporate customers, who have given pension fund money to financial institutions to manage, and who have a profit interest in investment performance – and would not look complacently at institutional use of their assets for private strategies and nonfiduciary ends. Public attention to investment performance has become much more widespread and important to institutional investors. Customers study relative performance, communicate with one another and with institutional managers, and apply rewards and punishments accordingly (most obviously, in allocations of pension fund money among accounts).

When a concern for investment performance is strongly operative on institutional investors, the investors must be prepared to move into and out of securities in large volume, depending on the outlook for particular industries and companies. The turnover rate of performance-oriented portfolios will be high. Thus a Morgan, when it comes to view a favored area like "metals and minerals" less favorably, reduces its impressive holdings in this area on a massive scale (its employee benefit plan assets in metals and minerals fell from $640 million to $69 million between 1968 and 1973). Such fluidity reduces the control significance of institutional investors holdings, as their lack of permanence makes them less formidable a threat to a management than the holdings of investors less prone to "abandon ship" at the slightest sign of malaise.

Growth in size, bureaucratization, and concern over possible violation of inside information rules have led to the separation and functional specialization of trust departments in banks. The trust departments of the larger banking institutions are profit centers with considerable autonomy and with prerogatives that are protected to some degree by law. The use of trust assets for control and larger bank strategies would violate internal bank rules and the ethic of the trust investment function as seen by its participants. Such violations occur, but rarely. Thus functional specialization tends to reinforce the focus on investment performance and strict portfolio management.

Institutional investors are also constrained from using stock ownership as a control vehicle by business relationships with the companies in which they own stock. Diversified institutional investors frequently do business – sometimes a great deal of it – with owned companies, and the business and personal linkages between the investor and investee management are often extensive. Portfolio management involves numerous contacts with portfolio companies in the pursuit of investment information – a flow that would be seriously disturbed by hostile acts in voting or tendering stock.

Nondiversified institutional investors are also linked to companies in ways that often constrain their independence from management. Foundations still present a fairly varied picture: Some are quite independent of both the originating family and management (Irvine, A&P), others are close to a family that has ceased to control the company (Kresge, Rockefeller), and still others are dominated by or closely linked to the management of the company (Duke Power, Johnson & Johnson). Managements have a keen interest in a large stockholding foundation and often succeed in establishing relations that neutralize the independence of foundations with large holdings in their companies.

Employee stock savings and profit-sharing plans, which constitute the most important institutional owner of very large holdings in large corporations, are even more reliably promanagement than the foundations. For the minority, where the trustee or management itself votes the shares, management domination of the voting block is clear. In the majority of ESPs, with "pass-through" rights, the trustee can vote unvoted shares at his discretion, which means that the one unified block of votes under these plans is assuredly promanagement. The voting behavior of employee-owners of pass-through shares is harder to assess, but support for management is likely for these reasons: (1) The stock held in the plan is contributed by the company (management), in whole or in part, and is generally regarded by the employee-recipients as management largess. (2) The employees with the most stock are those with longest tenure and closest ties to the company. (3) The employees are subject to more extensive management influence and persuasion than other shareholders.

Other institutional owners like investment companies and governmental retirement funds are less profoundly influenced by linkages to company managements, although these are not entirely absent (especially in investment companies). But such institutions have never been activist investors either, mainly because of their specialization in security evaluation and the absence of obvious benefits from efforts to control.

An investor with relatively modest holdings (1 to 10 percent) does not pose a threat to a large corporation unless it aggressively pursues control. Such aggression is discouraged by all the constraints mentioned and by the difficulty, if not futility, of attempting to convert moderate stockholdings into control. Control efforts by institutional investors are so rarely encountered that corporate managements warmly welcome large institutional purchases of the stock (especially by institutions with whom they do business) for their favorable price effects and as manifestation of loyalty. It is assumed that the institutions will vote their proxies with management and managements are rarely disappointed in this regard.[75]

Although the major institutional investors have been extremely passive and promanagement in using their proxies, they have tried to exercise influence on occasion. Financing plans that involve eliminating the preemptive rights of stockholders, or otherwise altering the capital structure in ways deemed inappropriate, are sometimes the object of such action. Stock option plans occasionally arouse institutional ire. But the most important basis for intervention is a merger proposal, which often leads to telephone calls, letters, and visits, in which reasoning or threats, or both, are used. Institutional investor attempts to influence decisions rarely involve the use of proxies and voting machinery, which are widely thought to be ex post facto and ineffectual. And the effect of institutional intervention is far from reliable, especially if the management has already come to a decision before intercession gets underway.

When institutional pressure *is* effective, it is often a result of management's conviction that the objections are sufficiently intense and widespread to threaten the price of the company's stock. There is no evidence that institutional investors collude in either voting their stock or buying and selling securities. They have shown very little interest at all in the voting of shares; it has been a bother, with the added disadvantage of suggesting a degree of power that is not felt.[76] As investors, they are very much preoccupied with investment performance. From this standpoint, the use of their investment securities for collective strategic and power ploys would not serve their own interest. This is especially so in light of the probable futility of such endeavors, given the usual size of their holdings, the number and variety of institutions that would have to be organized, and the legal and economic problems inherent in any effort at market rigging. Nonetheless, the institutions may present a common front, without planned collective action, where their interests are perceived as identical, as in opposing an ill-conceived merger. Thus, although their ownership may be too diffused and uncoordinated and constraints on its use too severe for them to exercise great influence by voting power, their ability to affect the price of the company's stock (and the credit standing of the company as a borrower) by buying and selling stock freely is the institutional investor's primary basis of influence. Institutional disaffection and a low stock price will weaken the management's status with other stockholders and open up the possibility of either other stockholder initiatives or a takeover bid from outside.

An important constraint on management behavior thus lies in the size, mobility, and performance orientation of many institutional investors. Aggressors in takeover bids can mobilize institutions to "warehouse" stock (helping the bidder finance the acquisition) in exchange for guarantees on ultimate selling prices.[77] Loss of institutional support thus affects management in direct and indirect ways – the value of management stockholdings and stock options declines, financing and merger plans based on favorable stock prices are made more difficult, and management security is diminished. Management status is also weakened within the organization and among members of the businesss and financial elite, with further potential effects on company and important outsider morale and support. The considerable attention and time devoted by management to investor (and investment community) relations are a testimonial to the importance of these matters for managerial welfare.[78]

The threat of financial control

Concern over financial control has been grounded, in part, on fear of the sheer aggregation of power that would follow from a unification of banking and industrial interests. Such close linkages have been common in continental Europe (especially in Germany), and in Japan, where banks have long been organized as financial conglomerates, combining investment banking functions, direct stock ownership, and short-term lending.[79] In contrast with this so-called "continental model," law and tradition in Great Britain, Canada, and the United States brought forth banking institutions with more restricted functions centering in short-term lending. Continental practice was (and remains) conducive to bank control of industry, whereas the British–Canadian–U.S. tradition has limited bank control and made for a looser system of bank-industry relationships.[80] Except for transitional periods, like the Morgan era and the 1920s, financial domination of the large corporation and the development of bank-based networks of real control have been unusual and on a downward trend over the past 80 years.

Another source of concern has been the scope of the banker's activities, which might induce efforts to mediate between firms and even across industry lines in the interest of avoiding "excessive" competition. The benefits to the banker from such policy might be more secure credits as a lender, higher prices and dividends on owned or managed stock, promoter's profits and commissions where coordination called for combining competing firms, and a reputation for business statesmanship. For bankers to take this route, they would have to have a *lot* of breadth of view and considerable power. J. P. Morgan was reputed to have been concerned with excessive competition and to have been influenced in his promotional endeavors by a desire to bring "order" to business.[81] And he had a great deal of power, probably more than any of his successors, because of his extraordinary prestige, an exceptionally high level of financial concentration and coordination, and the limited strength of competitive centers of power, such as governments.

Bankers of the 1970s, by contrast, seem more narrowly and opportunistically profit oriented, more passive in relation to large social forces, and less powerful. Even in industries like the airlines, where bank credit extensions and fiduciary stockholdings have been very large, bank impact on major industry policies seems to have been modest.[82] The bankers have focused on deposits, loans, and arrangements that would provide proper rewards and protections for the risks incurred. They have been innovative in developing ways to lend to weakening borrowers with profit and security for themselves, but capturing profitable business – not the imposition of order or reform – has been the order of the day.

Concern has also been expressed that banker alliances with dominant firms might lead to discrimination against potential new competitors. According to William Shepherd, "banking structure tends to replicate itself throughout other markets,"[83] reflecting both the interest of banking oligopolists in protecting their investments, as well as the pressures of the dominant firms themselves desirous of avoiding competition. There may be some truth to this, although its relevance to the U.S. economy in the 1970s appears to be limited. It should be noted that causality does not run in one direction only, from banking to industry, although it is possible that an oligopolistic banking structure might contribute to further industrial concentration. Very small and new businesses have always had problems in raising funds because of risk, high transaction costs per dollar of loan, and the limited geographic scope of the market for small business loans – factors independent of the kind of industrywide calculations suggested by Shepherd. Furthermore, although U.S. banking markets are generally oligopolistic, industry leaders do business heavily with *national* oligopolists; small firms do business in hundreds of local oligopolistic markets. A small new firm, in short, would be doing business with banks that are hardly likely to be interested in industrywide effects; whereas firms that achieve a modicum of success may well have options that extend over quite a few submarkets.[84] If local bankers do discriminate against small firms on other than risk-return calculations or arbitrary local factors, this is likely to be the result of a local bank doing a favor for a nationwide firm in anticipation of possible rewards or penalties. For example, it was claimed that local bankers on boards of transit companies urged the purchase of GM buses in hopes of eliciting deposits from that automotive giant.[85] Given the decentralization of the U.S. banking structure, it seems more likely that financial discrimination against new competitors would flow from large non-financial firms to banks rather than the other way around. (Other barriers to entry, such as scale, rapidity of technical change, and product differentiation, seem more formidable and relevant in the United States.)

Bankers undoubtedly do use their power positions in companies to further their own interests, most obviously in trying to corral a greater fraction of customer deposits and loan business. Whether they can do this without providing commensurate service, or whether they can impose noncompetitive rates or balance requirements, will depend on their degree of company control and/or their market power. With weak borrowers they may be able to extract their "pound of flesh,"[86] although they are subject to the constraints of internal policy rules and public relations considerations, among other factors. The bankers may urge or cooperate in programs of excessive company borrowing, although this can run counter to self-interest in solvency. In the airlines case, the banks' failure to constrain overbuilding to excess capacity in the 1960s illustrates the possibility of banker contribution to overexpansion when adequate creditor protection is available. But real evidence of banker encouragement and positive impetus is lacking. With a borrower class such as public authorities, banker influence appears to have biased investment toward physical facilities with predictable financial returns, resulting in "overborrowing, overspending, and overconstructing," and a tendency "to ignore costs and benefits to the public at large and sometimes to competing private interests – costs that will not show up on the corporate books."[87]

Banker influence over large private corporations is usually more modest. With bank market power limited and the relationship one of reciprocity, banker influence tends to be one of constraint and ideological influence, exercised by a participant in a community-of-interest system. On the rare occasions when bankers have taken control of sizable companies in recent years – almost invariably the result of a borrower's extreme financial distress and consequent inability to meet bank payments – they have tended to clean house and get out, either forcing liquidation or putting the companies in the hands of managers who are given considerable autonomy.[88] If the company's assets are highly marketable, this may result in a ruthless dismantling of the company, without regard to the social costs.[89]

In the past century major adverse results of financial control in the United States have been associated with speculative rather than banking interests. The neglect and plundering of the Erie and the Missouri, Kansas, and Texas railroads by Daniel Drew and Jay Gould set a standard that successors have rarely matched.[90] In the years between 1880 and 1883 Jay Gould alone controlled 12 railroads accounting for 15 percent of all U.S. mileage, along with Western Union Telegraph and Manhattan Elevated.[91] In the public utilities sector in the late 1920s some of the holding company entrepreneurs came close to the Drew–Gould models, and their negative contributions to the general inflation and subsequent collapse of security values were significant. But the conglomerators and empire builders of the 1960s and 1970s (such as Geneen, Ling, Bludhorn, Lindner, Ricklis, and Seabrook) were only pale reflections of a more flamboyant past – wheeling and dealing in companies to no particular social advantage,[92] engaging in occasional peccadilloes at company and shareholder expense,[93] but falling far short of the level and scope of abuses of their predecessors. Their preoccupation with influencing stock prices through growth, with heavy reliance on accounting and tax and market gimmickry, and their occasional self-dealing excesses, have brought some of them close to the edge of speculative control. However, disclosure laws and legal constraints on insider trading and market manipulation have seriously limited activities in the traditional malign channels by leaders of the largest companies.

Financial influence over the large corporation in the 1970s

There has been a *decline* in banker control of the large corporation in the twentieth century. In 1900–1901, a quarter of the 200 largest companies were financially controlled; in 1929, an eighth; and in 1975, only a single firm out of 200.[94] In 1900 and 1929 banker control was based on sizable ownership holdings or on strategic position obtained through promotion or reorganization (often combined with ownership). Investment banker promotional activities in very large corporations no longer yield the ownership and the strategic position that they produced in earlier years; reorganizations are less frequent among the giants and no longer result in banker control by means of voting trusts; and the greater size and bureaucratization of large corporations, and the changed legal environment, make the seizure of control by speculative interests more difficult.

The only company among the 200 largest classed here as banker controlled is Union Pacific, a company in which the old Harriman interests were still strong in 1975, although on the verge of becoming subordinate to management. As the Union Pacific 10-K report of 1974 noted in December of that year, the Interstate Commerce Commission (ICC) found that the

> company is controlled by the Harriman interests (which the ICC apparently regards as composed of members of the Harriman family and their associates and the private banking firm of Brown Brothers, Harriman and Co. in which Messrs. Harriman, Lovett, and Gerry, directors of Union Pacific Corporation and certain subsidiaries are partners).

The company denied this allegation, but the sheer numbers of the Harriman–Brown Brothers group still on the board, its historical status in the organization (E. E. Harriman was honorary chairman; Lovett was president until 1968), and its continued domination of the executive committee in 1974 made the ICC conclusion plausible. The ICC claimed that the Harriman interests still controlled 3 percent of the voting stock in 1974, which would make this the largest unified block, although not of great significance for control in and of itself. Harriman, Lovett, and Gerry were all at least 65 years old in 1974, and their imminent departures from the Union Pacific board foretold a near end to Harriman–Brown Brothers' uniquely long domination of the affairs of Union Pacific.

Ten years ago Atlantic Coast Line Railroad Co. (now Seaboard Coast Line Industries, Inc.) would have been classed as bank controlled, with 51.7 percent of the voting stock owned, with sole voting rights, by the Mercantile-Safe Deposit and Trust Company of Baltimore, Maryland. This enormous holding stemmed from huge personal ownership by the Walters, Newcomer, and Jenkins families, who dominated both the railroad holding company and the Safe Deposit and Trust Company of Baltimore (an important predecessor of Mercantile-Safe Deposit). But in early 1972, just prior to a dividend reduction by Seaboard, a large block of stock was sold. Questions arose about the possible misuse of inside information by the bank,[95] which was well represented in the inner circles of power at Seaboard. By the end of 1974 Mercantile holdings of voting stock at Seaboard had fallen below 3 percent, and its residual power rested largely on two officer representatives on the board, one still chairman of the executive committee. This is a marginal case of financial control, with power in transition. But

Table 4.13. *Financial control, significant influence, and representation in the large corporation, 1975*

	200 largest nonfinancials		100 largest industrials	
	No.	%	No.	%
1. Outright control	1	0.5	—	
2. Significant influence, probably significant in decision-making process [a]	40	20.0	15	15
3. Other representation on boards [b]	117	58.5	66	66
a. Major institutions	(85)	(42.5)	(57)	(57)
b. Local institutions	(32)	(16.0)	(9)	(9)
Total	158	79.0	81	81

Includes as instrumentalities of financial control commercial banks, investment banks, and insurance companies.

[a] Taken from "Financial constraint" (subdivision 2) on Tables 3.1, 3.2, and 3.3.
[b] Does not include any cases already taken into account under "Significant influence."

the stock divestments and adverse publicity that resulted from the 1972 stock sale seem to have tilted the balance of power toward inside management control, although Mercantile Bank interest remained significant in the mid-1970s.

Table 4.13 shows the extent of financial control, significant influence, and representation in the large corporation in 1975. Although only one company – Union Pacific – was classified as under outright financial control, significant influence by financial institutions was present in a substantial minority of large companies. *Significant influence* as used here means having some power and input in policymaking, but usually a constraining and negative power short of ultimate authority. It is synonymous with partial control, in contrast with full control. There is no mechanical rule that provides a dependable basis for determining significant influence, and the complexity and limited information on the source of key decisions makes arbitrariness inescapable. Companies were classed as subject to significant financial influence in this study if: (1) There was publicly available or privately disclosed information indicating a substantial banker input into the making of key decisions (usually either in top management selection or in major investment choices);[96] (2) they were, or recently had been, in dire financial straits, with high debt–equity ratios, requiring special emergency financing, or subject to the imposition of severe restrictive convenants; and (3) the number of bankers on the board of directors, their status, and their historic position suggest real influence. In most cases where companies were subject to significant financial influence, it was manifest in more than one of these categories. Thus, in the case of Arlen Realty, a high official of Citibank was on the Arlen board (3), and Arlen was in dire financial straits in 1975 (2) – by 1978, with a further deterioration in Arlen's status, a new president was installed who was recommended by Citibank (1).[97] In Pan Am's case, in the mid-1970s severe restrictive covenants were in place (2) and renewals of revolving credits were regular occasions for the displacement of Pan Am top executives (1).[98]

Several mechanical rules were followed in applying criterion (3). If a major bank was represented on the executive committee of a relatively weak nonfinancial, I automatically classified it as a case where there was probably significant influence (e.g., Citibank vis-à-vis Owens-Illinois and Arlen Realty; Morgan Guaranty Trust in its relations with Panhandle Eastern Gas and Santa Fe Industries). When a major financial institution was represented on the board, but not the executive committee, of a large firm, it was classed as subject to probable significant influence if the imbalance of power was great and the relationship was of long standing (e.g., Citibank vis-à-vis Long Island Lighting; Morgan in relation to Niagara Mohawk Power and Champion International). Where the nonfinancial corporation was a strong and highly solvent enterprise, significant influence was deemed probable only where financial representation was more extensive (e.g., three major New York banks on the board of Phelps Dodge, three financial representatives on the board of GTE, with a long background of banker influence in the cases of both Phelps Dodge and GTE). Some adjustments were made on the basis of special knowledge, and banker presence was given greater weight where companies were in financial difficulties.[99]

These criteria produce a relatively high (probably upper limit) estimate of financial sharing in control, because some reliance is placed on mechanical numbers like board and committee membership, and financial condition, which may have very little effect on final decision-making power. On the other hand, in a number of these cases the latent power of financial institutions may be great and the constraints they impose on managers without overt instructions or explicit actions may be severe. Table 4.13 also indicates that potential financial influence through board representation is not exhausted by the category of "Significant influence" – in 117 further cases among the 200 largest, there is financial representation on boards, including 85 instances of representation by major institutions.

Concluding note

The impact of financial enterprises on the large nonfinancial corporations of the 1970s has novel features, as compared with the past. Direct and decisive control has declined in importance and is rare, but shared power in the sense of important minority and/or constraining influence on decision making is applicable in perhaps as many as a fifth of the large companies. The financial view of sound policy is pressed home to managers by a still wider array of banker representatives on boards and personal, business, and market influences of financial institutions as creditors and owners of stock.

Financial power in the 1970s appears to constitute a strongly conservative force, accommodating and serving the dominant nonfinancial elements in the community. It does not dominate the large corporation, but what influence it has tends to press for actions that will enhance creditworthiness and profit growth. Its natural tendency is to affiliate with "profit machines" and managements that know how to guide them and then to give them free reign. If these managements see the future as requiring a stream of acquisitions, financial institutions will compete to finance them. Institutional passivity in voting behavior tends to reinforce management control of the large corporation; its support of customer merger strategies, to which the largest firms are essentially immune as victims, seems to reinforce tendencies toward concentration, but as an accommodation process rather than as one involving active initiation.

5

Government and the Large Corporation

It is frequently suggested that government enterprise and regulation have so altered the character of the economy that government – not private owners or managers – actually has control over business decision making.[1] In this chapter I will examine the role of government as a producer and the extent to which the government itself has come to occupy a place among the largest producing entities. I will also look at the extent to which government regulation of business has encroached on business decision making and prerogatives. As a prelude to examining these issues, I briefly discuss the evolving relationship between business and government and the changing role of government in the United States and other developed countries.

Government and business: the background

The level of government involvement in business in the United States from the late eighteenth century to the present has followed a U-shaped pattern: There was extensive government intervention in the pre-Civil War period (major subsidies, joint ventures with active government participation, and direct government production),[2] then a quasi-laissez-faire period between the Civil War and the end of the nineteenth century, followed by a gradual upswing of government intervention in the twentieth century, which accelerated after 1930.[3] In each of these periods there were subtrends and sometimes contradictory crosscurrents interrupting the main drift. In the earlier interventionist period, government action reflected a wide spectrum of interests and the government played an active role, such as in constructing public works.[4] In the quasi-laissez-faire period that followed, government policy was conservative and intervention more limited, although opportunistic exceptions were still made, as in the aggressive use of tariff protection and the huge contributions to the transcontinental railroads.[5]

In the twentieth century there have been increasing demands for government action and a weakening of the ideological constraints on government intervention. As in the pre-Civil War activist era, a broader base of interests has succeeded in eliciting government responses. The passing of William McKinley in 1901 marked the end of an era of relatively unconstrained business domination of national politics. In the words of economic historian Jonathan Hughes:

> The long Victorian boom was ending, and as a counterpart to organization designed to protect the interests of the investors – the Morgan specialty – the pendulum swung back from the business oligarchy and the "Billion Dollar Congress" era toward political democracy. The "little man," the farmer, the small-town businessman and the worker began once again to be courted by politicians.[6]

Governments at all levels became, and continue to become, larger economic factors.

Business has had a complex and contradictory relationship with government. Business enterprise has never been monolithic. At various times some business sectors have felt threatened by others and have pressed for and successfully mobilized government protection. This resulted in antitrust laws, railroad regulation, anti-chain store and branch bank legislation, and resale price maintenance laws, all mainly rooted in small business responses to economic pressures.[7] Big business has also resorted to government protection and subsidy in the face of exceptional costs and risks (e.g., railroads, advanced weapons systems) or "unfair competition" from abroad (the basis for the U.S. steel industry's recent successful appeal for protection). In a world of multinational business and rapid technological change, demands for assistance, protection, and support have been on the upswing.[8] Business has also contributed to the rise of big government by its support of, or acquiescence in, militarization and a forward foreign policy.[9]

Finally, a variety of "problems" are spun off by business in its process of growth – such as structural unemployment, waste disposal sites – which it does not internalize but compels government and the larger society to deal with as best they can. Thus, on the one hand, business has contributed greatly to the rise of big government by its own externalization of social costs and ad hoc mobilization of government – most often to restrain, or offset by subsidy, competition from domestic or foreign producers. On the other hand, business has felt harried and threatened by increasing government intervention, even when of its own creation. Government intervention has a variable impact on businesses, and even its business beneficiaries and sponsors may object to regulatory detail while supporting the overall thrust of the relevant regulatory policy. Business is further troubled over the growth of government social welfare intervention – admitted to be necessary in a complex social order but regularly criticized for overgenerosity and mismanagement. Business has felt a loss of power, freedom of action, and control.[10] This might seem paradoxical following the strongly probusiness administrations of Nixon and Ford and Carter's eager search for a formula to reestablish "business confidence," but it reflects the fact that business power has suffered a *relative* decline since 1929 and that a contributing factor is that governments have become large, bureaucratic power centers, broadly responsive to business interests but not completely so.[11]

The economic role of governments

Governments – federal, state, and local – have risen in importance as economic entities in the United States in the twentieth century by virtually any measure. Government accounted for 3.8 percent of employed labor in 1900, 7 percent in 1929, and 19.1 percent in 1978. The government share of expenditures for goods and services increased from about 4 percent of the gross national product (GNP) in 1900 to 8.2 percent in 1929 to 20.5 percent in 1978. Gross government outlays in 1978 were still much larger – 35.9 percent of GNP. But compensation of government employees, as a proportion of national income, has increased by a much smaller magnitude: from about 5.5 percent in 1900, to 5.8 percent in 1929, to 13.3 percent in 1978.[12]

In 1978 gross government outlays totaled $763.4 billion. This huge figure, however, includes not only government purchases of goods and services but also $327.9 billion in transfer payments under social security and various subsidy and welfare programs. These are important, but they involve a government-sponsored rechanneling of income flows by taxing and transferring revenue to other parties, rather than any direct government product or demand for output. If we subtract transfer payments from gross government outlays, we arrive at a figure of $435.5 billion for all purchases of goods and services. By subtracting further the compensation of government employees ($229.6 billion in 1978), we find $204.9 billion to be the net figure for government purchases of goods from the outside – clearly a manifestation of government power and importance in the economy, but with production, however, remaining in the private sector and the government serving as consumer.

Direct government output for 1978 is approximated by the figure for compensation of government employees – $229.6 billion, which was 10.8 percent of GNP, in contrast with 20.5 percent for all purchases of goods and services and 35.9 percent for gross outlays. Of the 17.5 million government employees in 1978, 12.7 million (72.5 percent) were employees of state and local governments. Of the 4.8 million federal employees, 2.1 million were in the armed forces and another 900,000 were civilian employees of the defense department, leaving 1.8 million performing all civil government operations. Of these, 35 percent were in the postal service and 45 percent were in education. Of the 12.7 million state and local government employees, 6.5 million (54 percent) were in the field of education.

Government oulays and output in 1978 were clearly concentrated in limited and traditional areas. National defense accounted for two-thirds of federal employment (a fifth of its *civilian* employment) and two-thirds of federal purchases of goods and services; education and highway construction accounted for about half of state and local government gross outlays; and social welfare spending under retirement, unemployment, health, and other programs was a major factor in both federal and nonfederal government expenditures.

Despite the impressive numbers involved in social welfare spending, the United States has lagged behind the major Western industrial powers in this area – social welfare payments as a percent of GNP have been far larger in Austria, West Germany, Canada, Great Britain, Italy, and Sweden.[13] Furthermore, the financing of social welfare in the United States has been especially regressive, with the lower income households essentially financing their own benefits through social security taxes (as opposed to financing social welfare out of general tax revenues). This is done in part to mitigate business fears that social security and welfare payments will involve some kind of redistribution of income by class. About 25 percent of public assistance outlays, however, now come out of general revenue of all governments.

To a considerable extent, government productive activities have been confined to doing what private business cannot do, or does not care to do itself, and many of these activities support, complement, and promote private business interests. For example, expenditures on defense and the global spread of U.S. military forces and power have moved in close parallel with the enormous post-World War II expansion of U.S. investment and sales abroad,[14] and the serviceability to business of "containment" and associated protective strategies is beyond doubt.[15] Because many of the advanced weapons systems purchased by the Defense Department have been very expensive and risky, even the largest contractors have not had equity positions capable of sustaining genuine market bids. But these companies have been protected by government subsidization of research, provision of government capital,[16] "golden handshakes,"[17] and assorted other modes of transference of costs and risks to the public sector. Weapons procurement and research have been contracted out to private organizations, resulting in a decline in in-house weapons production and research capability on the part of the military services.[18] Thus defense, which accounts for 65 percent of federal purchases of goods and services, has become an increasingly important sphere of *private* enterprise.

Other sizable government outlays in the United States are in the areas of postal service, police and fire protection, sanitation and sewage, and parks and recreation – all of which have increased in cost as a function of population growth, urbanization, and inflation. Public enterprise in the United States has been largely confined to these areas, along with the provision and management of local transit systems, courts, airports, libraries, museums, hospitals, and other social service entities. Some 16 states are in the retail liquor business (usually on a legal monopoly basis); most cities provide water; and many cities supply electricity. Most cities that supply electricity buy it wholesale from federal projects or private producers (nonprivately produced power accounts for about 25 percent of total output).[19] There are several significant government producers of power, all dating to the Great Depression or earlier (Tennessee Valley Authority, 1933; State Power Authority of New York, 1931; and the Los Angeles Department of Water and Power, 1925). But government as producer in the United States has been kept almost entirely out of agriculture, trade, mining, and manufacturing; and the bulk of the enormous resources deployed by government in the finance sector services private financial institutions, not the public.

The relatively limited role of public enterprise in the United States may be explained by the fact that public enterprise is only one of a number of alternatives, preferable from some standpoints but objectionable from others. If required scale is too large and risks too great for private enterprise, public enterprise is one option, but subsidized and protected private enterprise is another. If monopoly power is inherent in scale economies, or if competition might threaten important values (airline safety, for example), regulation is an alternative to public enterprise. If the external social benefits or costs of projects are potentially important – as in the case of regional development, education, the arts, pollution-prone industries, or public transport facilities – taxes, subsidies, and regulations are alternatives to public ownership and control (as is simply ignoring the external effects). Public enterprise might be used to bring competition to oligopolistic industries, but antitrust laws, direct regulation, and the acceptance of oligopoly are other alternatives.

In the United States, to an exceptional degree, regulated, subsidized, and risk-underwritten private enterprise have been preferred to public enterprise. In other advanced Western countries, government ownership of facilities such as rail and air transport; electric, gas, and water utilities; coal, iron, and steel; and commercial and savings banks is common.[20] West European government enterprise has occasionally even been able to penetrate into advanced technological sectors like aerospace, petroleum, and chemicals.[21] But in the United States, public enterprise has been confined to a modest position in the utilities (especially water but also electricity), and to otherwise complementary and supportive functions. In fact, the United States stands at or near the bottom of a list of major industrial powers in percentage of assets and sales of public enterprise in the "materials sectors" of the economy.[22] The U.S. government is becoming an important producer in rail transport (Amtrak, Conrail), but only in a bailout role, to preserve the operation of public and commercial facilities where private enterprise options seem unfeasible. With Chrysler in dire straits and the automobile industry in general in relative decline and shakeout, the government's bailout role may well be extended.

Both the limits on public enterprise and character and scope of government regulation in the United States have been greatly influenced by special cultural and political circumstances. One such circumstance is that a socialist-oriented political constiuency that would provide broadly based support for government enterprise on grounds of either principle or interest has been almost completely absent in this country.[23] Business has also been more hostile to public enterprise in the United States than in Europe, in part because of the individualistic American tradition and ideology and also over fear of encroachment by a potentially competitive power capable of being mobilized by adversary groups.[24] Business influence on government in the United States does not appear to be less than that in France, Italy, West Germany, or Japan, but it has been more ad hoc and distant. Business has not needed government here as much as elsewhere, and partly for this reason business is less frequently engaged in close collaboration with government and thus less trusting of it.[25] U.S. business has even fought bitterly against extensions of government enterprise designed to serve a purely supportive function – the establishment of the Federal Reserve System, for example, was opposed by the American Bankers Association – and even more aggressively when the government would encroach on terrain that business is engaged in or could service with government subsidization.

Since 1932, Congress, under the prodding of business, has made periodic surveys of government enterprise that is competitive with private business, with a view toward minimizing government competition.[26] This campaign has been successful, and, ironically, the result has often been a protection of competitors from competition. Government competition can be formidable,[27] but it has been effectively foreclosed in the United States, even where oligopoly power is solidly entrenched and sustained by government subsidy. A second irony is that government *regulation* has been American business' preferred choice over public enterprise,[28] so that the peculiarly duplicative, bureaucratic and anticompetitive American solution in the regulated sector has its fundamental root in the fact that "the basis for the demand for public ownership is gone." [29]

Government representation among the largest corporations

Studies of the largest corporations are generally confined to privately owned corporations. But with governments now accounting for a fifth of GNP (although little more than a tenth as producer), the question arises, where would government entities stand in a large company universe defined to include them? Assuming an asset-based standard of size, paralleling that used in Chapter 3, one must resolve the issues of organizational form and the nature of activity to be included in order to answer this question.

In their 1932 classic, *The Modern Corporation and Private Property*, Berle and Means mentioned that "even the government is beginning to employ the corporate device – witness, for example, the Port of New York Authority," [30] suggesting that the corporate form might come to prevail in government ventures. The implication was that the corporate form itself is of main importance, but questions may be raised as to whether this is plausible for government activity. The main division in government organization is between governmental corporate bodies, on the one hand, and departments or divisions of governments, on the other. A government corporate body may have more autonomy and more authority to borrow money in public markets than a government department or division. Among the important purposes in establishing government corporations, in fact, was the desire to insulate them from the vagaries of the political process, to bring them closer to private business in managerial independence, and to permit the issuing of securities in circumstances where nonautonomous noncorporate public bodies were subject to tax and debt limits.[31]

Although this distinction between government corporations and departments may be meaningful for some purposes, it is not useful here. For one thing, there has been a proliferation of thousands of special public authorities and special districts in the United States that fall somewhere between an old-style public corporation and a department or division of government. More importantly, the choice between forms is sometimes of little substantive importance; some departments perform the same functions as government corporations, with similar levels of autonomy and debt-issuing capability. For example, the California Department of Water Resources can issue its own bonds, which are its sole responsibility. The Los Angeles Department of Water and Power can also issue its own revenue bonds within prescribed limits, and has a five-person board, whereas in 1974 the Government National Mortgage Association (GNMA) was a "corporation" without a board, mainly funded by public borrowing. The New York State Power Authority is a corporation but also a subdivision of the state of New York. Because the distinction between corporate body and department is not consistent in use or functional relevance, for purposes of this assessment of the importance of large government corporations I will include as a large corporation any distinguishable government body that meets the asset-size and activity standard.

As for the activity criterion, I will exclude such unique government outputs as national defense and social welfare [32] and confine matters to government entities that produce outputs sold to consumers or private industry or that produce for the government itself outputs identical in character with those produced for the private sector. The latter would include the General Services Administration (GSA), mainly in the business of construction supervision and property management, with assets of $11 billion at the end of 1974, whose services are confined to the federal government itself. The Forest Service, on the other hand, owner-manager of some 183 million acres of national forests, and easily meeting our asset standard, is excluded on the ground that much of its service is intended to be outside of the market system. Besides the GSA, other government entities that qualify for inclusion in the universe of large corporations on both a size and activity basis are in the following businesses (asset size figures given are for 1974–1975):

1. Constructing, owning, and managing water resource facilities (mainly storage and transmission plant and equipment). Three government entities would be included: Metropolitan Water District of California (assets about $1.7 billion), California Superintendent of Water Resources (assets about $2.5 billion), and Puerto Rico Water Resources Authority (assets about $1 billion).

2. Constructing, owning, and managing houses, apartments, and public buildings. Four government entities would be included: GSA (assets about $11 billion); New York City Housing Authority (assets about $2.2 billion), New York State Dormitory Authority (assets about $2.5 billion), and Pennsylvania General State Authority (assets about $2.1 billion).

3. Constructing, owning, and managing roads, transport facilities,[33] and ports. Three government entities would be included: The Port Authority of New York and New Jersey (assets about $3.9 billion), San

Francisco Bart (assets $1.6 billion), and New Jersey
Turnpike (assets about $1.4 billion).

4. Constructing, owning, and managing electric power
   facilities. Three government entities would be included: Tennessee Valley Authority (assets about
   $5.5 billion), Los Angeles Department of Water and
   Power (assets about $2.6 billion), and New York
   State Power Authority (assets about $2.2 billion).

5. Constructing, owning, and general supervising of
   nuclear research and processing facilities. One government entity would be included: Atomic Energy
   Commission [34] (assets about $14 billion).

6. Purchasing, selling, and storing agricultural commodities. One government entity would be included: Commodity Credit Corporation (assets
   about $6 billion).

7. Operating a postal system. One government entity
   would be included: U.S. Postal Service (assets about
   $1.7 billion).

Using the size and activity criteria previously discussed, in a
broadened classification system, one would include 16 government entities among the 200 largest nonfinancial corporations in
the United States in 1975. Their total assets of $62.4 billion are
only 8.6 percent of the grand total of assets of the 200 (see Table
3.1). The Atomic Energy Commission (AEC) and GSA held 40
percent of the assets of these 16 government entities. The AEC's
1974 assets reflected the large government investment in research
facilities and plants to process nuclear raw materials and to produce fissionable outputs, including atomic weapons. But, to a
large extent, the research and production activities of the AEC
were carried out by private contractors – in 1970 the AEC itself
accounted for only 5 percent of all the employees hired by it and
its contractors.[35] Also, the AEC and its successors have been precluded from any participation in the commercial nuclear reactor
market, which has been reserved for the "tight oligopoly structure
[mainly GE and Westinghouse] of the older electrical equipment
industry." [36] Thus the bulk of underlying research costs have been
socialized, material supply has been partially subsidized,[37] risks
have been underwritten by government or reduced by government fiat,[38] and the probability is that the serious fuel-recycling

and waste-disposal problems will be resolved at public expense.[39] Business' frequently reiterated view that government encroachment and lack of aid and support for business is the root of the U.S. economic malaise ignores the history of industries like nuclear energy, where subsidization has been massive and commercial possibilities have been reserved for private enterprise.

The place of government among large financial entities is greater than in the nonfinancial field. In a recomputation of the 50 largest financials, nine government entities would find a place. But even more than in the nonfinancial sector, the government's role is supportive of, or complementary to, private financial institutions. The government provides only marginal competition to the private sector in serving final consumers of financial services (mainly in agricultural lending, where farmers' political power was able to make a dent in the traditional limitations on the government role).

Occasionally, special circumstances have thrust the federal government into ownership and control of substantial facilities competitive with private business. But the government has rarely been able to sustain its position and has typically withdrawn to allow private business full sway. This was true of its takeover of the railroads, its investment in shipbuilding, and its seizures of foreign firms during World War I. A similar process of entry and liquidation took place during and after World War II.[40] For example, General Aniline and Film was taken over as enemy property in 1942, but the controlling stock investment was sold off in 1965. The government's huge World War II production facilities were also duly resold at the war's end, and in such a way as to slightly enhance the power of preexisting firms.[41] Government holdings in the power industry dating from the 1930s have not been divested, but their scope has been sharply confined and their acceptance has been closely related to their abandonment of any competitive threat to private utilities.[42]

Government regulation

It is not easy to assess the government's role as regulator and the degree of its encroachment on business decision making, partly because of the great variety of regulation and the difficulty of measuring its quality or effectiveness, now and in the past. An index of the number of regulators or government outlays on regulation would, for one thing, understate compliance costs in the private sector, and the changing character of regulation makes any assumption of proportionality between government and private inputs implausible. The effectiveness with which the mission(s) of regulation is (are) carried out must also be considered. Regulation would not be significantly more important now than in 1929 if the much larger number of regulators engaged mainly in paper shuffling and in well-publicized but largely symbolic interventions, with only marginal effect on economic activity. The importance of regulation can easily be inflated by simply assuming that the impressive nominal powers of regulators are realized in fact.[43]

The ends sought by regulation and the nature of its sponsorship must also be taken into account. Regulation may be imposed on business against its will, or it may be positively desired by business to facilitate business ends. Again, it is important to differentiate nominal and real objectives. Particular regulations are always nominally established as in the general public interest, even when blatantly servicing a narrow special interest at public expense. Furthermore, real objectives may be transformed over time – often from a public interest orientation to protection of a special interest in the process of regulatory stagnation of capture.[44]

In connection with the purpose of regulation, it is important to distinguish between the two major classes of regulation. The first is the traditional or "old" regulation of "natural monopolies" by commissions, with a trade-off made between state grants of a monopoly franchise, protection against entry, and the right of eminent domain, on the one hand, and state (via commission) control over prices, rates of return, services, and the like, on the other. The second is the "new" or social regulation – such as that implemented by the Environmental Protection Agency (EPA), the Occupational Safety and Health Agency (OSHA), and the relatively new bodies dealing with consumer and highway safety – which crosses industry lines to implement legislation presumably aimed at preserving the environment from the externalities of modern technology.

The differences between these two classes of regulation are numerous and important. Among them are the following.

First, the "old regulation" (OR) is usually characterized by detailed controls over the most strategic business variables, notably, prices charged, allowable entry, and services that may (or must) be rendered. These are the variables that private cartels seek to control but are prevented from doing (at least in flagrant ways) in the United States by the antitrust laws. Publicly supervised cartels are allowed to fix these variables because public service commissions presumably engage in surveillance and control in the public interest.[45]

The "new regulation" (NR), by contrast, is aimed at more narrowly defining the framework or ground rules within which business operates. But it also uses methods of direct and detailed intervention in applying its ground rules to specific cases. Disclosure requirements under the securities laws present a typical case of NR, with a general rule of truthfulness but with detailed rules for proper submissions, timing of prospectuses, and security issues. The NR is, in fact, not really new. It has important antecedents in the food, drug, child labor, and worker-safety laws that date back to the beginning of the century. But the recent surge of ground rules presents an immediate challenge to managerial prerogatives. They also threaten more serious cost consequences. Both the OR and the NR involve a great deal of paperwork, inspections by government officials, and negotiations on the meeting of requirements in the specified areas. But the NR, nevertheless, differs from OR in that firms are left free to invest and fix prices as they see fit within the bounds of new social welfare constraints.

Second, a further distinction between OR and NR is that OR was often brought into existence by the desires of industry members to avoid pricecutting, entry of competitors, or public ownership of natural monopolies. This was not the sole basis of all commission regulation – pressures from those abused or threatened by monopoly power and discrimination were sometimes a factor – but the protective element underlying OR was large.[46] The NR, by contrast, usually came into existence contrary to the desires of, and with varying degrees of hostility from, the business community and was usually a response to urgent demands for protection against abuses (SEC) or externalized social costs (OSHA).

Third, whatever the initiating source of the old and new regulation, by and large the old regulators g dually have been brought into friendly alliance with the regulated. The new regulators have been less amenable, partly because they are newer, partly because their assigned functions bring them into more fundamental conflict with the regulated, and partly because they cover a great many industries and are not so readily subject to "regulatory capture" as are regulatory bodies serving particular industries.[47]

Finally, the really large social costs of business regulation are attributable to the OR – as in the transportation sector – where cartel regulation has resulted in inflated prices and substantial resource misallocation.[48] In these cases, private costs are not offset by any significant public benefits – the only beneficiaries are the private firms that are regulated and protected by the government-sponsored cartel. The NR, as the OR, involves direct regulatory costs (inspectors, private compliance outlays, etc.), but these are offset by potentially large public benefits,[49] so that at worst the social deficit would be small and the potential for large positive net results under efficient management seems clear. The fact that "regulation" has become an acknowledged massive and threatening evil only with the rise of NR, and that the NR – not the really costly OR – is the subject of so much of the animus and criticism, tells us a great deal about the preferences and power of the business community.

The decline of the cartel-regulated sector in the universe of large corporations

Cartel regulation (OR) has been the traditional basis for division between a regulated and unregulated sector. Among the 200 largest corporations in 1975, how many were regulated in this traditional sense and how does this compare with the past? Classification problems arise immediately. Only part of large diversified companies may be under formal, detailed regulation; in fact, many regulated companies in stagnant fields, such as railroading, have tried to diversify out of their relatively unprofitable regulated activities. For example, in 1975 only 19 percent of Illinois Central Industries' gross sales came from its railroad operations, and it was clearly no longer a railroad company alone. I will include a large company as "regulated" (subject to substantial government regulatory constraint) if 15 percent of its gross sales are in a formally regulated sector.

Table 5.1 shows that on this liberal criterion, 79 (39.5 percent) of the 200 largest companies, accounting for 39.9 percent of the assets and 18.7 percent of the sales, were in the "regulated sector" in 1975. The table also shows that since 1929–1930, the regulated sector has *declined* among the very largest firms, accounting for a smaller number of companies and an even smaller proportion of assets. (And the decline in assets is understated because of the

Table 5.1. *Representation of regulated companies in the 200 largest nonfinancial corporations, 1929–1930 and 1974–1975*

	1929–1930	1974–1975
Number of companies	94	79
Percent of 200	47.0	39.5
Assets of regulated companies ($ billions)	81.1	288.1
Percent of assets of 200	62.6	39.9
Sales of regulated companies ($ billions)	NA	131.9
Percent of sales of 200	NA	18.7
Composition of regulated sector		
Utilities (percent of regulated total in		
parenthesis)	52 (55.3)	54 (68.4)
Railroads	42 (44.7)	11 (13.9)
Other transport	—	8[a] (10.1)
Other	—	6[b] (7.6)

[a] Includes five airlines, two companies in the shipping business (ocean and truck), and one in the bus business.
[b] Includes four companies with large financial subsidiaries, two in the dairy business.

lower fraction of regulated assets of the companies classed as regulated in the later period.) The decline in regulation is largely a result of the disappearance of many railroads from the 200 largest companies. Railroads accounted for 42 of the Berle and Means 200 giants, but only 11 of the 200 largest in the mid-1970s (including the Penn Central, in receivership, and Illinois Central Industries, rapidly diversifying out of railroading). Seven of the 100 largest industrials are subject to substantial regulatory constraint. Of these, only International Telegraph and Telephone (ITT) and Tenneco were among the top 50 industrials in the mid-1970s.

Economic growth has clearly reduced the importance of the traditional regulated sectors; electric power and gas maintained their position after 1929, but the transport sector's share of the national income fell from 7.6 to 3.8 percent between 1929 and 1972 (see Table 6.1), and the railroad's proportion of that diminished share fell relative to trucking and airlines. The high growth areas of the economy have been relatively free of both government enterprise and extensive regulation by commission.

It is often asserted that regulation has become so all-encompassing as to render the concept of a regulated sector obsolete – that *all* firms are regulated. Industries such as pharmaceuticals and chemicals, for example, are subject to increasing "product-entry," production-safety, and waste disposal controls. The petroleum industry is subject not only to environmental controls over plant location, waste disposal, noise, and product availability,[50] but also to state controls over crude production, commission regulation of pipelines and natural gas prices, and, since 1959, federal regulation of oil imports. From 1973 into 1980 the prices of gasoline and other oil company products were subject to price controls and various rules on allocation, on a "temporary" basis.[51] Government intervention in these industries has increased markedly since 1929 and its scope is clearly on an uptrend. But apart from the price and allocation controls applied to the oil industry (which, incidentally, merely further intervention introduced at the behest of oil industry members in earlier years of "oversupply"), even the more extensively regulated industries such as chemicals and drugs retain considerable freedom of action on prices, product composition, finance, and volume of capital investment; and the constraints on location, production methods, direction of investment, and products, although increasingly important, are far from comprehensive. Government controls are mainly boundary-fixing and veto-type constraints, frequently only applicable to specific products, plants, or marketing areas.

The effectiveness of regulation

Although there can be no doubt that the NR has grown markedly and that the protests and sense of loss of control of the business community are based on a changing reality, many of the complaints reflect the novelty rather than the real importance of new regulatory encroachments. Thus far the scope and effectiveness of the NR have been sharply limited by business' success in weakening the content and constraining the enforcement of the new legislation. The process of attrition has been multileveled; if regulation appears threatening at one level, it may be neutralized at another.

The first level is the enabling legislation and its revision,[52] where regulation may be critically affected by limitations on information-gathering powers,[53] decision processes, and remedies.[54] Jurisdiction may be made too narrow or hopelessly broad,[55] and the processes and remedies may be made so cumbrous as to assure limited action and to provide for extended delay via appeals, hearings, and litigation. Built-in procedural delay may completely stultify regulation in areas where change is rapid, as in control of deceptive and false advertising. This area is inherently difficult to regulate anyway, but regulation is rendered totally innocuous when the regulatory process cannot be completed before a shift to new advertising programs would occur in any case.[56] If the probability of regulatory discipline is small and penalties are mild – generally the case – both the level of prosecution and the deterrent effect of the regulation may be very small. If the threat of regulatory discipline becomes severe, the "overly enterprising" regulatory body may be subject to congressional investigation and harassment,[57] its functions may be curtailed or transferred to a more pliable agency,[58] or its actions may be subject to direct congressional veto. Curtailment and veto have most seriously threatened the Federal Trade Commission (FTC) in 1979–1980,[59] but legislative revision, or its threat, has affected many agencies.[60]

A second level of potential business influence over regulation is in its funding. This influence is exercised indirectly through business' political connections, which have enabled it to reward deserving regulators and to contain unfriendly behavior. An Interstate Commerce Commission (ICC) serving as a bulwark of its regulated clientele becomes the most affluent of regulatory bodies;[61] agencies going strongly counter to industry desires and interests are subject to budgetary pressures and threatened cuts.[62] More important, funding defines the potential scope and quality of enforcement. William Cary, former chairman of the SEC, claims that in general "the regulatory agencies have been traditionally starved for funds."[63] Whether or not this is so, it is clearly possible to achieve "deregulation through budget slashing"[64] or token regulation via appropriations completely out of line with responsibilities. Financial stringency – actual or threatened – has made for dependence on political and industry allies for information and expertise,[65] limited experimentation, restricted scope of enforcement, and increased vulnerability to political and legal attacks and attrition strategies. This has been especially pertinent to the Food and Drug Administration (FDA) and the new agencies in the fields of pollution control and product and worker safety, which have aroused the ire of the business community. In 1972, for example, Congress directed the EPA to review and reregister all the pesticides that came on the market in the last 30 years, some 50 thousand of them. The agency was unable to meet an October 1976 deadline, in part because of "a failure of Congress to give any appreciable resources to do the job."[66]

A third level of industry input is through political control over the regulators themselves. Politicians frequently intervene in the regulatory process. One of the Nixon administration's responses to business' hostility to the new social regulation was an order put out by the Office of Management and Budget (OMB) on October 5, 1971, requiring all federal agencies *except* the independent regulatory commissions to clear with the White House any regulations "pertaining to environmental quality, consumer protection, and occupational and public health and safety" that would "impose significant costs on, or negative benefits to, non-Federal sectors."[67] The Carter administration's economists have also showed an unusual interest in the inflationary potential of curbing cotton dust and coke oven emissions[68] (although this may reflect frustration at an inability to attack inflation at any substantial source).

It is well known that many regulators are drawn from the regulated industries or anticipate going there after a regulatory stint. Roger Noll, Merton Peck, and John McGowan found that 21 of 33 commissioners leaving the Federal Communications Commission (FCC) between 1945 and 1970 became affiliated with the communications industry as employees or as lawyers and engineers who were practicing before the FCC.[69] The so-called "revolving door" is also widely prevalent at the staff level.[70] As Cole and Oettinger point out, "Such rapid turnover increases the chances of what Ralph Nader calls 'the deferred bribe,' which is not money. Being cooperative is a way to keep career options open, to prove to prospective employers that one is knowledgeable, efficient – and agreeable."[71] Actually, many commissioners and staff members who "revolve" perform creditably during their tenure in public service, but significant numbers reflect industry perspectives to a degree incompatible with agency objectives. Their initiatives and influence not only weaken regulation directly but also produce a pervasive cynicism, demoralization, and the exit of potentially effective bureaucrats.[72] The resultant self-fulfilling prophecy of a corrupt and lackadaisical public service is an industry plus.

Beyond the "revolving door" phenomenon, the regulated industries often have a significant influence on the appointments process – they are typically given the opportunity to express their

views on proposed commissioners, they are occasionally successful in pushing their own candidates, and they are almost always
successful "in excluding persons who are regarded as opposed to
the interests of the regulated."[73] Public interest and consumer
groups have rarely been allowed to participate in the identification
and selection of potential nominees – "General public comment is
confined to the time after the nomination is made, and consumer
groups must necessarily center their efforts on the Senate and confirmation hearings."[74] Proceedings before regulatory bodies –
long confined largely to nonpublic negotiations between regulators and regulated – have always been characterized by an enormous imbalance in participation (and expertise mobilized) between the regulated firms and consumer-public interests. In
theory, the regulators represent the public interest, but this has
not generally been true. The process is changing, but a huge imbalance remains,[75] and must affect regulation.

Business also affects the regulatory process through litigation
and the mobilization of public opinion and political power. Litigation is often based on ambiguities in the law or built-in appeal
procedures that permit delay, absorb resources, and effectively
neutralize the regulatory process.[76] The capacity of business to
mobilize public opinion and political influence is based on enormous resources,[77] dependable access to extensive media connections,[78] and the power to threaten employment cutbacks and reduction of service if faced with serious regulatory pressures.[79] A
regulatory institution – like OSHA – that arouses general industry
ire, is given a steadily bad press that focuses on its absurdities and
business' complaints of harassment, ignoring the regulators' limited resources and any positive accomplishments.[80]

The power and willingness of business to resist vary, depending
on the strength and enmity of the businesses involved and the nature and prospective cost of the regulatory threat. Where the affected businesses are powerful and unified, and the threatened
costs are considerable, business opposition can blunt both captious
and quite reasonable regulatory efforts. For example, the environmental cost of automobile emissions was under public debate by
the 1940s, and starting in the early 1950s government officials
from southern California approached the automobile companies
for relief on the smog problem. But the automobile industry's
powers of resistance were sufficiently great to stall the state of
California for 10 years, delay the setting of any federal emission
standard for another half decade, and hamper any effective federal

controls into the third decade after the California appeal.[81] The industry is so important that several times its assertion of inability to meet a standard has left politicians and regulators with little option but to acquiesce.[82] Because its actions affect millions of jobs, the industry can be pushed only slowly, and it can push back. The EPA, placed in charge of emissions control regulation, moved very cautiously in dealing with a behemoth of such huge impact. For example, it decided to accept a 60 percent compliance rate for assembly line tests of vehicles in order to implement a major program in a manner "not unreasonably burdensome to the auto companies."[83] This low rate weakened the possibility of any recall program, and the Inspection and Maintenance Program of the EPA never got off the ground – with the result that "the Act's strategy for control of emissions from automobiles has been so crippled by the combination of EPA's poor performance, OMB's interference, contractors' failures, and states' objections that the standards simply are not being enforced."[84]

With reference to the traditional regulation that is industry specific (OR), there is a fairly broad consensus among students of regulation that there are built-in tendencies toward ultimate domination of the regulatory process by the regulated industry itself.[85] Some analysts also contend that there has been a deterioration in regulation from a pre-World War I antimonopoly/public interest emphasis to a new era anticompetitive bias – manifested in oil prorationing and hot oil legislation, the Highway Act of 1935, and the Civil Aeronautics Act of 1938.[86] Although it is often assumed that the quality of regulatory personnel and public interest has been on the rise, this is also disputed. In 1960 James M. Landis asserted that "it is generally admitted by most observers that since World War II a deterioration in the quality of our administrative personnel has taken place, both at the top level and throughout the staff."[87] The acceptance and institutionalization of extensive industry representation on regulatory bodies as compatible with the public interest have contributed to this deterioration in the 1970s.[88] Close observers of OR say that "there is an incredible love affair going on between the regulators and the regulated" and that "if there were no CAB, the airlines would invent one."[89] Owen and Braeutigam note that "With the exception of natural gas suppliers, whose prices have been held below competitive levels, every industry violently resisted the Ford administration deregulation program."[90]

Some serious abuses, such as insider manipulation and trading on privileged information, and the draining of corporate income into insider-controlled affiliates, have been significantly reduced since 1930. But these are benefits of the NR. In the case of OR, however, the revolving door, friendly and protective regulators, and the anticompetitive proclivities of traditional regulation have been extended and have become institutionalized – at substantial social cost. The restraints on entry and on price competition have tended to keep prices and rates of return (or costs) higher than otherwise, to a degree that has almost surely offset the fact that price regulation has sometimes prevented price increases that airlines or utilities would otherwise have imposed.[91] In the transportation sector, specialists claim that regulation has cost the consumer dearly, for the benefit of some, but by no means all, of the regulated.[92] In the electric utility business, the regulatory substitute for competition has yielded an unenterprising, constrained monopoly solution, with a capped rate of return imposed on top of an uncontrolled (and inflated) cost structure.[93] Thus, although there is clearly *more* and *more efficient* regulation in the formally regulated sector, from the public interest viewpoint regulation may be somewhat less effective.[94]

The "new" or "social" regulations of work and product safety, waste disposal, the use of inside information, and corporate disclosure are very much more extensive now than before 1930, and their impact on business has been substantial. Rules on pollution control in particular involve major outlays that businesses would not make voluntarily. Work and product safety regulations may require costly installations and testing and sometimes the ultimate rejection of products that would otherwise be salable. Very large firms are sometimes especially hard hit by these social regulations, as they are image conscious and their size makes them obvious targets. On the other hand, they are better able to afford the legal and other expenses of fighting or adapting to regulation, and their policies may often have been closer to conforming with the new rules than in the case of smaller firms.

As noted earlier, however, business has not been a helpless victim of the NR; its power to contain, mitigate, and avoid regulation, although far from complete, remains potent. The mobility and economic importance of business frequently gives it bargaining leverage in specific cases. The legal and financial resources of many of the new regulatory agencies have been fixed at modest levels, and their reach and effectiveness have been limited.

Many conservative critiques of the NR agree that it has been ineffective, but they rarely attribute this to business' powers of attrition. In business publications, also, the NR is commonly viewed as a "tilting at windmills," although this idea is not integrated into any larger framework of analysis of regulation and its limits. Thus, with respect to OSHA, *Business Week* has noted that despite the huge outcries over OSHA's nit-picking, its body of inspectors was so small that "The typical business establishment will see an OSHA inspector every 77 years, about as often as we see Halley's comet."[95] A detailed business school study of the impact of OSHA on the chemical industry confirms a very limited effect:

> The conversion of consensus exposure standards to mandatory legal requirements does not appear to have had a significant impact on exposure-monitoring activities in the chemical industry. The early spurt of self-inspection activity in the companies studied associated with the onset of regulation does not appear to have extended beyond physical safety hazards to more subtle health hazards. Few firms perceived that federal regulation based on existing consensus standards posed any real problems in their operations, particularly in light of the government's prior record of enforcement in the health area.[96]

In its comments on the new toxic substances legislation of 1976, *Business Week* reported a series of industry victories in the final language of the act, such as the fact that the chemical companies must provide EPA with data on new chemicals only 90 days before production is to commence, with EPA given 45 days to notify of a prohibition and the company given the right to submit a counterargument. If EPA persists in opposing production, it must seek a court injunction. *Business Week* notes further that "Inadequate funding may preclude Schweitzer's 45-person staff from treading heavily on industry even if it wanted to."[97] Another business publication, trying to explain in the early 1970s why the FDA displays an "inability to do more than handle day-to-day crises," stresses the fact that "the agency now has a $37 million budget to regulate a $6 billion-a-year industry."[98] In commenting on the Consumer Product Safety Commission's (CPSC) limited performance, *Business Week* noted that the gross imbalance between responsibilities and resources led the CPSC to encourage industry self-regulation by means of voluntary standards and the reporting of previously unforeseen hazards.[99]

In sum, the NR has been given large responsibilities and limited capabilities, financial and legal. The result is that its impact, although real, has left business in the United States with a great deal of decision-making freedom. In explaining the great surge of foreign direct investment in this country, *Forbes* magazine quotes Hans Schudel, president of a German-owned U.S. affiliate, the Stinnes Corporation, who extolls the U.S. market as exceeding all others in attractiveness because of "how liberally you can conduct your business."[100]

Concluding note

Capitalism as a system imposes constraints on government, and these constraints are fixed mainly by the requirements of business. This results first and automatically from the strategic position of business in carrying out basic economic functions, and thus in making key decisions on production, investment, and employment that are crucial to community welfare.[101] Secondarily, this strategic position is also closely associated with disproportionate command over resources, expertise, and the flow of information. Division among business often weakens or cancels out this integral power, which is not total in any case.[102] But on many fundamentals, business is unified, and even where it is not, individual business interests can often overwhelm nonbusiness opposition.

Given this centrality of business functions, a sag in "business confidence" may have potent effects – and the greater business' sensitivity to political and reformist threats, the narrower the range of discretion of politicians in pursuing reform. This sensitivity has been steadily enhanced by the gradual internationalization of money and capital markets. Policies that are "unsound" from the perspective of multinational banks and nonfinancial companies, large private wealthholders, and foreign central banks can induce massive shifts into and out of currencies, with serious consequences for exchange rates.[103] Policy actions and personnel selection for high administrative office (e.g., secretary of the treasury, chairman of the Federal Reserve) that will "restore confidence" may be virtually compulsory for governments of countries that are integrated into the international financial system.

The strategic role (and power) of business also helps explain the frequency with which other interest groups – local politicians, unions, and black organizations such as the National Association for the Advancement of Colored People – join with business on issues such as environmental controls, which hit business directly but can also affect local tax revenues and jobs. More generally, given its strategic position in influencing production and jobs, investment and export subsidies and other benefits to business will often be supported (or only weakly opposed) by second-order beneficiaries; benefits to others that threaten business will be opposed by both business and its trickle-down allies (unless they are the direct recipients of these benefits).

Despite its continuing preeminence and power, and its considerable influence over government, business has suffered a relative decline from its pre-1930s position of almost exclusive domination of government policy. The federal government itself is a far more important semi-independent power entity. Organized labor and other nonbusiness constituencies are now vocal claimants in the political arena. The welfare state has brought with it new financial burdens to business, a tighter labor market, and a number of worrisome interventions constraining business freedom of action and threatening still further cost increases.

Government as a business competitor has been kept in firm check. And the "old regulation" by commission has not been unduly troubling to the business community. But the "new regulation" has been disturbing, with its more detailed, multi-industry intrusions into areas of long-standing managerial discretion and its cost- and liability-enlarging potential. Much of the threat of the NR has been successfully deflected by business, but the EPA-related burdens and those incurred to reduce some occupational hazards have been real enough. These burdens have been especially painful to business because of their imposition at a time of accelerating international competition and structural maladjustments besetting important U.S. industries. Given the continued duality in business' attitudes toward government – viewing it as an adversary and power threat and demanding more support from it – business reactions to recent problems have been confused and inconsistent. A powerful campaign has been mounted to contain government; reduce its size – or rate of growth – especially as regards social welfare functions; and diminish its regulatory encroachments, again, especially with respect to the NR. On the other hand, business clamors for government protection, decisive efforts to control inflation, and more consistent and vigorous external actions. This is a whipsaw treatment of government that discredits it and diminishes its moral authority and power when responding to nonbusiness demands, although expecting efficiency and responsiveness in favored directions. Carried out by such a powerful interest group as the business community, this reaction to government holds forth the possibility of a policy stalemate, immobilization of the state, and more erratic and irrational government responses to intensifying conflict.

6

The Centralization of Corporate Power

Up to this point I have looked at the large firm as an independent and autonomous entity, usually controlled by its management, but sometimes dominated or significantly influenced by specific external interests (large owners, bankers, government). In this chapter I examine the linkages between large companies that fall short of control but that might qualify the assumption of autonomy. These include interlocking directors, joint business ventures, and participation by corporate officials in supracorporate business, political, and social associations. This leads to a discussion of intercorporate interest groups, their evolution, and current status.

Much of the interest in the large corporation, interlocks, and the evolution of interest groups stems from the possible impact of corporate size and collective action on market power and the economic and political consequences of that power. In this chapter, therefore, I broaden the discussion to take a brief look, first, at the overall importance of the large corporation and how its importance has changed over time (the measurement and evaluation of concentration). Most of the chapter deals with intercorporate ties, their evolution, and significance. I then consider, also, the decentralizing forces that have tended to offset the effects of the growth in size and integration of the large firms.

Trends in corporate size

There is a long Jeffersonian tradition in the United States, in which great business size has been feared and opposed – as much for its incompatibility with basic social and political values as for its purely economic consequences.[1] The rise of big business has meant the displacement of many small producers and distributors by a relatively few larger ones, with a concomitant change in the social and political order. Between 1850 and 1900, with rapid industrialization, the rise of the railroad, and the relative decline in farming, there was a major increase in the proportion of business done by large firms in the United States. Many industries had reached high concentration levels by the turn of the century. Subsequently, business' absolute size increased markedly, but whether *relative* size – overall and especially in specific markets – increased thereafter has been subject to dispute.[2] There is also continuing debate over the change in the power of family- and banker-based "interest groups," and the degree of unity and coordination of big business over the past 75–80 years.

A distinction must be made between changes in absolute firm size, size relative to all other firms, and size relative to the position of others in specific markets. Economists tend to disparage the use of absolute size as a relevant measure and even relative size when considered apart from specific markets. If market size expands with sufficient rapidity, absolute size may increase while market concentration diminishes. If size discrepancies among firms are large, however, and if great size carries pecuniary and strategic advantages, absolute size could gradually and indirectly affect market structure and behavior. This matter has been long debated, especially in connection with the significance of conglomeration, and a good case has been made that bigness *has* private growth and survival value.[3] Still other potential economic effects of absolute size are its contribution to diffused ownership (and thus management control) and bureaucratization, which may affect incentives, the organization of work, and the speed and character of business responses to economic signals. The growth in firm size also alters the power of business organizations relative to the individual citizen (even with an unchanged size structure of business firms). To a great extent, it was the growth in business size and power that elicited the countervailing emergence of unions and the growth of government.[4] Bigness *beyond* business was to a great extent a response to bigness *in* business.

Large firms have clearly increased in absolute size over time. But their predominance does not extend to all sectors of the economy. In 1975 large firms (defined as those with assets of $250 million or more) controlled less than a third of the assets in four major sectors – agriculture, construction, trade, and services – which together accounted for 37.5 percent of national income (see Table 6.1).[5] Large firms controlled more than half of the assets in four other major sectors – mining, manufacturing, transport and

Table 6.1. *Numbers and assets of corporations by sector and company size, 1975*

Sector	Number of corporations	Percent of national income	(Percent of national income in 1929)	Firms with assets under $100 million		Firms with assets $100 million to under $250		Firms with assets $250 million or over	
				No.	% of assets	No.	% of assets	No.	% of assets
All	2,023,647	—	—	2,019,621	27.2	2,144	7.7	1,882	65.1
Agriculture, forestry, fisheries	56,280	3.4	(9.5)	56,270	88.6	—	—	10	11.4
Mining	14,242	1.4	(2.3)	14,172	26.1	38	8.8	32	65.1
Construction	141,219	4.9	(4.3)	141,175	83.6	—	—	44	16.4
Manufacturing	217,354	25.0	(24.9)	216,509	20.9	397	6.6	448	72.5
Transport, communications, and utilities	80,701	7.7	(10.8)	80,388	8.5	104	3.7	209	87.8
Trade	614,632	15.7	(15.3)	614,407	70.1	141	6.7	84	23.2
Services	435,672	13.5	(11.7)	435,604	75.7	37	6.2	31	18.1
Banking, finance, real estate	411,846	11.6	(14.5)	409,395	23.1	1,391	9.2	1,060	67.7
Other (mainly government)	—	16.8	(6.7)	—	—	—	—	—	—

Source: Internal Revenue Service, *Statistics of Income – 1975, Corporate Income Tax Returns* (Washington, D.C.: Government Printing Office, 1979).

utilities, and banking and finance – which accounted for 45.6 percent of national income – and in all nonfinancial sectors taken together. But the number of large firms should be taken into account in evaluating these statistics. In manufacturing there were 448 large firms that together controlled 72.5 percent of the assets. The 200 largest accounted for 43 percent of the value added in manufacturing and 31 percent of manufacturing employment.

Plant size in manufacturing, as measured by the number of employees, has not increased greatly since the 1920s, although the capital investment in, and productivity of, such plants certainly has.[6] Very large firms have many plants, and centralization of employment in manufacturing by *firms* is considerably greater than by establishment. Unfortunately, data are not published regularly on firm as opposed to establishment (plant) employment, but some indication of the centralization of employment in manufacturing is given by the fact that the 200 largest accounted for 31 percent of employment. A detailed study by the Bureau of Economics of the Department of Commerce in 1954 showed that whereas about 32 percent of manufacturing employment in 1951 was in *establishments* with 1,000 or more employees, 50.6 percent was in *firms* with 1,000 or more employees.[7] For all industries a finer subdivision for 1950 showed 37.9 percent of employees in firms with 1,000 or more employees, and of these, 18.9 percent worked in 200 firms with 10,000 or more employees.[8]

Large firms in manufacturing are large because they are multiplant operations. A sample taken by the author of 10 of the largest manufacturing companies in 1975 showed a range in the number of plants extending from 63 to 328, with 8 of the firms having over 100 plants. This multiplant structure includes separate lines of activity and crosses national borders. In the mid-1970s 90 of the 100 largest manufacturing companies were active in 4 or more industries, 33 were active in more than 10 industries; by contrast, only 31 of a sample of 100 medium-sized manufacturing firms were active in 4 or more industries, none in 10 or more.[9] The overseas commitment of 223 large manufacturing companies in 1970 was also extensive, with their majority-owned subsidiaries controlling assets amounting to 21 percent of the companies' total assets.[10]

Whether the growth in size of large U.S. companies has kept pace with overall economic growth is the subject of studies of trends in "aggregate concentration." *Aggregate concentration* is the measure of the importance of some small set of firms relative to all firms or some other system total. The measure became pop-

Table 6.2. *Concentration in the 200 largest nonfinancial corporations,*
1909–1975

Year	Assets[b]	Sales[b]	Net income	Employment including government	Employment excluding government
			Percentage[a] accounted for by the 200 largest in:		
1909	33.0	—			
1929	49.2	—	43.2[c]		
1933	57.0	29.9			
1975	34.9	24.2	38.4	15.1	18.7

[a] Percentage of total for all nonfinancial corporations.
[b] Figures for 1909, 1929, and 1933 are taken from National Resources Committee, *The Structure of the American Economy, Part 1. Basic Characteristics* (Washington, D.C.: Government Printing Office, 1939), p. 107; for 1975, computed from company data and IRS asset totals.
[c] Adolf Berle and Gardiner Means, *The Modern Corporation and Private Property* (New York: Macmillan, 1932), p. 29.

ularized with Berle and Means's focus on the 200 largest nonfinancial corporations and their growing relative importance in the system.[11] Aggregate concentration measures have become fairly widely used but are scorned by many economists because of their weak statistical underpinning and their uncertain economic significance. In an age of increasing multinationality, business diversification, large price-level changes, and tax and accounting variation related to size and industrial composition of firm, concentration ratios become difficult to apply and interpret. Changes in the relative importance of the 200 largest, or the 100 largest industrials, even apart from statistical problems of accuracy, comparability, and consistency, do not relate directly to concepts such as markets or industries and have uncertain behavior/performance implications.[12] Nonetheless, an increase in aggregate concentration describes a measured growth in centralization of control over economic resources – its consequences may be hard to disentangle, but sizable changes in such measure will have social effects.

Aggregate concentration reached a temporary peak during the last years of the great merger movement of 1890–1904, although the actual level attained is not known. Tables 6.2 and 6.3 show estimates for changes in aggregate concentration from 1909 to the

Table 6.3. *Concentration in the 100 largest manufacturing and industrial firms, 1909–1975*

	100 largest industrials [a]		100 largest manufacturing firms [c]	
Year	Percent of all industrial assets	Percent of industrial profits after taxes	Year	Percent of all manufacturing assets
1909	17.7	—	1925	36.1
1919	16.6	—	1929	39.7
1929	25.5	44.0	1935	42.3
1935	28.0	—	1941	39.6
1948	26.7	29.8	1947	39.3
1958	29.8	—	1950	39.8
1974	29.2 [b]	31.8 [b]	1955	44.3
			1960	46.4
			1965	46.5
			1968	49.3
			1970	48.5 [d]
			1973	47.6 [d]

[a] Included in industrials are manufacturing, trade, services, and construction industries. Excluded are utilities, railroads, and financial institutions. Based on computations by N. R. Collins and L. E. Preston, "The Size Structure of the Largest Industrial Firms," *American Economic Review,* December 1961, p. 989.
[b] My own computations, using comparable definition of industrials and an IRS asset and net income base.
[c] Taken from Federal Trade Commission, *Economic Report on Corporate Mergers* (Washington, D.C.: Government Printing Office, 1969), p. 173.
[d] The 1970 and 1973 figures taken from David W. Penn, "Aggregate Concentration: A Statistical Note," *Antitrust Bulletin,* Spring 1976, p. 93. There was a statistical procedure change that dropped the 1973 figure below that shown in the ongoing Federal Trade Commission series; the figure shown here is on the old basis of computation.

mid-1970s for the 100 largest industrials and the 200 largest non-financials. Table 6.2 indicates a major increase in the importance of the large firm up to the early 1930s and a subsequent decline. The rise reflects the increasing importance and concentration of the electric and gas business; the decline is related to the relative sluggishness in the growth of the capital-intensive railroad sector and the government-enforced decentralization of the utility industry. The more versatile industrial and manufacturing sectors (Table 6.3) display no major downturns, but show significant shifts upward, followed by temporary plateaus. The table describes a sharp upward movement in percent of assets held by the 100 largest industrials between 1909 and 1929, with only a slight upward movement thereafter. It shows a relatively stable fraction of assets held by the largest 100 manufacturing firms from 1929–1950, followed by a substantial upswing through 1968.

Thus a major centralization of economic activity and power continued, even after the great merger movement of 1890–1904, at least up to the Great Depression. Industrial concentration increased markedly from 1909–1935, as did the relative asset holdings of the 200 largest nonfinancials. By the end of the 1920s almost 50 percent of the assets of all nonfinancial corporations were controlled by the 200 largest (up from an estimated 33 percent in 1909), and a quarter of industrial assets were controlled by the 100 largest industrials (up from 17.7 percent in 1909); and the U.S. economic system had assumed its present form – with relatively stable oligopolies dominating a great many core industries. After 1920 there was also a major increase in diversification growth by large firms, both internal and via combination, and the stage was set for the extensive growth of divisionalized and conglomerate enterprises.[13] Since World War II there has been an accelerated globalization of U.S., West European, and Japanese business and an extension and interpenetration of national markets[14] – with complex effects on national concentration measures.

The concurrent impact of all these size and aggregate concentration trends on *market* concentration is in considerable dispute. The issue is rendered moot by the limited quality of data available for longer time periods, the changes in product composition over time, and the uncertain effects of improved transport and communications on the scope of markets. Even at a given point in time, it is not easy to identify a "product" (given the usual continuum of substitutes) and to determine its relevant market.

National concentration ratios were already high for many products in 1900 and markets were narrow in geographic scope; thus it may well be true, as claimed by some analysts, that long-term changes in market concentration have been slight.[15] There has been an increase in average concentration in industrial markets since World War II, which is the only period for which relatively strong data are available. F. M. Scherer views this increase as "modest," whereas Willard F. Mueller and Larry G. Hamm consider it more alarming, given the simultaneous rise of cross-market penetration, the much greater increase in aggregate concentration, and the disproportionate increases in concentration in consumer goods industries.[16] Scherer notes that some 43 percent of manufacturing industries in the early 1970s had four-firm concentration ratios of 40 percent or higher on a national basis – and that many actual markets are local or regional in scope. He concludes, therefore, that "something in excess of half [of these manufacturing industries, by number] can be categorized as oligopolistic."[17] Industries in which products are intensively advertised have shown major increases in concentration since 1947.[18] Thus differentiated oligopoly – with leading firms integrated both vertically and across increasing numbers of industry lines – has extended its dominance in the manufacturing business in recent decades.

The market power of the largest firms has probably increased since 1900, and perhaps even since 1929. The regulated sector, widely characterized by governmental sponsorship of cartellike behavior, is far more important now than at the turn of the century. In the unregulated sector, also, the market power of large firms has probably increased on average, based on several factors – the greater importance of product differentiation and intensive advertising;[19] a secular increase in barriers to entry;[20] the reduced turnover rate of the largest firms; the greater homogeneity in class, education, and outlook of the corporate leadership; more efficient communications; and a more extensive array of ties that bind firms together. The more conservative and less competitive business practices and strategies that have evolved since the turn of the century, especially the displacement of price cutting and price warfare by nonprice methods of competition,[21] are important evidence of enhanced market power.

Supracorporate centralization

Corporate power depends not only on the resources and market control of individual companies but also on the extent to which companies coordinate their behavior and activities. Collective action may result from structural ties between firms that integrate their interest and facilitate coordination between them – such as a common ownership interest – or it may arise out of a recognized common interest or mutual business interdependence with minimal personal contact and communications among the companies and their officials. In between these extremes is a wide spectrum of linkages, such as interlocking directorates; common membership in trade associations, government advisory bodies, and public affairs groups; and personal connections of officials through clubs and other social bases of contact. Such ties are natural and inevitable, arising in part out of business, social, and class affiliations, but also emerging as forms of "interfirm organization"[22] as businesses strive to reduce uncertainty and to bring minimum stability to their market environments. The nature, strength, and role of these ties may change markedly over time and in some cases may be subject to legal constraints (coordinated market behavior, for example, is restricted by antitrust laws). Intercorporate linkages may facilitate ideological harmony and political coordination and have little impact on market behavior, or vice versa, or they may contribute to both. The number of corporate ties are so great and their individual effect so uncertain that this is virtually *terra incognita.*

The channels through which supracorporate linkages can influence corporate behavior may be classed under the headings *command, communication,* and *community of interest.* Coordination by means of command is based on common authority – as with common family ownership interest in several companies sufficient to dominate them all (the Du Pont family vis-à-vis the Du Pont Company, GM, and U.S. Rubber in 1930). In the Du Pont case the linkage rested on legal, ownership-based control. A number of popular theories of financial control contend that bank creditor/owner power amounts to the power of command, and in early discussions of "interest groups" there was often an explicit or implicit suggestion that the core elements (Rockefeller family, Morgan) had sufficient power over the constituent companies to be able to coordinate by command. In Brandeis's analysis of centralization of power in the years before World War I the interlocking director was viewed primarily as an instrument of control – in fact, as "the most potent instrument of the money trust."[23]

Virtually all intercorporate ties involve communication between companies. Communication may provide knowledge that can increase efficiency and reduce market imperfections. It may also facilitate collusive market behavior by reducing uncertainty of response and by encouraging and permitting negotiation of complex issues and conflicts.[24] Communications can take place without formal ties (e.g., by ad hoc telephone calls), and in principle at least may occur even without personal contact, as in cases where oligopolistic rivals learn through experience how to forecast and interpret one another's response.[25] Communication also occurs through formal business ties such as interlocking directorates.

It is difficult to assess the significance of specific linkages such as interlocking directorates, because there are so many modes of communication – formal and informal, direct and indirect – that it is hard to say whether any one particular mode has unique importance. The law prohibits a direct interlock between Du Pont and Union Carbide, but it does not prohibit common membership of officers and directors of the two companies on other boards or organizations; two directors of Du Pont are on company boards on which directors of Union Carbide also serve. Furthermore, Irving Shapiro of Du Pont and F. Perry Wilson of Union Carbide were both members of the executive committee of the Business Roundtable, and Shapiro and William Sneath of Carbide were policy committee members of the Business Roundtable in the late 1970s.[26] And the law does not prohibit the executives of Du Pont and Union Carbide from playing golf or calling one another on the telephone to talk about the weather. Only a few selected vehicles of communication between competitors are prohibited; otherwise, interfirm communications are subject only to rules on *what* may be communicated via the large number of available channels. Obviously, policing the subject matter of intercompany communication at times of innocent merriment or joint efforts in the social interest (e.g., lobbying against a department of consumer affairs, or serving on an advisory body to a government department) is not easy.

Direct communication about prices to be charged, or markets to be divided up, would, of course, be illegal; but it happens frequently anyway, as indicated by the number of successful antitrust prosecutions, which are almost surely the tip of the iceberg.[27] The smaller the number of firms in a particular market, the easier the coordination by direct communication or by learning to read and adapt to indirect signals. Thus the largest firms, insofar as they operate in markets of few sellers, tend to have less severe communications problems than smaller firms in more atomistic industries.[28] On the other hand, pricing and marketing decisions may be so decentralized in large divisionalized companies that corporate leaders, meeting together in groups like the Business Roundtable, may only infrequently discuss such matters. In some cases very limited communication may be required, and a short, high-level exchange may suffice. In other cases pricing and market-sharing problems may require extended negotiations, involving frequent contact between corporate officials.[29] Competitors do assemble and communicate through organizations like the Round-table, where explicit coordination does occur on matters being fought in the political arena, potentially on issues of the market-place.

In contrast with the ties of command, the ties of communication are not binding or compelling. They expedite collective action and provide means for mitigation of conflicts of interest, which, without communication, might more often yield open warfare "of benefit only to the consumer."[30] But sometimes conflicts are too serious to be overcome or the ties of proximity and ready communication, which often bind, may bring out personal hostility that exacerbates conflict.

The third channel through which intercorporate ties affect corporate behavior is by bringing about a closer *community of interest,* that is, the feeling among the corporate leadership of a mutuality and interdependence of business needs and obligations and a sense of shared goals. At one extreme, community of interest exists where there is power of command, because the commanding authority's interest dominates the behavior of each of the controlled entities. At the other extreme, community of interest may rest merely on the shared values of members of a social class or the recognition of joint concerns by otherwise unconnected leaders of the same industry. Community of interest is strengthened by communication and personal relationships, and thus by joint membership on business, charitable, and advisory boards.

Interlocking directorates among the largest corporations

Director interlocks have received the greatest attention in discussions of intercorporate ties, partly because of their conspicuousness and partly because of the belief in their significance, going back to the Morgan era and Brandeis's attacks on the practice as "the root of many evils [and offensive to] laws human and divine."[31] The concern about interlocks has focused on their centralizing and anticompetitive potential – their possible use as instruments of command and as means of communications between competitors *and* as devices making for community of interest among competitors and establishing privileged positions for suppliers, banks, and customers.

An important distinction should be made between direct and indirect interlocks. A direct interlock between two companies exists when a single individual is on the board of directors of both; for example, when William O. Beers serves as director of both Kraftco and Manufacturers Hanover Trust (MHT). An indirect interlock exists when two directors, each from a different company, meet on the board of a third company. An indirect interlock existed in the late 1970s between MHT and Chase Manhattan Bank because both Beers, a director of MHT, and Norma Pace, a director of Chase, sat on the board of Sears Roebuck. Direct interlocks are more important linkages than indirect ones, because in direct interlocks the director is exposed to the problems and personnel of both companies and has a fiduciary obligation to both. For example, William O. Beers was not only intimately acquainted with the problems and personnel of Kraftco, where he was chief executive officer for some years, but he also met regularly with the board and top officers of MHT, was informed about their problems, and was obligated as a director to help them solve those problems. With indirect interlocks the directors' responsibilities pertain only to the problems of a third company; the problems of the companies they represent are not at issue. And the communication link between the indirectly interlocked companies is only one on one; that is, the director of A meets only one director of B on the board of C, whereas in a direct interlock, the director of A meets with the entire board of B.

Whether direct or indirect, officer interlocks are likely to be more important than interlocks mediated by outside directors. Outside directors of large companies frequently have little power, whereas inside directors, who are also top officers, normally formulate and implement key decisions. An officer interlock, therefore, means a more direct connection between key decision makers and a greater potential for negotiation and the exercise of power. It also has symbolic significance as a display of closeness, because an inside director is more clearly identified with the represented corporation than is an outside director. Because William O. Beers was the top officer of Kraftco, his serving as a director on the board of MHT implied a closer link than would an interlock mediated by an outside director. Furthermore, John Mc-Gillicuddy, president of MHT, served on the Kraftco board, so that

Table 6.4. *Distribution of directors among the 200 largest nonfinancial corporations, and 200 largest nonfinancials plus 50 largest financials, 1975*

200 largest nonfinancials			200 largest nonfinancials plus 50 largest financials		
Number of directorships	Frequency	%	Number of directorships	Frequency	%
1	2058	86.4	1	2363	79.9
2	249	10.4	2	394	13.3
3	59	2.5	3	136	4.6
4	15	0.6	4	45	1.5
5	2	0.1	5	17	0.6
6	—	—	6	3	0.1
7	—	—	7	1	—
Total	2383	100		2959	100

there was a reciprocal officer interlock between the two companies. This implies an even closer relationship and, in fact, MHT has long been the lead bank for Kraftco, lending it money and serving in numerous service and trust functions.

As potential mechanisms of control, direct interlocks are obviously more important than indirect ones; it is hard to imagine how indirect interlocks would serve that role at all.[32] Direct officer interlocks would also seem more potent for command functions than direct nonofficer linkages, but this may be misleading; control is usually established through large stock acquisitions, loan foreclosures, or proxy contests, with interlocks *following* the establishment of a power position – and nonofficer directors may suffice for command surveillance. For communications purposes, direct and officer interlocks have an edge over indirect and nonofficer relations. The superiority of direct and officer interlocks also holds in building communities of interests.

Most directors of the largest companies do not have an interlocking relationship with any other large company. Of the 2,959 directors of the 250 largest in 1975 (including the 50 largest financials), 2,363, or 79.9 percent, were directors of only one of this universe of companies; and as shown in Table 6.4, if attention is confined to the 200 largest nonfinancials, 86.4 percent of the directors are one-giant directors. Out of 2,959 directors of the 250 largest, 596 sat on two or more large company boards. The number of company linkages among the 250 accounted for by multiple-board directors amounted to 1,082 in 1975.[33] This means that 1,082 pairs of companies among the 250 shared a common director (out of a possible 31,125). This is a modest decrease in the number of interlocks from the recent past and a sharp decline from the pre-Clayton Act days. For the largest 250, th⸱ number of interlocks fell from 1,423 in 1935, to 1,240 in 1965, to 1,082 in 1975. For a longer time perspective, reaching back to the Morgan–Baker era, David Bunting shows the number of interlocks among a set of 167 very large companies changing as follows:[34]

Year	Number of Interlocks
1899	1,294
1912	1,800
1919	1,174
1935	822
1964	741
1974	685

In addition to the large decline in number of interlocks among large companies after 1912, Bunting also shows that multiple-interlocking both by the same individual and between pairs of companies fell off greatly after 1912, which reinforces the likelihood that the direct interlock plays a smaller role in control and coordination than it did prior to the passage of the Clayton Act in 1914.

The direct interlocks among the 250 largest corporations are extensive. Table 6.5 shows that only 15 of the 200 largest nonfinancials and only one of the 50 largest financials have no interlocks within the 250. One financial institution is directly interlocked with 42 others among the 250, and one nonfinancial (AT&T and its largest subsidiaries) is directly interlocked with 76 of the 250. The intercompany linkages involving the largest financials are more numerous than those involving the largest nonfinancials; 17 out of 50 large financials (34 percent) as compared with only 25 out of 200 large nonfinancials (12.5 percent) are directly interlocked with 15 or more members of the 250 set.

The power and prestige of the 250 largest corporations make

Table 6.5. *Number of companies among the 250 largest connected by direct interlocks, 1975*

Number of other companies in the 250 to which company is linked	Among 200 largest nonfinancials	Among 50 largest financials
None	15	1
5 or more	131	42
10 or more	69	29
15 or more	25	17

their officers sought after as outside directors and give them the capacity to attract, as directors, officers from these same prestigious companies. Of the total of 3,060 directors of the large corporations,[35] 1,298, or 42.4 percent, were officers of another member of the set, and these same 1,298 directors held 43.6 percent of the total directorships. Over half (53.8 percent) of the directors who held three or more large company directorships were officers of other large companies. One hundred twenty-two of the 200 nonfinancial giants and 41 of the 50 largest financials provided officers as directors to other members of the 250; 19 of the 250 provided officers as directors to five or more of the 250. One bank (Citibank) provided officers as directors to 16 other companies, and 1 nonfinancial corporation (AT&T and its largest affiliates) provided officers as directors to 21 of the 250. Only 79 of the 250 largest corporations did not have an officer of another member of the 250 on their board, and 120 of the 250 had officers of two or more of the other members of the set on their board. Forty-one of the 200 largest nonfinancials had reciprocal officer interlocks with other members of the 250 (one had four); 22 of the 50 large financials had one or more reciprocal officer interlocks (one had five).

The Clayton Act of 1914 prohibited direct interlocks among large firms that are "competitors." And there was a major decline in direct interlocks among competitors following the enactment of this legislation, despite the well-known virtual nonenforcement of Section 8 of the Clayton Act.[36] Bunting shows that between 1912 and 1969 horizontal interlocks among large transportation companies and among banks were almost completely eliminated.[37] There was little change in direct interlocking within what Bunting calls "industry," but even using a broad industry classification system to test the intraindustry interlocks among the 250 largest, direct interlocks were relatively sparse in 1975. There were only 17 interlocked pairs that fell within the same (two-digit) standard industrial classification (SIC) class in 1975, of which nine were in the financial sector. In the nonfinancial sector, Allied Chemical and Warner Lambert, both in the chemical and drug fields had a common director; Pacific Power and Light and Pacific Lighting shared a common director; and six other pairings, more remote from a product-competition standpoint, can be identified. Among the nine in the financial sector, American Express, for example, had a common director with Chase, Chemical, and MHT; and common directorships were shared by Citicorp and First National Bank of Boston and by First Bank System and First Chicago Corporation. It should be reiterated that these findings, which suggest very modest direct interlocking among large competitors, relate to *main* SIC class only; a great many more would be added to the list if the numerous secondary-product interests of the often diversified giants were considered. Also, although direct interlocking among competitors is relatively modest, as I describe subsequently indirect interlocks and other linkages between them are extensive.

Other intercorporate linkages

Interlocking directors are only one form of intercorporate connection. Others are indirect interlocks, joint ventures, trade and other business associations, and government advisory committees. The aggregate of these "other" linkages is very impressive.

Indirect Interlocks

It should be noted that indirect interlocks, linking competitors, were unaffected by the Clayton Act. They are not so powerful ties as direct interlocks, but they are not negligible, especially as many of them involve officers of competing firms. For example, in the mid- and late 1970s the officers of three major New York Banks met together as outside directors on the board of Phelps Dodge.[38] A 1978 Senate study, *Interlocking Directorates Among the Major U.S. Corporations,* showed that in 1976 the 13 largest U.S. corporations not only had an impressive 249 direct interlocks, but they also had an enormous total of 5,547 indirect interlocks.[39] The study also examined direct and indirect interlocks between companies in the automobile, energy, and telecommunications industries. GM, Ford, and Chrysler had no direct interlocks, but they had 21 indirect interlocks;[40] Exxon had no direct interlocks with its major competitors, but it had 6 indirect interlocks with Mobil, 4 with Arco, 1 with Shell, 6 with Standard of California, 2 with Standard of Indiana, and 2 with Texaco;[41] AT&T had no direct interlocks with IBM, ITT, and General Telephone, but it had 22, 4, and 2 indirect interlocks with those companies, respectively.[42] These are all points of communication between competitors, and the numbers of contacts involved are large.

Joint Ventures

The Webb–Pomerene Act of 1918, allowing the formation of export cartels, was an important step in the trend toward the use of *joint ventures,* which have become extremely important vehicles for collective action in a number of key industries. The joint venture is a major form of business organization in the oil and gas, iron and steel, mining and chemicals industries and links together a considerable number of competitors. The nature and extent of interfirm organization in a joint venture is variable, a great many involving only a contractual agreement to bid together or for one of the partners (usually a government) underwriting expenses, with the other partner exploring and working a property at cost plus a fixed percentage of the profits. Some companies pool resources to explore, do research, or work a property, with one of the partners being assigned the job of managing the company. A sizable number of joint ventures involve two or more companies contributing resources, sharing in or choosing management, and distributing revenues in an agreed-on basis. These are *quasi-mergers* in which ownership interests are fused.

Joint ventures have received remarkably little attention from antitrust authorities, partly as a result of their number, variety, and complexity. Justification for joint ventures is given on the grounds of the magnitude of outlays and risks, in some cases, or the marginality and inconsequence of the project in many others. When scarce and concentrated resources are involved, joint ventures may seem a lesser evil than the monopolization of these resources by single interests. In the iron industry, for example, the joint venture was a means of securing a supply of iron in the face of shrinking open market opportunities.[43] In part, however, the joint venture has become institutionalized by long-standing practice, extensive use, the power of its users, its political aspects, and the sheer inability of antitrust law and authority to cope with its complexities.[44]

In the case of oil, important joint ventures have sometimes been a product of political negotiations in which the state participated in dividing up among national majors the spoils of successful pursuit of the "national" and/or oil industry interests (Iran);[45] or they have sometimes been arranged and negotiated by industry majors for their own strategic interests, with the backup support of the state. In the mid-1920s the U.S. government fought strenuously to help Exxon and Mobil gain admission to the Iraq Petroleum Company, which successfully united British Petroleum (BP), Royal Dutch/Shell, Exxon, and Mobil in a joint venture that led to the 1928 Red Line Achnacarry agreement – both the joint venture and the cartel agreement were, on their face, violations of U.S. antitrust laws.[46] Many joint ventures and long-term supply contracts were explicit parts of international cartel agreements, designed to unify concession control and to regularize the handling of regional oil surpluses and deficits.[47] Whatever the rationale – fear of oil shortage, strategic interest, oil company power – the U.S. government has sponsored explicitly anticompetitive joint ventures in oil and disregarded their incompatibility with antitrust law principles.[48]

A great deal of important evidence has come to light showing that the formation and change in composition of major joint ventures like Caltex and Aramco were designed specifically to avoid new competition and to contain and control supplies that threatened to destabilize markets. In joining Aramco, Exxon felt that one of the major advantages would be "easing the pressure that would otherwise come from Caltex in their efforts to expand their outlets."[49] The arrangements, concluded in 1947, allowed Exxon and Mobil to limit the expansion of Aramco output and to absorb into their worldwide marketing facilities oil that might be "distress oil" or that might induce Socal (Standard Oil of California) or Texaco to expand their distribution facilities too aggressively. During the golden age of Aramco, and into the 1970s, the price of the bulk of Persian Gulf crude oil was fixed by agreement of representatives of four major U.S. oil companies.[50] Given the importance of this source of supply, the pricing and production decisions on Aramco crude necessarily defined and limited the pricing and marketing strategies of the Aramco partners elsewhere. Blair has argued that Exxon and Mobil were in a command position based on common (Rockefeller) control in 1946–1947, and he presented some modest evidence of Exxon–Mobil domination of Aramco policy.[51] Whatever the truth, it is clear that for such an important enterprise as Aramco, collective negotiations and decision making beyond the joint venture were implicit in the decisions pertaining to the joint venture itself. Texaco and Socal appear to have been constrained by Exxon and Mobil, who opted for higher prices, slower expansion, and avoidance of market disturbance, consistent with their larger vested interests.

In huge joint ventures like Aramco and Caltex the parameters of the venture – the rate of output of the raw material and its price – are at the heart of the business of the parent firms and would appear necessarily to draw the top executives into communication or collective decision making. This is often not the case with lesser joint ventures, which may involve only local divisional (or subdivisional) communication or mechanical implementation (as in the case of pipelines). The communication link is there in each case, but may not involve high-level personnel, except in the small minority of joint ventures of major proportions or significance relative to company size.

By their very nature, joint ventures also would seem to create a clear community of interest between the partners, who have combined their resources and have a legally contracted common interest. If the joint venture is very important, the firms may be tied together in ways that require a collective decision on price and production, essentially precluding any significant competition between them. Thus if firms that draw crude oil, or iron ore, in predetermined proportions agree to increase overall raw materials production, they must also agree on the marketability of the finished product and on reasonable prices. It is estimated that in the late 1960s and early 1970s Exxon and Royal Dutch/Shell were joint participants in over 150 joint ventures outside the United States.[52] In considering the proposed linkage of Socal with Exxon via Aramco in 1946, some Socal directors objected on the grounds that the tie would preclude any Aramco advance relative to Shell: "Jersey [Exxon], therefore, could never get ahead of Shell because the more Venezuelan, Iraqi and Indonesian crude oil available to Jersey the more became available to Shell . . . the more they develop and produce in these areas, the greater they allow the Shell position to build up."[53] Oil company joint ventures link together the major producers on a scale that is unduplicated in any other industry; some indication of the scope of these linkages is shown in Table 6.6. This matrix table, probably an understatement of the

Table 6.6. Joint ventures among the 20 largest U.S. oil companies in the early and mid-1970s

	Arco	Exxon	Shell	Sohio	Stand. Ind.	Mobil	Socal	Texaco	Gulf	Sun	Conoco	Getty	Union	Cities Serv.	Amerada Hess	Phillips	Marathon	Ashland	Tenneco	Occidental	Total
Arco																					0
Exxon	220																				220
Shell	15	186																			201
Sohio	139	9	48																		196
Stand. Ind.	112	10	10	1																	133
Mobil	12	55	46	41	6																160
Socal	19	18	98	18	6	31															190
Texaco	15	31	45	27	8	31	100														257
Gulf	10	21	22	35	7	14	15	23													147
Sun	147	4	5	7	106	4	4	8	6												291

																				Total
Conoco	10	12	13	13	6	8	11	12	26	6											117
Getty	16	11	8	20	8	8	9	10	12	3	12										117
Union	28	4	5	19	30	5	9	9	4	9	5	5									132
Cities Serv.	7	5	8	3	5	6	1	11	7	13	16	4	6								92
Am. Hess	1	1	2	3	70	1	0	0	0	0	4	16	2	0							100
Phillips	14	4	4	11	6	95	10	5	5	15	8	6	3	5	3						194
Marathon	15	6	9	2	3	5	4	5	3	3	10	4	8	5	5	1					88
Ashland	5	2	12	2	3	1	2	2	2	3	2	3	2	2	4	5	2				54
Tenneco	3	3	1	1	1	9	1	3	1	2	3	2	5	2	1	4	1	1			44
Occidental	2	1	1	1	3	1	2	2	1	0	1	2	1	1	0	1	0	1	1		22
Total	790	383	337	204	268	219	168	90	67	54	61	42	27	15	13	11	3	2	1		2755

For purposes of this tabulation, Royal Dutch/Shell and Shell Oil Company, and BP and Standard Oil of Ohio, are considered as single entities.

Source: Published documents of companies (especially 10-Ks and annual reports), Moody's, and the two doctoral dissertations cited in note 52.

actual totals, shows over 2,700 joint venture ties among the 20 oil giants. Some companies use joint ventures more than others, but each company does participate in them and, as shown in Table 6.7, over 90 percent of the possible combinations among the 20 largest oil companies have been realized via joint ventures.

Many of the joint ventures are relatively insignificant, but Table 6.7 shows that more than half (55.8 percent) of the possible combinations of the 20 large oil company sample were achieved by *major* joint ventures (defined as involving a collective investment of $10 million or more). And this is probably an underestimate, given the limited data available.

In the iron and steel industry the iron-producing companies – almost all virtually appendages of groups of steel companies, and many owned outright by the steel companies – allocate a good part of production to the joint venture partners on the basis of percentage of stock held;[54] thus decisions on the rate of output of iron ore by a subsidiary are inherently linked to questions of final output and price plans of the joint owners of the subsidiary. This inducement to collective action is reinforced by the common involvement of the ore-owning partners in more than one joint subsidiary, as shown in Figure 6.1 for the early post-World War II linkages centering in the Hanna iron ore interests.

These ties go a long way beyond common interest in maximizing collective profits. Furthermore, even though firms that share a joint subsidiary may have conflicting interests, as well as difficulty reaching an accord on handling the joint venture itself, the partial fusion of interests should tend to make for better mutual understanding, sense of common purpose, ease of adjustment, and avoidance of undue hostility. The European Economic Community (EEC), in considering whether to allow a joint venture between GE and the Weir Group Ltd., noted that because the two companies compete in power engineering at both the vertical and horizontal levels:

> the very creation of the joint venture in which the parties took joint control amounted to a restriction of competition, regardless even of the specific restrictive provisions of the agreement . . . In addition, the existence of the joint venture was seen by the Commission as providing opportunities and inducements to the parties to enlarge their common activities so as to impair free competition between themselves in areas outside sodium circulators where they retain independent interests.[55]

Table 6.7. *Interlocks and other ties among 20 oil company majors and among a 20-company control sample of large corporations, 1975*

Type of linkage	Oil company pairs connected by particular linkage (190 possible ties)		Control company pairs connected by particular linkage (190 possible ties)		Total oil company ties		Total control company ties	
	(1) No.	(2) % of 190	(3) No.	(4) % of 190	(5) No.	(6) % of total[a]	(7) No.	(8) % of total[a]
Direct interlock	0	0	6	3.2	0	0	6	.9
Indirect interlock	46	24.2	79	41.6	70	5.2	114	17.8
Major joint venture	106	55.8	0	0	254	18.8	0	0
Minor joint venture	176	92.6	1	0.5	2,501	0	1	0
Common auditor	27	14.2	21	11.1	27	2.0	21	3.3
Common investment bank	42	22.1	40	21.1	42	3.1	41	6.4
Common representation on federal advisory board	190	100.0	52	27.4	697	51.5	94	14.7
Common major club membership	135	71.1	172	90.5	354	0	447	0
Common representation on nongovernment advisory or research body	112	58.9	128	67.4	263	19.4	364	56.9
Common legal counsel	0	0	0	0	0	0		
Common major ownership of voting stock	0	0	0	0	0	0		
Total no. of ties					4,208	100.0	1,088	100.0
Mean no. of ties					210.4		54.5	
Total minus clubs					3,854		641	
Mean (minus clubs)					192.7		32.1	
Total minus clubs and minor joint ventures					1,353		640	
Mean (minus clubs and minor joint ventures)					67.7		32.0	

[a]Total ties minus clubs and minor joint ventures.

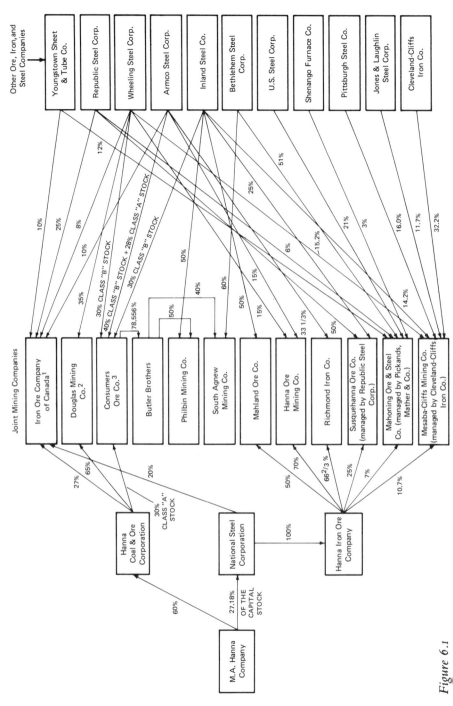

Figure 6.1

The argument that joint ventures are required to spread risk is a strong one, but it hardly suffices as a general explanation and rationale. On the basis of risk we would anticipate a relatively great use of the joint venture by small companies, incapable of self-insuring through diversification. But the number of joint participations rises steadily with size,[56] and the greatest users are companies like Exxon and Royal Dutch/Shell, not industry minors. Joint ventures have an obvious anticompetitive potential, but it is not easy to prove that this is an objective – or that joint ventures have affected competition. Walter J. Mead succeeded in showing that joint venture bidding on oil and gas leases reduced the likelihood of the partners bidding against one another in other lease bids in the same general area.[57] Other studies, as well as the data in Table 6.6, indicate that a very large proportion of joint ventures is among direct competitors, that many others are among companies with vertical relationships, and that joint ventures tend to be most prevalent where there are intermediate degrees of concentration and special interfirm coordination is most needed.[58] There is also some indication that the spurt in joint venture activity in the 1950s was stimulated by the Celler–Kefauver Amendment of 1950, which increased the difficulty of arranging traditional mergers.[59] Jeffrey Pfeffer and Phillip Nowak conclude that "joint ventures are a form of inter-firm linkage used to reduce competitive and buyer–seller interdependence, to establish, in Cyert and March's terms, a 'negotiated environment.' "[60] According to Richard E. Caves and Masu Uekusa, Japanese experience shows that companies involved in joint ventures are significantly less vigorous rivals than wholly owned subsidiaries of a

---

Figure 6.1. Interrelations between the M. A. Hanna Company and other ore, iron, and steel companies, 1950. [1]*As a stockholder, National has the right to contract for the purchase of 20 percent of the production of the Iron Ore Co. of Canada for the first 25 years of its operations.* [2]*Hanna Coal & Ore Corp. owns 65 percent of Douglas Mining Co. but is entitled to receive only 30 percent of the reserves. Wheeling Steel Corp. owns 35 percent but is entitled to 70 percent of the reserves of Douglas Mining Co.* [3]*Hanna Coal & Ore Corp. owns 30 percent of Consumers Ore Co. but is not entitled to any of the ore reserves controlled by Consumers Ore Co. through its subsidiary, Butler Brothers.* (Source: *Federal Trade Commission,* Control of Iron Ore, *report published by the House Judiciary Committee, December 1952.*)

single parent, and the Japanese government has encouraged joint ventures precisely for this reason – that is, to allow "admitting foreign capital and securing foreign technology without turning loose a major new competitive threat on Japanese product markets."[61]

In both the oil and steel industries, basic structural factors – especially the substantial vertical integration of the steel majors and oil "sisters," and the durable oligopolistic conditions overall – are undoubtedly crucial in explaining the modest rivalry and generally successful avoidance of price competition. (As regards oil, Blair concluded that "the seven international majors have succeeded to a remarkable degree in limiting to a predetermined rate the growth of overall supply.")[62] But these are not *highly* concentrated industries, and their products are relatively homogenous, so that more vigorous rivalry might have been expected. Perhaps the harmonizing and integrating effects of the joint venture, widely prevalent in these industries, has added to the spirit of live and let live.[63]

Trade and Other Business Organizations

The number of trade organizations grew steadily following the Civil War, especially in the 1890s and thereafter. A sharp increase in the number of associations followed the passage of the Clayton Act (from about 800 in 1912 to some 2,000 in 1919).[64] World War I was probably the main stimulus to that rapid growth, but the further major expansion of trade associations in the 1920s and in the National Recovery Administration (NRA) period was closely connected with a quest for business "stability." A. R. Burns wrote that from 1912–1932, "these associations were enthusiastically welcomed as a means of coordinating the policies of sellers in a variety of industries . . . 'without relinquishing the fruits that spring from individual initiative.' "[65] The 1920s was the golden age of the "open price association," a trade association featuring the dissemination of information with an intent to discourage price competition. The federal government actively encouraged the organization of trade associations in the early 1920s, and again during the NRA period, and one of the leaders of the trade association movement observed in 1934 that:

> Practically, under the Harding, Coolidge and Hoover administrations industry enjoyed, to all intents and purposes, a moratorium from the Sherman Act, and, through the more

or less effective trade associations which were developed in most of our industries, competition was, to a very considerable extent, controlled. The Department of Justice acted with great restraint and intelligence and only enforced the Sherman Act against those industries that violated the laws in a flagrant and unreasonable manner.[66]

The great age of trade association growth and stabilization activities ended with the termination of the NRA in 1935; for a while thereafter their numbers stabilized, and their role in collective action was reduced as they became subject to significant antitrust constraints when they engaged in explicit efforts to fix prices or divide markets. Their numbers increased again during and after World War II. According to one recent estimate, there are about 2,800 national trade associations and some 40,000 associations all together if local affiliates and independents are included.[67] Almost all industries have trade associations, and in most of them the principal firms are leading members. Trade associations are less active in industry coordination of price and output policy than they were before 1930, but they serve for communication, education, lobbying, and the development of an esprit de corps.

There are numerous other organized bodies within which leaders of the largest corporations meet together for business, conviviality, and social and political efforts. The Business Council, originally an official advisory committee to the Department of Commerce, now exists as an unaffiliated body and holds membership meetings four times a year for policy discussions with government officials.[68] Private business may be transacted in connection with such gatherings – the chairmen of Utah International and GE, for example, got together for detailed discussions of their merger in Washington, D.C., following a meeting of the Business Council, in which they were both members.[69] The Business Roundtable, organized in 1972, has superseded the Business Council in importance and power, partly because of its open activism and attempt to influence policy. The Roundtable has attained influence through direct get-togethers between its prestigious members (the heads of some 180 large corporations) and high-level government officials.[70]

The U.S. Chamber of Commerce and the National Association of Manufacturers (NAM) have long been major national organizations representing business interests in which leading business executives meet. There are a great many other research and policy advisory bodies, sponsored largely by business, in which business people participate in running (overseeing) the organizations, serving on various committees, and attending meetings. Among the more important of these bodies are the Conference Board, Committee for Economic Development, American Enterprise Institute, Institute for Defense Analysis, the Rand Corporation, the Atlantic Council, the Council on Foreign Relations, the Foreign Policy Association, and the National Planning Association.[71] These organizations reflect and implement the power of business, but they also play a role as vehicles for communication and the development of community of interest and collective behavior. From this standpoint the number of points of contact afforded by these organizations is large.

Businesspeople often meet and form acquaintances and close personal ties at schools or in social clubs. A disproportionate number of directors of large corporations come from families sending their children to the elite private schools and colleges of America,[72] and directors are heavily represented among the major social clubs.[73] How much these relationships are a source of cohesiveness and avenues of communication is debatable, but the number of potential points of contact that these schools and social clubs afford is again very large.

Government Advisory Committees

An underrated basis of competitor linkage is the government advisory body. As in the case of the trade association, the government advisory body was greatly stimulated by wartime mobilization (in both the First and Second World Wars), in which the government brought in industry advisors and managers to cope with the problems of urgent and large-scale government intervention. Business found participation in such bodies a good means of getting to know and gaining access to officials, and thus the opportunity to acquire influence through a steady input of information, expertise, and viewpoint. Out of World War I, for example, came the American Petroleum Institute, founded in 1919, and "World War II brought the formal and apparently permanent return of the [oil] industry to the inner structure of the American Government."[74] Although the elaborate World War II advisory apparatus was disbanded, an Oil and Gas Division for limited planning, liaison, and other functions was retained, and the National Petroleum Council was organized in 1946 "to advise, inform, and make recommendations as requested by the Department of the Interior regarding any matter relating to petroleum or the petroleum industry."[75] In 1974 the council had 126 members, representing not only many small independents but also 33 of the 200 largest nonfinancial corporations, including virtually all the large oil, natural gas, and pipeline companies.

Advisory committees have always been an appendage of federal government bodies, but they proliferated greatly after World War II, paralleling the increase in government contracting and regulatory activities. As noted in one study of an important advisory committee, the Industry Advisory Council of the Department of Defense, such committees "complement the work of the broader policy planning groups by overseeing the bureaucracy which is to implement those policies."[76] This particular body, which functioned between 1962 and 1972, brought together three times a year approximately 25 high executives of competitors, such as Boeing, General Dynamics, Grumman, Hughes Aircraft, Lockheed, McDonnell-Douglas, Northrop, IBM, Sperry Rand, Honeywell, GE, and the like. The minutes of the Industry Advisory Council reveal that in many respects it functioned for the Department of Defense like a board of fairly strong outside directors;[77] views were interchanged with the insiders, and those of the outsiders had some weight. The interests of the advisory group in higher profits and in expedited procedures were carefully attended to, and the Pentagon aided the outsiders' pursuit of foreign military sales by serving as a marketing arm. In turn, the outsiders energetically supported the policy of the insiders (e.g., on the desirability of pursuing the Vietnam War). And for both insiders and outsiders a spirit of camaraderie prevailed.

The number of advisory bodies is large – 820 of them with 18,742 members in December 1979[78] – representation of competing industry members on industry-related committees is prevalent, and the committees are generally closed to the public. All this is so, despite the requirements of openness and balanced representation under the Federal Advisory Committee Act of 1972. Although the act led to the abandonment of the Industry Advisory Council – no meetings were held after the law took effect, and the council was officially abolished in 1974 as no longer serving its original purpose[79] – the number of advisory committees and their membership has dropped only moderately since 1972 and improvements in openness and balance have been modest. This has resulted from the law's vagueness, the availability of evasive techniques, the lack of vigorous enforcement and – underlying all these – the interests and desires of the major (governmental and business) participants in advisory committees.[80]

In literally scores of industries the government advisory body is a vehicle through which major competitors meet regularly, under government imprimatur, with de facto exemption from anti-trust,[81] to advise the government on matters of common interest. This has not only been a real plus for business in getting its views across and gaining a desired access to government,[82] but it has also been a vehicle through which businesspeople of the same trade can get together on a regular basis, with the public excluded.

The importance of intercorporate linkages

It is difficult to quantify ties between companies, partly because the data are not readily accessible for some of them and partly because these ties vary in importance. Nevertheless, Table 6.7 provides a rough order of magnitude of some intercorporate link-ages. A simple count has been used rather than a necessarily arbi-trary system of weights for different types of intercorporate ties. Bank linkages through common creditor relationships are ex-cluded because reliable information was not obtainable on the lead banks of the sample companies.[83] Obviously not all types of per-sonal and business ties between corporate leaders could be consid-ered.

The selected intercorporate ties were examined in detail for two samples: one of 20 large oil companies among the 200 largest non-financials; the second, a random (control) sample of 20 others from among the 200 largest. Each of the sets of 20 had a maximum potential number of combinations among them of 190.

Table 6.7 shows the number of company pairs among the oil companies and control companies for each type of linkage and the total number of each type of linkage within each set. For example, columns (1) and (2) show that there were 176 minor joint venture pairings of oil companies, which means that 92.6 percent of the possible combinations of the 20 oil companies were realized by a minor joint venture. Columns (3) and (4) show that joint venture activity among the control companies was slight. Column (5) shows that there were 2,501 minor joint ventures that stemmed from the 176 pairings of the 20 oil companies, which constitute more than half of the total number of ties of any kind among the oil companies.

Table 6.7 shows that there were relatively few interlocking directorates in 1975 – no direct interlocks among the 20 largest oil companies and only six direct interlocks among members of the control sample. Forty-six pairings of oil companies and 79 pairings of the 20 control companies were linked by indirect interlocks, accounting for a total of 70 and 114 indirect interlocks, respectively. Linkages based on joint ventures and common membership on federal advisory bodies tower over other forms of connection among the 20 oil companies; common club membership and joint association on private advisory and research bodies are next by numerical count, well ahead of the remaining bases of linkages. All 190 possible pairings of the 20 oil companies occurred in linkages based on participation in government advisory bodies, resulting in 697 aggregate ties, and even the 20 control group companies had 52 pairings and 94 aggregate ties based on federal advisory body linkages. It should be kept in mind that club membership often yields ties that are weak and that many minor joint venture ties are of little consequence to policymaking. But Table 6.7 makes clear that the business community has a huge number of supraindustry connections that bind its members together not only by economic ties but also socially, politically, and ideologically.

Interest groups

Analysts of the large corporation and corporate power have long been intrigued with the idea of supracorporate collectivities of corporations, large and small, integrated and controlled by some common power entity such as an entrepreneurial family or a powerful bank. The interest group idea was a logical outgrowth of pre-World War I economic developments. At that time it was possible to isolate sets of large corporations that were closely aligned with J. P. Morgan, George F. Baker, and James Stillman – "the inner group," controlling seven New York banks, according to the Pujo report – as well as a Kuhn Loeb group, Dillon, Read and Lee Higginson (a Boston group), and the Illinois Trust, First National, and Continental Bank of Chicago (a Chicago group).[84] Some of the entities within these groups were banker controlled, and many of the others had been promoted by and had a special financial relationship with an investment banking firm, although the extent of banker control and the significance of the groupings are somewhat nebulous. These interest groups were friendly rivals, whose many common interests unified their behavior and made it possible to speak of a larger "money power":

> It can hardly be expected that the banks, trust companies, and other institutions that are thus seeking participation from this inner group would be likely to engage in business of a character that would be displeasing to the latter or that would interfere with their plans or prestige. And so the protections that can be offered by the members of this inner group constitutes the safest refuge of our great industrial combinations and railroad systems against future competition. The powerful grip of these gentlemen is upon the throttle that controls the wheels of credit and upon their signal those wheels will turn or stop.[85]

The concept of an interest group and the attempt to estimate its significance reached its apogee in Paul Sweezy's Appendix 13, "Interest Groupings in the American Economy," published in 1939.[86] For Sweezy, an interest group was a set of companies either under common control or subject to "a significant element of control in common." Sweezy recognized that director interlocks between a bank and an industrial company do not prove bank control and that "knowledge of the relationship on which interlocking directorates are based" is critical to assessing their significance. Sweezy gave weight to historical linkages, number and character of interlocks, ownership, and business connections. This approach yielded eight "interest groups" as of the mid-1930s – Morgan–First National, Rockefeller, Kuhn Loeb, Mellon, Chicago, Du Pont, Cleveland, and Boston – with assets of $61 billion, or 62 percent of the assets of the 250 largest corporations.

The degree of integration of the members of Sweezy's interest groups was highly variable. The Du Pont, Mellon, and Rockefeller groups, in their prime, were linked together by centralized control, which rested on a solid foundation of majority or substantial minority ownership. The Cleveland group, although not characterized by a central locus of control, was also based on a complex system of interlocking ownership interests. Historic banking relationships and interlocks of uncertain and variable effect were the basis of the other four interest groups. In the case of the "Chicago" group the integration rested "solely on the basis of interlocking directorates" of such number as to signify "a substantial community of interest between the firms involved." Such a community of interests is clearly a far cry from common control, and a consistent use of multiple interlocks as the basis for defining an interest group would have yielded a great many more interest groups. Sweezy noted, for example, that even in the 1930s AT&T and its major subsidiaries had large numbers of interlocks and banking relationships with the various acknowledged interest groups, but he suggested that these did not define a Bell-centered interest group, "as they form a bond between the major groups and apparently independent corporations . . ." Why the Chicago interlocks define a "community of interest" group but the Bell interlocks do not is unclear. In a curious inconsistency AT&T was included as part of the Morgan–First National group, whose membership was based not on ownership control but "upon long-standing financial relations and the very great prestige attaching to the Morgan and First National firms." This certainly involved a community-of-interest relationship between the two financial institutions and AT&T, but even partial control of AT&T by the banks in 1935 was dubious.

The Kuhn Loeb interest group, which Sweezy claimed to be "less closely knit" than the Morgan–First National group and more in the nature of a loose alliance, was allegedly based on long and durable financial relationships between the investment bank and various railroads – including the Pennsylvania Railroad and Union Pacific. The Pennsylvania Railroad is generally considered to have been solidly management controlled during this period; Union Pacific was still a Harriman family and Brown Brothers Harriman-controlled company, and was so designated by the Interstate Commerce Commission as late as 1974. This "interest group" may have been nonexistent in whole or in part even in 1935.

Forty or more years later, in the late 1970s, all four of the owner-based interest groups were still identifiable, although in altered (usually contracted) form. The four banker-dominated and interlock-based community-of-interest systems, of uncertain validity in the 1930s, are not distinguishable collectivities today.

Of the four owner-based interest groups, the Rockefeller group has shriveled the most (as measured by continued dominance over large companies, not total assets or income). Rockefeller holdings in all the great oil companies have fallen to noncontrol levels; and given the long absence of the family from managerial participation, Rockefeller control of these companies is a thing of the past. It is possible that the residual stockholdings, the importance of the Chase Manhattan Bank, and the wealth and prestige of the family establish some base of potential influence and community of interest among the oil companies, but this is of doubtful significance, given the long nonexercise of power, the strength and financial options of the oil companies, and their large number of non-Rockefeller points of contact and bases of community of interest. Among the 250 largest, only the Chase is still Rockefeller controlled, based more on continued family participation in top management than in family stock ownership, which was reportedly under 5 percent in 1974.[87]

In 1935 the Du Pont group included four of the 250 largest companies: E. I. Du Pont, U.S. Rubber, GM, and the National Bank of Detroit. In 1975 the Du Pont group included only one of the 250 largest – the chemical company. GM control was lost as a result of a 1949 antitrust action in which the government sought divestiture of GM stock by the Du Pont interests. The government's position was sustained by the Supreme Court in 1957 and led to a major divestment in the 1960s.

The National Bank of Detroit was closely affiliated with GM and fell out of the Du Pont orbit of power with the GM separation. Control of U.S. Rubber was given up by a long-term divestment that brought ownership well below 5 percent in the mid-1970s (down from 15.7 percent of the common in 1937).

The Mellon group, which Sweezy described in 1939 as "probably the best integrated and most compact," remained the most intact of the groups in the mid-1970s, with its three main constituents – Gulf, Alcoa, and Mellon Bank – still in the 250 largest and still subject to substantial Mellon family influence or control. This is still a fairly close-knit system, with extensive interlocking, family representation on boards (although now indirect), and family ownership still in excess of 10 percent. But Mellon holdings have declined markedly since 1938, and with negligible family participation in management of its companies, even this interest group seems to be in its last decade or so of collective control.

The Cleveland group was probably never subject to common control but represents a classic case of interlocking interest among a local business elite that made for a durable community-of-interest system. Four of the members of Sweezy's 1935 group remained in the 250 largest – Republic Steel, Youngstown Sheet and Tube (now a part of Lykes Youngstown), Inland Steel, and Goodyear Tire and Rubber. Of these, the three steel companies are still linked together by substantial joint venture interests, indirect interlocks, and other local connections. This is an instance in which Sweezy probably understated the interest group membership for the mid-1930s. National Steel, Armco, Eaton, and to a lesser extent Bethlehem Steel, among the current 250 largest, were also closely bound by vertical interlocks, common banking relations, common legal counsel, common ownership, and extensive joint venture relationships. Especially noteworthy has been the integrating role of Cleveland–Cliffs and M. A. Hanna Company, both mainly in the iron ore and mining business, and interlocked with a great many steel companies. Cleveland–Cliffs had equity investments for many years in Inland Steel, Jones and Laughlin, Youngstown Sheet and Tube, and Republic Steel, and reciprocal investments and joint ventures with these and other steel companies.[88] M. A. Hanna and Hanna Mining arguably control National Steel via the largest block of stock and two top Hanna Mining officers who serve on the National Steel board. Hanna's extensive network of joint ventures and vertical interlocks with National Steel and other steel companies is shown in Figure 6.1. The Cleveland group, like the old Rockefeller group, has special significance in its extensive coverage of a major industry – in this case iron and steel companies, mainly located in Cleveland but not confined there.

The forces weakening investment banker power and strengthening the autonomy of nonfinancials further loosened the ties among the members of the four banker-dominated and interlock-based interest groups described by Sweezy – Morgan–First National, Kuhn Loeb, Chicago, and Boston groups – and made them hardly differentiable from a great many other community-of-interest blocs. Morgan was broken into separate commercial banking and investment banking entities in the 1930s, and its two progeny have no special power over firms such as U.S. Steel, GE, AT&T, and ITT. Interlocks and business relationships exist between Morgan Guaranty, Morgan Stanley, Citibank, and many other of the old constituents of the Morgan–First National interest group. But the relationships hardly constitute a meaningful control group. These ties are similar to community-of-interest relationships that generally characterize the higher reaches of business enterprise.

The main potential focal point of contemporary "interest groups" would seem to be the great commercial banks, with their extensive customer relationships based mainly on credit extensions. Perhaps some forms of interest groups also could be identified around some of the very largest industrials. Tables 6.8 and 6.9 show the sets of companies linked with Citibank and Morgan

Table 6.8. *Direct interlocks and ownership links of Citicorp and Citibank with other members of the 250 largest corporations, 1975*

Corporation	Inside represen- tation of Citicorp	Outside represen- tation	Total inter- locks	Citicorp and Citibank stock holdings with sole power to vote (%)
(A) *Citicorp and Citibank with an officer on another board*				
1. Arlen Realty and Development	1	1	2	—
2. Beatrice Foods	1	—	1	1.1
3. City Investing	1	—	1	—
4. General Electric	1	—	1	1.6
5. W. R. Grace	1	2	3	—
6. Kraftco	1	1	2	—
7. Long Island Lighting	1	—	1	—
8. Monsanto	1	1	2	—
9. Mutual of New York	1	—	1	—
10. National Cash Register	1	1	2	—
11. Owens-Illinois	1	—	1	—
12. J. C. Penney	1	1	2	3.0
13. Phelps Dodge	1	—	1	—
14. Santa Fe Industries	1	—	1	—
15. Sears Roebuck	1	—	1	1.1
16. United Aircraft	1	1	2	—
(B) *Citicorp outside director-based interlocks*				
17. Aetna Life and Casualty		1	1	—
18. Allied Stores		1	1	—
19. American Telephone and Telegraph		4	4	0.1
20. Boeing		3	3	—
21. Continental Can		1	1	—
22. Du Pont		1	1	0.6
23. Eastman Kodak		1	1	1.5
24. Equitable Life Assurance		1	1	—
25. Exxon		1	1	0.6
26. First National Boston Corporation		1	1	—
27. Ford Motor Co.		1	1	0.7
28. General Motors		1	1	0.4
29. Ingersoll-Rand		1	1	—
30. International Business Machines		3	3	1.5
31. Kennecott Copper		2	2	—

Table 6.8 *(cont.)*

Corporation	Inside represen- tation of Citicorp	Outside represen- tation	Total inter- locks	Citicorp and Citibank stock holdings with sole power to vote (%)
32. Mobil Oil	1	1		0.4
33. New England Mutual	1	1		—
34. New York Life	1	1		—
35. Pepsico	1	1		—
36. Proctor and Gamble	1	1		0.2
37. Radio Corporation of America	1	1		—
38. Standard Oil of California	2	2		—
39. Union Pacific	1	1		—
40. United States Steel	1	1		—
41. Westinghouse	2	2		0.1
42. Xerox	1	1		4.4

(C) *Citicorp and Citibank stock holdings of 2 percent or more with sole power to vote, not associated with an interlock*

43. Arco	3.4
44. Caterpillar Tractor	2.8
45. Coca-Cola	2.9
46. Continental Telephone	3.4
47. Federated Department Stores	2.8
48. First Bank System	2.6
49. First International Bankshares	2.2
50. Florida Power & Light	2.2
51. FMC	2.2
52. Honeywell	3.7
53. Johnson & Johnson	3.0
54. S. S. Kresge	3.5
55. J. P. Morgan	3.5
56. Pennzoil	4.6
57. Philip Morris	3.0
58. Travelers	2.0
59. TRW	3.6
60. United Telecommunications	2.9

Table 6.9. *Direct interlocks and ownership links of J. P. Morgan and Morgan Guaranty Trust with other members of the 250 largest corporations, 1975*

Corporation	Inside representation of Morgan	Outside representation	Total interlocks	Morgan stock holdings with sole power to vote (%)
(A) *Morgan with an officer on another board*				
1. Bethlehem Steel	1	1	2	—
2. Champion International	1	1	2	4.4
3. Continental Corporation	1	—	1	—
4. General Electric	1	2	3	0.2
5. General Motors	1	1	2	1.2
6. Kennecott Copper	1	—	1	4.6
7. Niagara Mohawk Power	1	—	1	—
8. Panhandle Eastern Pipeline	1	—	1	—
9. Santa Fe Industries	1	—	1	—
10. Southern Railway	1	1	2	1.9
(B) *Morgan outside director-based interlocks*				
11. Aetna Life and Casualty		2	2	0.4
12. American Telephone and Telegraph		1	1	0.1
13. Burlington Northern		1	1	—
14. Coca-Cola		1	1	3.5
15. Continental Oil		1	1	—
16. CPC International		1	1	—
17. Du Pont		1	1	—
18. Eastman Kodak		1	1	2.0
19. Exxon		1	1	0.8
20. Federated Department Stores		1	1	3.9
21. Ford Motor Co.		1	1	3.0
22. Ingersoll-Rand		1	1	—
23. International Business Machines		1	1	3.0
24. John Hancock		1	1	—
25. Metropolitan		1	1	—
26. Missouri Pacific System		1	1	—
27. New York Life		1	1	—
28. Proctor and Gamble		1	1	3.1
29. Prudential		1	1	—
30. Ralston Purina		1	1	4.3
31. Sears Roebuck		1	1	2.3
32. Singer		1	1	—

Table 6.9 (*cont.*)

Corporation	Inside represen- tation of Morgan	Outside represen- tation	Total inter- locks	Morgan stock holdings with sole power to vote (%)
33. Union Carbide	1	1	—
34. United Aircraft	1	1	—
35. United States Steel	2	2	—
(C) *Morgan stock holdings of 2 percent or more with sole power to vote, not associated* *with an interlock*				
36. American Airlines				2.4
37. American Cyanamid				3.0
38. American Express				5.8
39. Bankamerica Corporation				2.4
40. Burlington Industries				7.7
41. Citicorp				3.5
42. Connecticut General				7.5
43. B. F. Goodrich				2.3
44. Goodyear Tire				5.0
45. Halliburton				3.7
46. International Paper				6.7
47. Kraftco				2.5
48. S. S. Kresge				5.4
49. Marathon Oil				2.8
50. Mobil Oil				2.5
51. Owens-Illinois				2.3
52. J. C. Penney				4.5
53. Pepsico				8.2
54. Pfizer				2.6
55. Philip Morris				7.9
56. Westinghouse				2.4
57. Xerox				3.5

Guaranty[89] by direct interlocks and by large trust department stockholdings as of early 1975. The tables are confined to connections among the 250 largest; the interest group systems would be considerably enlarged if lesser companies were included. Each table is divided into three parts: (A) showing interlocks and trust department stock ownership (with sole bank voting rights) where the bank has an officer on the board; (B) showing other direct interlocks and associated ownership; and (C) showing cases of trust department ownership in excess of 2 percent (with sole bank voting rights) where there is no accompanying directorship.

Table 6.8 shows that in 1975 Citibank had direct interlocks with 42 of the 250 largest corporations. In 16 of these cases (A) it had one of its own officers on the board of one of the 250, and in the other 26 cases (B) a Citibank outside director was on the board of another giant. In 13 of the 42 interlock relationships there was more than one interlock between Citibank and the other members of the 250 set. In 15 of the 42 instances of a direct Citibank interlock the Citibank trust department held stock with sole bank voting rights in 1975 – in only 2 cases, however, in excess of 2 percent (J. C. Penney, 3 percent, and Xerox, 4.4 percent). In 18 additional cases, however, where Citibank had no direct interlock, the bank held 2 percent or more of the stock of one of the 250 giants with sole bank voting rights. The largest percentage holding was in Pennzoil, 4.6 percent, and three of the large holdings were in bank holding companies, including a 3.5 percent holding in J. P. Morgan. In virtually all of the cases where Citibank had an officer on another board or the outside company had a representative on the board of Citibank, Citibank had an important banking relationship with the interlocked company.

Table 6.9 shows a similar set of linkages for Morgan Guaranty, with 10 Morgan officer interlocks with other members of the 250, 25 other direct interlocks, and 7 cases of multiple interlocks. Morgan's stockholdings in interlock companies, and its large holdings without interlocks, were more impressive in number and size than those of Citibank. In 16 of the interlock cases, Morgan held at least some stock with the sole right to vote; in 10 of these cases the holding amounting to 2 percent or more of the company's voting stock; and in 22 additional cases where it had no interlock Morgan held 2 percent or more, in 8 of them the Morgan holding ranging from 5 percent to 8.2 percent of the voting stock. Just as Citibank held 3.5 percent of Morgan voting stock, so Morgan held 3.5 percent of Citicorp voting stock. As with Citibank, banking relationships generally accompanied Morgan officerships on other boards and other company officer representation on Morgan's board.

Although the major banks are the most important community-of-interest centers that draw large firms together in interlock systems, one nonfinancial outdoes all financial institutions in this regard, namely, the Bell system. AT&T alone has only slightly fewer interlocks with other members of the 250 largest companies than either Citibank or Morgan. AT&T also has huge subsidiaries that would easily make the largest 250 list in their own right; and AT&T has long encouraged these affiliates to build goodwill by judicious selection of prestigious directors – which the subsidiaries have done. They are part of a unified power complex that is capable of being mobilized in time of need.[90] Table 6.10 shows for AT&T and its seven subsidiaries with individual assets in excess of $5 billion in 1975 the same interlock information as was provided in the preceding tables for Citibank and Morgan. The Bell system is shown to have officer representation on the boards of 21 of the 250 largest, including nine of the largest banks and six of the largest insurance companies; it has direct interlocks with 76 separate members of the 250 universe, including 30 of the 50 largest financial institutions; and it has multiple interlocks with 32 of the 250 largest.

What do these linkages mean in terms of control and integration? Interlocks between very large companies, with rare exceptions, do not reflect control by one corporation over another. This is clearly true of the AT&T system of interlocks, which is not associated with significant direct stock ownership[91] and where the service provided by the core company, although monopolized, is subject to common carrier regulation limiting discriminatory abuse. The stockholdings of the large banks, especially those of Morgan, are impressive, and even though they are not of control size or apparently used with control intent, their magnitude is such as to make bank opinion of more than passing interest to corporate managers. When accompanied by interlocks and lines of credit, they may give added weight to bank judgments and recommendations. And when other banks and powerful investors agree with Morgan Guaranty on issues of corporate policy, corporations will be under moral pressure and implicit threats of still greater force.

Nevertheless, with companies as powerful as GE, Proctor & Gamble, IBM, Sears, J. C. Penney, and Xerox, the banks do not have the power to command; these autonomous entities of great individual power are merely participating in ties of mutual exchange. Even where there is an imbalance of power and occasional weakness vis-à-vis the bank – as between say Citibank and Arlen Realty, or Morgan and Niagara Mohawk or Champion International – this is still not an area of bank command but of degrees of

Corporation	Number of AT&T system officers	Outside directors only	Total inter-locks
(A) *Companies on which an AT&T or affiliate officer sits on the board*			
1. Bankers Trust New York	2	—	2
2. Chase Manhattan Corporation	1	—	1
3. Chemical New York Corporation	1	1	2
4. Citicorp	1	3	4
5. Continental Corporation	1	1	2
6. CPC International	1	—	1
7. Crocker National Corporation	1	3	4
8. First National Boston Corporation	1	—	1
9. Ingersoll-Rand	1	1	2
10. John Hancock Mutual	1	2	3
11. Kraftco	1	1	2
12. Manufacturers Hanover Corporation	1	2	3
13. Metropolitan	1	1	2
14. J. P. Morgan	1	—	1
15. Mutual of New York	1	2	3
16. New York Life	1	2	3
17. Northern Natural Gas	1	—	1
18. Northwest Bancorporation	1	—	1
19. J. C. Penney	1	2	3
20. Prudential	1	2	3
21. United States Steel	1	1	2
(B) *Companies interlocked by outside directors of AT&T group*			
22. Allied Stores		1	1
23. American Can		3	3
24. American Express		2	2
25. Baltimore Gas & Electric		1	1
26. Bankamerica Corporation		2	2
27. Bank of New York		1	1
28. Boeing		1	1
29. Burroughs		1	1
30. Caterpillar Tractor		1	1
31. Charter New York Corporation		1	1
32. Chrysler		2	2
33. Continental Illinois		1	1
34. Continental Oil		1	1
35. Deere		1	1
36. Dresser Industries		1	1
37. Eastern Airlines		2	2
38. Equitable Life Assurance		1	1

Table 6.10 (*cont.*)

Corporation	Number of AT&T system officers	Outside directors only	Total inter-locks
39. Exxon		1	1
40. Federated Department Stores		2	2
41. First City Bancorporation of Texas		1	1
42. General Foods		1	1
43. General Motors		1	1
44. W. R. Grace		1	1
45. International Business Machines		2	2
46. International Harvester		1	1
47. International Paper		1	1
48. Kennecott Copper		1	1
49. Ling Temco Vought		1	1
50. Marine Midland Banks		2	2
51. Massachusetts Mutual		1	1
52. McDonnell Douglas		2	2
53. Mobil Oil		1	1
54. National Steel		1	1
55. NCNB Corporation		1	1
56. New England Mutual		2	2
57. Northwestern Mutual		3	3
58. Pacific Gas and Electric		2	2
59. Pacific Lighting		2	2
60. Panhandle Eastern Pipeline		1	1
61. Republic of Texas Corporation		1	1
62. Republic Steel		1	1
63. R. J. Reynolds Industries		1	1
64. Santa Fe Industries		2	2
65. Seaboard Coast Line Industries		1	1
66. Security Pacific Corporation		1	1
67. Southern California Edison		2	2
68. Southern Company		1	1
69. Southern Railway		1	1
70. Texaco		1	1
71. Union Carbide		1	1
72. Union Electric		1	1
73. Union Oil		1	1
74. Union Pacific		1	1
75. Western Bankcorp		2	2
76. F. W. Woolworth		2	2

influence, depending on circumstances, issues at stake, and personalities. Although Morgan is credited in Tables 3.1 and 3.2 with more than nominal influence in 7 of the 57 companies shown in Table 6.9, and Citibank had similar power in 5 of the 60 companies in Table 6.8, these are not cases of banker control but instances where the banks were deemed likely to have a significant, though still usually only a constraining, influence in decision making.

What is most impressive about these linkages is the total spectrum of personal and business contacts among the leadership of the dominant financial and industrial corporations of the United States, including the leaders of ostensibly competitive firms. Directors of Ford and GM meet on the boards of both Citibank and Morgan. AT&T, IBM, RCA, GE, Westinghouse, and Xerox meet on the Citibank board, and AT&T and IBM meet on the Morgan board. Union Carbide and Du Pont meet on the Morgan board. Bethlehem and U.S. Steel meet on the Morgan board. Kraftco, Beatrice Foods, and Pepsico meet on the Citibank board. Aetna, John Hancock, Metropolitan, New York Life, and Prudential meet on the Morgan board. Caterpillar Tractor, John Deere, and International Harvester are linked together by AT&T system directorships. Some of these linkages are via outside directors, but the fact remains that an extraordinary number of directors of major competitors in a wide array of major industries are in formal legal contact through common directorships of these two great banks and AT&T.

Dissociative factors

The centralizing and integrating forces previously described have been strong. To round out the picture on centralizing tendencies, however, it is important to consider some of the counteracting factors, both governmental and private, that also have been at work.

Role of Government

The role of government in the process has been complex. Just as in agriculture, where the government strives to improve productivity and at the same time contracts for output reduction, so also in relation to industrial organization it may successively or simultaneously pursue contradictory policies. It has often encouraged centralization and collective business action, as in its previous sponsorship of trade associations and more recent support of business advisory bodies; its military contracting policies both in war and peace; its war plant disposal practices; its sanctioning of collective international relationships among large companies; and its various tax and subsidy programs, enhancing the power of the largest businesses.

On the other hand, the Public Utility Holding Company Act of 1935 led to the splitting up of many centralized utility systems, and the Glass Steagall Act of 1933 forced the separation of scores of investment bank affiliates from commercial banks and prevented further close (ownership) association between the two. The tradition of keeping separate the ownership and control of commercial banks from the nonfinancial sector, formalized in the Bank Holding Company Act of 1956, has also been a significant governmental constraint against centralization.

Antitrust policy has been of varying effect – in some periods hardly interfering with the merger process, perhaps even encouraging it, at other times acting as a deterrent – but overall it has probably exercised a net constraint on concentration.[92] In the pre-World War I cases brought against Standard Oil and American Tobacco, antitrust forced important divestments and the stage was set for an antitrust policy that allowed shared monopoly (oligopoly) but precluded single-firm monopoly by merger. After World War II, and especially after the Celler–Kefauver Amendment of 1950, merger between large competitors was made increasingly difficult. But this policy did not apply to banks until the 1960s, and a great number of large bank mergers had already taken place, altering the structure of banking in many city markets.[93] Even so, banking is relatively decentralized in the United States, and in the last decade or so the trend toward increased concentration has been halted.[94]

Antitrust law has been compatible with a great many acquisitions by large firms of companies other than major direct competitors, principally where the acquired firms are in other (even if closely related) product lines. The result has been continued domination of the large merger field by the 200 largest companies, which acquired two-thirds of the assets of all large mining and manufacturing firms that were absorbed between 1948 and 1968.[95] In contrast with the 1920s, and even the period immediately preceding the Celler–Kafauver Amendment, large firm mergers of recent decades have been mainly product- or market-extension mergers, so that the encroachment on competition is less clear and direct than in cases of horizontal or vertical mergers. The competitive impact may even be positive if a more vigorous rival comes into a market from a completely unrelated area.[96] But acquiring firms have tended to enter related fields where they already had a small position (oil companies into chemicals), or where interproduct competition was already present and growing (oil companies into coal and uranium, glass and can companies into plastics and paper), and it is clear that *de novo* entry rather than entry via merger would be more compatible with a policy of competition.

Market Expansion, Multinational Growth, and Their Impact on Centralization

Although national market concentration ratios in the United States have increased on average since World War II, other changes have tended to undermine market positions. The drift has been toward the breakdown of market barriers and the enlargement of geographical market scope. This process has been profoundly influenced by technological change in transportation and communications, which has permitted the movement of goods and messages over greater distances with more flexibility and at lower cost. This has tended to integrate markets both within and among countries.

With a more systematic crossing of national boundaries, the markets for computers, steel, cigarettes, automobiles, or bank loans become larger, and all the multinational producers of a given product become potential rivals. In this respect, multinational expansion has been a factor making for deconcentration in markets for the many products now supplied by a wider array of international sources. International coordination, collective action, and *esprit de corps* among international rivals are less developed than among domestic firms in home markets,[97] and multinational expansion might be expected to intensify competition for this reason as well. Before World War II there was an extensive network of cartels and other international combines, sometimes state sponsored, that involved detailed market sharing and widespread international entry restrictions.[98] Many cartels were abandoned during and after the war, and restrictions on foreign entry were also lessened, reflecting in part the interest of U.S. multinationals in moving into foreign terrain. Although protectionism, the joint venture, and various types of collusion still prevail in many international markets, there has been a marked reduction in restrictionism and cartel controls in comparison with the earlier period.

It should be pointed out, however, that each national market continues to be more or less protected, and depending on the power of the domestic producers and the state itself, foreign firms sell on sufferance. Price restraint may be a condition of sufferance. Also, multinationals compete with major foreign rivals in already highly concentrated markets and in many of them these firms often meet the same large foreign firms. Raymond Vernon stresses the fact that on a global basis there is a strong, almost "universal tendency toward declining concentration," with world industrial leadership "being dispersed at a rapid rate."[99] He also recognizes that this statement may contain misleading implications for structure and competition in particular markets. Entry abroad is typically into tightly knit oligopolistic markets, which the entrant may disturb but usually not very seriously; the tendency is for oligopoly to persist.[100] Because a complex of forces is at work, the results can vary, depending on circumstances.

In the European Economic Community (EEC) U.S. entry into the auto and electrical machinery industries altered market shares and disturbed patterns of market behavior, adding to the procompetitive effects of the concurrent reduction of common market tariff barriers and the introduction of an antimonopoly policy.[101] But even under these favorable circumstances, powerful offsetting trends have preserved oligopolistic structures. A decline in the number of competitors and an increase in concentration occurred "in almost all countries and industries" of the EEC during the 1960s,[102] and a 1977 EEC study disclosed that in over 100 EEC product markets, the largest firm had a market share of 50 percent or more.[103] In England, in the breakfast cereals industry, subject to substantial multinational penetration and with Kellogg the market leader, oligopoly has remained stable for a considerable period (five firms have over 90 percent of the market) and price competition has remained nonexistent.[104] With the onset of multinational entry, Vernon notes that U.S. and European firms quickly developed a "complex system of partnerships, alliances, and conventions" in many industries "aimed at ensuring that they would move in step with one another and would avoid any outbreak of virulent competition."[105]

The situation in Third World markets is likely to be even less favorable: Few domestic firms are able to compete successfully with the multinationals, which leaves the state and foreign majors as the only important rivals in highly concentrated and increasingly denationalized markets.[106] Thus the competitive impact of the new entry may be compromised by both a diminution in numbers of independent local firms and by policies of restraint under conditions of "linked oligopoly." This is apart from even more basic issues of economic and political dependency, and the overall impact on these societies of the intensive marketing of developed countries' consumer goods packages.[107]

Although the post–World War II era has been characterized by a reduction in international cartels, as compared with the interwar period, the expansion of multinational activity and interpenetration of national economies during the past several decades has led to a new network of international linkages. The extensive transnational joint ventures in the petroleum business were noted earlier. A survey of the 10-Ks and Moody's for the 100 largest U.S. industrials in 1975 shows that 67 of them had joint ventures with one or more foreign companies, encompassing 56 separate foreign firms in 15 countries, for a total of 1,131 joint subsidiaries. This is a gross underestimation, resulting from the severely limited disclosure requirements governing joint ventures, as previously discussed. Direct intercorporate ownership between international rivals is also apparently extensive but is subject to minimal disclosure and has been inadequately studied. Olivier Pastré tabulated the 1975 stockholdings of the 100 U.S. companies that were most heavily invested in France and found 819 separate individual holdings of 1 percent or more covering many hundreds of French companies (but fewer than 819 companies, as there were many cases of several U.S. companies with large holdings in the same French entity).[108]

Direct board interlocks among competing multinationals of different countries are also of growing importance, although they are still of minor significance for the top parent institutions. In 1975, 30 of the 200 largest U.S. nonfinancials had one or more foreign directors, comprising only 2 percent of the total directors of the 200. Disproportionate numbers were Canadian, and several cases where there were multiple interlocks were merely instances of strong ownership interest (Royal Dutch/Shell–Shell; British Petroleum and Sohio). Interlocks appear to be more important among subsidaries, but they have been subject to very little investigation as yet. There are also supranational groupings, binding together the worldwide economic elite, such as the boards and advisory bodies of the International Monetary Fund, the World Bank, the International Chamber of Commerce, the Bilderberg group,[109] and the International Energy Agency (IEA);[110] but with the possible exception of the IEA, they are unimpressive coordinators of industry members, in comparison with the numerous industry and governmental cross-industry national advisory and research bodies.

These international centralizing and coordinating processes have tended to constrain rivalry and keep it within responsible bounds, and in the race between world market expansion, on the one hand, and increased business size and coordination, on the other, there has been something close to a stalemate during the past three decades. The impact of this expansion on individual markets is unclear, as oligopoly and oligopolistic behavior have persisted despite some new firm entry, denationalization has been widespread (reducing the size of local competitive fringes), and more intensive product differentiation has increased in importance in world and local market structures.

The Limits of Solidarity: Technological Change and Intercorporate Warfare

As was shown earlier, large domestic corporations are linked together in a great many networks that allow them to communicate and cooperate on a number of levels, which may serve to restrain competition in some forms and under some conditions. Offsetting these network constraints are the growth of managerial autonomy (even if it is a constrained autonomy), the weakening of both the investment banker and owner-based interest groups of earlier decades, and the more institutionalized profit orientation of the modern giant. The large corporation is a technologically based, profit-cum-growth machine, and when profitable growth opportunities appear that will damage other large entities, there are powerful internal pressures to move ahead.

Many of these pressures have arisen as a result of the high rate of technological change – especially in the electronics, petroleum, and chemicals industries – that has tended to bring new products into competition with old products and newer and cheaper materials into competition with traditional materials. For example, steel has been subjected to competition from aluminum and plastics, among other materials, as the producers of the substitute products have adapted them to specific industrial and commercial uses. Oil-chemical-plastics producers have entered the packaging and container markets and wreaked havoc among the major companies – such as International Paper, PPG, Owens-Illinois – that are the traditional suppliers of those materials.[111] Procter & Gamble has entered the paper market, to the great discomfiture of Scott Paper, and made a powerful thrust into the coffee market in opposition to the dominant giant, General Foods; and Procter & Gamble is reported to be developing products and contemplating entry into markets that will bring it into collision with Johnson & Johnson, Coca-Cola, Pepsico, and Ralston Purina, among others.[112]

The high technology of the communications equipment field, which encompasses the transmittal, processing, display, and storage of information, has brought a whole host of formerly separate industries – such as radio, television, telephone, copier, and computer – into an overlapping and competitive relationship with one another, so that 3M, Litton, Xerox, RCA, GE, GTE, ITT, NCR, and IBM are all jostling for position and abutting against AT&T. AT&T's control has been weakening since 1968, when attachments of outside equipment to Bell lines became permissible; its greatest problem is preserving its position in the business information transmission market in the face of new technologies that could bypass it altogether.

Thus the pressure for profits, and the profit opportunities opened up by technology in the traditional domains of others, have frequently disrupted intercorporate solidarity and resulted in more or less severe warfare. In some cases this has involved the simple crossing of industry lines with competitive new product offerings, as in the entry of a materials and parts manufacturer like Texas Instruments into a number of final product markets such as digital watches, calculators, and computers; Procter & Gamble into the coffee and potato chip businesses; and IBM into the copier machine field. Some of these new entries have involved significant price cutting as well as the offering and advertising of a new product.

Intercorporate warfare among the giants often takes the form of lawsuits based on alleged exclusions from vertically integrated monopolistic market positions. Both Litton and ITT have been suing AT&T for exclusion from the telephone equipment market, and ITT has been pursuing a major private antitrust suit against

GTE since 1967 along similar lines. The ITT suit against GTE led to a 1972 decree, under appeal, that would force a drastic divestment of telephone properties by GTE.[113] Westinghouse has been denouncing and suing Gulf – both classed by Sweezy as part of the Mellon interest group in the 1930s – for its participation in the uranium cartel and for contributing to the uranium price rise that has caused Westinghouse so much grief.[114] The following companies, to give just a small sample, have also been in fairly serious litigation with one another in recent years: Smithkline Corporation and Eli Lilly; H. J. Heinz and Campbell Soup; du Pont and Pepsico; Southern Company and Jim Walter Corporation; SCM and Xerox; Mobil and Superior Oil; Philadelphia Electric Company versus Singer and Rockwell International.

These illustrations of continued conflict among the giants, periodical encroachments on one another's domains, and even open price competition, legal warfare, and personal denunciations are intended to show that in the community of interest networks of corporate America there still lurks a considerable amount of autonomy, which surfaces when enhanced profit opportunities overpower commonality of interest.

The more aggressive intercorporate struggles usually have occurred between relatively unlinked companies. In its long fight to constrain imports of Japanese television sets, for example, Zenith gradually came to exclude Sony, with whom it entered into significant licensing arrangements in the 1970s. Sony was one of several Japanese manufacturers sued by Zenith in 1974 for unfair competitive practices, but the issues between the two companies were settled out of court in 1977. A *Wall Street Journal* report noted that "John J. Nevin, Zenith's chairman and president, often has specifically excluded Sony from his charges of unfair competition from Japan. Recently, Zenith acquired rights to market and sell video player-recorders based on Sony technology."[115] Another *Wall Street Journal* report explains RCA's benign attitude toward Japanese entry as a result, at least in part, of "lucrative licensing arrangements" with Japanese companies.[116]

Among domestic companies that are aggressive invaders of the turf of other U.S. companies, interlocks with rivals and potential rivals seem to be exceptionally sparse. Procter & Gamble, for example, an aggressive entrant into a series of consumers goods markets, has no direct and few if any indirect interlocks with any other company that produces the "products normally sold through food, drug and variety stores,"[117] which it sees as its natural market. Its interlocks involve suppliers, customers (Kresge, Federated Department Stores, Sears, Kroger, Penney), financial institutions, and unrelated industrials. GTE has no direct or indirect interlocks with ITT, and ITT has no direct and only a few indirect interlocks with AT&T, IBM, RCA, Westinghouse, and GE (four, three, one, two, and one indirect interlocks, respectively).

AT&T has no direct interlock with IBM, although IBM had two direct interlocks with major AT&T subsidiaries in 1975, as shown in Table 6.10. But AT& T had 22 indirect interlocks with IBM (plus three through Western Electric). Whether these and other connections between the two giants have affected IBM's willingness to compete is an interesting question. "Other connections," in this instance, include the fact that the Bell System is one of the world's largest customers for IBM computers;[118] the possibility of a threat to this business was discussed among IBM management in considering when and how to move into the emerging communications–data processing field.[119] IBM seems to have moved slowly in challenging AT&T. In 1974 *Business Week* noted that "IBM chairman Frank T. Cary and AT&T's de Butts seem almost as anxious to preserve détente as Secretary Kissinger and Premier Brezhnev."[120] IBM bought into a satellite venture in 1974, but it made little effort to penetrate the specialized equipment market, in which it was already involved in Europe.

In assessing the impact of interlocks and other ties, one has the problem of determining cause and effect. If Procter & Gamble has no links with companies on its "hit list," this may be a result of its anticipation of the competitive onslaught. A company contemplating an aggressive move against another company may shed itself of conflicting and encumbering interlocks. If the companies are already in overlapping fields, such as GTE and ITT, direct interlocks may be precluded by the Clayton Act. But changes may occur that make potential competitors out of companies with an historic network of linkages, in which case linkages could obstruct rivalry (although other scenarios are obviously possible). The elaborate network of indirect interlocks between AT&T and IBM could be an anticompetitive factor, although in this case an important vertical business relationship, related in part to sheer size, seems to have been the most potent barrier to entry.

The competitive effect of the crossing of product lines by companies with new products or cheaper materials is often offset in some degree by preemptive moves of the threatened companies

and industries, as in the oil company absorption of coal and uranium resources and the can company mergers with glass manufacturers. This reduces the number of rivals in product markets that
are in process of fusion, with potential negative effects on interproduct competition. It could also slow up technological development in fields where vested interests elsewhere are less than eager to enlarge competitive sources of supply. It could even lead,
in some circumstances, to the elimination of a competitive source
of supply, particularly if, for example, the supply source requires
an important infrastructure of long-term and expensive fixed
equipment (such as tracks or power lines). In the transportation
field, for example, National City Lines, a company affiliated with
GM, acquired control of 46 local streetcar systems operating in 45
cities in 16 states.[121] Petroleum and tire companies contributed –
along with GM – to the financing of this operation, in which the
acquired streetcar systems were quickly supplanted by passenger
buses, procured from GM. This was hardly the sole factor involved in the motorization of local transit and rapid decline in
electric-powered streetcars in big cities, but it helped.

The power of giant companies was also manifest in the organization of huge government subsidies for highways. In 1932 a National Highway Users Conference was organized with the stated
purpose of obtaining an exclusive allocation of gasoline taxes for
highway construction. The auto, petroleum, and tire interests that
established and supported this group achieved resounding success,
into the mid- and late-1970s staving off efforts to allocate highway
"trust funds" to local rapid transit or railway improvement. Adams and Dirlam note that,

> Had Congress been asked to finance highways out of general
> tax revenues, it would have been far more difficult to process
> the $70 billion spent on the Interstate Highway system
> through the appropriations screen. Congress certainly would
> not have allocated that amount to highways while spending
> only $795 million, or 1 percent, on rail transportation.[122]

Concluding note

The centralization of economic power in the United States has
increased markedly since 1900, even since 1929. The individual
has been further submerged in a mass society, increasingly dominated by organized groups – business, government, labor, and as-

sorted other collectivities.[123] Business centralization considered by itself has also increased significantly in the twentieth century, in the sense of a great enlargement in the average size of business unit, as measured, for example, by employees per firm. The entire distribution of firms by size has drifted upward over time. This has reflected, in part, changes in output and occupational distribution, most notably the decline in agriculture and the rise in large-scale sectors such as manufacturing, electric and gas utilities, and transport. It has also been a consequence of the steady growth of the multiplant firm, a development that has rested in turn on the rise in importance of mass distribution – national and international – and other forces that have pushed large firms toward product and market diversification. Aggregate concentration also increased markedly in the beginning of the twentieth century, at least until the early 1930s. Since then it has shown a more complex pattern of movement: declining sharply from its depression peak, then stabilizing and moving up slightly, according to broader measures of economic activity – rising substantially in manufacturing alone.

Aggregate concentration was already high in 1900, with the country in the midst of its greatest merger movement and with a financial structure more concentrated than in 1980. The subsequent rapid growth of markets and technological change caused deconcentration in many industries, and the family-owned and banker-based interest groups of earlier years tended to weaken. The large corporations of today are less frequently tied together in closely knit groups than in the past, but communication among them is more efficient and extensive and there are a very large number of looser linkages, points of contact, and common connections that make for varying degrees of community of interest. These may help explain why the rivalry among the large corporations, although still very much alive, involves more widespread adherence to mutually protective rules of the game – particularly, the channeling of rivalry into forms of competition that do not involve price cutting. Other factors also contribute to a more constrained rivalry, including greater stability of the core firms in many industries (with a resultant incentive toward live-and-let-live policies), the increased importance and high costs of product differentiation and technological change, and the greater role of government as regulator, contractor, and business partner.

The internationalization of business has tended to diminish centralization in one sense, making markets more open and global and thus adding foreign majors to the set of relevant suppliers. On the other hand, internationalization has enhanced the power of the multinational corporations within individual states. This is not evident in domestic market concentration ratios, which have increased only moderately over the past several decades, but it is observable in aggregate concentration changes in the post-World War II era. It is also evident that the flexibility of international corporations enhances their bargaining strength with organized labor, as they can easily relocate to better investment climes. As regards government, the matter is more complex; on the one hand, the multinational depends heavily on government for support; on the other, internationalization increases the power of maneuver of private interests and private initiatives in hostile environments frequently set the stage for government intervention. The multinational corporation thus has a paradoxical effect: It increases the importance of the state, which is appealed to for aid and protection by both expanding multinationals and threatened domestic interests, and it weakens the power of the state, which has lost control over events, becoming both reactive (rather than initiative) and paralyzed by the conflicting requirements of domestic interests and international pressures and obligations.[124]

7

Power, Responsibility, and Conflicting Imperatives

In this final chapter I will summarize and enlarge on earlier findings and then extend the discussion to related policy issues, some
of the mechanisms proposed for resolving them, and the prospects
and promise of implementing such reforms. Special attention will
be given to corporate responsiveness to social issues, both voluntary and under various forms of community pressure; fuller disclosure; and some major proposals for altering the machinery of
corporate governance, as devices for solving problems in this age
of dominance by the large corporation. A brief concluding section
addresses the broader and more speculative prospects of change in
the corporate order as it faces the difficult challenges of the late
twentieth century.

Major themes and some policy implications

This book has stressed a number of themes on the control and
power of the large corporation that have implications for policy
and the future development of the business system.

First, the corporation has become ever more dominant in economic life over the past 80 years. And within the increasingly
dominant corporate world the largest 100 or 200 corporations
are not only vastly larger today than in 1900, but they have also
become relatively more important as well. It should be noted,
however, that the largest corporations wielded considerable
power even in 1900. There was no "golden age" of small-business
dominance and unconstrained competition at the turn of the
century – competition was widespread and frequently intense, but
monopoly power and collusion were also widely prevalent and
centralization of economic power was already at a high level. In
fact, large firms were grouped together in more unified interest
groups in the earlier years – banker control and the "money trust"

were near their zenith in 1900, and both finance-dominated and ownership-based interest groups have been on a secular decline through most of this century.

Still, the largest nonfinancial firms today are connected with one another through an extensive though loose network of inter-locks, joint ventures, advisory bodies, and other social, political, and trade groups. These connections are enhanced in importance by the efficiency of modern communications and by the maturity of many major industries, whose top firm membership has stabi-lized, and a consequent tendency toward policies of live-and-let-live and constrained rivalry. The market power of the largest firms probably has increased on average, and price competition has diminished in this process of growth and maturation, but ri-valry among them persists and large firms invade one another's product and geographic turf at least as readily now as in the past. The welfare implications of this shift away from price competi-tion, along with the persistence and refinement of nonprice forms of rivalry, are complex[1] – but it clearly has enhanced the impor-tance of the largest firms. The post-World War II increase in ag-gregate concentration, the more rapid pace of technological and product change, and an intensified international rivalry have in-creased the weight of large firms in determining the rate of invest-ment, the level of employment, and the state of the national bal-ance of payments.

The internationalization of the activities of the largest corpora-tions has enhanced their power in other ways. The domestic size of large firms tends to be exaggerated insofar as their markets and facilities are located abroad, but the multinational dispersion of international corporations increases their mobility and their free-dom from effective government control. The growth of large multinational corporations links economies together ever more closely by virtue of normal corporate operations; by the same to-ken, policy actions contrary to the interests of international cor-porations would induce massive shifts in money balances, invest-ment, and the location of production across political boundaries. This prospect reduces the discretionary power of national author-ities, who are constrained not so much by individual companies as by an international corporate order whose normal market re-sponses impose themselves as a coordinating force on national policymakers.

Second, the large corporation in the United States has preserved its autonomy to a remarkable degree during the twentieth century. External financial control has declined since 1900. Government intervention has clearly been on the upswing, but offsetting its effects on business autonomy have been the large firms' improved communication systems, greater product diversification and geographic dispersion, and enhanced mobility.

The relationship between government and business has been obscured by a tendency to exaggerate both the degree of conflict between business and government and the scope and impact of government regulation. Contrary to the current cliché, government and business are not merely "adversaries," they are often allies and partners. Also neglected in conventional portrayals of an all-enveloping leviathan is the continued remarkable success of the U.S. business community in confining government to complementary and supportive functions (roads, schools, police, a military establishment) – systematically excluding it from producing things like tanks and refined oil. Regulation by government commission has frequently been at the request of business; the current intraindustry struggles over deregulation point up the fact that strategic business sectors *want* government to protect and serve it. Furthermore, industries and firms regulated by government commission have been in relative decline since 1930 as a result of their sluggish growth – reducing government's proportionate control of the largest firms and their activities in the sphere where regulation most seriously affects business decision making. Social regulation has increased markedly since 1930, but its impact has been mainly to establish behavior limits in selected areas of concern, and its reach and encroachment on major business decisions have been greatly exaggerated.

Third, there has been a major shift in the pattern of control of the large corporation since 1900, with a decline in direct control by both substantial ownership and financial interests and an increase in direct control by managers who own relatively little stock and yet possess considerable decision-making authority. This shift to management control has come largely at the expense of financial control, which was widespread in the boom eras of the turn of the century and the late 1920s. The shift in the locus of control resulted from the lower turnover rate among the increasingly diversified large companies; the diffusion of individual ownership with growth in company size, merger activity, and the dissipation of large family blocks of stock; the increased importance of the management function in these complex giants, adding impetus to the displacement of family managers by professionals; and the importance of strategic position for corporate control.

Even in 1900, however, *majority*-ownership control of the large corporation was rare, so that the separation of *most* ownership from any direct say in management was already the prevailing pattern. What is more, control by speculative and other financial interests – often owning, at least temporarily, substantial blocks of stock – and the seriously abusive exploitation of strategic position by controlling insiders, were far more prevalent than in the modern (post-1930) era. The separation of ownership from control increased markedly after 1900, and, everything else being equal, should have resulted in still greater abuse of ordinary shareowners by managers and controlling minority interests. But everything else has not been equal, and, as noted, separation was great enough in 1900 so that, in conjunction with the economic opportunities, structural arrangements, and the political/legal environment of the time, abuses of the noncontrolling owners were more serious then than in the mature managerial system of the 1970s.

Fourth, the large corporations, with their growth in size and complexity in the twentieth century, have evolved from personalized, ad hoc, loose structures into more systematically organized entities, usually characterized by a top-level decision-making authority and a series of operating divisions carrying out the buying, producing, and selling functions. These divisions are sometimes organized on functional lines, often according to major product lines and sometimes a combination of both. These changes in internal structure, combining centralized control and direction with decentralized operations and subplanning, has allowed – simultaneously – more flexible and extensive growth (without loss of control) and the imposition by the control group of more rigorous standards of profit performance on the underlying operating entities and their subbureaucracies. This internal rationalization process has tended to preserve a profit orientation; and as a function of size and need for control these organizational and role changes have made for a convergence in objectives among companies with varying control forms.[2]

Fifth, there has been considerable speculation on the effect of the shift to management control on corporate objectives and performance. The speculation has run the gamut from those claiming a new sense of corporate responsibility to the larger community on one side to those emphasizing the new possibilities of managerial self-aggrandizement on the other. Nonprofit-maximizing behavior by managers has gained some limited support in empirical studies that have shown a superior profit performance in owner- as opposed to management-dominated firms; but the evidence is not consistent, and all sources of bias have not been removed from such analyses. The position developed in this book is that the broad objective of both large managerial- and owner-dominated firms tends to be profitable growth. In managerial companies, varying weights are given to profitability and growth in company size, but the two are seen as linked together both functionally and in managerial strategies, with growth viewed as successful only with a profit payoff. Owner-dominated firms have had a similar matrix of objectives – they are not undeviating profit maximizers any more than managerial firms.

Managerial objectives are shaped and constrained to a considerable degree by owner-creditor power, which exercises its influence through many channels, including stock and credit market pricing, board representation, large-owner inquiries and suggestions, peer group rating, and the underlying threat of displacement by internal power realignments or takeovers from the outside. Owner-creditor power underlies business ideology and the rules of the game that define success and fix limits to self-aggrandizement. Selection processes in movement up the corporate ladder, as well as the market for managerial talent, give critical weight to profit-related variables. Managers rate themselves on this basis, as do their peers – fellow officers, outside directors, bankers, and large stockholders.

Managerial discretion in very large corporations is also circumscribed by group decision-making, bureaucratization, and divisionalization. In many large companies, whereas a single individual often has preeminent power, a number of top managers contribute to the making of key decisions; and a great many decisions are made on the basis of pressures from within the organization. Collective decision making tends to bring to the surface the values guiding decisions and in the process tends to force these values into acceptable channels. The discretion of managers – whether owners, hired managers, or controlling nonowner/managers – is also likely to be affected by the need to standardize and bring order in organizations of great size and complexity. This requires control processes, rules of behavior, and standards of evaluation that serve to limit discretion and channel behavior in accordance with rational rules of control.

Thus a number of basic forces, some evolving side by side with the managerial revolution itself (size, decentralization of operation, professionalization of management), have tended to constrain independent managers, limit the range of their discretion, and press them toward a profit orientation at least as unequivocal as that of owner/managers. This leaves room for a certain amount of "expense preference," the periodic emergence and cutting back of organizational "slack," and other modes of sharing in corporate surpluses by active managers, but these are neither new nor demonstrably a special feature of managerial firms. In principle, the argument for larger discretion on the part of independent managers was never very persuasive in the first place. An owner/manager has greater discretion than a nonowner/manager because the legal and moral case for an unusual application of corporate resources is greater for the former (they are the *owner-manager*'s assets)[3] and because the owner-manager's control position is likely to be more secure. The contrary view seems to be based on a confusion of discretion with *interest;* owner/managers, it is assumed, would pursue profits, because this is in their interest, whereas nonowner/managers, lacking in personal incentive to maximize profits, will be free to pursue other ends.[4] It should be obvious, however, that the owner/manager does not *have* to pursue profits and that the nonowner/manager may be under strong pressure to seek profits. Lack of direct interest in profits could lead nonowner/managers to search for reasons to pursue other objectives and to be more "image conscious" and responsive to external pressures. This is still not a matter of greater discretion but of different interest. The autonomous manager may be more willing to respond to outside pressures but may be less capable of independent actions.

Finally, if the shift to managerial control did lead to significant, negative performance effects – such as lower rates of return, excessive growth, and expense preference – what policy conclusions would follow? A number of analysts have asserted (and given evidence) that managerial discretion and potential abuse depend on market power, so that further argument is provided for the case against allowing great market power. In addition, if abuse and inefficiency are demonstrably related to management control, this provides a rationale for constraining increased size per se. It is huge size that leads to a diffusion of ownership and thus to managerial control, so that if managerialism has net detrimental effects, growth in size also does.[5] It would hardly be feasible to force a retention of large ownership blocks. Thus the only way to prevent further diffusion of ownership would be by constraining growth in absolute size; the only route to more concentrated ownership would be a policy of active decentralization. On its face, the latter is not a feasible strategy, but the strength of the case against growth in size is enhanced if managerial control produces its own unique inefficiencies.

It follows from the analysis developed in this book, however, that the conventional view is misdirected. The main impact of the managerial revolution has been the creation of a larger, more bureaucratic and rational profit-seeking entity. The control groups of these firms do pay themselves generously, and, under the impetus of high personal tax rates, have developed elaborate systems of compensation by deferred money payments, stock options and bonuses, and expense account perquisites of large scope and ingenuity. Insiders and affiliated persons also sometimes benefit from the advantages of inside information in buying and selling company stock and occasionally from sales of property by or to the corporation and other forms of misuse of strategic position. But abuses of these types have declined markedly in large corporations as a result of changes in the law, publicity, shifts in rules of the game, and sheer size and bureaucratization itself. Self-dealing and privileged information abuses, which were massive in the very large corporations in 1900, and large in 1929, are moderate in the mid- and late 1970s. They remain far more serious, as is tax evasion, for companies, managements, and controlling stockholders of smaller and less bureaucratized and exposed companies.[6]

Furthermore, there are far more important issues affected by corporate choices and power than managerial expense preference and overemphasis on sales growth rather than return on equity. Among them are the following.

1. How to control effectively the externalities of workplace and total environment, which have grown enormously in importance with economic growth and the industrial/scientific revolution.[7]

2. How to adjust to a prospective decline in the rate of growth of net output per capita and to the limited supply of "positional goods."[8] In a society attuned

to rapid growth and expanding opportunities for personal economic advancement, the necessary changes in attitudes and values and the avoidance of polarization and communal conflict may be difficult.

3. Barring a change in values and a shift to a non-growth, less competitive, and closed system, a pressing issue must be how to increase the rate of technological advance to offset the effects of the growing costs of controlling externalities and intensifying worldwide competition.

4. How to cope with the serious social costs of rapid technological change and the effects of great business size and mobility on the nature, quality, and security of work and problems of workforce adaptability and unemployment.[9]

5. How to deal with multinational economic and financial integration and its weakening effects on governmental powers and capacity for initiative. Corporate expansion and the maturing of an efficient world capital market have made political boundaries obsolete, reducing governments' knowledge of and control over these market-straddling activities and entities.[10] Yet political unification has not made parallel advances and may even have diminished over the past 30 years.

6. How to constrain inflationary pressures, which have become more severe and "built-in" in a world of large governments, with limited autonomy vis-à-vis core national power groups, committed to economic growth and high employment but constrained in policy options and effectiveness by the openness and integration of the world economy, rapid financial innovation,[11] and the absence of domestic consensus. Internal distribution struggles over the more slowly growing "income pie" are transmuted into inflationary pressures,[12] and may be resolvable only by some new consensus or imposed rule on the mechanics and outcome of income sharing.

7. How to contain and reverse the international arms race, which is draining world resources and threatening international stability.[13]

8. How to alleviate the extreme poverty afflicting the

Third World and the increasing inequality between rich and poor nations.[14] Although this is primarily a Third World problem, economic and political linkages bind nations together and give the choices of each nation an international significance. Third World countries may be encouraged to buy more arms;[15] to develop large-scale, export-oriented agriculture;[16] to redistribute land and otherwise aid the rural masses – or they might be allowed greater leeway to go it alone.[17] The multinationals of the industrialized world, and their governments and financial support institutions, have been powerful forces pressing toward the first two options, discouraging the last two.

The motives and power of the large corporation – and the system of large corporations – will have obvious and large bearing on the capacity of societies to address these problems in the coming decades. In such a context, corporate diligence in the pursuit of profits has no simple relationship to welfare. Insofar as it fosters improved efficiency and technological advance, the search for profitable growth frequently has an important social payoff – this has been the great source of strength of the "modern Prometheus" (capitalism) over the past two centuries. But most of the problems just enumerated are the built-in and cumulating negatives of the same drive for profitable growth that produced the huge productivity advances of the past. Some of these problems are the undesired secondary effects of the means corporations employ to pursue profitable ends. Others flow from the corporations' power to limit the problems that may be addressed and society's power to deal with them.

Whether capitalism will be able to cope with problems of such severity that seem to flow from its most fundamental properties and needs is a moot question. The answer may well vary by country, as differences in size, economic and social structure, traditions, and degree of integration into the world market make for substantial differences in adaptability. This book is concerned mainly with the corporate system of the United States. In the section that follows I will examine some of the proposals designed to bridge the gap between the corporation's drive for profits and the requirement of a well-behaved and responsive corporate order. In a concluding section I will return to a broader analysis of the corporate system of this country and its near-term prospects.

Corporate reform and its limits

Much of the interest in the growth of the large corporation and the "managerial revolution" derives from unease over the drift of the corporate system, a questioning of its capacity to cope with contemporary problems, and concern over its reformability either from within or by external imposition. In this section I review briefly some of the main contemporary proposals for liberal reform of the managerial corporation, which stress either voluntary changes from within, the possibilities of change through community pressures, or legislatively imposed rules, focusing on modes of board selection and corporate governance.

Corporate Responsibility

This is an age of "corporate responsibility," at least in the sense of an increased emphasis on responsible corporate behavior as a potentially significant means of solving social problems. In part, this is a function of heightened awareness of the problems themselves, which has led to appeals for solutions in many directions, including voluntary actions of those with power – namely, the corporate leadership. It is also related to the rise of public interest activists in the 1960s and 1970s, who have pressed for responsive corporate behavior. A belief in corporate responsibility as a viable machinery of reform also derives from the facts and theories of centralization and managerialism, which describe a concentrated economic structure led by managers who have discretionary power to act.[18] A segment of the corporate leadership itself expounds and welcomes an emphasis on corporate responsibility, partly out of fear that if the business system itself does not address problems, the government will step in and fill the breach.

Evolution of Corporate Social Responsibility. The acceptance by business and the business leadership of a responsibility to society beyond producing goods and abiding by the law has a long history. This responsibility has been expressed for many years in charitable contributions, in public service functions (participation in school boards, fund raising for hospitals, churches, colleges, and so forth), and in the idea that business leaders serve a trustee function. The notion of a special responsibility to society inhering in the wealth and power of the business leader dates back to pre-Calvinist doctrines of Christian charity, which persisted in spite of the triumph of Puritanism, "a creed which transformed the acquisition of wealth from a drudgery or a temptation into a moral duty . . . The good Christian was not wholly dissimilar from the economic man."[19] Under the Puritan doctrines, if wealth was a product of hard work (and God's grace), no sharing was necessary, especially if the likely beneficiaries were designed for poverty or might be encouraged in their bad habits by receiving unearned income. Thomas C. Cochran notes that in the nineteenth century, "poverty in America savored of sin," an attitude that helped to make possible a substantial reduction in government aid to the indigent between 1875 and 1900, despite a great increase in the number of needy.[20] Even now, the widespread belief persists that although there are deserving poor, there are also large numbers of *undeserving* poor who take advantage of the largess offered by the community at the expense of the active members of society.

In earlier years, sharing by the wealthy through charity was often thought less important than job creation through the reinvestment of profits, and magnates such as John Jacob Astor and Cornelius Vanderbilt, who left almost nothing to charity, were widely applauded in the press for their preoccupation with output and employment creation.[21] This view has also retained an important place in contemporary ideology and provides a groundwork for the frequent denial of any corporate responsibility beyond simple profit-making activity.[22]

The notion of the business leader as steward or trustee has been a long-standing feature of the ideological landscape. For a long time, this notion was tied to religious doctrine – especially Christian fundamentalism. The churches of the pre-World War I era were strong on social messages – generally compatible with and supportive of business – stressing the importance of self-help, hard work, and adjustment to the world as it is.[23] Business espoused these same doctrines, which justified their preeminence and sanctified harsh social policies. One of the most famous expressions of business' attitude, containing a quasi-religious overlay, was George Baer's 1902 response to an appeal for Christian behavior in treating the striking coal miners: "The rights and interests of the laboring man will be protected and cared for – not by the labor agitators, but by the Christian men to whom God in His infinite wisdom has given the control of the property interests of the country."[24]

But the businessman was often viewed (and often viewed himself) as a steward of God with eleemosynary obligations.[25] And he helped fill part of the welfare gap left by an almost laissez-faire government in earlier years. Business giving for community welfare was fairly extensive by 1900, and Cochran believes that it may have been more important than the private gifts of executives.[26] Business leaders sometimes saw their position as requiring generous disposition of their wealth on strictly pragmatic grounds: If social efficiency and progress necessitate great inequality, concentrated wealth must be properly and generously used to avoid social upheaval. In the words of Andrew Carnegie, the man of wealth must "consider all surplus revenues which come to him simply as trust funds, which he is called upon to administer, and strictly bound as a matter of duty to administer in a manner which, in his judgment, is best calculated to produce the most beneficial results for the community."[27]

Carnegie was speaking about personal wealth, not corporate assets. The idea that the corporation has community obligations is more complicated, given its legal obligations to public stockholders and creditors. Nevertheless, the corporation was long thought to have some obligation to behave as a good citizen, especially to its own workers, but also in relation to local community needs. Companies frequently assumed patriarchal, protective postures toward their workers. In early years the emphasis was on protecting workers from idleness and temptation, rather than from occupational hazards or economic insecurity. The widespread phenomenon of company towns and company-owned housing frequently gave corporations de facto social responsibilities, and they served as the providers of quasi-governmental, off-the-job services. The patriarchal role (at least with respect to the labor force) was also a facet of the long struggle, from the nineteenth century through the 1920s, to deflect unionism.

Baer's sanctimonious language, previously quoted, although widely denounced as blasphemous and used effectively against him, did capture the depth of business antipathy to labor organization and its patronizing attitude toward the work force. A more sophisticated paternalism associated with the National Civic Federation[28] emerged early in the century, however, and reached its peak in the "welfare capitalism" of the 1920s.[29] Its most eloquent spokesman in the latter period, Owen D. Young of General Electric, claimed that labor and capital were now "partners in a common enterprise," where conflict was being reduced, efforts were being made to make work more zestful and more democratically organized, and profit sharing and worker ownership were being

extended along with various other self-help and benefits programs.[30] Changes along these lines were modest, however, and
were made in a strongly antiunion context, with union prevention
an important objective and effect.

The corporate leadership has always looked upon itself as
"doing good" and serving the community mainly if not exclusively by its ordinary productive activities. "Profits through service," a popular business formula of the 1920s,[31] meant service in
producing goods, not charitable contributions or concern with the
external effects of business actions. In the 1920s progressivism in
business meant high wages, profit sharing, and other obligations
to one's own workers, but obligations that extended beyond the
immediate corporate nexus are hard to find.

During the 1920s and 1930s fascism took hold in a number of
advanced Western states. In the ideology of fascism (sometimes
referred to as "corporatism"), "natural leaders" – including top
businesspeople – served as stewards of society, entrusted to balance private and social interests. In the United States a phase of
rapid trade association growth was taking place. These developments, as well as prevailing economic conditions, helped to produce the National Recovery Administration (NRA) and a business
movement for self-government in industry.[32] The Swope Plan of
1930 called for joint trade association – Federal Trade Commission
regulation of each industry and self-government of business under
government supervision; it also included spin-off benefits to labor.

Only in recent times have obligations to the community at large
been viewed as part of corporate responsibility. Thus an oft-
quoted statement by Frank Abrams, chairman of Standard Oil
Company of New Jersey (now Exxon), in 1946, described the role
of the modern manager as maintaining "an equitable and working
balance among the claims of the various directly interested groups
– stockholders, employees, customers, and the public at large."[33]
And in his McKinsey Foundation Lectures of 1962, Thomas Watson, Jr. of IBM called explicitly for a business perspective that
goes beyond the traditional responsibility to the company's own
workers:

> The manager of a large organizaton may have done a fine job
> in demonstrating what he can do for his people. But let him
> go one step beyond this and recognize that people who are
> not working for large organizations – or those who are not
> working at all – may have even greater need for partial assis-

tance with some of their problems than his employees do. He might well remember this before he automatically criticizes a piece of legislation aimed at helping those people.[34]

Watson's position is still rare among American business leaders, and he himself says that he would be "one of the first to admit that it is a good deal easier to state this proposition [the importance of attention to 'public need'] than to put it into practice."[35] Watson was appealing to the business community, in fact, not to actually *do* more for society but, rather, to cease its total negativism toward domestic social welfare programs.[36]

The traditional business view still maintains its predominance: Business' primary responsibility is to the organization and its owners; business responsibility to society at large is mainly, if not exclusively, to produce goods that meet the test of the market and in accordance with law. As noted by Thornton F. Bradshaw of Arco, corporations "depart from this purpose at their own peril."[37] Bradshaw notes that the rules may change and that in business society "the businessman has a very large responsibility for helping to change the rules."[38] This is what Watson was talking about, urging businesspeople to *allow* the rules to be changed. Bradshaw says the same, without implying, as Watson did, that business has been an obstacle to rule changes. Bradshaw urges business to work within the rules to achieve social goals, but he stresses the limits of "competitive tolerance" and the need for outside follow-up efforts to carry on the programs started by business. Bradshaw concludes that in the end there is "one last rule: Obey Friedman's law and make a profit. That will create jobs, and that is the most revolutionary concept there is."[39]

The Theory of Corporate Responsibility. In the usage that has evolved over the past decade or so "corporate responsibility" means business obligations beyond those traditionally assigned, that is, other than producing goods for a profit within a framework of law and customary behavior. An important distinction should be drawn between responsible actions that are at the expense of stockholder and corporate profits and those that are not. When beneficent corporate actions can be justified as consistent with the long-run profit interest of the corporation, the management of the company is not faced with a hard choice or conflict of interest. For example, charitable, educational, and public service contributions of corporate resources are regularly justified because they enhance the corporate image and result in better sales, easier recruitment, and so forth. They may be defended as necessary public relations and as obligatory evidence of corporate responsiveness. But defense of these contributions strictly in terms of their benefits to the public, independent of corporate interests, is not only a rarity, it would be regarded as evidence of irresponsibility and softheadedness. The internal corporate standard is ultimate profitability, and the key question debated is the profit effectiveness of corporate actions.

Because the profitability standard is so obviously important as a basis of corporate actions, it is regularly put forward by social critics trying to affect corporate behavior from the outside. Thus corporations are told that foot-dragging on minority hiring is profit-inefficient because the unprogressive company will be forced by law into a costly and hurry-up process of conforming to the new legal standards. In an important sense, community, activist, and public interest group demands and campaigns have become part of the environment influencing expected profitability. For example, the activists' success in getting laws that required minority hiring passed *made* a progressive anticipatory hiring policy profit-effective, *ex post facto*. Sufficient adverse publicity besetting Dow for the production of napalm had "image" effects on other sales and recruitment that converted napalm profitability into an overall company loss.

The dominance of the profitability standard in corporate determinations is based, in part, on legal constraints. Arbitrary use of corporate resources for noncorporate purposes can be challenged by stockholders. Only in recent times have legislatures and courts established the right of corporate managers to give gifts to charities and educational institutions,[40] and corporate largess for purposes not readily reconciled with profit-effectiveness is still subject to legal challenge. Obviously, if all the stockholders accepted some particular nonprofit-oriented disposition of company assets, there would not be a problem. But the views of stockholders are not easily ascertained, and some fraction of a large stockholder group is likely to be negative. By and large, given the social composition and interests of stockholders, one would expect a relatively conservative response on these matters. Furthermore, even if the general run of stockholders were socially progressive, managers would face the problem of dissenting minority holders and their claims and suits for managerial "waste" of corporate resources.

Complementing the legal constraint, and perhaps more fundamental, are the internal and external pressures on corporate managers to increase and protect profitability. The modern corporation's profit and investment centers, which have goals fixed in pecuniary terms, make nonprofit goals especially hard to translate into action, despite general expressions of philosophic preference by top management.[41]

Managerialism and Corporate Responsibility. Economists' studies of manager versus owner performance generally start from the assumption that the managerial revolution should lead to risk aversion, satisficing, an emphasis on growth per se, and more direct managerial pursuit of self-advantage ("expense preference"). These views, which I have already discussed – and questioned – would seem to point to far more plausible outcomes of managerial control in a world of competition and personal striving than the emergence of a new managerial ethic of social responsiveness. Nevertheless, the latter possibility has been claimed, or implied, often and optimistically. Much of the literature supportive of the new responsibility is exhortative or has a strong public relations tinge. As noted, many corporate executives encourage the idea of corporate responsibility to preempt attempts at solutions by others (mainly government), and liberal activists use such claims as a basis for appeals and pressures for better business behavior.

In fact, the only reputable proponent of enhanced corporate responsibility as an outcome of the managerial revolution has been A. A. Berle himself. In *The Modern Corporation and Private Property,* Berle and Means raised the question of how managers, insulated from traditional owner control, might use that new found power. They noted three possibilities: continuing to serve as trustees devoted to the interests of the powerless stockholders, plundering in the managerial interest, or serving the interest of society at large.[42] In the end, they came out for the third alternative, not as the actual functioning characteristic of managerial capitalism, but as one likely to emerge in the future. In their words:

> It is conceivable, – indeed it seems almost essential if the corporate system is to survive, – that the control of the great corporations should develop into a purely neutral technocracy, balancing a variety of claims by various groups in the community and assigning to each a portion of the income stream on the basis of public policy rather than private cupidity.[43]

There followed some speculations on the jockeying for power between the state and large corporations, in which domination of the state by the corporations is put forward as one possibility, but the basic extrapolation is for business practice to be "increasingly assuming the aspect of economic statesmanship." This was not a very analytical treatment, but its economic elements can nevertheless be broken down into these constituents: (1) separation of ownership and control has given managers the discretionary power to move in several directions; (2) although self-interest might cause this new power to be used by managers for their own advantage, because there is no longer any moral basis for owner or managerial claims, those of the community at large will tend to prevail. How this will come about is unstated, but its occurrence supposedly follows from the fact that it is necessary for system survival. (This proof is on a par with a hypothetical assertion during the Triassic Age that the dinosaur will change because it must!)

Although the later Berle writings became a little more assured that the "essential" change would occur, they never added much on the details and mechanics. In *The Twentieth Century Capitalist Revolution,* Berle brings in a "corporate conscience," which, however, is a vague composite of public relations, actions responsive to public opinion or to pressures or threats by government, and the long-run interest of managers in system survival.[44] There is very little in the way of "conscience" in view here – the managers are responding to pressure from outside or to self-interested calculations. This conscience would seem to have little connection to the separation of ownership and control, although in *Power Without Property* Berle does suggest that nonowning managers may pay more attention to public opinion than owner/controllers.[45] Surprisingly, Berle, although a lawyer, neglects mention of the legal encumbrances on managerial use of the resources of publicly owned companies, in contrast with the greater rights of owner/managers in private companies.

Berle's remarks on corporate responsibility and the corporate conscience were so undeveloped as to amount to an expression of an ideological position rather than to serious analysis. Berle's first writing on the subject, in *The Modern Corporation and Private Property,* greatly overstated the loss of stockholders' power and the separation and discretion of managers, possibly in the interest of yielding more dramatic conclusions. Even if the extreme separation hypothesis held, Berle provided no basis for rejecting the alternative inference that the independent managers would feather their own nests. If, furthermore, management power is greatly constrained by owner/creditor interests, a key premise of the Berle forecast of a new corporate responsibility is undermined. No mention is made by him of the impact of competitive pressures, which persist in varying degrees in a world of oligopolies. These constraints and pressures point toward a continued profit orientation, as does the interest of the organization as a whole. Berle also completely disregarded the long-discussed possible effects of great size and bureaucratization in submerging individual values to the demands and interests of the organization as a whole. In his 1824 essay, "On Corporate Bodies," subtitled "Corporations have no soul," William Hazlitt wrote that:

> Corporate bodies are more corrupt and profligate than individuals, because they have more power to do mischief, and are less amenable to disgrace or punishment. They feel neither shame, remorse, gratitude, nor good-will . . . The refinements of private judgment are referred to and negatived in a committee of the whole body, while the projects and interests of the Corporation meet with a secret but powerful support in the self-love of the different members. Remonstrance – opposition, is fruitless, troublesome, invidious: it answers to no one end: and a conformity to the sense of the company is found to be no less necessary to a reputation for a good-fellowship than to a quiet life.[46]

John Z. De Lorean says much the same thing in 1979, based on his long experience as an executive with General Motors:

> The system has a different morality as a group than the people do as individuals, which permits it to willfully produce ineffective or dangerous products, deal dictatorially and often unfairly with suppliers, pay bribes for business, abrogate the rights of employees by demanding blind loyalty to management or tamper with the democratic process of government through illegal political contributions.[47]

Bureaucratic pressures and the disciplined pursuit of overall corporate objectives tend to be greater in large organizations. Community pressures and interests are less personally felt and tend to be lost in bureaucratic processes dominated by a market-based profit-loss calculus. One of the benefits of large size, conglomeration, diversification, and multinationalization is precisely the ability to move around, to take advantage of cheaper and better disciplined labor and a superior tax climate.[48] In a world of competitive political units – local, state, and national – increased capital mobility means a greater ability to extract tax and other concessions to induce (or prevent) corporate movement.[49] Greater capital mobility also allows the aborting of labor's attempts to improve wages and working conditions, through a threatened or actual change in location. With profit motive and competitive pressures intact, market forces should produce organizations that are better structured to abandon individual plants and communities in the interests of company profits as a whole. In an important sense, the success of large corporations follows in part from their being *designed* to be less "responsible" than smaller local enterprises.

A. A. Berle assumed that the corporate managerial leadership responds neither to owner/creditor/organizational pressures nor to compelling interests of its own but, rather, to public opinion and governmental prods. The corporate managers, in his words, resemble "a professional civil service far more than a group of property-owning and property-minded entrepreneurs."[50] In contrast with the disinterested and passive trustees envisaged by Berle, managers primarily concerned with the impact of environmental controls on profits might try hard to avoid such controls by spending money to alter public opinion or to stymie the enactment or enforcement of environmental control laws, or by shifts (or threats of movement) to better investment climes.

Managerial Versus Owner Responsibility – The Record. Berle did not provide further analysis or empirical evidence to suggest that non-owning managers would be more accommodating to the public good than owner/entrepreneurs. The greater discretion of the non-owning manager was questioned earlier in this book, and the pressures on both top and middle managers were seen to be quite intense in the managerial corporation. Empirical evidence is not available on corporate largess by control type, but corporate giving declines as a percentage of profits as company size increases. Corporate charitable contributions have hovered around the 1 percent mark since 1944, with peaks in 1945 (1.35 percent), 1953 (1.22 percent), and 1969 (1.24 percent) – clearly not approaching the tax deductible limit of 5 percent.[51] This suggests that any discretionary power of managers to loosen corporate purse strings to serve larger social needs has not been exercised, or is not overcoming counteracting factors.

Another indicator of social responsibility might be the extent to which companies attach weight to the damage done to community and workers, resulting from relocation decisions. Responsible companies would take these matters into account; impersonal profit-maximizing companies would ignore such externalities – for which they have no legal obligation. There is much episodic information on "abandonments" and divestments,[52] but solid evidence on shutdown rates by firm size and ownership characteristics is sparse. Barry Bluestone and Bennett Harrison show a higher rate of shutdowns – relative to both openings and acquisitions – of New England business establishments by conglomerates than by either independent or other corporate owners, "For every new job created by an independently owned business between 1969 and 1976, 1.6 jobs were destroyed in metalworking and 1 in department stores. But in establishments controlled by conglomerates, for every job created, 4.6 jobs were destroyed in metalworking, while 4 were eliminated in department stores."[53]

Bluestone and Harrison also show that the rate of shutdowns of large manufacturing establishments was higher in the South than in any other part of the country, which they said indicated the accelerating rate at which capital has been able to "outrun" labor:

> It took 75 years for the Northeast to lose the bulk of its old mill-based industry to the Sunbelt and to foreign countries. Yet already, within a much shorter time span, the South has witnessed the overseas migration of textiles, apparel and other non-durables. To select just one industry, between 1971 and 1976, almost 60% of all textile mill closings in the United States – in both union and non-union plants – occurred in the South.[54]

The evidence is inconclusive but suggests that large managerial corporations may be taking advantage of their greater flexibility to abandon local communities and workers more readily than small local enterprises. As noted earlier, this would appear to be the logical outcome of the workings of a market that is efficient in the private but not in a social sense. It implies that large, profit-seeking companies under competitive pressure have a structural bias *toward* irresponsibility, in the sense of greater capability of externalization of social costs through abandonment.

The responses of large managerial firms in the last decade to appeals and pressures in the area of pollution control have been profit-protective and have not displayed greater than average concern with nonindustry (larger community) values. U.S. Steel was described by the deputy administrator of the Environmental Protection Agency (EPA) in 1976 as having "compiled a record of environmental recalcitrance second to none,"[55] and other major managerial firms in the steel business also have struggled furiously against environmental controls.[56] General Motors and Union Carbide, leading managerial firms in the automobile and chemical industries, have both been singled out for criticism of their undistinguished performance on environmental issues, and another sizable managerial firm, Hooker Chemical Company, a subsidiary of Occidental Petroleum, has been the subject of exceptional publicity for its role in the contamination of Love Canal and its extensive and sometimes illegal dumping of toxic chemical wastes elsewhere.[57] In the paper and pulp industry a Council on Economic Priorities study of 1970–1971 showed the two leading firms in the industry, International Paper and Crown Zellerbach, both managerial, as being uncooperative in providing data and having undistinguished performance records in pollution control.[58] The two companies that were praised for leadership and innovation in pollution control were Weyerhaeuser and Owens-Illinois, the former still owner controlled, the latter long dominated by the Levis family and probably owner controlled well into the 1960s, when the basic plant designs and control policies were established.[59] The poorest performers, as rated by the council, were St. Regis, Potlatch, and Diamond International, three managerial firms.[60]

In the area of occupational health, the greatest scandals of recent times have been fairly evenly distributed between managerial and owner-dominated firms. In the handling of asbestos, the Tyler, Texas plant owned jointly by PPG and Corning, both owner-dominated firms, provided the materials for a classic case study of occupational hazards and company misbehavior by Paul Brodeur in his book *Expendable Americans.*[61] But industry leader and management-dominated Johns Manville has fought both disclosure and improved safety standards in this hazardous business for decades.[62] Allied Chemical, a firm with strong professional management but a powerful minority-owner contingent on the board, was responsible for the serious mishandling of Kepone, which led to numerous employee casualties and major water pollution – followed by substantial fines and damage suits against that company.[63] Owner-dominated Rohm and Haas moved slowly in protecting employees from the chemical BCME, despite a surge in lung cancer cases in 1962 – the production process was not substantially self-contained until 1968, and the workers were not informed of the mounting evidence that BCME caused lung cancer until 1971.[64] And one of the greatest occupational calamities in modern American history took place under the auspices of the management-controlled firm, Union Carbide, during the cutting of the Gauley Bridge tunnel through silica rock in 1929–1931 in West Virginia, where working conditions were such as to have cost an estimated 476 lives and left 1,500 disabled.[65]

There also appears to be little difference between managerial and owner-dominated firms in their willingness to sacrifice sales and profits in the interest of enhancing consumer health and safety. On automobile safety questions, the major American companies have not been innovators and they vigorously resisted pressures toward seat belts, air safety bags, and other safety changes. Owner-controlled Ford did take a brief, early, seat-belt initiative,[66] but otherwise there has been little difference between the majors. Because GM has been the industry leader, and a dominant firm, its behavior may have been controlling and restrictive of its rivals' options, but neither on safety nor other social issues[67] has GM's performance been encouraging as to the promise of managerial social responsibility. Also relevant is the behavior of the large managerial firms selling cigarettes, which provides impressive evidence of the ease with which management-dominated firms can rationalize aggressive efforts to market unhealthful products where the rewards are sufficiently great.[68]

Berle and other spokesmen for a new statesmanship have pointed to the new professionalism of modern management and to its capacity to take a longer view, which may require attention to the total environment in which the enterprise operates. Ignored, however, is the need for the new professionals to display their capabilities by "delivering the goods" in a reasonably short time.[69] Insofar as large businesses' plans extend into the more distant future, it is almost always in regard to variables over which the firms have some direct interest and potential control, such as access to supplies of raw materials and positioning in markets with significant expected growth. Concern about ecology and the breathability of the air or whether catastrophic weapons will actually be used, or even the preservation of a local urban community, are matters over which the large firms assume they have little control, and, for this and other reasons, these matters fall outside their planning calculus.

The most important "other reason" is that the responsibility for external costs – such as pollution and the hazards of work, consumption, and the general environment – is still very much at issue in the public arena, and business is fighting strenuously to prevent the internalization of these costs that are being pressed upon it. The costs involved are potentially enormous, and although the pressures on business have built up, its resistance also has intensified. Business' reaction in this area has been that of an interested faction, not that of disinterested statesmanship, as Berle suggested. The drive to preserve and expand profits remains dominant in the managerial firm and continues to be reinforced by competitive pressures. Because environmental controls vary in different parts of the United States, as well as between domestic and foreign producers, they not only add the burden of higher costs, but they also threaten competitive disadvantage. This adds to the intensity of resistance to environmental controls and readiness to move production facilities to superior investment climates.[70]

Berle failed to take adequate account of competitive pressures as a constraint on corporate statesmanship. These pressures are sometimes mitigated when there is rapid growth and unique market position, which then allow for greater largess and freedom of action. The leadership of a Xerox or IBM in their golden years, for example, may have taken a more statesmanlike position on some public issues and enlarged their gift-giving and funding of public service programs. But these appear to be special cases of little overall importance. In areas where corporate profits and growth are seriously at stake, even firms in their bonanza years cannot be counted on to sacrifice profits voluntarily.[71] Sometimes, short-term profits are sacrificed in the interest of long-term profits. Sometimes hazards to society and to the company itself are recognized as so costly that accommodation must be made, and the company will face up to these costs instead of continuing to pretend that they are not there or fighting strenuously against government attempts to compel internalization. The Kepone affair, for example, was sufficiently costly and traumatic to Allied Chemical that it triggered the creation of environmental control officers and environmental control procedures, as well as threats of firings for nonreporting of occupational hazards.[72]

In short, the assumption that managerial firms will acquiesce readily to social pressure or needs has no real support in fact or theory. They resist at least as energetically as owner-dominated firms, both resorting to varying combinations of the traditional modes of resistance to community pressures – public relations, litigation, lobbying, bribery, threats to politicians and local communities, or moving to more congenial environs. This may all be done on the grounds of the long-run interest of society in preserving the well-being of the geese that lay the golden eggs. Berle presumably meant more by the new statesmanship and corporate conscience than business' appeals to its own strategic importance and the need to protect its incentives, but he failed to recognize the ease with which corporate/owner self-interest could be transmuted into long-run social interest.

Corporate Responses to External Pressures

The traditional drive toward profitable growth and the force of competition, still powerful and compelling, continue to render voluntary corporate responsibility and the corporate conscience extremely weak reeds on which to base hopes for resolving current socioeconomic problems. According to Berle, the force of external pressures from government and "public opinion" helps produce a corporate conscience. The emergence of a great many consumer-oriented public interest groups in recent decades has given "public opinion" more organizational support and bite and raises the question of whether these organizations, if not a new corporate morality, may be able to induce substantial change in corporate behavior.

There are three major routes through which external pressures are exerted on the corporation:[73] (1) the machinery of corporate democracy – essentially putting up candidates for the board or proposing matters to be voted upon by stockholders in proxies; (2) publicity, boycotts, and withdrawals of business; and (3) lawsuits to force or terminate corporate actions, to activate government regulatory bodies, or to collect damages for alleged corporate abuses. These means are often used together and may be combined with campaigns in the political arena, seeking legislative and regulatory changes.

Board Selection and the Proxy Machinery. Attempts to utilize the proxy machinery are usually viewed by their sponsors as a means of achieving goals through publicity, rather than by winning a majority of votes. This is, in fact, the *only* realistic possibility for proxy-voting campaigns, none of which has ever won a large minority of votes for a proposed director candidate,[74] and whose power to garner votes for other public interest proposals has been modest.

In the most extensive public interest group effort to influence board selection – campaign GM, led by a Washington-based and Nader-affiliated Project on Corporate Responsibility – the group failed in two successive years to obtain 5 percent of the total vote for its proposals.[75] One proposal was to increase the GM directorate by three members, and a trio of public interest directors was named and put forward by the project. Another was to broaden GM's director constituency base to include employees, dealers, and vehicle users. All the proposals were resoundingly defeated.

The project did, however, get two of its proposals included in a GM proxy statement – over GM's strong objections – a significant development, especially because one was a resolution with a social rather than financial content.

Campaign GM was of great concern to the GM management; the selection of Leon Sullivan to the GM board and the appointment of a board Public Policy Committee was their response. But although the public interest groups won several partial victories in Campaign GM, the limits of corporate electoral politics were clearly evidenced. The campaign was carried out during a period of reformist enthusiasm and prosperity. Significant resources were absorbed in the campaign and were used to put up a very prestigious group of nominees for election. The fact that such a group could not make a respectable showing points up the inherent limits of director reform via corporate democracy. Shareholder interests, and management influence over owners and domination of the proxy machinery, seem capable of overpowering any electoral campaign based on appeals to good citizenship. If public interest groups do influence board selection, it is not by direct and electoral processes; it is through voluntary actions of the insiders. Thus the choices of new directors and policy changes are those of the management, not the outsiders. The staying power of challengers is doubtful in the face of sure electoral defeat, carefully calculated management concessions, the ebbs and flows of activist energies, and their less solid institutional base. Efforts by Campaign GM and organizers such as Saul Alinsky to mobilize a middle-class reformer/stockholder constituency on a more permanent basis never got off the ground, foundering on false premises concerning the interest and motivation of small stockholders.[76] Campaign GM ran only two electoral campaigns, then broadened its efforts, and lapsed in the mid-1970s. Other electoral efforts by outsiders interested in responsible (as opposed to more profitable) corporate behavior have been less successful than Campaign GM.

It seems reasonable to conclude, and is generally recognized by reformers, that gaining directorships through the processes of corporate democracy as now constituted, is close to impossible. In some proposals for reform, however, it is suggested that corporate democracy might be altered through legal measures, forcing more disclosure, cumulative voting, and new requirements for director composition and selection methods.

Most campaigns attempting to make corporate activity more responsive to the public interest, including electoral efforts like

Campaign GM, have tried to exercise influence through publicity and moral and economic pressure rather than by effecting board composition changes. During the Vietnam War, corporations such as Dow, GE, and Honeywell were targets of organized campaigns that involved investigation of corporate activities in military contracting; dissemination of information on profits and weapons production; and participation at annual meetings, ranging from polite efforts to ask questions and introduce resolutions to picketing and disruptive acts. These activities broadened and escalated in the late 1960s and early 1970s, no doubt in reaction to the Vietnam War and Nixon's domestic policies, but also reflecting deep-seated social forces that were carving out a more durable place for organized public interest groups.[77]

Public Interest Groups and Campaigns. Whatever the sources, the past decade has witnessed a great proliferation of groups and coalitions, some local and oriented to bread-and-butter issues like redlining, employment discrimination, and electric utility rates, others more national and global in orientation, focusing on issues such as strip mining, illegal political contributions, and corporate investment in South Africa.[78] A significant proportion of the groups specialize in areas such as television programming for children, auto safety, nutrition, health issues, environmental conservation, military issues, or energy issues. Some have focused on particular companies. An important set of public interest groups specializes in "making the law work," serving as public interest spokesmen and women before legislators to seek changes in the law (or oppose unwanted changes), seeking enforcement of existing law, and serving as public advocate in commission processes. Some groups have attempted to form and provide advice to grassroots organizations and local affiliates, others have prepared manuals for activist tactics and strategies; some have developed research specialties, others concentrate on coordination and tactical work. The number of these groups is unknown, but Jeffrey M. Berry, who attempted to locate and study *national* public interest groups in the early 1970s, found 83 of them with Washington offices, which he estimated to constitute at least 80 percent of the total.[79]

Public interest groups concerned with corporations are often small, serviced by relatively young, inexperienced, and transitory volunteers. There are important exceptions, however, including a number of Nader-affiliated groups, and, perhaps most important, the Interfaith Center on Corporate Responsibility (ICCR). The ICCR obtains continuity by its role in coordination of church-based efforts to influence corporations toward social betterment. The "consciousness raising" of Vatican II and the ferment of the 1960s led many churches to organize committees and allocate resources in an effort to help solve social problems. Because the churches have large assets and extensive holdings of corporate securities, church activists quickly gravitated to the dual questions of the morality of holding certain securities (maintaining "clean" portfolios) and the possibility of exercising positive moral influence on corporations whose securities were held.[80]

Reform Through Investor Activism. "Clean" portfolios have been of increasing interest not only to church activists but to other constituencies such as college students, who have exercised pressure on college endowment funds; labor unions, directing some pension investment and with potential influence over a much larger volume of trusteed pension fund assets; foundations; and public pension funds. Portfolios seem to be responsive to public interest issues in rough proportion to their distance from the corporate community. There is an especially sharp break between those that are "in business" (banks, insurance companies, and investment companies) and those that are not (college endowments, churches, unions, public pension funds, foundations). Within each of these two broad classes the same pattern holds – for example, among those "in business," banks, which are closest to the corporate community are least responsive, insurance and investment companies are somewhat more so.

"Ethical investor" behavior could influence corporate decision making through threatened impact on security prices or through other effects of negative publicity. The impact of a cleansing of portfolios on corporate behavior will depend in large measure on the size of the portfolios subject to activist concern, the unity of action of their managers, and market responses to net sales of activist stock. The size of activist portfolios is highly uncertain. College endowments hold only about 1 percent of corporate stock outstanding; foundations, about 2.6 percent; churches, perhaps 2 percent.[81] The total stockholdings of these groups thus amounts to about 5.6 percent of all stock outstanding and approximately 15 percent of all institutional holdings. Profit-oriented holdings clearly dominate the totals, not the institutions most likely to be moved by activist appeals. And only a modest percentage of the most promising institutional totals are likely to be responsive at all to socially oriented appeals.

Even the churches are far from unified on issues of corporate and investor responsibilities. Some 170 church bodies make up the membership of the ICCR, but most of these are small orders with limited assets; the larger diocesan bodies, with larger holdings, may occasionally be induced to join the ICCR on a particular issue, but by and large, they retain a more conservative stance. Members of the business community are important to churches, both as contributors and as lay officers (including investment advisors), which makes for a nonactivist orientation. College endowments also present a complex picture – some investments are constrained by the terms of the gifts, and business advisors are often important in managing university portfolios. University endowment activism, pressed by students, is highly discontinuous and varies by school in intensity and effectiveness.

If activist-influenced portfolios were to sell off the stocks and bonds of disfavored companies, and if the price effects were significant, this could serve as a threat and a discipline. The price effects could be significant if large sums were involved and if market offsets did not exist. There is no systematic study as yet of the market effects of activist-based sell-offs, but they appear to have been small thus far. Not only are the portfolios involved relatively small, but many activists have chosen to hold on to stocks as a basis for positive stockholder intervention. Furthermore, the vast bulk of investors are preoccupied with risk-return considerations. Morally based sell-offs would, in consequence, have little effect on price if alert "amoral" investors took advantage of small deviations in risk-return relationships and bought up the "underpriced" securities. A still further possibility is that activist sales may be offset, or more than offset, by conservative "counteractivist" buying. Public interest activists are likely to command smaller holdings than conservatives, who may choose to "reward" companies for the behavior that activists condemn. There is no quantitative evidence on this subject, but such reactions are known to occur.[82]

Activists' stockholder interventions have a greater potential impact on corporate behavior than the selling of their stock. Intervention includes attending annual stockholders' meetings, assembling proxies to be voted at these meetings, submitting proposals to management for inclusion in proxy statements, and petitioning and negotiating with management. Stockholders have used these same techniques in their own interest for decades to improve disclosure, enhance and protect their rights, and contain managerial self-dealing. In the late 1960s and 1970s social activists increasingly used these vehicles. Such interventions have, in fact, become institutionalized with the assistance of Securities and Exchange Commission (SEC) proxy rules, which require corporations to allow dissident stockholders access to the proxy statements sent out to shareholders and voted upon at annual meetings. SEC rules define the conditions of acceptability for proposals, including technical matters such as lead time of submission, and substantive matters such as truthfulness and the nature of matters to be discussed. Long-standing SEC rules not only barred proposals bearing on the conduct of the ordinary business operations of the issuer, but also those submitted "primarily for the purpose of promoting general economic, political, racial, religious, social or similar causes." Until the 1970s the SEC almost invariably sided with company managements in restricting the scope of proposal submissions; but with Campaign GM, other activist pressures, and some court clarifications, the SEC moved to a more neutral ground. Proxy rule revisions in 1972 and 1976 further eased access; most notable was the change in language relating to "general causes" – the 1972 revision permitted exclusion of a proposal only if the issue raised was "not significantly related to the business of the issuer or not within the control of the issuer." The 1976 revisions proposed replacing the "ordinary business" restriction with a narrower basis of exclusion. Although this proposal was not adopted, the SEC did narrow the scope of matters excluded from discussion.[83]

One of the prime functions of the ICCR is to coordinate the preparation and submission of proxy resolutions. In 1978 more than 75 church groups sponsored 62 resolutions to 48 different companies under the auspices of ICCR.[84] Of the 48 companies, 19 were addressed on loans to or other involvement in South Africa – the focal point of activist proxy pressures in the past few years. But proxy proposals ranged widely, encompassing redlining, equal employment opportunity policies, advertisers' support of violent television programs, and sale of infant formula in Third World countries.

It is difficult to assess the impact of these efforts. Frequently proxy proposals are parts of larger campaigns that may include boycotts, withdrawal of business from offending institutions, and widespread publicity. Campaign sponsors may try to obtain support from institutions – such as foundations, insurance companies, and even banks – with greater influence on managements. Early in the campaign, sponsors usually try to meet with managements to press their case and seek compromise of hostilities.

The Infant Formula Campaign. Some of the campaigns have been sustained for a long time and have had some effect on corporate behavior. In 1974 an ICCR-coordinated campaign was begun to get U.S. producers and sellers of powdered baby milk to alter their aggressive sales policies in Third World countries, where deficient sanitary conditions were alleged to make bottle feeding far more hazardous than breast feeding.[85] A full-time staff person has been in charge of this campaign – still functioning in 1980 – which has included investigation and publication of the facts on the Third World marketing and impact of infant formula, mobilization of church and other investor allies to pressure the companies, discussions and negotiations with managements as means of securing disclosure and the alteration of company practices, and legal and congressional actions to influence corporate behavior.

A lawsuit was filed against Bristol-Myers, one of the major producers of infant formula, by an ICCR member, the Sisters of the Precious Blood. The sisters introduced into the court record the product of an extensive research effort, including affidavits on damage to infants collected from over 15 Third World countries. The legal case, however, centered on the charge that Bristol-Myers made "false and misleading statements" about their overseas promotion and sales of infant formula. The case was dismissed by a district judge in May 1977 on the ground that irreparable damage had not been caused to stockholders. An appeal was initiated by the sisters that was ended by a negotiated settlement with Bristol-Myers in what amounted to a significant victory for the campaign. Bristol-Myers agreed to submit a detailed report to its stockholders, in which each party explained its position; the company agreed to change certain of its marketing practices; and the two sides agreed that they would "plan to continue to exchange views in an atmosphere of mutual respect for each other's good faith."[86]

The ICCR campaign and the lawsuit against Bristol-Myers stimulated the formation of a larger national coalition called IN-FACT (Infant Formula Action), which not only continued action against the U.S. sellers of infant formula but also helped to organize a boycott of Swiss-based Nestlé, the largest seller of baby formula to the Third World, to induce it to desist in its marketing practices. Activist pressures led to a Government Accounting Office study of the problem at the request of Senators George McGovern and Charles Percy and extensive Senate hearings in 1978.

This well-organized campaign is still in progress, but it has already accomplished the following: Extensive publicity has raised questions about the propriety of marketing of baby formula in Third World countries, and especially specific hard-sell practices. This issue has reached stockholders and employees of the companies involved through proxy resolutions and news reports. Dialogues have been initiated with the managements of all the major companies involved. Even Nestlé, strongly resistant to criticism of its practices, has been sufficiently concerned about the adverse publicity and the effects of the INFACT-organized boycott to begin negotiations. The negotiations and publicity have led to some changes in marketing practice. The critics have been especially concerned about the companies' denigration of breast feeding, use of hired nurses as saleswomen, other tactics identifying the product with medical authority, and failure to communicate adequately the dangers of failing to abide by all requisite conditions for sanitary use (especially refrigeration and sterilization). In the preliminary settlement, Bristol-Myers agreed to have product labels state that "breast milk is best for your infant and is the preferred feeding whenever possible." The company also agreed to expand both its instructions on product use and its warnings against misuse. The settlement also stipulated that no free samples were to be given out and that "Mothercraft nurses are to be clearly identified as company employees . . ."[87]

Sales of infant formula to Third World countries have risen steadily during the campaign, which does not prove total ineffectiveness but demonstrates that larger forces (including perhaps a genuine demand factor, as well as a powerful marketing effort) have tended to dominate. The directors of the campaign recognize that company sales efforts are multipronged and that "the companies are responding to their critics while at the same time attempting to maintain, or even increase, their market shares. The changes that these firms have made to date do not significantly alter the outcome of formula promotion in terms of human life."[88] The prime focus of advertising has been switched from the mass market to the medical profession, hospitals, and government health services. Its powers to penetrate the defenses of poor mothers for whom the economics and healthfulness of the infant formula is dubious remains unimpaired. The companies' self-imposed codes of ethics (partly in response to both criticisms and proposals for regulation) suffer from lack of independent scrutiny and inherent conflicts of interest. The campaign managers recognize that, given company incentives to sell and the impossibility of outside pressures controlling all the complex possibilities of marketing, proper controls cannot be achieved by voluntary managerial responses to external pressures that lack coercive power.

The Campaign Against South African Investment. Another sustained campaign has been directed at U.S. corporations doing business with the racist government in South Africa. This campaign has been mounted by several organizations, the main ones being the ICCR and the American Committee on Africa (ACOA).[89] This campaign is older, larger, and more broad gauged (in scope and support) than the infant formula campaign. Public support for this campaign has been strong because South Africa's apartheid system of racial segregation and economic and political discrimination runs counter to the "human rights" values espoused by the Western credo and because the black community in America identifies with the victims of apartheid. This public support adds potency to external pressures on the corporate sector. On the other hand, South Africa is a large and growing market open to U.S. business, which finds the opportunities there attractive and has built up a large stake. The book value of investments of U.S. companies in South Africa at the end of 1976 was $1.6 billion, U.S. bank loans to South Africa totaled $2.2 billion, and the more than 350 U.S. companies with subsidiaries operating there increased their investment by more than 300 percent between 1960 and 1975. Thus a relatively powerful "moral" constituency has had to confront formidable vested interests and perceived profit opportunities.

Although the moral constituency is large, its membership is unorganized and only episodically responsive to campaign efforts. The organizations actually carrying out the campaign are small and have limited financial resources. The ACOA, perhaps the largest of the activist groups specializing in Africa, had a 10-person staff and a total budget of $264,000 in 1977. The ICCR, the other central coordinator of the South Africa campaign, allocated fewer people and a smaller budget to this cause. The *Wall Street Journal* notes that:

> These funds are dwarfed by the reported $4 million that South Africa is spending on advertising and public relations

in the U.S. just to sell its Krugerrand gold coins to U.S. investors. And they are only a fraction of the public-relations budgets of the U.S. corporations that are the principal targets of ACOA's stinging broadsides.[90]

The South African government made payments to the public relations firm of Sydney S. Baron in New York amounting to $650,000 in 1977.[91] A 1979 South African scandal led to the disclosure of a secret expenditure of at least $13 million by the South African government in an influencing-buying campaign, including $11 million or more spent in the United States in trying to acquire control of news media.[92]

The corporations have been asked and pressured to withdraw entirely from South Africa, to refuse to make new investments there, to stop buying from or selling to South Africa or the South African government, and (in the case of banks) to terminate lending to the South African government or business entities. Often, the campaign has involved appeals and proxy resolutions for information on the companies' involvement in South Africa, including information on sales to the South African government and the number of black and white employees in the companies and their wage scales and working conditions. The companies have uniformly opposed resolutions for limiting their freedom of action in South Africa, although, on occasion, they have voluntarily agreed to prepare a report on South African operations for stockholder distribution and (much less frequently) to refrain from further investment pending clarification of South African racial policies. In 1977, out of 13 resolutions voted upon by stockholders on lending to South Africa, withdrawal, or nonexpansion of investments, only three received enough support to be eligible for reconsideration in 1978.[93]

Congressional hearings and reports, boycotts, and a variety of approaches to company managements have also brought pressure to bear on the companies. There have been some results, but thus far these have been modest. As with the baby formula campaign, publicity has been fairly extensive. Many individual stockholders, institutional investors, and boards, as well as the general public, have been made aware of the fact that there is an issue. Whether the issue has been clarified is less certain. The South African government has spent a great deal more money in counterpropaganda than has the campaign, and the *companies* have also argued, spent money, and mobilized support[94] for their contention that (1) things are getting better in South Africa and (2) their presence is a

plus for the blacks of South Africa and weakens apartheid. Whatever the merits of the various arguments, the public has not gotten
a very clear perspective on the issues but, rather, a conflicting mé-
lange, with probably the most prevalent notion that U.S. companies are serving a progressive role in an improving situation.

Because of the publicity, there has been considerable top management attention to the South African issue by those companies
involved, far greater, in fact than company investment would justify. Companies have studied their South African operations
closely, issued reports on their activities, and have debated internally, as well as with outsiders, the proper course of action. Over
100 of these companies have endorsed the "Sullivan Principles,"
which entail commitments to improve working conditions, to increase job opportunities, and equalize pay for equal work done by
black and white workers in South Africa.

Critics of corporate involvement in South Africa say that the
Sullivan Principles, and top management pressures on their South
African subordinates, have produced some tangible but modest
gains for black workers. They also say, however, that the Sullivan
Principles fail on three fundamental counts: (1) they have a limited
economic impact, because black and white workers do not perform the same jobs; (2) they do not challenge the legally institutionalized framework of discrimination operating in South Africa;
and (3) they provide philosophical support for the idea that the
presence of U.S. corporations in South Africa will enhance the
well-being of South African blacks. U.S. companies claim that
they give jobs to blacks on the best terms available in South Africa
and that their presence has a democratizing influence overall. Critics claim that the support given by the U.S. presence and investing
and lending activities to the existing power structure and thus to
apartheid far outweighs the marginal effects of the economic up-
grading of some U.S.-employed blacks. Only 100,000 of the eight
million blacks in South Africa are employed by U.S. companies
and their subsidiaries. Critics also contend that the companies and
their personnel readily accommodate to apartheid and that the
companies' expanded presence and buildup of loans and direct investment further increase their dependence on and interrelationships with the South African government, and make more difficult a challenge to the host government by the companies or by
the U.S. government.[95]

The impact of activist pressures on the companies investing in
and lending to South Africa has been slight. Quite a few small

victories have been won. Three or four companies have sold off their South African operations, several banks have agreed to cease participation in loans to the South African government or its agencies, and several major companies (e.g., Ford, Control Data) have announced a freeze on new investment in South Africa, pending a clarification of apartheid policy. No major commitments have been reduced, however, and some of the smaller sell-offs and agreements to reduce loan participations may have been based on strictly economic considerations. The political instability in South Africa has probably had a far more powerful effect on the flow of U.S. investment than has activist pressures. Nonetheless, neither activist pressures nor political instability has halted the fairly steady and considerable enlargement of U.S. direct investment, sales, purchases, and lending over the past decade or so. It is possible that the rate of increase of these activities has been less than it otherwise would have been, but it has been substantial. Furthermore, many companies have stated that, South Africa being an area of substantial profit opportunity, they have no intention of being deflected from pursuit of those profits by extraneous issues. A typical remark was GM chairman Richard Gerstenberg's statement in 1972 that "South Africa is a growing country with a big future ahead of it, and General Motors is going to stay right here and grow with it."[96] The same *Business Week* article that quoted Gerstenberg stated that U.S. investments in South Africa were then averaging about an 18 percent return. It also asserted that the companies were feeling the pressure to practice a higher level of social responsibility, and Gerstenberg had just visited GM's South African plants to ensure that "GM is hastening the day of racial equality in South Africa." The companies thus claimed that their energetic participation in South Africa was consistent with their social responsibility.

More recently, other companies have reiterated their faith in South African opportunities and their determination to stay. GE was quite explicit that there were a number of factors that might influence its decision, including U.S. policy or market changes, "but one thing [that] would not influence it," a GE spokesman said, is "the requests of activist groups to get out because they say our presence supports apartheid."[97]

Perhaps the impact of U.S. investments, loans, and other economic involvement, on the apartheid system is debatable. The companies operating in South Africa uniformly analyze the facts in ways that justify business as usual. Despite formidable opposition, these companies appear to have made only marginal adjustments in lending and investing policies. Probably the most effective control on U.S. business in South Africa has been via the modest legislation, passed in the 1970s, limiting sales of high technology products (computers, other electronics, and arms) to the South African police and military establishment. This has disturbed the companies, both because of its direct effects and because of its implications for possible future restrictions. But this legislation should not obscure the fact that overall U.S. policy toward South Africa has been quietly supportive of the apartheid government and U.S. business expansion in that country. The U.S. government has provided export–import guarantees and friendly military and political relations have prevailed between the two countries. Under liberal administrations, there has been an escalation of antiapartheid rhetoric, but negligible action; under Nixon, there was an open warmth toward the South African political and military leadership.[98] All administrations, however, have accepted the business viewpoint that expanded U.S. business activity in South Africa is helpful to the victims of apartheid – a position not maintained by the bulk of the black leadership in South Africa.[99]

Structural change and corporate responsiveness

Appeals and pressures by moral constituencies have had only slight effect on corporate behavior. Nonetheless, many leaders of these moral constituencies persist in their hope for change through education, "consciousness-raising," and, ultimately, legislative intervention. They argue, in effect, that their strategies of words and threats are the best they can muster in an environment in which practical options are sparse. These (and other) reformers have also proposed and campaigned for structural changes, partly through persuasion, but also via changes in the law. Given the difficulties encountered since World War II in getting significant structural change through legislation, reform proposals have tended to be modest in scope.

The main legal changes proposed to influence corporate social behavior in the United States have involved either expanded disclosure or changes in the composition of the directorate.

Disclosure

Perhaps the most important of all liberal reforms designed to improve corporate behavior has been "full disclosure." Its successful incorporation into law and regulation in the 1930s followed a systemic disaster and revelations of serious abuses of inside information by corporate control groups. The enactment and institutionalization of a disclosure policy was also facilitated by its ideological virtue and its minimal disturbance of power relationships. Full information is a critical requirement for an efficient market, and the misuse of privileged information also carries a stigma of unfairness. A policy of disclosure is not easy to oppose on grounds of principle. And the enactment of a disclosure policy involved only the requirement of new information flows from the corporation to its stockholders and outsiders. Furthermore, the precise nature of the facts that had to be disclosed – the areas to be encompassed and the specific details to be presented – were circumscribed and subject to interpretation, negotiation, and litigation.

Disclosure, in and of itself, involves no significant change in behavior; its effects are through either induced avoidance of adverse publicity or actions by recipients of the disclosed information. If something potentially damaging has to be disclosed, there is considerable managerial leeway in terms of the format, emphasis, and context. To a degree, detrimental facts may be hidden, softened, or explained away. And even if adverse information must be disclosed, this hardly guarantees reform. Corporate responses to disclosure of adverse information vary, from "toughing it out," to making token gestures, to investing in image-making expenditures in lieu of substantive change. For example, the poor image of being a polluter may be offset by stress on the fact that closing down polluting factories eliminates jobs.[100]

There are other limitations on disclosure policy as a control system. Existing policy arose as a response to abuse of *investors* and is incorporated primarily in securities law and regulations. The information required under securities legislation appears in registration statements and prospectuses required of companies in connection with new issues, as well as in 10-Ks, proxy statements, and other reports to stockholders. The information provided in these documents includes compensation and company stock ownership of the top officers and board, major insider transactions with the company, balance sheets, income statements, and other financial data and matters that might be relevant to investor decision making. When the legislation was passed in 1933, however, there was minimal concern about the larger social impacts of the corporation and the importance of knowledge to consumers, employees, and others affected by corporate activities, although the enabling legislation did allow the SEC to promulgate rules "as necessary or appropriate in the public interest or for the protection of investors." The SEC has steadfastly interpreted this language to mean that *investor* protection is coextensive with the public interest.[101] The rise of public interest groups has brought pressures to loosen the investor-oriented confines of disclosure regulations. In recent years, influenced by this new constituency, the SEC has tried to make the scope of facts relevant to investors more elastic, as in its campaign for disclosure of corporate bribery payments and in its rule allowing investors to participate more actively in communications with stockholders through the proxy machinery. The SEC has been severely criticized by the business community for these actions, which are seen as overstepping the boundaries of SEC responsibilities.

For years, there has been pressure on the SEC to improve and to enlarge the scope of existing disclosure requirements. On matters such as corporate ownership the SEC has refused to press companies to disclose beneficial holdings and it remains difficult to assemble accurate ownership data for even the largest companies.[102] The SEC has also allowed companies great leeway in disclosure on subsidiaries and joint ventures, with the result that publicly available information on these matters is extremely inadequate. Similarly, with the diversification of large corporations, aggregate data have become less and less useful, but the SEC has been reluctant to force data disclosure by meaningful product lines.[103] Pressures have developed for required disclosure of corporate data on the hiring of minorities and women, occupational health hazards, impacts on environment, political outlays and commercial "special payments," and foreign business activities (sales, selling practices, profits, wages, working conditions, governmental relations). Business, however, has vigorously resisted these pressures on the grounds of confidentiality, adverse competitive effects, ease of misuse, and potential cost of the paperwork. This struggle will continue for a long time to come.

The virtues of disclosure are substantial and basic. As noted by President James Madison, "knowledge will forever govern ignorance," and the debate over disclosure is in one aspect a contest for power. Stockholders, workers, the general citizenry, and government cannot argue well, may not even be able to see an issue or its importance, without facts. Workers cannot defend themselves against occupational hazards unless they know what these hazards are.[104]

On the matters regularly subject to disclosure – such as management compensation and insider transactions – exposure has caused restraint and has been a significant preventive force (especially in the context of potential lawsuits by activists and stockholders). It is possible that more disclosure on social issues would also serve as a discipline and incentive, although much of the data would be less meaningful than something like insider transactions.

The weaknesses of disclosure are formidable, however, so much so that a reform program in which it is the centerpiece will be limited, not fundamental. As noted, disclosure involves no compulsion to change behavior and may be disregarded by managements that are not image sensitive. Furthermore, potential image damage may be offset by intensified public relations efforts. There are serious obstacles to getting the relevant facts and avoiding overloading[105] and inundation that weakens the entire disclosure enterprise. Facts do not speak for themselves; they require comparative data and a framework for evaluation. Management compensation and insider self-dealing transactions are unusual in that they require a minimum of context – first, because the public knows about salaries and bonuses from personal experience; second, because conflict-of-interest transactions are questionable in and of themselves. But data on toxic substances, women and minority employees, injuries, and volumes of particles thrown into the air may not convey much out of context.

Ultimately, concern about the potential image damage caused by disclosure may be completely overpowered by the basic profit drive. The infant formula case showed the various lines of retreat that a company may pursue without giving up very much. The South African case showed that where the stakes are great, even a large moral constituency opposing serious violations of human rights has been unable to bring about substantial change. When the corporate interest is important enough, counterpublicity is intensified; the primary media institutions and the government exercise great restraint and give what amounts to tacit support to the business interests involved;[106] and, in the end, disclosure is of little more effect than an appeal to management's social conscience.

Changes in Board Composition

Structural change in the board of directors has also been a long-standing reform favorite for improving corporate behavior. This is understandable, because the board is the legal policymaking body of the corporation, and board selection procedures have long been subject to debate. The domination of the proxy machinery by management, the effective disenfranchisement of the small stockholder, the obvious limits to the effectiveness of corporate democracy all come to a focus in the issue of board selection. If managements dominate boards and perpetuate their control by means of broken-down democratic machinery, why not change the selection processes? If large corporations have become quasi-public organizations, whose responsibilities ought to be coextensive with their power, should not the directorship reflect a broader base? If managements are engaging in questionable political payments, would it not be feasible to attack this problem by requiring independent directors to serve as quasi-auditors and ombudsmen?

As discussed in Chapter 2, however, control over the large corporation is valuable; its possessors will not give it up easily, and they have the resources and influence to protect their positions. Altering the structure and composition of corporate boards to the degree necessary to affect corporate objectives and decisions would require the mobilization of substantial power. Marginal changes in director composition do not affect the basic structure of power. To do that, it would be necessary to transfer board selection from the inside management and existing board to others, and the new group of directors would have to possess the knowledge, capacity, and homogeneity of objective to be able to take command. Reform proposals usually fall far short of the aforementioned, and characteristically do not even give promise of affecting the corporate decision-making process or corporate objectives at all.

More, and/or More Independent, Outside Directors. A prime focus of corporate reformers has been the inadequate power, surveillance, and action of outside directors. During the 1974–1977 "confessional period," with disclosure of widespread corporate political payoffs and external bribery, there was a renewal of the periodic outcry against director failures and a call for increased numbers of outside directors and/or audit committees composed only of outside directors. What is needed, it was said, is "directors who direct" – a rephrasing of the title of a 1934 landmark article by William O. Douglas (subsequently, SEC chairman and Supreme Court Justice) called "Directors Who Do Not Direct."[107] A primary requisite for active, as opposed to merely nominal and rubber-stamp, directors was said to be an outside directorate independent of top management, as only outside directors are in a position to maintain an objective view of issues, to serve as protectors of stockholder interests against potential management self-dealing, and perhaps also to act in some degree as agents of society at large.

The previously stated perspective shaped the SEC's response to the corporate bribery scandals of 1974–1977. In its settlements with companies that were voluntarily acknowledging illegal transactions, the SEC pressed the companies to increase the number of outside directors, to establish audit committees comprised entirely of outsiders, and to revamp internal procedures so that outside directors get more "bad news." In the view of former SEC Chairman Hills, "What is missing on too many boards is a truly independent character that has the practical capacity to monitor and change management,"[108] and the SEC urged voluntary actions by the New York Stock Exchange and industry at large to expand the role and increase the strength of outside directors.

The focus on the importance of the outside director had its legal embodiment in the Investment Company Act of 1940, which required that at least 40 percent of the directors of a registered investment company not be "affiliated" with the firm that manages its investments (the investment adviser), and that the investment management contract be approved annually by either a full stockholder vote or the vote of a majority of unaffiliated directors. The experience with the outside director requirement under the Investment Company Act is not an encouraging testimonial to the usefulness of conventional types of outside director reform. Changes in investment company practices on matters such as excessive management fee rates and the use of brokerage fees to induce the sale of investment company shares were brought about by external pressures – private litigation, SEC actions, and published criticism – not by the actions of independent directors. Cancellations of management contracts and transference to other advisers by vote of outside directors have been extremely rare, although poor advisory performance over extended periods has not been uncommon.[109]

The Investment Company Act machinery is not adequate for

providing independent directors because of its limited definition of an "affiliated" person and the fact that the act left the selection of directors in the hands of the controlling management group. The act defined *affiliated* to include the officers, directors, partners, employees, and substantial owners of the investment advisor or its parent company, and legal counsel of any member of the investment company system. An *unaffiliated* person could thus be a relative, close personal friend, or outside business associate of a key insider. This legislative standard is not very satisfactory, but the fact is that it would be very hard to fix criteria that would prevent insiders from selecting friendly, amenable, and dependent individuals if choice remains in their hands.

Many who appear to take the independent outsider role seriously give surprisingly little attention to the conditions required for director independence. This may be either because establishing conditions of real independence would be extraordinarily difficult or because no serious change is really desired. Increasing the *number* of outside directors is a very practical reform because it combines a stern and moral rhetoric with minimal de facto change in corporate arrangements and outcomes. Thus if there is pressure to do something, but one doesn't think anything *ought* to be done, there is nothing much better than an appeal to business to spruce up its independent directors, voluntarily.[110]

It is possible that the creation of more, and/or more independent, outside directors might be a small but useful step in the evolution of industrial policy. It may even be true that with a larger proportion of outsiders, and outsiders dominant on audit committees, illegal and unethical business practices may be subject to greater constraint. But this is by no means certain. Such practices may be hidden from the outsiders, or even get the approval of the outsiders, if corporate leaders feel that these practices are important for corporate welfare.[111] There is no reason to believe that outsiders selected in the traditional manner would substantially affect corporate policies that are "antisocial" in the sense of externalities abuses.

Constituency Directors. A proposal with more potential for bringing about change than the foregoing is the suggestion that some fraction of the board be made up of members of social groups that have an important stake in the corporation's activities. Among the possibilities would be the company's employees, owners, creditors, dealers, suppliers, customers, governments, and representatives of communities in which the company is located. Traditionally, owners, creditors, large suppliers, and customers have had representation on boards – the latter three not representing social groups, however, but rather particular private interests. Employee representation on boards is very uncommon among large corporations in the United States, as is that of governments.

There has been a certain amount of local community representation on boards, usually by local business representatives and community notables such as college presidents. The past decade has also witnessed the rise in representation of members of self-conscious collectivities, such as women and blacks. These selections, carefully controlled by corporate managements, do bring some pressure to accommodate to outside interests, but they have been of marginal importance in affecting corporate choices.

Clearly, the impact of constituency representation will depend on the number and the proportion of outsiders, their homogeneity, the mode of selection, and their designated and de facto role in decision making.[112] The more modest reform proposals call for systematically adding constituency representatives of a broad character, with these representatives constituting a board minority. This solution suffers from a number of weaknesses. First, identifying which constituencies are to be represented is problematic, and devising and implementing director selection procedures would be extremely difficult and expensive (for consumers, local communities affected by the corporate presence, even for suppliers or employees). Second, if constituencies each had minority representation, boards would be "towers of Babel," with a premium put on logrolling. If constituencies were a minority in the aggregate, and at loggerheads with one another, they might render board meetings unpleasant but have no significant effect on corporate behavior, thus leaving even more corporate business than at the present to be conducted by the insiders without board input. If these constituencies had real power, separately and in the aggregate, the objectives of the organization would be a distillation of the bargaining among the constituencies and the management. Because corporate activity would no longer be unified around the goal of profitable growth, and goals would be subject to periodic shifts, it seems likely that operational efficiency would be impaired. This would not be objectionable if the trade-off gain were value choices that took better account of externalities and overall community long-run needs and preferences. It is not clear, however, that constituency representation would achieve these results. Weakly represented constituencies might be ignored, with coalitions of stronger groups with common interests overriding the others – as happens to a considerable extent at present in labor–management collective bargaining arrangements, where other interests are rarely taken into account. In a system in which diverse and conflicting interests are represented, there is no reason to believe that each (or any) will be properly weighted into corporate decision making. For example, having an environmentalist on the board would hardly ensure a satisfactory corporate environment policy. Even if selected by an environmental constituency there might be problems of competence, breadth of vision, knowledge of corporate practice and strategies, possible cooptation or acceptance of minor trade-off concessions, and lack of power. Environmental impacts are complex, interactive, and additive. To safeguard the environment, individual company policies should be determined simultaneously with that of others, but this would require an overall planning strategy that would not automatically follow even from widespread adoption of constituency representation at the individual firm level.

Thus even if we assumed the practicality of significant or majority constituency representation on boards of large corporations, there would be no reason to expect a balanced incorporation of new and valid values into corporate decision making. Rather, the plausible expectation is arbitrary degrees of influence based on coalition bargaining for concessions that may often be antisocial. That this would adequately compensate for the loss of corporate focus on output and operational efficiency is debatable.

With constituency directors in a minority position, the traditional focus of corporate policy is less likely to be impaired or altered, and the impact of the constituency directors on corporate behavior would probably be small and highly erratic. This is especially likely if board selection remains in the hands of management, as the tendency is to select individuals not likely to "rock the boat." But even potential boat rockers may be ineffectual in the board setting because of their minority status, lack of knowledge and desire to avoid looking foolish, possible cooptation through concessions or other favors, and the tendency of outsiders to accept the board/management concept of the function of the corporations – namely, to protect and advance the interests of the organization by profitable growth. Even with worker participation on boards, the evidence suggests:

> that the ability of management to manage has not been impaired nor have overall enterprise objectives been changed. A process seems to take place in which workers' representatives'

orientation takes on a managerialist coloring and in which their activities become increasingly supportive of management strategies and goals . . . the interests of the most powerful, those at the top of the authority structure, assume a character of accepted values.[113]

In European countries, where constituency directors are required by law, or selected as common practice, company employees are the main or exclusive constituency represented. In the late 1970s, in seven European countries the law required representation of workers on large company boards. The German codetermination system, the best known and most fully developed, uses a dual board to accommodate the employee/director input. The management board is concerned with operating matters and has no constituency representatives, but the "supervisory board," comprised of between a third and a half labor representatives, has oversight responsibilities and power to select the top officers. Legislation in 1976 increased workers' representation from one-third to 50 percent in virtually all large companies (over 2,000 workers), although equality is diluted by the fact that the chairman always represents business and has an extra vote in case of deadlocks.[114]

The German system was imposed on strategic sectors of industry (coal and steel) by allied military authority after World War II, with the support of organized labor, partly in response to those industries' close collaboration with Nazi expansionism. It was extended by law to other sectors, initially with one-third worker representation – although expanded to the 50 percent level in the case of large companies in 1976, as noted. The expansion of worker representation was acceptable because the system had proved, on balance, more than tolerable to industry. The cost was that labor as *the* constituency group had to be more carefully attended to and its interests taken into somewhat greater account in decision making. In particular, it meant greater union power at the shop/floor level and parallel diminution of management authority in work scheduling, health and safety standards, and performance assessment. Codetermination also posed a potential threat to management's freedom of action in investment planning, mergers, and divestment, but this threat has not materialized in practice.

The advantages of codetermination to management have been substantial. One is that, apart from work scheduling and practices, organized labor's interventions in managerial areas have been modest, often even supportive of management. Other advantages have been better morale, greater labor peace, and improved productivity.[115] In fact, in Great Britain and Italy, several companies have voluntarily proposed worker representation on boards "to diffuse worker militance by pulling unions under the corporate umbrella."[116] Thus by giving the workers a role in management, the union leaders and bureaucracy tend to become more accepting of status quo arrangements and procedures. Already "sympathetic to the profit motive" in Germany, involvement in decision making, where the entire range of company problems is at issue, has made the labor leadership even more understanding of the management view, and part of the codetermination package has been union representation of the company position to the workers.[117] If the worker representatives attain a certain solidarity with management and come to feel a common interest in company prosperity (related to long-term job security), they may work together with management to diffuse more aggressive and radical labor tendencies – even to facilitate necessary cuts in employment, resulting from technological improvements or market shifts. For example, the number of coal miners in the Ruhr was reduced by 53 percent between 1957 and 1968, "almost without difficulty" from the labor side.[118] According to one German trade union leader, "just the fact that the partners steadily sit down with each other leads simultaneously and unconsciously to a situation in which one draws the interest of the other more or less into his thinking."[119]

Two major studies of codetermination in Germany have suggested that extensive labor participation on supervisory boards has not greatly affected corporate objectives, managerial ideology, or company freedom of action. Very few managerial decisions have been contested, as the worker representatives are or become committed to company objectives of profit and efficiency and confine their attention largely to pay structures and conditions of employment. Wage levels are not considered in the orbit of supervisory board discussion, and earnings growth in coal and steel was not higher than that in other sectors of German industry. Where employment cutbacks have been required, "employee's representatives have shown remarkable understanding of economic necessities."[120]

The situation in Germany is unique, of course. German labor evolved out of a background of paternalism with a long interlude of corporate state authoritarianism. Organized labor relies on its political influence with the Social Democratic Party to bring about legislated welfare gains. And wage settlements are arrived at in Germany by interest group negotiations (as compared with industry and firm settlements in the United States). German codetermination has had its successes during a period of rapid expansion and relatively well-sustained world prosperity. It has shown strain since the oil crisis of 1973–1974 and the gradual displacement of more conservative older workers with a new generation of workers. The successes of codetermination may be culture and history specific, and it is not clear that they will be maintained as conditions change in Germany. According to one study, codetermination has been a temporarily successful experiment in labor relations, with labor peace exchanged for greater labor input into decisions affecting working conditions, plus largely marginal advisory rights on other matters.[121]

In Sweden there are two worker/directors in each large company. Swedish labor is politically active and its party has dominated Swedish politics for most of the past 50 years. Sweden's small size and relative homogeneity have contributed to a system that has displayed considerable flexibility and has thrived under exceptional interventionist conditions. In Sweden the private corporation is used for public purposes by means of powerful and innovative tax stimuli, with full employment policies and strong egalitarian tax and welfare programs as complementary policies. The worker directorships and a 1976 codetermination law have given Swedish workers a considerable say in company matters, partly advisory, partly through participation in decisions on plant openings, closings, structural characteristics, and working conditions.[122] Many Swedish managers are concerned about potential paralysis of decision making and factory inefficiency. Others see the trend toward greater worker representation to be under control and to have advantages such as a wage-strike-productivity improvement trade-off. The experience under the new system has been too brief to warrant any final judgment.[123]

In the United States labor has rarely sought board representation. It is not thought to be an end (or means) worthy of the sacrifice of independence, characteristic of the "confrontation" labor relations system. Organized labor has been oriented to bread-and-butter gains via bargaining. The avoidance of directorships and closer collaboration with management could reflect the self-serving interests of the unions, but confrontation-model spokesmen and women claim that their position rests on the lack of value of minority constituency directorships. One or several worker representatives on the board, by law or otherwise, would make labor a "part of management," but faced with the prospect of being regularly outvoted. Board participation entails the responsibility of taking management and other corporate interests into account and thus qualifying the bargaining capabilities of labor. It is certainly not evident that the benefits of a board window and voice via a small minority position outweigh the resultant loss of freedom of union action from the standpoint of labor. The benefits to society at large from such representation are equally uncertain.

Government Representation or Choice of Board Members. There is both theoretical and practical merit to the government's selection of board members: The government is democratically elected and its selections would thus be at least indirectly responsible to the community at large; it represents the community by a traditional and accepted mechanism (democratic vote) that is not accessible to community groups. Government representation or choice is also frequently justifiable in terms of government direct or indirect support of business in the form of subsidies, tax exemptions, and the like. From a practical standpoint, also, its appointments and selections could be relatively inexpensive as compared with constituency elections. Governments are also relatively powerful and permanent entities, and under some conditions their representatives might be more independent and forceful than representatives of lesser constituencies.

Looking at government directorships a little more critically, however, one sees that the impact of government-chosen directors will depend on the power of the government vis-à-vis private corporations and the intended role of the government directors. The government's power relative to a single corporation is obviously great, but this is misleading as the government cannot impose a radical change in relationship between itself and one or a few corporations. Proposals for government directorships on all corporations, or all very large corporations, have been rare. The constituencies that define the government's agenda oppose such representation and have said "No." And the business constituency that excludes government/directors would also, by inference, be able to sharply limit the scope of any public interest proposals submitted by government/directors.

If we assume for the sake of argument that the government is independent of business, capable of fully exercising its potential power, and determined to impose its will on the large corporation, then a further question arises: would the government be satisfied with the right to select less than a majority of board members? If a majority of board members were to be government selected, this would clearly be incompatible with continued private majority ownership and theoretical obligations to owners.

Minority representation by a determined group of government selectees would give the government a "window" and some influence based on bargaining and the threat of more substantial intervention. But the government representatives could be systematically outvoted and bypassed, and the boardroom would be a scene of struggle. This is assuming that the government representatives tried to implement a vision of corporate purpose and accountability at variance with the standard corporate focus on profitable growth. No alternate set of criteria has been formulated on a systematic basis as yet, but if it were, and matters such as internalizing social costs were pushed by the government/directors, the outsiders could be outvoted.

If we make the more realistic assumption that government-selected minority directors would not be the bearers of new criteria of social costs and benefits, and do not represent a government free from business influence, then the likelihood of substantial impact via minority directors diminishes markedly. The fact is that even government corporations, with *all* directors selected by government authority, tend to behave pretty much like private corporations. The Tennessee Valley Authority, for example, has been a notorious polluter, and other government entities have been similarly bottom-line oriented, although there are exceptions even in the United States, where private enterprise is so overwhelmingly dominant.[124]

When government/directors constitute a minority in a private business, the likelihood is great that the goals of management will be accepted without much question. The variation will depend on government power, intent, and implementation procedures. The Communications Satellite Act of 1962, for example, provided for six industry-selected, six stockholder-selected, and three government-selected directors of the new Communications Satellite Corporation. The three government-selected directors are appointed by the president for staggered three-year terms. They do not represent the government, have no responsibilities associated with director selection, and are not required to have any expertise in the communications field. Herman Schwartz notes the fact that industry preferred to have three government-appointed directors to one official government observer, presumably because the latter would be more likely to be well-informed and would have a direct responsibility to government.[125] Schwartz also points out that the government/directors were incorporated into the act in response to claims that the distribution of powers and rights under the original version of the act involved "a complete surrender to AT&T and the other carriers."[126] Government-selected directors were provided by law to represent the public interest in this otherwise privately dominated entity. Schwartz argues convincingly that the mechanism chosen added no significant public interest input.

Another example of government-selected directors on the board of a private corporation is that of the Union Pacific Railroad, heavily financed by the federal government in the nineteenth century, with five out of 20 directors selected by the government. The directors were in a relatively advantageous position, with a quarter of the directorships, a specific purpose – to look after the government's large financial stake in the company – and some mandatory committee memberships; and they were obliged by law to produce an annual directors' report. Nevertheless, the experience was not encouraging on the promise of government directorships – although in some respects, political and economic circumstances may have been less favorable than at present.[127] The Union Pacific directors were largely excluded from the decision-making process and found themselves "relatively powerless both within the company and with the Government." The Credit Mobilier scandal, other self-dealing abuses, and ultimately bankruptcy occurred under this regime, which was abandoned in 1897. As early as 1869, the government directors wrote: "Of what avail is it to have five representatives of the Government in a board of twenty directors? And why, when the interests of the Government outweigh all other interests, should its voice in the management of the road be practically unheard?"[128]

In the contemporary corporate system, minority directors normally have little say in the making of key decisions. Financial and minority owner interests may sometimes exercise considerable influence, with a power to veto or otherwise affect specific decisions, and even to influence management succession, especially under conditions of financial difficulty or managerial weakness and turmoil. But power by financial or large ownership interests can be exercised without position on the board, and, as was noted earlier, the representation of financial interests on the board is often a service to the company rather than an eagerly sought vehicle for exercising influence. Labor's power rests on organization and bargaining strength and can be realized in bargaining processes; even the right to be consulted beforehand on decisions on layoffs or planned organization changes could be negotiated without board representation. Board minority representation might add little or nothing to union (or bank, or government) power or knowledge, and, as noted in regard to unions, might well compromise freedom of action in bargaining processes. Financial institutions in possession of inside information may be hamstrung in using this information with a directorship and thus in a fiduciary relationship to the company's stockholders.[129]

The minority director route, therefore, does not seem very promising as a vehicle for substantially influencing corporate ends and behavior. If board selection remains in the hands of the existing management, constituency minority directorships promise nothing. But even if board members are selected from the outside, especially by unions or government authority, minority status promises little in the way of substantive changes. The majority still rules. Union power and government legislation could exact more and exercise more influence through traditional channels.

Other Board Reforms. It is possible to envisage a great many ways in which boards of directors and corporate structures could be changed to enhance corporate responsiveness, especially if the impact of these changes on corporate growth and profitability would be small (or positive). Christopher Stone describes a number of these with considerable ingenuity in *Where the Law Ends, The Social Control of Corporate Behavior*.[130] Especially worthy of attention here are his proposal for "special public directors" (SPDs) to cope with "problem cases" and his recommendation for assuring that negative information (and liability) will be brought to the attention of top management and board.

SPDs would be appointed by a court or upon appeal to a federal corporations commission to cope with chronically irresponsible companies or companies in industries that have generic problems (occupational health [asbestos companies] or pollution [steel or paper]). SPDs would have typical board director responsibilities, as well as special functions and possibly more specific powers imposed by a court or negotiated with the company.[131] Their powers would include the gathering of information (especially company data) and making recommendations to the company, the courts, or regulatory bodies. Stone also suggests that SPDs might be given the power to fire people, or veto promotions, and even to shut down production. These more drastic powers would be much more vigorously resisted by business. A substitute for an SPD, Stone suggests, might be an internally appointed high-ranking officer, to be responsible for a specific area of concern.[132]

The other interesting proposal developed by Stone is that designed to "mend the corporation information net" by making sure that the higher-ups of a corporation get more negative information from below. If executives are made to know certain things they might rather not know about, they may act either because of their enhanced liability (they cannot plead ignorance) or because they foresee negative consequences that would be wise to avoid. The people at the top can be forced to look at bad news if corporations are required to establish routines for the internal communication of significant information, such as by designating specific officers to be responsible for obtaining and transmitting certain kinds of information to the board, requiring written reports from underlings to higher-ups on actions with high legal risk, and making the failure to gather and transmit certain kinds of information *prima facie* evidence of transgressions.[133]

Some of Stone's proposals are attractive, and if put into place in uncompromised form might make for more responsible corporate behavior in certain specific cases. But they are reforms that address symptoms, not fundamental sources of irresponsibility. This is not a fatal criticism if the symptoms are nasty and their basic sources are not amenable to easy attack. But Stone brushes too lightly past the difficulties that would tend to emasculate any lightweight efforts to reform a powerful and adaptable institution such as the large corporation. It is naïve to assume that corporate behavior may be finely tuned through external intervention. Reforms strongly opposed by business can be critically weakened at numerous levels in the political process – legislative (language, scope, enforcement powers, funding), administrative (appointments, procedures, enforcement), and by court challenges – with the result that many threats have been effectively contained. The more substantial the threatened change, the greater the opposition and likelihood that the proposal will be altered in ways that will reduce its potential effect; but even with modest innovations there are critical slips twixt proposal, legislation, and implementation.

There is also a tendency to underrate the corporations' ability to absorb new instructions, offices, and individuals with special responsibilities, without effect – whether by cooptation, obstruction, tokenism, public relations efforts, or otherwise. Externally imposed rules may be effective, even in the face of conflicting corporate interests, if the rules are clear, simple, and virtually self-enforcing (the number of minority group members to be hired by a particular date, the number of scrubbers of a certain type to be installed per stack). It is a far more difficult matter when the rules are vague, standards of evaluation are uncertain, and stress is placed on gathering information. The freedom of action of corporate underlings is not great, and even outsiders imposed on the corporations by law, such as bank examiners and commissioners of regulatory bodies, are under great pressure to see the corporate point of view.

These constraints on independence and power apply to corporate environmental and occupational health officers, and they would apply also to the SPDs and the lower-level personnel assigned to tasks of transmitting bad news. Stone recognizes these considerations, including the great difficulties that would accompany an attempt to define criteria for bad news deserving top-level attention, but he fails to see how seriously these problems undermine his proposals. But even if these proposals were passed as conceived by Stone, SPD and bad-news-transmittal requirements would have the effect equivalent to that of a flea on the back of a rhino. After passage through the political/corporate mill, they would be the equivalent of second-order fleas (flea on the flea) on the back of a rhino.

It is not possible to alter the structure of power without the mobilization of equivalent or greater power. Reform proposals that envisage radically transforming the control structure of corporations, stripping power from controlling top insiders and conveying it to outsiders can hardly be enacted without a major political struggle. Dominant power is not relinquished, revolutions are not accomplished by the passage of "riders" or carelessness by the vested interests. It is easy to conjure up proposals for altering corporate power structures; it is quite another thing to get such proposals enacted in forms that retain any bite.

Final comments

Remarks on the future of the corporate system rest heavily on the perspective of the viewer. In this book, the perspective throughout – in the analysis of the evolution of corporate goals, structure, and power in the United States, and the review of the proposed roads to corporate reform – stresses the continued primacy of corporate initiatives in economic change, the great powers of corporate resistance to reforms uncongenial to profitable growth, and the resultant strong tendencies toward political immobility. These tendencies are reinforced by this country's business structure, culture, and political traditions.

The primacy of corporate initiatives derives in large part from the successful preservation of corporate autonomy, corporate dominance over basic economic activities, and weak government. By weak, I do not mean incapable of maintaining internal order, lacking in military power, or even inability to exercise commanding authority against the will of business in specific cases – I mean unable to plan and implement effectively some coherent and rational vision of domestic economic and social policy. This is partly a consequence of the sheer magnitude and complexity of the U.S. economy[134] – rendered still less manageable by the extensive internationalization of its leading financial and nonfinancial companies – and the U.S. commitment to a relatively open world capitalist economic order. Add to this the facts of a division of government authority (federal, state, local); the absence of a tradition of efficiency, status, and integrity in government; and sharp social and economic conflict that leads to frequent political stalemate and government irresolution – and the result is government that does not control or initiate, but one that reacts and follows.

I have stressed the fact that despite the increase in size of government in the United States, the government has been confined to support functions and excluded from participation in primary economic activities. This role limitation helps make government a hostage to the business community. Just as managerial discretion is constrained by market forces, so government itself is subject to similar limitations in a dominantly private economy. Government can move only a limited distance in opposition to business desires, otherwise incentives will fail and the pace of economic activity will slacken. Government must either accommodate business or pose a credible threat of radical intervention in cases of business refusals to cooperate. A negligible role as producer reduces the credibility of a government threat both for reasons of dependency and lack of know-how and capacity to displace private with public enterprise.

The confinement of government to a support role also reflects the political power of business, which is an important secondary reason for the absence of a credible threat.[135] Since World War II, liberal democratic leaders in the United States have invariably chosen the route of accommodation under conditions of economic crisis – never engaging in serious confrontation and fundamental challenge.[136] Even at the high points of public disapproval of corporate conduct, business' political clout has always kept really threatening intervention – such as nationalization or the establishment of new public enterprises à la TVA – outside the realm of practical politics.[137] In short, government in the United States has gotten big, but in a functional sense it has been kept in its place – and in its dependent position, with business autonomy well preserved, government has not been well positioned to address major domestic problems with any effectiveness.

Special characteristics of the U.S. culture, economy, and society have also contributed to tendencies toward political immobility. The huge size and great ethnic and social diversity of the United States, which have brought the benefits of a large national market and considerable entrepreneurial and worker vitality, have made for fragmentation, disunity, and a consequent lack of social controllability.[138] Its strongly individualistic culture, perhaps advantageous during the age of the frontier, is inadaptive in an era of increasing interdependence and externalities, where large-scale cooperation, planning, and communal compromises and sacrifices are required. The layering of governments, the checks-and-balances system of authority, and the longtime and continuing hostility of much of the business community to the government and government intervention have contributed to a tradition of corrupt and lackadaisical government.[139] Even an efficient government, commanding the respect and support of all major interest groups in the community, would have a difficult time coping with economic developments in a country as large, and with business as externally involved, as that of the United States. Under the circumstances, the situation is analogous to a blindfolded man leading a herd of untamed buffaloes.

During the twentieth century, capitalism in the United States has demonstrated a significant capacity for adaptation and reform, with numerous serious abuses successfully curbed or eliminated altogether. But these victories came slowly, often incompletely, and were commonly subject to intense resistance. The United States has just passed through another cyclic phase of reform. The democratic upsurge of the 1960s and 1970s, although bringing some improvement in the treatment of the sick and aged, and in

other areas, has not been graciously accepted or conducive to social harmony; it has aroused further conflict over the excessive
largess to the undeserving poor, the unreasonable tax burdens on
the productive classes, and overregulation of business. Only the
bipartisan forces supporting more arms have been relatively immune to this assault.

The modern liberal illusion is that economic and social organization, values, and domestic and international economic and military policies are under some kind of conscious, planned control,
reflecting foresight and collective rational decision making; or that
what is lacking for rational control is a better selection of individuals to high office, a different mix of fine-tuning choices in policy
implementation, or some new inputs into the corporate decision-
making process via changes in corporate boards, disclosure, and
the like. My own view is sharply different. "As if by an invisible
hand" the collectivity of autonomous yet interdependent business
units, sharing the same broad outlook and profitable-growth objectives, pushes society and governments in directions of its own
choosing and preference, allowing the government to ratify *faits
accomplis* and to pick up some of the debris. Size, factionalism, and
indirect rule continue to fulfill Madison's expectations, and have
allowed the "permanent interests" of society to shape its course
and resist change with exceptional effectiveness.[140] This power of
resistance is underrated because the "permanent interests" can
shriek louder than the rest at encroachments on traditional prerogatives. But when threats are deemed serious and democratic
politics yield painful costs, business mobilizes its resources. The
result is a period of conservative "retrenchment" in which the
costs and menace of "Big Government," and threats of internal
and external subversion and aggression, provide the ideological
and political underpinning for a sharp curtailment or liquidation
of reform as with the post–World War I Red Scare, Palmer raids,
and subsequent new era of "normalcy"; the age of Cold War and
McCarthyism; and the late 1970s to early 1980s period of threatening regulatory burden, renewed Cold War, and rearmament.[141]

It is conceivable that despite the conflict and instability so evident today that substantial growth of real incomes will be sustain-
able for some decades to come and that traditional market processes and further incremental government adjustments will bring
under control the intensified inflationary pressures, cope adequately with the more rapid change, obsolescence, and structural
unemployment – and resultant social tensions – and ease us into a

slower growth world. One can conceive of gradual acceptance of an overall wage/price policy of guidelines and negotiated increases (and restraint), government taking up even more slack as employer of last resort, and greater and more explicit partnership arrangements between government and big business to deal with both internal and external needs, somewhat along the lines of French, Japanese, and Swedish models of guided capitalism. This is the most optimistic prospect, which assumes modest external shocks, very gradual change in economic conditions, and relatively benign social and business accommodation. The impact on the democratic system is likely to depend on the severity of factionalism, other challenges to business and government performance, and many unpredictable elements in a rapidly changing domestic and international scene. Less benign political arrangements are easy to imagine under plausible conditions of intensified internal conflict or external shock, such as the aftermath of a "nuclear exchange"; a breakdown in the international trading or financial system associated with local or regional military conflict; disruptions in supplies of critical raw materials; turns to autarchy and trade wars by and among several major powers; an international liquidity crisis; or severe internal social conflicts arising out of inflation, unemployment, and tax-spending (or nonspending) packages that are intolerable to large numbers.

The upsurge of democracy in the West over the past several decades has troubled many business leaders in the United States (and elsewhere), who yearn for greater governability and a more favorable climate of business.[142] In many Third World countries these matters have been rectified by martial law governments that have brought "law and order," with responses from U.S. business people that have ranged mainly from satisfaction to positive enthusiasm.[143] In a revised "stages of growth" model, instead of Third World political economies becoming like us, under conditions of slower growth, severe factionalism, and major systemic shock, we may become more like them.

The scenario is not implausible. Conservatism in the United States has regained vitality not by providing plausible, relevant, and consistent answers to serious questions but, rather, by liberal default – emerging in the wake of growing economic difficulties, social polarization (sometimes carefully stoked),[144] resistance to the welfare state, and the impact of militarization and foreign threats (also sometimes stoked).[145] Its ideological and intellectual components have involved an uncomfortable wedding of a refurbished doctrine of the free market that accommodates the multinational corporation, oligopoly, and small government in its economic package, along with "law and order" and more generous allotments to national defense in its political package.[146] The "New Conservatism" promises peace through even more arms and toughness, a coping with social problems by tighter monetary/fiscal policy, cuts in social outlays, and unleashing free enterprise; reducing the burdens of government by tax and budget cuts and massive deregulation. Although a good case can be made for substantial deregulation, there is no reason to believe that it will be the more costly cartel regulation that is likely to disappear in conservative deregulation programs. If business preferences substantially influence deregulation choices, we might expect a gutting of the Federal Trade Commission, the Occupational Safety and Health Agency, and the Food and Drug Administration, with the Interstate Commerce Commission, Federal Communications Commission, Department of Agriculture, and the Maritime Board left intact or with improved efficiency.[147]

The other main threads of New Conservative policy would inflict large social costs on the lower 80 percent of income-receiving units and increase polarization but still not get at the roots of the economic and social malaise. Conservatism disregards all but a few of the wide array of social and structural changes that underlie national problems, and neither conservative nor liberal remedies deal adequately with the basic forces at work. Japanese, German, and Swedish socioeconomic successes have been associated with modest armaments, extensive government intervention and "dirigisme," and relatively high levels of social accord and harmony. The arms escalation, stress on law and order, and harsh social policy drift of the New Conservatism in the United States look toward the Brazilian or Chilean models[148] rather than toward the more benign models of the industrialized world. They also conform well to the forecasts of Thorstein Veblen made near the turn of the century: "The direct cultural value of a warlike business policy is unequivocal . . . In this direction, evidently, lies the hope of a correction for 'social unrest' and similar disorders of civilized life."[149]

Criticism for economic and other difficulties is often focused on "Big Government." Governments throughout the Free World keep growing; their spheres of power have enlarged, and they possess increasingly formidable means of coercion. This trend, which has been evident for many decades and in many countries, surely represents the workings of some very basic social forces and the demands of major interest groups. The growth of government has closely followed perceived failings of the private market system, especially in terms of economic instability, income insecurity, and the proliferation of negative externalities. Some of these deficiencies of the market can be attributed to its very successes, which have generated more threatening externalities and created demands for things the market is not well suited to provide. It also may be true that the growth of government further weakens the market. This does not alter the fact that powerful underlying forces – not power-hungry bureaucrats or frustrated intellectuals[150] – are determining the main drift. Major business sectors have pressed for government intervention to carve out opportunities and protect their enlarging international interests, to help mitigate domestic and foreign competition, to stimulate growth by subsidy and expansive monetary/fiscal policies, and to assist with the burdens of increasing worker and societal demands (e.g., workmen's compensation, social security, nuclear waste disposal). Given the scope of the demand for more government intervention, and the established trend toward increased government size and power, it is a safe forecast that government's role will continue to grow.

The enlargement in size and role of government has been parallel to and has partly been induced by the growth in size and power of the large corporation. Big business has wanted big government – in selected spheres[151] – and the spread of large firms across national boundaries and their increased mobility has led to demands for governmental aid by injured businesspeople, abandoned workers, and ailing local communities. The "revolution of rising expectations" and the decline in passivity of a number of social groups in recent decades have added to demands on governments – demands that are often mutually incompatible and that governments have been hard pressed to meet. This underlies the paradox stressed earlier; that is, while government size and coercive power are increasing, stalemate and immobility in social and economic policy have become commonplace. This is manifested in inflation, stop-and-go economic policies, spreading authoritarian government (thus far confined to the Third World), and increasing social conflict and tension. These trends will continue, as will the dangers inherent in a world of slowing growth, intensifying internal conflict, and increasing economic interdependence without effective international economic or political authority.

We may be approaching full circle in the West, from the distant era when decentralized economic power was strategic to the emergence of personal freedom and the birth of a "new kind of community [the Greek city-state, that] rested on economic independence"[152] to the present stage of evolution where economic freedom has produced an environment dominated by vast, impersonal organizations that pride themselves on their rootlessness (the "international" corporations) and that respond only to material incentives. These corporations have helped create enormous wealth, but in the process they have broken down traditional community links and brought forth new problems whose solutions require protective and control mechanisms – private and governmental, local, national, and international – that do not now exist.[153] Governments have grown large and potent along with large firms, but they continue to lose the power of initiative in a world of increasingly rapid change, international mobility of resources, and internal political conflict and stalemates. As both governments and large firms continue to expand, a qualitative change in social relationships, in the distribution of power, and in the capacity of societies to respond to crises is taking place. The hope for the future must be that a series of survivable small shocks or minor catastrophes will occur, leading to the emergence of new ideologies, values, and institutional arrangements that will strengthen the powers of small groups and nations to protect themselves and to cope with the lack of international authority. The autonomy and power of the business system, the weakness of government, and the resultant immobility of the whole are such, however, that a bleaker forecast is plausible.

APPENDIX A

Control Classification of the 200 Largest Nonfinancial Corporations, Mid-1970s

Asset size is the basis of inclusion for the 200 companies listed here. The *Fortune Directories,* with end of 1974 data, were used as a starter. This was supplemented by a search for companies excluded arbitrarily by the criteria of *Fortune* selection, especially closely held businesses, companies that were not recognized in the *Fortune* classification system because of a limited industry listing, and any falling between *Fortune*'s categories. *Fortune* includes privately owned companies only if they provide regular financial statements. Thus Cargill, Continental Grain, and the various elements of the Bechtel and Howard Hughes systems have not appeared on the *Fortune* lists, among other closely held companies. Of these, however, only Cargill had an asset total that brought it into our 200, although the Bechtel and Hughes groups would have been included if the separate corporations in the groups had been consolidated. *Fortune* consolidates only if there is a parent-subsidiary relationship via majority stock ownership and the parent consolidates the accounts of the subsidiary in its own balance sheet. Thus, in *Fortune,* AT&T and Western Electric are both included as separate companies, AT&T as the largest utility and Western Electric as one of the 25 top industrials, because, although the latter is wholly owned, AT&T does not consolidate the accounts of Western (or Bell Laboratories) as it does its telephone subsidiaries. This is arbitrary and without economic rationale, and I have consolidated the two and excluded Western Electric from the 200 largest. With the Bechtel and Hughes groups, on the other hand, consolidation would not be of parents and subsidiaries, but of separate corporate entities under common control. On this rationale, a case could be made for consolidating Alcoa and Gulf. I have retained the separate corporate entity concept here in defining the 200 largest, consolidating only where there was intercorporate majority ownership control.

    Fortune also excludes industrial categories, such as construction, apparently on the ground of the small number of large firms in this industry. Using the asset criterion, only Halliburton among construction firms made it into the 200 largest presented here when this restriction was removed. City Investing also qualified for the 200 largest in 1974–1975 on an asset criterion but was excluded from the *Fortune* list because 50 percent of its sales were not derived from manufacturing and/or mining in that year.

Exclusions of companies on the basis of criteria such as irregular financial reporting, which caused the omission of Cargill, has only a small effect on the asset importance of ownership control among large companies – an omission that would be more consequential if the list were extended to the 500 largest. The failure to consolidate the assets of subsidiaries, as in the AT&T–Western Electric illustration previously cited, could result in an understatement of the asset importance of the 200 largest, as they do have a larger structure of subsidiaries than smaller companies. A study done for this writer by David Kronfeld, which consolidated the assets of subsidiaries of the largest companies on a consistent basis, indicated that the total assets of the largest companies were understated by only 5 percent as a result of nonconsolidation.

The control classification used here (column two) distinguishes between *direct* (proximate) and *ultimate* control (see Tables 3.1 and 3.2). The distinction is based on whether or not there is an intervening entity that directly controls a company. If there is a separate proximate control, it will usually be another corporation holding a minority ownership position (if the corporation holds a majority position, the controlled company would be viewed as a part of its parent). The form of ultimate control will depend on the nature of control of the controlling entity. In the case of Coca-Cola, for example, Coca-Cola International (CCI) owned a large minority block of Coca-Cola and could be said to constitute the direct locus of control, but the Woodruff family owned a controlling block of CCI and otherwise dominated CCI in the mid-1970s, so that ultimate control is shown as minority ownership control. It is possible to have more than one subdivision applicable to a single company, as in the case of Eastern Airlines, where ownership, financial interests, and government all have special influence over decision making. This is shown therefore as "B-1/2/3." Where there is a difference between proximate and ultimate control, as in the case of Coca-Cola, column two will show ultimate control first and then proximate control in brackets.

As described in Tables 3.1, 3.2, and 3.3, I use an eight-rubric classification system: A. Inside Management; B. Inside Management and Outside Board; C. Majority Ownership; D. Minority Ownership (with subdivisions): E. Intercorporate Ownership; F. Government; G. Financial; H. Receivership.

A and B together comprise cases of management control in the usual sense, the division resting on an assessment of the power of the outside directors in the sharing of control. Where the top insiders clearly dominate the board in representation, activity, and prestige, and the outsiders are correspondingly lacking in these characteristics and in sources of power, the company qualifies for class A. Where the outsiders are strong, active, and numerous, and/or company power is in transition (see Chapter 2 under "Stability and instability of control via strategic position."), or where the distribution of power at the top is uncertain, I have placed the company in class B. The distribution between A and B is thus somewhat arbitrary, more so than is the distinction between management contol (A + B) and the other control categories.

A subdivision classification system is used under the various major categories, most importantly, under Management Control (A and B), as a method of dealing with the frequent existence of shared power, where substantial ownership interests, outside financial groups, and government have special influence over corporate decision making, which still falls short of primary power over the selection of the top officers and the full range of key business decisions. Subdivision 1 also includes cases where the directors own a very sizable block of stock that gives them a respectable ownership stake (defined here as 1 percent to under 5 percent). The other major subdivisions are discussed in the text at various points – with respect to financial and government control in the relevant parts of Chapters 4 and 5.

The problems of dealing with minority ownership control are discussed in broad terms in Chapter 2 and in relationship to specific classification problems as well in Chapter 3. As used here, minority ownership control includes cases where the ownership is large enough to establish a presumption of control (10 percent or more), or where a group demonstrably in control (usually the active managers) own 5 percent or more of the voting stock. The subdivisions under minority control mean the following: 1 refers to the ownership of 10 percent or more of the voting stock and active participation in the management; 2, ownership of 10 percent or more, but not part of the active management; 3, ownership of 5 and under 10 percent by the control group, and active management involvement; 4, ownership of 5 and under 10 percent by a group not active in management, but still capable of exercising decisive power.

Where a company's stock is held in a large block by individuals or institutions not active in management, latent power must be assessed, which necessitates a case-by-case analysis, giving consideration to size of holding, representation on the board and board committees, and other evidence of influence such as the prestige, policy, and lines and record of intervention of the owner(s). Where the holding is in excess of 10 percent, with board representation as well, I have tended to posit control. Thus in cases like Alcoa and Gulf, with Mellon family holdings greater than 10 percent, and continued family representation on the boards, I have classified the companies as minority owner controlled, although management power in both companies has been steadily increasing and these could be viewed as instances of shared power, or as management control with a strong residual ownership constraint. These are transitional cases, with control shared in a slowly changing and uncertain fashion between the active management and second or third generation entrepreneurial family members. The method of handling such cases here gives an upward bias to the enumeration of ownership control in Tables 3.1, 3.2, and 3.3.

In many cases, basic structural facts – especially those pertaining to stockholdings and board composition and history – yield fairly straightforward information on corporate control. The locus of power of Amerada Hess, with Leon Hess the top officer and controlling 22 percent of the stock, is clear; as is the control of companies at the other end of the spectrum, with great financial solidity and extreme diffusion of stockholdings (GM, GE, AT&T, ITT). But in the great number of intermediate cases, structural facts are not sufficient. In these cases, information is often revealed when the placid surface of the power structure (as seen from the outside) is disturbed by a corporate trauma – the suicide of an Eli Black, the internal deposition of Robert Sarnoff, the resignation of Donald Kircher as chief executive officer of Singer in 1975, or the Security and Exchange Commission's pressure on Gulf or Phillips to disclose illegal payments and install corrective procedures. Such traumas often produce a flood of private and public disclosures that tell something about the pretrauma distribution of authority, and they may also identify a new power alignment at its point of installation. The balance of power may shift thereafter, so that inferences from the moment of truth lose their authority as time elapses and circumstances change.

In essence, the method pursued here has been to focus on structural facts, especially ownership and board composition, in an historic context, with close attention to strategic moments of truth and any other public manifestation of evidence on the locus of key decision-making power. In difficult cases, resort has been made to interviews with company officials, board members, and bank officers. In some cases, company officials have been willing to provide specific or at least order-of-magnitude figures for large family holdings, dispersed over a sizable number of nondirector relatives and foundations, none of which come near a 5 percent value that would require disclosure in a corporate proxy statement. Extensive use has been made of company histories, biographies of company officials, court records, government hearings and reports on industries and problem areas, and the rich array of newspaper and magazine articles on companies and strategic individuals. The table that follows in this appendix provides a complete list of the 200 nonfinancial companies included in this study, with their control classifications in the mid-1970s and the basis of and sources for that classification.

It is impossible to include all the "salient facts" that went into the construction of this table, but the third column provides a few that are strategic and of special interest in each case. "OD" stands for officer/director.

Primary sources of information are presented in summary form in column four. Many companies were subjected to fairly extensive investigation. General inquiries such as the Celler Committee investigation of conglomerates, the Metcalf Committee studies of corporate disclosure and ownership, the Patman Committee investigations of relationships banks and nonfinancial companies were examined, as well as commercial bank, investment company, and insurance company data on security holdings, biographies and company histories, brokerage firm reports, and business publications and services (Moodys, Value Line). Company documents such as annual reports, proxies, 10-Ks, prospectuses, and SEC reports on security transactions were examined, sometimes over an extended time period. The symbol "Ps" refers to the aggregate of public documents issued by a company. The symbol "I" refers to interviews carried out with company personnel; the number of such interviews is indicated in parenthesis. "SR" refers to a student report on a company; those cited here were of quality that afforded new material or insights, sometimes based on direct contacts and often tapping 30 or more biographical sources (exclusive of company documents). "WSJ" stand for *Wall Street Journal*, "BW," for *Business Week*, "NYT," for the *New York Times*. Space limitations restricted the inclusion of the vast bulk of materials that contributed to this assessment.

Company	Control classifi- cation	Salient facts	Primary sources of information
Allegheny Power System	A-3	OD ownership under 0.1%; stock diffused	Ps
Allied Chemical	B-1	Strong management; strong board of direc- tors owning just under 10% [a]	Ps; I(2); *For- tune* 10/54
Allied Stores	B-2	OD ownership under 0.5%; 2 bankers on executive committee; Prudential ownership 8% [b]	Ps; *Best's Mar- ket Guide*
Aluminum Company of America (Alcoa)	D-2(a)	Mellon family hold- ings c. 14.3% direct, 22% total	Ps; SR; WSJ 3/20/73; 4/5/73
Amax	D-1 (a)	Selection Trust, 11.5%; 3 directors, 4.7%; Socal, 20%	Ps; BW 8/2/76
Amerada Hess	D-1 (b)	CEO ownership, 22+%	Ps

Company	Control classifi-cation	Salient facts	Primary sources of information
American Airlines	B-2/3	OD ownership under 0.1%; heavy debt conc. in large N.Y. banks and insurance companies; restrictive covenants and financial representation on board relevant	Ps; SR
American Brands	A	OD ownership under 0.5%; inside board	Ps; I(1); SR; BW 2/10/73
American Can	A	OD ownership under 0.5%; Moore family also under 0.5% and role marginal by 1975	Ps; SR
American Cyanamid	A-1	OD ownership, 2.3%; inside board	Ps: I(1); BW 9/4/72, 3/24/75; *Forbes* 6/15/64; *Chemical Week* 1/3/73
American Electric Power	A-3	OD ownership under 0.1%; wide dispersion	Ps
American Natural Resources	A-3	OD ownership under 0.1%; wide dispersion	Ps
American Telephone & Telegraph (AT&T)	A-3	OD ownership under 0.1%; wide dispersion	Ps
Anaconda	A-2	OD ownership, 0.2%; financial difficulties in early 1970s; strong banker representation [c]	Ps; BW 12/1/75; Sen. Metcalf, *Congressional Record* 1/10/75
Arlen Realty & Development	C	Cohen, 29%; Levien, 14%; all directors, 53%	Ps; SR
Armco Steel	A	OD ownership under 0.5%	Ps; SR
Asarco	A	OD ownership under 0.5%	Ps; H. O'Con-nor, *The Guggenheims;* I. Marcosson, *Magic Metals*

Company	Control classifi- cation	Salient facts	Primary sources of information
Ashland Oil	A-1	OD ownership, 2.4%	Ps; Forbes 11/15/74
Atlantic Richfield (Arco)	A	OD ownership under 1%	Ps; BW 1/13/75; *Forbes* 7/15/76; NYT 3/19/72
Avco	D-4	Harringtons, 6.1%; OD ownership, 8.8%	Ps; Forbes 4/1/74
Baltimore Gas and Electric	A-3	OD ownership under 0.1%	Ps
Beatrice Foods	A-3	OD ownership under 1%	Ps; *Finance Magazine* 5/72; NYT 3/19/72
Bendix	A	OD ownership under 1.0%	Ps; *Forbes* 3/15/74
Bethlehem Steel	A	OD ownership under 0.1%	Ps
Boeing	A	OD ownership under 0.5%	Ps
Boise Cascade	B-1	OD ownership 1.3%, but 5 directors with 45,000 – 120,000 shares each	Ps, BW 6/1/74
Borden	A-2/3	OD ownership under 1%; Chemical Bank on executive commit- tee	Ps
Burlington Industries	A	OD ownership under 0.5%; Morgan, 7.7% sole voting rights	Ps; SR; BW 3/10/73, 3/2/74; *Fortune* 6/64
Burlington Northern	A-3	OD ownership under 1%	Ps
Burroughs	A	OD ownership under 0.5%	Ps; SR; BW 3/11/67; *Forbes* 11/1/68; *Michigan Business Review* 5/75
Cargill	C	90% owned by Cargill & MacMillan families	*Dun and Brad- street Report* 9/27/76; BW 5/10/79

Company	Control classification	Salient facts	Primary sources of information
Carolina Power & Light	A-2/3	OD ownership under 0.5%; CEO of Wachovia on board and relations extensive	Ps
Caterpillar Tractor	A	OD ownership under 0.5%	Ps
Celanese	A	OD ownership under 0.5%; Dreyfus, 6.1%	Ps; *Forbes* 8/1/76
Central and Southwest	A-3	OD ownership under 0.1%	Ps
Champion International	B-2	OD ownership under 1%; 2 Morgan interlocks, 4.4% sole voting stock & other relationships	Ps; BW 3/1/76; *Forbes* 1/1/74
Chessie System	B-1/3	OD ownership, 1.5%; 10 out of 11 outside directors, and several strong	Ps; *Forbes* 11/15/75
Chrysler	A	OD ownership under 0.5%	Ps
Cities Service	B-1/2	OD ownership, 2.8%; 3 banks on board, two on executive committee	Ps
City Investing	B-1/2/3	OD ownership, 1.8%, 3 out of 6 on the executive committee bankers	Ps
Cleveland Electric Illuminating	A-3	OD ownership under 0.5%	Ps
Coastal States Gas	D-1(b)/3	CEO ownership, 10.5%	Ps
Coca-Cola Company	D-4 [E-2]	Woodruffs, 5.1+%, 2 on board, R. D. Woodruff chairman of finance committee	Ps; SR
Colgate-Palmolive	B-1	OD ownership, 4.2%	Ps
Columbia Gas	A-3	OD ownership, 0.1%	Ps
Commonwealth Edison	A-3	OD ownership under 0.1%	Ps

Company	Control classifi- cation	Salient facts	Primary sources of information
Consolidated Edison	A-2/3	OD ownership under 0.1%; 2 major banks represented on board, financial difficulties	Ps
Consolidated Natural Gas	A-3	OD ownership, 0.1%	Ps
Consumers Power	A-3	OD ownership under 0.5%	Ps
Continental Can	A	OD ownership under 0.5%; National Bank of Detroit, 6.7% sole voting rights	Ps
Continental Oil	A	OD ownership under 1%	Ps
Continental Telephone	A-3	OD ownership under 0.5%	Ps
Control Data	A-1/2/3	OD ownership, 2.6%; financial difficulties in mid-1970s led to divi- dend restrictions, etc.	Ps (1974 10-K, pp. A14-19); BW 7/30/66; *Fortune* 2/68
CPC International	A-2	OD ownership, 0.5%; Chemical Bank on ex- ecutive committee	Ps
Crown Zellerbach	A-1	Zellerbach family and foundations about 1%; OD ownership, 0.4%	Ps
Deere	D-1(b)	Deere family, 15+%; CEO & family (Deere related), 3.6%	Ps; I(1)
Detroit Edison	A-3	OD ownership under 0.1%	Ps
Dow Chemical	D-3	Dow family at least 8.8% in 1972; 3 Dows on board in 1975	Ps; I(1); Metcalf Report of 1973
Dresser Industries	A	OD ownership under 0.5%	Ps; BW 5/24/76
Duke Power	A-1/3 [E-2]	Duke Endowment ownership 24% in 1975, but management dominated[d]	Ps: annual re- ports of Duke Endowment

Company	Control classifi-cation	Salient facts	Primary sources of information
E. I. Du Pont De Nemours (Du Pont)	D-1(a) [E-2]	Christiana Securities, a family holding company, held 28% in 1975	Ps; Metcalf Report of 1973
Duquesne Light	A-3	OD ownership under 0.1%	Ps
Eastern Airlines	B-1/2/3	Laurance Rockefeller ownership 2.3%, including entire pre-ferred-stock issue, with representation on board; financial diffi-culties and big debt in 1974	Ps; SR
Eastman Kodak	A	OD ownership under 0.5%	Ps
Eaton	A	OD ownership, 0.5%	Ps
El Paso Company	A-1/3	OD ownership, 1.2%	Ps
Exxon	A	OD ownership under 0.5%; Rockefellers 0.2% [e]	Ps
Federated Department Stores	A-1	OD ownership 1.3%; Ralph Lazarus, 1.1% in 1975	Ps
Firestone Tire & Rubber	D-1(b)	Firestone family ownership approximately 28%	Ps
Florida Power	A-3	OD ownership under 0.1%	Ps
Florida Power & Light	A-3	OD ownership under 0.1%	Ps
FMC	A	OD ownership under 0.5%; Chase, 7.5% sole voting rights, First National Bank of Boston, 6.2% sole voting rights	Ps
Ford Motor Company	D-1(b)	Ford family owned approximately 40% of voting shares	Ps; SR

Company	Control classifi- cation	Salient facts	Primary sources of information
General Electric	A	OD ownership under 0.1%	Ps: SR; BW 7/8/72; *Forbes* 3/15/74, 5/15/74
General Foods	A	OD ownership under 0.1%	Ps; SR; *Fortune* 3/64; BW 8/25/73
General Motors	A	OD ownership under 0.1%	Ps; SR, *Fortune* 1/72; BW 11/11/71, 3/16/74, 6/28/76; WSJ 2/5/74
General Public Utilities	A-3	OD ownership under 0.1%	Ps
General Telephone & Electronics (GTE)	A-2/3	OD ownership under 0.5%; banker controlled from reorganization in 1935 until 1951 *f*	Ps; I(2); *Fortune* 9/59; BW 12/16/72
General Tire & Rubber	D-1(b)	O'Neil family owned 20+%	Ps: SR; I(2); NYT 5/15/76
Georgia-Pacific	B-1	OD ownership, 2.3%; 3 nonofficer directors own 1.1 million shares	Ps
Getty Oil	C	Getty controlled 64% in 1974–1975	Ps
B. F. Goodrich	A-2	OD ownership under 0.5%; Weinberg, Goldman Sachs on executive committee – important in rebuff of Northwest Industries in 1969	Ps; SR; *Fortune* 7/69; *Forbes* 12/1/75
Goodyear Tire and Rubber	A	OD ownership under 0.5%; Morgan, 5% sole voting rights	Ps; SR
W. R. Grace	A-1	Graces at least 2.2%; Flick group 12% in 1976	Ps: I(1); BW 10/13/75, 1/8/75; WSJ 4/2/75

Company	Control classifi- cation	Salient facts	Primary sources of information
Greyhound	A-3	OD ownership under 0.5%	Ps: BW 9/31/75; *Forbes* 2/15/67, 6/1/74
Gulf States Utilities	A-3	OD ownership under 0.1%	Ps
Gulf Oil	D-2(a)	Mellon interests, 10.2%	Ps: CDE Transportation Directory
Gulf & Western Industries	D-3	CEO Bludhorn, 6.7%; OD ownership, 8.4%	Ps
Halliburton	A	OD ownership under 1%	Ps
Hercules	A	OD ownership under 1%	Ps
Honeywell	A	OD ownership under 0.5%	Ps
Houston Lighting & Power	A-3	OD ownership under 0.1%	Ps
International Business Machines (IBM)	A	OD ownership under 0.5%; T. Watson Jr., only 0.13%	Ps; *Fortune* 3/72; BW 1/22/72, 3/24/75
Illinois Central Industries	A-3	OD ownership under 1%; Union Pacific, 11.6% voted by 3 bank trustees	Ps: *Forbes* 3/15/71
Ingersoll-Rand	B-1	Grace and Phipps on board with 2.7% and long relationship	Ps; I(1); BW 6/22/74
Inland Steel	B-1	OD ownership, 1.6%; 2 Block brothers still on board though no longer officers	Ps
International Harvester	A	OD ownership under 1%; McCormick was CEO but family hold- ings small	Ps; I(2); SR; BW 3/17/75
International Paper	B	OD ownership under 0.5%; management in flux after Hinman dy- nasty (1940–1971); Morgan, 6.7% sole voting rights	Ps; NYT 12/16/73; BW 8/12/72, 4/28/73; *Forbes* 6/15/76

Company	Control classification	Salient facts	Primary sources of information
International Telephone & Telegraph (ITT)	A-3	OD ownership under 0.5%; Geneen in command into 1979	Ps; SR; BW 4/26/72, 8/11/73, 12/20/76; WSJ 7/13/79; Sampson, "The Geneen Machine," *New York,* 4/23/73
IU International	A-1/3	OD ownership, 2.1%	Ps
Johnson & Johnson	A-1 [E-2]	OD ownership, 2.9%; Johnson Foundation, 16%	Ps; SR
Kaiser Aluminum & Chemical	D-1(a) [E-2]	Kaiser Industries owned 38.3% in 1975; Kaiser family 38.7% of KI	Ps
Kennecott Copper	A-2	OD ownership under 0.5%; Page of Morgan on executive committee and Morgan important owner/lender (4.6% sole voting rights)	Ps; I(1)
Kraftco	A-2/3	OD ownership under 0.5%; 2 bankers on executive committee, including MHT	Ps; SR
K Mart	A-1	OD ownership, 9.7%, 9.2% of which was held by Stan Kresge [g]; Morgan, 5.4% sole voting rights	Ps; NYT 9/19/76
Litton	A-1	OD ownership, 4.1%	Ps; I(1); SR
Lockheed	B-1/2/3	OD ownership, 3.3%; period of severe financial difficulty & banker + government loans with severe constraints	Ps; NYT 10/8/75, 10/7/76, 10/17/76; WSJ 12/17/73, 6/11/76

Company	Control classifi- cation	Salient facts	Primary sources of information
Loews	D-1(b)/3	Tisch family owner- ship, 43.6%	Ps; SR; *Fortune* 5/71, 6/75; BW 4/12/69, 11/1/76
Long Island Lighting	B-2/3	OD ownership under 0.5%; strong board, long Citibank repre- sentation	Ps
LTV	A-2	OD ownership under 0.5%; bankers strong since brink of failure in 1970–1971	Ps; *Fortune* 6/73; *Forbes* 8/15/70, 4/15/75
Lykes–Youngstown	D-1(b)/3	Lykes family owner- ship, 12.3%	Ps
Marathon Oil	A	OD ownership under 0.5%	Ps; SR
McDonnell Douglas	D-1(b)	McDonnell family ownership, 19.3%	Ps
Middle South Utilities	A-3	OD ownership under 0.1%	Ps
Minnesota Mining & Manufacturing (3M)	D-2(a)	McKnight interests 7.4%; Ordway inter- ests 7.2%	Ps; SR; Huck, *Bread of the Tartan*
Mississippi River Corporation	A-1/3	OD ownership, 2.6%; took over majority control of Missouri Pacific in 1974; Capital Research, 5%	Ps
Mobil Oil	A	OD ownership under 0.5%	Ps; *Finance Magazine* 11/75
Monsanto	B	OD ownership under 1%; instability since Queeny retirement in 1965, earnings decline in early 1970s	Ps; SR; BW 11/4/72
NCR	B-2	OD ownership under 0.5%; financial diffi- culties in early 1970s, two bankers on board	Ps; BW 5/26/73; 12/8/73
National Steel	D-3 [E-3]	OD direct ownership 3.4%, but ODs important in M. A. Hanna, last reported as 13% [h]	Ps; I(2); SR

Company	Control classification	Salient facts	Primary sources of information
New England Electric System	A-3	OD ownership under 0.1%	Ps
Niagara Mohawk Power	B-2/3	OD ownership under 0.5%; managerial instability in early 1970s; strong banker presence	Ps: I(1)
Norfolk and Western Railway	A-2/3	OD ownership under 0.1%; Penn Central 12% voted by 3 independent trustees; 3 bankers on board, one on executive committee	Ps; I(1)
Northeast Utilities	A-3	OD ownership under 0.1%	Ps
Northern Natural Gas	A-3	OD ownership under 0.5%	Ps
Northern Indiana Public Service	A-3	OD ownership under 0.5%	Ps
Northern States Power	A-3	OD ownership under 0.1%	Ps
Occidental Petroleum	A-1	OD ownership, 2.3%, Armand Hammer 1.9%	Ps; BW 2/26/72
Ohio Edison	A-3	OD ownership, 0.1%	Ps
Owens-Illinois	B-2	OD ownership under 1%; Citibank strong in lending, presence on executive committee; Morgan, 2.3% sole voting rights	Ps; I(1); SR
Pacific Gas and Electric	A-3	OD ownership under 0.1%	Ps
Pacific Lighting	A-3	OD ownership under 1%	Ps
Pacific Power & Light	A-3	OD ownership under 0.5%	Ps
Pan American World Airways	B-2/3	OD ownership under 0.5%; major financial difficulties in early 1970s; bank power effective [i]	Ps; SR; NYT 3/11/73; BW 11/13/71; WSJ 10/31/74

Company	Control classification	Salient facts	Primary sources of information
Panhandle Eastern Pipeline	A-2/3	OD ownership under 0.5%; 2 bankers on executive committee including vice chairman of Morgan	Ps
Penn Central Transportation	H	In receivership	Ps
J. C. Penney	A	OD ownership under 0.5%; Chase 7.2%; Morgan 4.2%; Citibank, 3.4% sole voting rights	Ps; BW 8/10/74, 8/18/75
Pennsylvania Power & Light	A-3	OD ownership under 0.1%	Ps
Pennzoil	A-1	OD ownership, 3.1%; Liedtke Brothers 1.4%	Ps; BW 3/23/74; *Forbes* 5/1/74, 9/15/74
Peoples Gas	B-2/3	OD ownership under 0.1%; strong board, including investment banker on executive committee	Ps
Pepsico	A-1	OD ownership, 2.2%; Herman Lay 1.7%; Morgan, 8.6% sole voting rights	Ps; SR
Pfizer	A	OD ownership under 1%	Ps; BW 6/16/63; *Fortune* 8/65; *Chemical Week* 10/13/71; *Barrons* 7/23/73
Phelps Dodge	B-2	OD ownership under 0.5%; strong board; 3 major bank representatives	Ps; I(1)
Philadelphia Electric	A-3	OD ownership under 0.1%	Ps
Philip Morris	A-1	OD ownership, 1.2%; Cullmans 0.6%; Morgan, 7.7% sole voting rights	Ps; SR; BW 1/27/73, 12/6/76

Company	Control classification	Salient facts	Primary sources of information
Phillips Petroleum	A	OD ownership under 0.1%	Ps; BW 3/10/73
Potomac Electric Power	A-3	OD ownership under 0.1%	Ps
PPG Industries	D-2(a)	Pitcairn ownership, 15.7%, 3 board representatives	Ps; *Fortune* 6/15/67
Procter & Gamble	A	OD ownership under 0.5%	Ps
Public Service Electric and Gas	B-2/3	OD ownership under 0.1%; heavy banker representation on board and on executive committee	Ps
Ralston Purina	D-2(a)	Danforths controlled 19.7%	Ps
Rapid-American	D-1(b)/2	Ricklis ownership, 14.5%, but in financial difficulty and under severe banker constraint	Ps; BW 3/25/72, 2/16/74, 11/3/75; WSJ 11/16/76
RCA	B-1/2	OD ownership under 0.5% but 3 individuals who each acquired blocks of 1 million shares, were on board; Lehman and Lazard on executive committee	Ps
Republic Steel	A	OD ownership under 0.5%; closely interlocked with other Cleveland corporations[j]	Ps; SR; BW 6/9/73
Reynolds Metals	D-1(b)	Reynolds family ownership, 17.7%	Ps
R. J. Reynolds Industries	A-1	OD ownership, 4.2% (McLean ownership, 3.5%); various Reynolds trusts and Wachovia holdings over 5%	PS; SR; NYT 5/20/73

Company	Control classification	Salient facts	Primary sources of information
Rockwell International	A-1	OD ownership, 4.4%; Rockwells ownership, 3.3%	Ps
Safeway Stores	B-1	OD ownership, 1.8%, McGowans ownership, 1.4%, 2 McGowans on executive committee and other strong board representation	Ps; NYT 1/13/74
Santa Fe Industries	A-2/3	OD ownership under 0.1%; strong banker representation on executive committee	Ps; *Forbes* 5/1/75, 5/1/76
Seaboard Coast Line Industries	A-2/3	Mercantile officer on executive committee[k]; OD ownership under 0.5%	Ps; *Forbes* 5/1/74
Joseph E. Seagram & Sons	D-1(b)	Bronfman family ownership, 32.6%	Ps
Sears Roebuck	A	OD ownership under 1%	Ps; WSJ 2/10/75; BW 10/5/75; *Forbes* 10/1/74
Shell Oil	A [E-1]	Shell Petroleum N.Y. (Subsidiary of Royal Dutch/Shell), 69.4%	Ps; NYT 6/20/76; Beaton, *Enterprise in Oil*
Signal Industries	A-1	OD ownership, 1.6%	Ps; BW 1/5/74, *Forbes* 11/15/76
Singer	B	OD ownership under 0.5%; poor performance & management transition in 1974–1975	Ps; SR; *Fortune* 12/75; *Forbes* 1/15/74, 1/15/77
Southern Railway	B-3	OD ownership under 0.5%; strong board	Ps; I(1); *Forbes* 5/1/74
Southern California Edison	A-2/3	OD ownership under 0.1%; strong banker representation, 2 on executive committee	Ps

Company	Control classification	Salient facts	Primary sources of information
Southern Company	A-3	OD ownership under 0.1%	Ps
Southern Pacific	B-3	OD ownership under 0.5%; strong and numerous outside board, mainly customers	Ps; SR
Sperry Rand	A	OD ownership under 0.1%	Ps; SR; *Forbes* 4/1/75; BW 2/24/71
St. Regis Paper	A-1/2	OD ownership, 2.8%; 2 representatives of financial institutions on executive committee	Ps; I(1)
Standard Oil of California	A	OD ownership under 0.1%; Rockefellers ownership, 2.3%; Chase, 1.8% sole voting rights	Ps; BW 12/7/74; *Forbes* 10/1/75
Standard Oil of Indiana	A	OD ownership under 0.5%	Ps; SR; *Financial World* 11/8/72; WSJ 1/6/75; BW 11/23/74
Standard Oil of Ohio	F [E-2][1]	BP (51% owned by British government) owned 25% of voting stock, 3 director representatives from BP	Ps
Sun Oil	D-2(a)	Pew family interests, 36.5%	Ps: SR; Rottenberg, "Sun Gods," *Philadelphia Magazine,* 9/75; BW 7/27/74
Tenneco	A-3	OD ownership under 0.5%	Ps; SR
Texaco	A	OD ownership under 1%	Ps: BW 12/11/71; *Forbes* 2/1/75
Texas Eastern Transmission	B-1/3	OD ownership, 2.6%	Ps

Company	Control classifi-cation	Salient facts	Primary sources of information
Texas Utilities	A-3	OD ownership under 0.1%	Ps
Textron	A-1	OD ownership, 2.1%	Ps; BW 6/8/74
Transco Companies	D-1/3	OD ownership, 2.2%; Stone & Webster, 8.2%	Ps
Trans World Airlines (TWA)	B-2/3	OD ownership under 1%; financial difficul-ties in early 1970s in-creased banker influ-ence	Ps; I(1); SR; WSJ 1/7/76, 11/19/75; BW 7/7/75, 8/9/76
TRW	A-1	OD ownership, 1.6%	Ps; SR
UAL	B-2/3	OD ownership under 1%; 2 bankers on ex-ecutive committee	Ps; SR; BW 1/16/74, 6/29/74
Union Carbide	A	OD ownership under 0.1%	Ps
Union Electric	A-2/3	OD ownership under 0.1%; strong bank presence on executive committee	Ps
Union Oil	A	OD ownership under 1%	Ps; SR
Union Pacific	G-3	OD ownership under 1%, and Harriman in-terests also under 1%, but Harriman–Brown Brothers strategic po-sition strong[m]	Ps; SR; *Forbes* 6/1/77
Uniroyal	A-1/2	OD ownership under 1%, Du Pont interests under 5%; 2 financial institutional represen-tatives on executive committee as financial position weakens	Ps; I (1)
U.S. Steel	A	OD ownership under 0.1%	Ps; NYT 2/29/71; BW 3/9/74
United Technologies	A	OD ownership under 1%	Ps: I(3); *Forbes* 4/15/75

Company	Control classification	Salient facts	Primary sources of information
United Telecommunications	A-1/2/3	OD ownership, 1.9%; 2 bankers on executive committee; Citibank, 2.3% sole voting rights	Ps
Virginia Electric & Power	A-3	OD ownership under 0.1%	Ps
Warner Lambert	A-1	OD ownership, 2%	Ps; SR
Western Union	A-3	OD ownership under 0.5%	Ps; BW 6/8/74
Westinghouse	A-2	OD ownership under 0.5%; financial difficulties and strong bank presence in 1975	Ps; SR; BW 10/2/71, 7/20/74, 2/3/75
Weyerhauser	D-3	OD ownership, 6.35%	Ps; *Duns Review* 4/73; BW 5/25/75, *Forbes* 9/15/75
Williams Companies	D-3	Williams family ownership, 7.25%	Ps
F. W. Woolworth	B-1	OD ownership, 2%; old families still potent on board	Ps; *Fortune* 1/60; BW 6/29/74, 3/31/75
Xerox	A	OD ownership under 0.5%	Ps; *Duns Review* 12/72; BW 5/4/74, 4/5/76

[a] A brief discussion of the Allied Chemical control situation is given in Chapter 2 under "Active versus latent control."

[b] Institutional holdings of voting stock by banks, insurance companies, investment companies, and nonprofit organizations are shown in this appendix where they are 5 percent or more of the total, with full voting rights held by the institution. Banks frequently have partial or no voting rights over trust department stock; insurance companies and investment companies usually have full voting rights. A discussion of the quantitative importance and power implications of institutional stock holdings is provided in Chapter 4 under "Institutional stock ownership."

[c] Anaconda had serious financial difficulties in the early 1970s, associated mainly with the expropriation of its properties in Chile. John Place, a vice-chairman of

Chase, was named CEO of Anaconda in 1971, which led to the claim that Anaconda was banker controlled. It is clear that banker power was great at that time and that Place was acceptable to the bankers, whose approval was surely a necessary condition for appointment at that time. Whether he was a representative of Chase is more dubious. He had lost out in the contest for number two man at Chase and was reportedly looking for his own top spot – circumstances that raise doubts as to his permanent loyalty to Chase. He subsequently consolidated his power and was clearly in charge of Anaconda by 1975, with bankers on the board, but by then they were in no position to command. See Robert Walker, "A Banker for Anaconda," *New York Times,* May 23, 1971; Senator Lee Metcalf, "The Relationship Between the Anaconda Company and Major Banks," *Congressional Record,* January 10, 1975; Letter from John Place, put into the *Congressional Record* by Senator Metcalf, Jan. 10, 1975.

[d] The relationship of the Duke Endowment to control of the Duke Power Company is discussed in Chapter 3 under "The decline in family control."

[e] On the question of Rockefeller power in the oil companies and the issue of family power more broadly, see Chapter 3 under "The decline in family control."

[f] The problems involved in assessing control of GTE are discussed in Chapter 4 under "Bank directorships."

[g] See the discussion of control of Kresge in Chapter 2 under "Active versus latent control."

[h] The officers and directors of National Steel owned less than 5 percent of its voting stock in 1975, according to the company's proxy statement. But several of the key company officers were also owners and officers of M. A. Hanna Company, which had divested from about 26 percent in 1929 to a lesser figure, but probably still over 10 percent, by 1975. For these reasons, I classify National Steel as directly controlled by an outside corporation, ultimately by minority ownership interests.

[i] See Chapter 4 under "Restrictive covenants."

[j] See the discussion of the Cleveland system of interlocks in Chapter 6 under "Interest groups."

[k] See Chapter 4 under "Financial influence over the large corporation in the 1970s" for further discussion of this case.

[l] This anomalous case is one in which the proximate control of a major U.S. company is in the hands of a foreign company, which in turn is under the legal control of the British government via a 51 percent stock ownership.

[m] This case is discussed in Chapter 4 under "Financial influence over the large corporation in the 1970s."

Control Classification of a Sample of 40 of the Largest Nonfinancial Corporations, 1900–1901

In contrast with Tables 3.1 through 3.3, 5 of the 40 companies shown on Table 3.4 and listed here are included as instances of shared control – for example, Northern Pacific is shown as controlled by both the Great Northern interests of James J. Hill (minority control) and the Morgan interests (financial control). In part, this use of shared control is a result of the more limited and sketchy quality of data for the earlier period – but this was also an era of unusual banker entrepreneurship and aggressive empire building by groups of people sharing power in the process.

To maintain symmetry with the tables for 1975, I use the following symbols in the classification columns: "AB" for Management Control (without attempting any distinction between the two); "C" for majority ownership control; "D" for minority ownership control; "E" for intercorporate control; "G" for financial control – but with parenthetical indication of banker (b) or speculator (s) involvement. Two control letters separated by a slash are used to indicate shared control in five cases.

Company	Proximate control	Ultimate Control
Amalgamated Copper	G(s)	G(s)
American Sugar Refining	AB	AB
American Telephone and Telegraph	AB	AB
Armour	C	C
Asarco	D	D
Atchison, Topeka and Santa Fe	AB/G(b)	AB/G(b)
Baltimore and Ohio	E	AB
Burlington	AB	AB
Chesapeake & Ohio	E	AB
Chicago, Milwaukee and St. Paul	D	D
Consolidated Gas	AB/G(a)	AB/G(s)
Consolidated Tobacco	C	C
Crucible Steel	D	D
Du Pont Powder	C	C
General Electric	G(b)	G(b)
Great Northern Railroad	D	D
International Paper	D	D
Lackawanna Steel	C	C
Massachusetts Electric	AB	AB
Metropolitan Securities	G(s)	G(s)
Missouri Pacific Railroad	D	D
Pennsylvania Railroad	AB	AB
Peoples Gas	D	D
Philadelphia Electric	AB/G(s)	AB/G(s)
Pittsburgh Coal	G(s)	G(s)
Pullman	D	D
National Biscuit	G(s)	G(s)
New York Central Railroad	D/G(b)	D/G(b)
Northern Pacific Railroad	D/G(b)	D/G(b)
Reading Railroad	G(b)	G(b)
Rock Island Railroad	G(s)	G(s)
Southern Pacific Railroad	E	D
Southern Railway	G(b)	G(b)
Standard Oil	C	C
Union Pacific Railroad	D	D
Union Traction	G(s)	G(s)
U.S. Leather	D	D
U.S. Rubber	D	D
U.S. Steel	G(b)	G(b)
Western Union	AB	AB

The Relationship Between Control Form and Performance for 72 Large Nonfinancial Firms, 1967–1976

A statistical analysis of the relationship between control form and economic performance for 72 large companies, for the 10-year period 1967–1976, is summarized in tabular form here. The six main headings are the performance variables used in the analysis – rate of return on equity (ownership interest), abbreviated as ROE; rate of return on total investment (ROI); growth in earnings per share; sales growth; payout rate (the ratio of dividends to earnings); and risk. The risk accepted by a firm in its choice of activities is measured here by the fluctuations in its ROE during the period in question (more precisely, the standard deviation of ROE). The other performance measures are included as mean values for the applicable years.

The control forms used in the analysis were simply Management Control versus Ownership Control, but the latter was subdivided into cases of *strong* ownership control (where the control group owned 20 percent or more of the voting stock) and *weak* ownership control (where the controlling owners held more than 5 percent but under 20 percent of the stock). Presumably, any performance differences would show up with greater clarity where there is strong control. Of the 72 companies studied here, 45 were classed as management controlled, 19 were under strong ownership control, 8 under weak ownership control. In the tabulation, C_s indicates that only the strong ownership control cases were included in the analysis; C indicates that all ownership control cases were included.

In testing for the effect of control form, one must correct for other variables that may also influence performance. The most obvious are the nature of the companies' business and company size. In this analysis the companies are sorted by principal activity into 15 industries, corresponding to two-digit classes in the Standard Industrial Classification system (e.g., food, chemicals). Industry, designated by "I" in the analysis, commonly shows powerful effects on performance variables. Asset size is also included as an independent variable, shown as "A" and computed as an average for the period examined. Some of the performance variables are also included as independent variables in the analysis of other performance variables where we would expect an important relationship between the two. For example, firms that incur more risk do so in the hope of higher returns and would anticipate a positive risk-return relationship. Including risk as an independent variable in the analysis of factors influencing ROE does yield a statistically significant result in one case (see column two of the table). In other cases, also, performance variables were used as independent variables, although they are not shown on the table unless they proved to be statistically significant.

In company selection, in order to make meaningful comparisons, only relatively undiversified companies were included; conglomerates such as ITT and LTV were ignored. The fact that there were many more management-controlled than owner-controlled companies in the large company universe imposed a constraint, as some industrial classes were lacking in owner-dominated companies. Most of the companies included were among the 100 largest industrials, but a handful from the next hundred were brought in to bolster a few industry classes (a list of the 72 companies appears after the statistical tabulation). Four of the 72 companies were involved in mergers that seriously affected the performance data for the earlier five-year period (1967–1971), and they were excluded from the analysis of those years and for the entire 10-year span – for those two sets, the sample is confined to the remaining 68 companies. For the years 1972–1976, two columns are shown – the first, including 68 companies maintaining consistency with the analysis for 1967–1971; the second, covering all 72 companies.

A covariance analysis was used here, based on the SPSS (Statistical Package for the Social Sciences) program. The numbers shown on the table are probability values, so that to meet a 5 percent significance test standard the value should read 0.05 or less. Thus for the first performance variable, ROE, the table shows for 1967–1976 a probability value for C of 0.757 (M−), indicating no significant relation between control form and ROE. The situation is not much improved by a strong control comparison (C_s = 0.677 (M+)). The M+ for the latter, in fact, shows that ROE is positively related to management control, although the relationship is not statistically significant at a 5 or 10 percent probability level. R^2 is the conventional statistical measure of the variability explained by the factors included in the analysis. Thus an R^2 of 0.651 in the last column, row 4, indicates that 65 percent of the variation in the performance variable is explained by the factors used as independent variables in this analysis.

As seen from the table, the main hypothesized relationship in the literature on the effects of managerialism – that management control yields a lower rate of return to investors – is given very limited support in this analysis, where neither ROE nor ROI display any significant relationship

	1967–1971	1972–1976 (1) (68 companies)	1967–1976 (2) (72 companies)	1967–1976
Return on Equity (ROE)				
C	$C = 0.923$ $I = 0.000$ $R^2 = 0.624$	$C = 0.394$ $I = 0.000$ $R^2 = 0.646$	$C = 0.567(M-)$ $I = 0.000$ $A = 0.116$	$C = 0.757(M-)$ $I = 0.000$ $R^2 = 0.640$
C_s	$C_s = 0.700$ $I = 0.001$ $R^2 = 0.611$	$C_s = 0.837$ $I = 0.001$ $\text{Risk} = 0.040$ $R^2 = 0.196$	$C_s = 0.773(M+)$ $I = 0.001$ $R^2 = 0.625$	$C_s = 0.677(M+)$ $I = 0.001$ $R^2 = 0.651$
Return on Investment (ROI)				
C	$C = 0.984$ $I = 0.000$ $R^2 = 0.664$	$C = 0.542$ $I = 0.000$ $A = 0.065$ $R^2 = 0.646$	$C = 0.623(M-)$ $I = 0.000$ $A = 0.049$ $R^2 = 0.616$	$C = 0.804(M-)$ $I = 0.000$ $A = 0.070(+)$ $R^2 = 0.669$
C_s	$C_s = 0.545$ $I = 0.000$ $R^2 = 0.662$	$C_s = 0.642$ $I = 0.002$ $\text{Risk} = 0.080$ $R^2 = 0.675$	$C_s = 0.691(M+)$ $I = 0.001$ $A = 0.080$ $R^2 = 0.620$	$C_s = 0.527(M+)$ $I = 0.000$ $R^2 = 0.689$
Payout Rate				
C	$C = 0.169$ $I = 0.005$ $R^2 = 0.395$	$C = 0.058$ $A = 0.063$ $R^2 = 0.207$	$C = 0.066(M+)$ $A = 0.066(+)$ $R^2 = 0.264$	$C = 0.080(M+)$ $I = 0.018$ $R^2 = 0.387$
C_s	$C_s = 0.107$ $I = 0.011$ $R^2 = 0.419$	$C_s = 0.075$ $I = 0.039$ $A = 0.046$ $R^2 = 0.374$	$C_s = 0.072(M+)$ $I = 0.013$ $A = 0.048(+)$ $R^2 = 0.430$	$C_s = 0.079(M+)$ $I = 0.037$ $R^2 = 0.402$

Risk

C

C	= 0.178	C	= 0.014	C	= 0.011(M−)	C	= 0.055(M−)
I	= 0.000	I	= 0.000	I	= 0.000	I	= 0.000
A	= 0.024	R^2	= 0.722	R^2	= 0.624	R^2	= 0.656
R^2	= 0.720						

C_s

C_s	= 0.176	C_s	= 0.215	C_s	= 0.047(M−)	C_s	= 0.496(M−)
I	= 0.000	I	= 0.000	I	= 0.000	I	= 0.000
A	= 0.021	ROE	= 0.014	R^2	= 0.634	R^2	= 0.717
R^2	= 0.729	R^2	= 0.775				

Sales Growth

C

C	= 0.131(M+)	C	= 0.001(M−)	C	= 0.001(M−)	C	= 0.292(M−)
I	= 0.002	I	= 0.000	I	= 0.000	I	= 0.000
Risk	= 0.001	Risk	= 0.021	Risk	= 0.022	Risk	= 0.003(+)
R^2	= 0.586	R^2	= 0.542	R^2	= 0.538	R^2	= 0.546(+)

C_s

C_s	= 0.135(M+)	C_s	= 0.001(M−)	C_s	= 0.001(M−)	C_s	= 0.140(M−)
I	= 0.002	I	= 0.000	I	= 0.000	I	= 0.000
Risk	= 0.001	Risk	= 0.020	Risk	= 0.035	Risk	= 0.002
R^2	= 0.604	R^2	= 0.542	R^2	= 0.532	ROE	= 0.115
						R^2	= 0.558

Growth in Earnings per Share

C

C	= 0.001(−)	C	= 0.795(M−)	C	= 0.794	C	= 0.536(M−)
I	= 0.000	R^2	= 0.260	R^2	= 0.260	R^2	= 0.236
A	= 0.022						
R^2	= 0.451						

C_s

C_s	= 0.002(M−)	C_s	= 0.733(M−)	C_s	= 0.718(M−)	C_s	= 0.481(M−)
I	= 0.000	R^2	= 0.261	R^2	= 0.339	R^2	= 0.237
A	= 0.018						
R^2	= 0.450						

List of companies included in analysis of control and performance,
1967–1976

Alcoa	Firestone Tire	National Steel
Amax	Ford Motor	Owens-Illinois
Amerada Hess	General Foods	Pepsico
American Brands	General Mills	Pfizer
American Cyanamid	GM	Philip Morris
American Home Products	General Tire	Phillips Petroleum
Armco Steel	Georgia Pacific	PPG Industries
Asarco	Getty	Ralston Purina
Arco	Goodrich	Republic Steel
Ashland Oil	Goodyear	Reynolds Metals
Beatrice Foods	Gulf Oil	Rohm & Haas
Bethlehem Steel	International Harvester	G. D. Searle
Boeing	International Paper	Shell Oil
Borden	Kaiser Aluminum	Squibb
Burlington Industries	Kennecott	Standard Oil of Cal.
Carnation	Kraftco	Standard Indiana
Chrysler	Eli Lilly	Standard Ohio
Coca-Cola	Loews	J. P. Stevens
Continental Oil	Lykes-Youngstown	Sun Oil
Crown Zellerbach	Marathon Oil	Union Carbide
Deere	McDonnell-Douglas	Union Oil
Dow	Merck	Upjohn
Du Pont	Mobil Oil	Warner Lambert
Exxon	Monsanto	Weyerhauser

to form of control. Growth in earnings per share also shows no significant relationship to control form for the entire period or for 1972–1976, but it does display a significant relationship for 1967–1971, thus giving some support to the main hypothesis. Payout rate is shown here to be significantly related to control form (at the 10 percent significance level for the 1972–1976 years and for the decade as a whole), but the relationship has the wrong sign, showing managerial control to be associated with a higher payout rate, whereas "a major component of the managerial theory is the hypothesis that a greater percentage of internal funds are retained and invested than are warranted to maximize stockholder welfare." (Henry Grabowski and Dennis Mueller, "Managerial and Stockholder Welfare Models of Firm Expenditures," *Review of Economics and Statistics,* February 1972, p. 9.) The risk measure shows statistical significance again for the 1972–1976 years and the entire decade, and here the sign is in conformity with the usual hypothesis that managerial control is associated with risk avoidance. Sales growth shows a statistically significant relationship to control form for 1972–1976, although not for the earlier years or the entire decade. But except for the years 1967–1971 (for which the relationship is not statistically significant), the sign is not consistent with the hypothesis that manager-dominated firms strive more than owner-dominated firms for growth – the minus signs indicate a negative relationship between managerial control and rate of sales growth.

Notes

Chapter 1. Corporate Control: Background and Issues

1 See testimony of Federal Trade Commission Chairman Michael Pertschuk in U.S., Congress, Senate, Judiciary Committee, Subcommittee on Antitrust and Monopoly, *Mergers and Industrial Concentration*, 95th Cong., 2d sess. (Washington, D.C.: Government Printing Office, 1978), p. 155.

2 See M. A. Adelman, "The Measurement of Industrial Concentration," *Review of Economics and Statistics*, November 1951, pp. 261–296; Joe S. Bain, *Industrial Organization*, 2d ed. (New York: Wiley, 1968), Chaps. 4–6; Alfred D. Chandler, Jr., "The Structure of American Industry in the Twentieth Century: A Historical Overview," *Business History Review*, Autumn 1969, pp. 255–298; Carl Kaysen and Donald F. Turner, *Antitrust Policy* (Cambridge, Mass.: Harvard University Press, 1959), Chap. 2; G. W. Nutter, *The Extent of Enterprise Monopoly in the United States, 1899–1939* (Chicago: University of Chicago Press, 1951); William G. Shepherd, *Market Power and Economic Welfare* (New York: Random House, 1970), Chaps. 7 and 10; F. M. Scherer, *Industrial Market Structure and Economic Performance* (Skokie, Ill.: Rand McNally, 1980), Chaps. 3–4.

3 See esp. Bain, *Industrial Organization;* Kaysen and Turner, *Antitrust Policy;* Shepherd, *Market Power;* and Scherer, *Industrial Market Structure.*

4 See Bain, *Industrial Organization* and Scherer, *Industrial Market Structure.* See also Paolo Sylos-Labini, *Oligopoly and Technical Progress* (Cambridge, Mass.: Harvard University Press, 1962) and Franco Modigliani, "New Developments on the Oligopoly Front," *Journal of Political Economy*, June 1958, pp. 215–232.

5 The competitive challenge that underlies dynamic oligopoly behavior is frequently based on either rapid technological change in the industry, which enforces technological progressiveness as a simple condition of survival, or the fact of producer orientation to export markets, where formidable domestic and other foreign competition must be met head on.

6 Japanese firms, for example, have at least two sources of internal

pressure that give them an expansionist and technologically progressive orientation: (1) their high fixed costs of labor, resulting from their traditional and patriarchal system of lifetime employment and (2) their extensive resort to bank borrowing and very high debt-to-equity ratios, which drive them toward aggressive efforts to expand earnings to provide assured cover for their heavy fixed-interest and amortization payments. See Richard E. Caves and Masu Uekusa, *Industrial Organization In Japan* (Washington, D.C.: Brookings Institution, 1976), pp. 37–41; Ezra F. Vogel, *Japan as Number One, Lessons for America* (Cambridge, Mass.: Harvard University Press, 1979), pp. 135–137.

7 See Mary Kaldor, *The Disintegrating West* (New York: Hill and Wang, 1978), Chaps. 1–3. On the loss of technological flexibility in the automobile and steel industry, see William J. Abernathy, *The Productivity Dilemma: Roadblocks to Innovation in the Automobile Industry* (Baltimore, Md.: Johns Hopkins, 1978); Walter Adams and Joel Dirlam, "Big Steel, Invention and Innovation," *Quarterly Journal of Economics,* May 1966, 167–189; D. Ault, "The Continued Deterioration of the Competitive Ability of the U.S. Steel Industry: The Development of Continuous Casting," *Western Economic Journal,* March 1973, 89–97; U.S., Congress, Senate, Judiciary Committee, Subcommittee on Antitrust and Monopoly, *Study of Administered Prices in the Steel Industry,* 85th Cong., 2d sess. (Washington, D.C.: Government Printing Office, 1958).

8 See Walter Adams and Joel B. Dirlam, "Private Planning and Social Efficiency," in A. P. Jacquemin and H. W. deJong, eds., *Markets, Corporate Behaviour and the State,* Nijenrode Studies in Economics, Vol. I (The Hague: Martinus Nijhoff, 1976), pp. 216–223; Emma Rothschild, *Paradise Lost: The Decline of the Automobile-Industrial Age* (New York: Vintage, 1973).

9 Ralph E. Lapp, *The Weapons Culture* (Baltimore, Md.: Penguin Books, 1969), esp. Introduction, Chaps. 1, 2, and 8; Herbert F. York, *Race to Oblivion: A Participant's View of the Arms Race* (New York: Simon & Schuster, 1970); Mary Kaldor, *The Disintegrating West* (New York: Hill and Wang, 1978), esp. Chaps. 1, 2, and 7; Emma Rothschild, "Boom and Bust: Department of Defense Annual Report, Fiscal Year 1981," *New York Review of Books,* April 3, 1980, pp. 31–34.

10 Francis M. Bator, "The Anatomy of Market Failure," *Quarterly Journal of Economics,* August 1958, pp. 351–379; Allen V. Kneese and Blair T. Bower, *Managing Water Quality: Economics, Technology, Institutions* (Baltimore, Md.: Johns Hopkins, 1968), Chap. 5.

11 A pure public good is consumed nonexhaustively, as the consumption by one individual of, say, national defense, does not reduce that of another, and the social cost of extending consumption to another individual is therefore zero. In this case the ideal price would also be

zero. See Neil M. Singer, *Public Microeconomics* (Boston: Little, Brown, 1972), Chap. 6.

12 Francis M. Bator, *The Question of Government Spending* (New York: Harper & Row, 1969); James Buchanan, *The Demand and Supply of Public Goods* (Chicago: Rand McNally, 1969).

13 On the theory of work effort trade-off, see Tibor Scitovsky, *Welfare and Competition* (Chicago, Ill.: Richard D. Irwin, 1951), Chap. 5. On technology and its negative impacts on this trade-off, see Ivar Berg, Marcia Freedman, and Michael Freeman, *Managers and Work Reform, A Limited Engagement* (New York: Free Press, 1978); Harry Braverman, *Labor and Monopoly Capital: The Degradation of Work in the Twentieth Century* (New York: Monthly Review Press, 1974); David F. Noble, *America by Design: Science, Technology and the Rise of Corporate Capitalism* (New York: Alfred Knopf, 1977); Richard C. Edwards, *Contested Terrain: The Transformation of the Workplace in the 20th Century* (New York: Basic Books, 1979). On the negative social effects of business strategies of mobility and abandonments, see Barry Castleman, "The Export of Hazardous Factories to Developing Nations" (Washington, D.C.: Environmental Defense Fund, 1977); Barry Bluestone and Bennett Harrison, *Capital and Communities: The Causes and Consequences of Private Disinvestment* (Washington, D.C.: The Progressive Alliance, 1980). See also the series on runaway shops put out by the North American Congress on Latin America: "Electronics: the Global Industry," April 1977; "Capital's Flight: The Apparel Industry Moves South," March 1977; "Hit and Run: Runaway Shops On the Mexican Border," July–August 1975.

14 Although the traditional liberal view has been that a return to a more decentralized industrial structure would be a public benefit, this perspective has fallen out of favor in recent years – partly because of the utopian character of proposals to effect serious decentralization, and also because of the widely held beliefs (1) that larger size means a higher rate of technical innovation and (2) that economies of scale make for irreducibly small numbers that now require oligopoly. Lester Thurow rejects antitrust on the somewhat inconsistent grounds that it hasn't worked ("antitrust laws do not, in fact produce competitive industries") and that competition remains potent ("General Motors is part of a competitive industry") – or would be with freer trade ("If competitive markets are desired, the appropriate policy should be to reduce barriers to free trade"). *The Zero-Sum Society* (New York: Basic Books, 1980), pp. 127, 146.

15 With high monopoly profits, the trade-off between additional profits and the extra effort needed to acquire them eventually favors relaxed effort. An often quoted phrase expressing this idea is that "it may well be that the best of all monopoly profits is a quiet life."

J. R. Hicks, "Annual Survey of Economic Theory: The Theory of Monopoly," *Econometrica,* January 1935, p. 8.

16 A. A. Berle, Jr., and Gardiner C. Means, *The Modern Corporation and Private Property* (New York: Macmillan, 1932).

17 Ibid., p. 18.

18 Ibid., p. 85.

19 Ibid., p. 94.

20 Ibid., pp. 8–9, 121ff, 345–346.

21 Newton Booth, "The Issues of the Day," a speech given in San Francisco, August 12, 1873, quoted in Alfred D. Chandler, Jr., *The Railroads* (New York: Harcourt Brace & World, 1965), p. 56.

22 Ibid.

23 Charles Francis Adams, Jr., and Henry Adams, *Chapters of Erie* (Ithaca, N.Y.: Cornell University Press, 1956), p. 3. Essay originally written in 1869.

24 Ibid., p. 61.

25 *Report of the Committee Appointed Pursuant to House Resolutions 429 and 504 to Investigate the Concentration of Control of Money and Credit,* H. Rpt. No. 1593, 62d Cong., 3rd sess. (Washington, D.C.: Government Printing Office, 1913), pp. 146–147.

26 Ibid., p. 147.

27 Edwin P. Hoyt, Jr., *The Guggenheims and the American Dream* (New York: Funk & Wagnalls, 1967), pp. 193–194.

28 Thorstein Veblen, *The Theory of Business Enterprise* (New York: Charles Scribner, 1904), pp. 157, 174–175.

29 Ibid., pp. 26–35.

30 Thorstein Veblen, *Absentee Ownership* (New York: B. W. Huebsch, 1923), pp. 331–332, 338–341.

31 See Chap. 3, Table 3.6, and the discussion under "Diffusion of Ownership."

32 According to William Z. Ripley, the real innovations of the 1920s were not the use of voting trusts and layered holding companies but, rather, the new, or at least newly widespread, use of disenfranchised stock – the setting off of preferred shares as nonvoting and the increased use of separate classes of common, with nonvoting offered to the public and voting stock reserved for the insiders. The latter were sometimes even referred to boldly as "Management Shares," reserved for the promoters as a bonus and assuring them unconstrained control. *Main Street and Wall Street* (Boston: Little, Brown, 1927), pp. 84–87.

33 Ibid., p. 128.

34 J. M. Keynes, "The End of Laissez-Faire" (1926), in *Essays in Persuasion* (London: Rupert Hart-Davis, 1951), p. 314.

35 Ibid., p. 315.

36 Adam Smith, *An Inquiry into the Nature and Causes of the Wealth of*

Nations (New York: Random House, 1919), p. 700. (Originally published in 1776.)

37 H. G. Manne, "Mergers and the Market for Corporate Control," *Journal of Political Economy,* April 1965, pp. 110–112; R. A. Gordon, *Business Leadership in the Large Corporation* (Berkeley: University of California Press, 1961), passim; J. K. Galbraith, *The New Industrial State* (Boston: Houghton Mifflin, 1967), Chaps. 6–7; Paul A. Baran and Paul M. Sweezy, *Monopoly Capital* (New York: Monthly Review Press, 1966), Chap. 2.

38 O. E. Williamson, "Managerial Discretion and Business Behavior," *American Economic Review,* December 1963, pp. 1032–1057; R. Rees, "A Reconsideration of the Expense Preference Theory of the Firm," *Economica,* August 1974, pp. 295–307.

39 William J. Baumol, "The Theory of the Expansion of the Firm," *American Economic Review,* December 1962, pp. 1078–1087; John Williamson, "Profit, Growth and Sales Maximization," *Economica,* February 1966, pp. 1–16.

40 See Chap. 3, under "The persistence of ownership influence and the profit incentive,'' and Appendix C.

41 The main policy conclusion deduced by investigators in this field is that invigorated competition is desirable, because any deviations from profit maximization are contrained by the rigors of active competition. See John Palmer, "The Profit Performance Effects of the Separation of Ownership from Control in Large U.S. Industrial Corporations," *Bell Journal of Economics and Management Science,* Spring 1973, pp. 293–303; Oliver Williamson, *The Economics of Discretionary Behavior* (Englewood Cliffs, N.J.: Prentice-Hall, 1964), p. 169. A competitive policy would follow, of course, from conventional neoclassical principles independent of any effects of managerialism, but a small increment is added to the competitive case by these analyses. See further, Chap. 7 under "Major themes and some policy implications."

42 Milton Friedman, who stresses the "relative unimportance" of business monopoly and the continued viability of competition, states in regard to the claim "that the corporation has become a social institution that is a law unto itself, with irresponsible executives who do not serve the interests of their shareholders" that "This charge is not true." Period. *Capitalism and Freedom* (Chicago: University of Chicago Press, 1962), pp. 121, 135.

43 Manne, "Mergers and the Market for Corporate Control"; also R. Marris, *The Economic Theory of "Managerial" Capitalism* (New York: Free Press, 1964).

44 See esp. A. A. Berle, Jr., *The Twentieth Century Capitalist Revolution* (New York: Harcourt Brace, 1954).

45 See Ralph Nader and Mark J. Green, *Corporate Power in America* (New York: Grossman, 1973); Christopher D. Stone, *Where the Law*

Ends: The Social Control of Corporate Behavior (New York: Harper & Row, 1975).

46 Berle and Means, *The Modern Corporation*, p. 356.

47 Baran and Sweezy, *Monopoly Capital*, p. 35.

48 See Chap. 3, under "The persistence of ownership influence and the profit incentive."

49 William Leonard Crum, "On the Alleged Concentration of Economic Power," *American Economic Review*, March 1934, p. 73.

50 See esp. the chaps. by Demsetz, Brozen, Weston, and Ornstein in J. Fred Weston and Stanley Ornstein, eds., *The Impact of Large Firms on the U.S. Economy* (Lexington, Mass.: Lexington Books, 1973).

51 See Chap. 3, under "The evolution of control of the large corporation: 1900–75."

52 Philip H. Burch, Jr., *The Managerial Revolution Reassessed: Family Control in America's Large Corporations* (Lexington, Mass.: Lexington Books, 1972), pp. 102–103.

53 See Chap. 3, notes 2 and 17.

54 Crum, "On the Alleged Concentration of Economic Power," p. 71.

55 U.S. Temporary National Economic Committee, Monograph No. 29, *The Distribution of Ownership in the 200 Largest Nonfinancial Corporations*, 76th Cong., 3rd sess., (Washington, D.C.: Government Printing Office, 1940), p. 99.

56 Louis D. Brandeis, *Other People's Money, and How the Bankers Use It* (Washington, D.C.: National Home Library Foundation, 1933); Rudolph Hilferding, *Das Finanzkapital* (Vienna: Wiener Volksbuchhandlung, 1923); Lenin, *Imperialism* (New York: Vanguard Press, 1926).

57 National Resources Committee, *The Structure of the American Economy, Part I, Basic Characteristics* (Washington, D.C.: Government Printing Office, 1939).

58 U.S., Congress, House, Committee on Banking and Currency, Subcommittee on Domestic Finance, staff report on *Commercial Banks and Their Trust Activities: Emerging Influence on the American Economy*, Vol. 1 (Washington, D.C.: Government Printing Office, 1968).

59 Burnham's managerial order was only a hypothetical one, to which society was only *tending;* managers finally achieve *ownership* control as well as strategic position when the managerial revolution becomes a reality. According to Burnham, control via strategic position "will shift ownership unambiguously to the new controlling, a new dominant, class." But "the finance-capitalists are still the ruling class in the United States; the final control is still in their hands." Just how and why a shift will occur and its consequences were left quite vague. James Burnham, *The Managerial Revolution* (New York: John Day, 1941), pp. 95–97.

60 Trade union power is not addressed in this book, in part because

unions in the United States have made no serious effort to obtain direct control or to participate in the broad decision processes of large companies. Their influence and power are real but they are exercised through bargaining, and they have been confined almost entirely to wage and working condition issues, ignoring the many other key corporate decisions. Unions clearly influence corporate decisions in the important spheres of union interest, but as with government in fixing the parameters of a social regulation, they bargain on the terms of outcomes to which the corporate leaders must then adapt. The same point may be made regarding citizens and public interest groups to which the corporation may have to respond and with which it sometimes negotiates a settlement (see Chap. 7 under "Corporate responses to external pressures").

Chapter 2. Control and Strategic Position

1   For example, the workers, union, and local officials will be deeply concerned with any decision to move a headquarters or producing facility; the investment community will be much more interested in a decision on dividend rate or major acquisition plan; and the federal government might be especially interested in an acquisition of a competitor or supplier or a plan to enter a cost-plus engineering contract with the Soviet Union.

2   This comes close to Galbraith's notion of a "technostructure" dominating an organization. See J. K. Galbraith, *The New Industrial State* (Boston: Houghton Mifflin, 1967), Chap. 6.

3   Amitai Etzioni, *Modern Organizations* (Englewood Cliffs, N.J.: Prentice-Hall, 1964), pp. 10–13; James F. March and Herbert A. Simon, *Organizations* (New York: John Wiley, 1958), pp. 38–39. G. W. Dalton, L. B. Barnes, and A. Zaleznick, *The Distribution of Authority in Formal Organizations* (Cambridge, Mass.: MIT, 1968); Roderick Martin, *The Sociology of Power* (London: Routledge & Kegan Paul, 1977), Chap. 8; C. Perrow, "Departmental Power and Perspective in Industrial Firms," in M. N. Zald (ed.), *Power in Organizations* (Nashville, Tenn.: Vanderbilt University Press, 1970).

4   Alfred P. Sloan describes a good case history of this in the abandonment of the copper-cooled engine by General Motors in 1923 because of nonacceptance by the divisions. See *My Years with General Motors* (Garden City, N.Y.: Doubleday, 1963), pp. 86–89.

5   It may be argued that worker organizations are not properly regarded as external to the firm – rather, they are constituent parts of the organization and share in decision making and thus in control. It may be true that unions should be regarded as integral parts of business firms for many purposes but not as control entities as that term is developed here, for reasons spelled out in note 60 of Chap. 1.

6   James D. Thompson describes the use of "cooperative strategies" by organizations as a means of achieving power through an exchange of commitments between parties. It reduces uncertainty for *A* by also reducing it for *B*. Cooptation is one form of cooperation in which new elements are introduced into a leadership or policy-determining structure. It gains the cooperation of the new element but places it "in a position to raise questions and perhaps exert influence on other aspects of the organization." James D. Thompson, *Organizations in Action* (McGraw-Hill, New York: 1967), p. 35. See also, Peter M. Blau, *Exchange and Power in Social Life* (New York: John Wiley, 1964), pp. 120ff; William Dill, "Business Organizations," in J. G. March (ed.), *Handbook of Organizations* (Chicago: Rand McNally, 1965), pp. 1076–1077.

7   Thompson, *Organizations,* pp. 4–6, in which a closed system is determinate, the variables and relationships are few enough for us to comprehend, and we have control over or can reliably predict all of the relevant relationships.

8   This is a leading theme of Alfred D. Chandler, Jr. in *The Visible Hand, The Managerial Revolution in American Business* (Cambridge, Mass.: Harvard University Press, 1977). Chandler's view is that "Top managers, in addition to evaluating and coordinating the work of middle managers, took the place of the market in allocating resources for future production and distribution" (p. 7). Another main theme in *The Visible Hand* is that organizational changes over the past century have enhanced the capability and power of top management: "These new structures and controls also permitted the top managers to evaluate with more precision the performance of the middle- and lower-level managers and to select for top management with more assurance" (p. 451). This, along with the new professionalism, "further enhanced the economic power of the large industrial enterprises and the men who managed them" (p. 454).

It is argued in organizational analyses that complex organizations tend to be managed by coalitions of varying size. Three subpropositions are relevant here: "When power is widely distributed, an *inner circle* emerges to conduct coalition business." "The organization with dispersed bases of power is immobilized unless there exists an effective inner circle." "In the organization with dispersed power, the central power figure is the individual who can manage the coalition." Thompson, *Organizations,* pp. 140–142. Thompson goes on to argue that a dominant individual can lead but can act only with the consent of the dominant coalition, and neither can alter the main drift of the organization: "In the highly complex organization, in our opinion, neither the central power figure nor the inner circle (nor their combination) can reverse the direction of organizational movement at will." pp. 142–143.

9   Allied Chemical was formed in 1920 by the merger of five compa-

nies that were family dominated, including two Solvay companies. For an account of the history and internal struggles into the 1950s, see Edmund L. Van Dusen, "You'd Hardly Know Allied Chemical," *Fortune,* October 1954, pp. 119ff.

10 This is a point stressed by Chandler in explaining the relative importance of "finance" in the control structure of various industries in different periods. He notes that in the 1890–1904 merger era, financial interests were less important in industrials than in the railroads: "For one thing, many experienced manufacturers who had owned and operated the firms entering the merger often stayed on the board and continued to have an influence on top management decisions. For another, the capital requirements of the industrials were smaller than those of the railroads. In most cases, too, the consolidations were able to generate a higher return than railroads. Because they had less continuing need for outside funds, fewer financiers came on their boards, and those that did rarely had the power – albeit a veto power – that they had on the railroads. In only a few cases where particularly heavy outside financing was required did financiers outnumber managers on boards of industrials, and such cases became less and less frequent." Chandler, *Visible Hand,* p. 416. The same theme is pursued in explaining relative financial control in specific industries and sectors; see pp. 198–199, 237–238, 298, 305, 311, and 477.

11 Annual meetings may be made uncomfortable, but even more painful have been the lawsuits for breach of duty and other claimed derelictions. See Robert J. Cole, "The Director at Bay," *New York Times,* October 17, 1971; Jeremy Bacon, "Directors Under Pressure," and S. H. Gillespie, "Directors' Liability Problems," *Conference Board Record,* February 1972.

12 Herbert A. Simon, *Administrative Behavior* (New York: Free Press, 1967), p. xii.

13 I refer here to the methods of maintaining control of basic decision-making of the overall organization, not the methods by which top-level decisions are implemented within the organization.

14 In the case of railroads, which were the most important large corporations of the nineteenth century, "an essential of successful promotion, usually, is the reservation . . . of a controlling interest in the capital stock as a whole." Railroad organizers often set up construction companies through which all of the railroad securities were channeled, with the bond issues then sold to the public, the stock used in part as a bonus for bond sales, but the bulk kept by the promoters. William Z. Ripley, *Railroads, Finance and Organization* (New York: Longmans, Green, 1915), pp. 15, 35, 41. See also Julius Grodinsky, *Jay Gould* (Philadelphia: University of Pennsylvania, 1957), pp. 114–115. In the promotion of many of the great combi-

nations around the turn of the century, the promoters frequently took a sizable block of newly issued common stock as part of their promotion fee. The Morgan syndicate took 1,299,975 shares, half common and half preferred, for organizing the U.S. Steel combine of 1901. The promoters were sometimes able to increase greatly their proportion of the total stock held by buying out companies and shareholders with newly issued bonds. In the case of the American Tobacco Company this procedure allowed six insiders, formerly minority owners of constituent companies, to control more than half the common stock of the combine – and just prior to developments that were highly favorable to common stock ownership. See Report of the U.S. Commissioner of Corporations, vol. 1, February 25, 1909, reprinted in part in William Z. Ripley (ed.), *Trusts, Pools and Corporations* (New York: Ginn, 1916), Chap. 8.

15 This adds to "normal" attrition resulting from death and estate taxes, dispersion by gift and estate division among entrepreneurial families, and further distributions, based on tax and diversification factors.

16 An illustration of this point was provided by Irenee Du Pont in 1973, when he was quoted in "A management leapfrog at Du Pont," *Business Week,* December 15, 1973, p. 49: "As for not succeeding himself to the post the family has controlled through most of the company's history, Irenee Du Pont once told a visitor that 'as a stockholder, I wouldn't vote for me.' He adds: 'This company must be run by the best people able to run it. There are only 1,000 or so descendants, and half don't qualify because of age. It would be a remarkable quirk if among the blood relations there were several candidates with the immense mental ability needed to run this company.' "

17 As noted by Arthur J. Goldberg, reflecting on his experience on the TWA board: "At the very best, outside directors of almost all large corporate enterprises under the present system cannot acquire more than a smattering of knowledge about any large and far-flung company of which they are directors . . . The outside director is simply unable to gather enough independent information to act as a watchdog or sometimes even to ask good questions." "Debate on Outside Directors," *New York Times,* October 29, 1972, Sec. 3, p. 1. See the similar remarks of Martin Stone and Rodney C. Gott, then CEOs of Monogram Industries and AMF, Inc., "The board: It's obsolete unless overhauled," *Business Week,* May 22, 1971, pp. 50, 55.

Alfred D. Chandler gives expertise, information, and managerial organizational capability great weight in explaining the gradual domination of salaried managers in the large corporation. In *The Visible Hand,* p. 491, he states that "by 1917 representatives of an entrepreneurial family or a banking house almost never took part in middle management decisions on prices, deliveries, wages, and employment required in the coordinating of current flows. Even in top management decisions concerning the allocation of resources, their power remained essentially negative. They could say no, but unless they themselves were trained managers with long experience in the same industry and even the same company, they had neither the information nor the experience to propose positive alternative courses of action."

18   See Robin Marris, *The Economic Theory of Managerial Capitalism* (New York: Basic Books, 1964), p. 17.

19   For the case of Penn Central see Staff Report of the SEC, U.S., Congress, House, Committee on Interstate and Foreign Commerce, Special Subcommittee on Investigations, *The Financial Collapse of the Penn Central Company* (Washington, D.C.: Government Printing Office), pp. 151–172.

20   Although the holders of a majority of voting shares of stock can eventually displace a board, and thus may be said to possess ultimate power of control, the board is not an "agent" of the shareholders in the strict legal sense, removable without the need to show cause, as an officer may be removed by the board itself. In 1958 one court even held that a *sole* shareholder could not remove directors during their term without cause. [*Frank* vs. *Anthony,* 107 So. 2d. 136 (Fla. DCA, 1958)]. Statutory requirements give boards an important degree of autonomy, which appears to be based partly on traditional practice and usages, and also on a curious guardian theory of corporate organizations, imposed by state fiat. See Robert A. Kessler, "The Statutory Requirement of a Board of Directors: A Corporate Anachronism," *University of Chicago Law Review,* vol. 27, 1960, pp. 696–736.

21   E. J. Kahn says that Asa Candler, Sr. kept a majority of Coca Cola shares before 1916 "so that he could – as he often did – dismiss a suggestion that he didn't cotton to with a brusque 'I vote fifty-one per cent against it.' " *The Big Drink, The Story of Coca Cola* (New York: Random House, 1960), p. 60.

22   That outside directors are "delving more deeply into the affairs of the companies they oversee" is allegedly shown by the fact that 84 percent had audit committees versus 72 percent in 1974, and the number of companies providing directors with reports in advance of meetings increased from 83 to 86 percent between 1974 and 1975! ("Outside directors get more involved," *Business Week,* February 17, 1975, p. 27.) Elsewhere, it is said that "The payoff scandals are producing 'a fundamental transformation in the outlook of outside directors on their responsibilities,' asserts Victor Palmieri, a Los Angeles business consultant." B. E. Calme and Eric Morgenthaler, "The Hot Seat: Outside Directors Get More Careful, Tougher After Payoff Scandal," *Wall Street Journal,* March 24, 1976, p. 1. See also,

"End of the directors' rubber stamp," *Business Week,* September 10, 1979, pp. 72ff.

23 Boards whose function appears to be mainly to meet this legal requirement are referred to by Stanley Vance as "constitutional" boards; see his "New Dimensions for Boards of Directors," *Conference Board Record,* November 1971, pp. 53–54.

24 Jeremy Bacon and James K. Brown, *Corporate Directorship Practices: Role, Selection and Legal Status of the Board* (New York, Conference Board, 1975), p. 25.

25 A deposition in the Mead corporation struggle to fend off a takeover by Occidental Oil Company revealed that the CEO of Occidental, Armand Hammer, had obtained undated letters of resignation from eight Occidental directors, one an outside director. Stephen Sansweet, "Fending Off Suitors: Hostile Merger Moves Meet Fierce Opposition . . ." *Wall Street Journal,* April 3, 1979, p. 39.

26 As noted by Ian K. McGregor, when he was a CEO of Amax, "In any company's history, there is an ebb and flow of the interface between management's responsibility and the board's. Generally speaking, the board gets more involved in management decisions in a time of change, in a time of expansion, in a time of weakness in the management. On the other hand, an established, capable management usually pushed the interface further up the line." Conference Board, *The Board of Directors: New Challenges, New Directions* (New York: Conference Board, 1971), p. 27.

27 See John C. Baker, *Directors and Their Functions* (Boston, Mass.: Harvard Graduate School of Business, 1945); Courtney C. Brown, *Putting The Corporate Board to Work* (New York: Macmillan, 1976); Robert A. Gordon, *Business Leadership in the Large Corporation* (Washington, D.C.: Brookings, 1961), Chap. 6; Myles Mace, *Directors: Myths and Realities* (Boston, Mass.: Harvard Graduate School of Business, 1971); Bacon and Brown, *Corporate Directorship Practices.*

28 Testimony Taken Before the Joint Committee of the Senate and Assembly of the State of New York to Investigate and Examine into the Business and Affairs of Life Insurance Companies Doing Business in the State of New York (Armstrong Committee Hearings), testimony of September 29, 1905, vol. 2, p. 1299.

29 Bacon and Brown, *Corporate Directorship Practices,* p. 7.

30 Jeremy Bacon, *The Board of Directors: Perspectives and Practices in Nine Countries* (New York: The Conference Board, 1977), p. 83.

31 Stanley Vance, "Director Diversity: New Dimensions in the Boardroom," *Directors & Boards,* Spring 1977, p. 41.

32 Quoted in Mace, *Directors,* p. 47.

33 Bacon and Brown, *Corporate Directorship Practices,* p. 28.

34 Quoted in Allan Nevins and Frank Ernest Hill, *Ford, Decline and Rebirth, 1933–1962* (New York: Charles Scribner, 1963), p. 315.

35 Noyes E. Leech and Robert H. Mundheim, *The Outside Director of the Public Corporation* (New York: Korn/Ferry International, 1976), pp. 5–9.

36 Courtney C. Brown, *Putting the Corporate Board to Work*, pp. 22–23; see also Bacon and Brown, *Corporate Directorship Practices*, p. 29.

37 Jeremy Bacon, *Corporate Directorship Practices: Membership and Committees of the Board* (New York: Conference Board, 1973), p. 51.

38 Korn/Ferry International, *Board of Directors, Sixth Annual Study*, February 1979, p. 5; Bacon, *Board of Directors*, p. 86.

39 Brown, *Putting the Corporate Board to Work*, p. 23.

40 "A black director pushes reforms at GM," *Business Week*, April 10, 1971, p. 100.

41 A contrary view assumes that a sheer increase in numbers makes for a greater impact: "Outside directors are having more impact because there are more of them." ("Outside directors get more involved," *Business Week*, February 17, 1975, p. 27.)

42 In his satirical but serious article "Preserving the importance of the board," *Harvard Business Review*, July–August 1977, Milton C. Lauenstein, a professional director, notes that "Especially if the board is sufficiently large, the opportunity for any individual member to have substantial part in the discussions can be kept near zero by following the 'rule of 80 and 10.' Management should use at least 80% of available meeting time in its own presentations and should spend at least 10 minutes answering any question raised by a director." p. 37. On his calculations, a careful manager can confine each outside director to about 24 minutes per year for questions and answers to these questions.

43 Bacon, *Corporate Directorship Practices: Perspectives and Practices*, p. 1.

44 Ibid., pp. 84–85.

45 Korn/Ferry International, *Board of Directors*, p. 10.

46 Occasionally, splits in the ranks of the top insiders are felt at the board level and realignments occur, as in the RCA case where some insiders and outsiders joined forces against Robert Sarnoff and his management and outsider director allies ("Why Robert Sarnoff quit at RCA," *Business Week*, November 24, 1975, pp. 76–81); or Genesco, where The *Wall Street Journal* account is titled, "Revolt of the Troops: Demotion of Genesco's Chief Was Set in Motion by a Trip by Two Inside Directors to See Outsider," (*Wall Street Journal*, January 5, 1977, p. 26).

47 This point was raised effectively by John C. Baker in his 1945 study of boards of directors; see Baker, *Directors and their Functions*, pp. 23–27.

48 The New York Stock Exchange requirement is given in full in Jeremy Bacon, *Corporate Directorship Practices: The Audit Committee*, (*New York: Conference Board*, 1979), p. 10.

49 Bacon, *Corporate Directorship Practices: Membership and Committees,* p.v.
50 For example, a news report on Lynn Townsend's decision to resign as head of Chrysler cites John McGillicuddy, president of Manufacturers Hanover Trust and on the board of Chrysler, as a "close friend" of Townsend. See Agis Salpukas, "Townsend Decision to Quit Chrysler Believed His Own," *New York Times,* July 5, 1975, p. 23.
51 Among the many limitations on the SEC's requirement of disclosure of director transactions are: (1) Amounts need be disclosed only "where practicable". (2) No information need be provided where there is no "material interest," where business done is at rates determined by competitive bids or by governmental authority, and where the interest is in bank services, such as trustee, depository, transfer agent, and the like. (3) This information requirement is subject to negligible policing by the SEC.
52 For purposes of this study a substantial volume of business includes cases where: (1) a law firm – whether or not the official legal counsel of the company – received fees of $100,000 or more in 1974 or 1975; (2) as banker or investment banker, a company obtained fees of $100,000 or more in 1974 or 1975; (3) a firm sold the corporation goods valued at $500,000 or more in 1974 or 1975; (4) a firm bought goods worth $500,000 or more from the company in 1974 or 1975.
53 See Lewis D. Solomon, "Restructuring the Corporate Board of Directors: Fond Hope – Faint Promise?" *Michigan Law Review,* March 1978, pp. 585–586; Mace, *Directors,* p. 89.
54 Myles Mace observes that although some directors who own or represent large blocks of stock are passive and compliant, "There is some evidence that if the owner of the stock had come into possession of it through his own efforts, such as an entrepreneur developing his own business and then selling it to a larger company for its shares, the entrepreneur will take a very active role as a director of the acquiring company. If the outside director with large stockholdings is a second or third generation heir of an entrepreneur, his involvement as an active director is less likely." "The President and the Board of Directors," *Harvard Business Review,* March–April 1973, pp. 44–45.
55 Average director compensation for 542 companies responding to Korn/Ferry was $11,250 in 1978; $15,770 for corporations with sales of $1 billion or more. And fees are rising steadily. A professional director with half a dozen directorships has a substantial stake in maintaining a market for his or her services. Korn/Ferry International, *Board of Directors,* p. 5.
56 Juanita Kreps was not present at that meeting of Eastman Kodak. See Marylin Bender, "Management: Scrutinizing the Corporate

Boardroom," *New York Times,* May 14, 1976, p. D.1. Kreps was one of the two public directors selected for the board of the New York Stock Exchange, the other being Jerome Holland, a black professional director. A 1973 news report on their activities claimed that the two were, in the description of several industry members, "the most silent members of the group during discussions. 'I've never heard them speak at all,' said one director in what is perhaps something of an overstatement." See Vartanig G. Vartan, "Public Directors Cautious at Big Board," *New York Times,* May 21, 1973. Kreps and Holland were, respectively, tied for first place in women representation and tops for black representation on the boards of our 250 large companies in 1975.

57　W. Stewart Pinkerton, Jr., "The Outsider: Don Mitchell Discovers Problems and Rewards of Being on 12 Boards," *Wall Street Journal,* August 17, 1970.

58　Thomas C. Hayes, "New Look on Corporate Boards," *New York Times,* October 11, 1979, p. D.4.

59　This grand total includes the directors of the 250 largest companies along with the directors of all of their subsidiaries with assets in excess of $5 billion.

60　Of all the categories discussed here, this is the one posing the most serious problem of accuracy, as "black" is not something recorded in proxy statements or annual reports. Information on this matter was derived from pictures provided in perhaps half the proxy statements and annual reports and from information culled from various *Who's Whos,* including *Who's Who Among Black Americans,* and various news and periodical items on the companies' policies of broadening directorates to include minorities. There may be a few omissions, but they are probably very small in number.

61　Korn/Ferry International, *Board of Directors,* p. 12.

62　Mace, *Directors,* p. 92.

63　Ibid., p. 93.

64　John Mayer of the Mellon Bank, expressing opposition to constituency directors on the ground that activists might go over the heads of the board to the public, noted that "You would hate to be the hostage of a guy like that." Quoted in "The board: It's obsolete unless overhauled," *Business Week,* May 22, 1971, p. 58.

65　Patricia Harris reported that once when she had made some critical point the chairman told her she should have raised the matter privately. See Marylin Bender, "Outside Directors," *New York Times,* July 15, 1973, sec. 3, p. 1. See also Mace, *Directors,* pp. 77–80.

66　Brown, *Putting the Corporate Board to Work,* p. 24.

67　On the importance of the outside directors as a peer group defining ethical standards and thereby circumscribing managerial behavior, see Mace, *Directors,* pp. 26–27.

68 Howard Hughes, controlling 78 percent of the voting stock of TWA, lost control of TWA in 1960–1961 because of the need to set up a banker-dominated voting trust as a condition for getting the necessary financing for TWA. In 1961 these voting trustees altered the TWA board from Hughes domination to banker-management preeminence. A loss of control through financial exigencies for a small company subject to 80 percent family ownership is described in "A financial expert for beleaguered Barwick," *Business Week,* May 19, 1975, p. 58.

69 See Robert L. Sorenson, *Some Economic Implications of the Separation of Ownership and Control in the United States,* Ph.D. dissertation, Virginia Polytechnic Institute, 1971, pp. 125–126.

70 William A. McEachern, *Managerial Control and Performance* (Lexington, Mass.: Lexington Books, 1975), p. 31.

71 The present writer was able to identify 20 instances of involuntary ousters of top managers among the 200 largest nonfinancials in the years 1965–1974. Of these 20, four were companies where substantial ownership interests participated in the ouster, a number that corresponds closely to the overall proportion of ownership-control cases to be found in the universe of the 200 largest (as shown on Table 3.2). In six of the remaining cases, banker influence under conditions of financial distress was great and contributed to the displacement, whereas in ten, the change seems to have occurred almost entirely from within the organization. Of the turnover cases subject to significant external influence (large owner or banker), only two involved companies among the very largest, namely, Gulf and 3M.

72 See George Kennan, *A. H. Harriman, A Biography,* vol. 1 (Boston: Houghton Mifflin, 1922), pp. 357–358.

73 For further discussion of takeovers, see Chap. 3, under "Other market and owner-related forces".

74 A brief account of these difficulties, including the huge losses in the joint venture General Atomic, is given in Michael Jensen, "Gulf: Its Troubles Get Deeper," *New York Times,* January 4, 1976, sec. 3, p. 1.

75 Since retiring as chairman of Consolidated Foods in 1960, Nathan Cummings "has managed the firings of two chairmen." One of the firees, William Buzick, claimed that Cummings "would call me at any time from anywhere in the world, seven days a week" and would frequently undercut his authority by telling other officers how things should be done. See David M. Elsner, "Hanging On: Retired Chief Officer of Consolidated Foods Isn't a Retiring Sort," *Wall Street Journal,* March 29, 1976. According to Spencer Stuart, chairman of Spencer Stuart & Associates, when a domineering executive "retires," "the first guy in as his successor – maybe even the

first two or three – usually doesn't have a chance." See "The men who still hang on to the reins," *Business Week,* October 2, 1971, pp. 40–42.

76 Mary Bralove, "Power Struggle: At United Brands Co. Fight for Control Came After Honduran Payoff," *Wall Street Journal,* May 7, 1975; James Carberry and Liz Gallese, "Top Banana: Who Is Mr. Milstein? Head of United Brands Is Keeping Low Profile," *Wall Street Journal,* May 13, 1977.

77 See Myles Mace, "The President and the Board of Directors," *Harvard Business Review,* March–April 1972, p. 45.

Chapter 3. Control of the Large Corporation: Evolution and Present Status

1 The proxy statement of International Harvester showed Mr. McCormick and his immediate family holding 127,041 shares, or 0.46 percent, of the outstanding, in early 1975.

2 After stating that "it is now generally agreed in most business circles that working control of any large company can usually be obtained through possession of something like 4 or 5 percent of the voting stock," Philip Burch illustrates the conservativeness of this figure as follows: "In its March 1, 1967 issue, for example, *Forbes* pointed out (p. 36) that the Harriman (or Brown Bros. Harriman interests) still retained undisputed control over the Union Pacific RR, even though they held barely 3 percent of the outstanding common stock." (*The Managerial Revolution Reassessed,* p. 25 and note 36). In addition to the *nonsequitur* or cause and effect, Burch cites no evidence for his 4 to 5 percent figure, and as can be inferred from the present text, I consider this figure wrong and without support from business people close to the questions of control and takeover problems.

3 Generous stock bonus and option plans can raise management holdings to quite respectable levels once managements are in a position to provide themselves with these inducements to serve the corporate interest; for example, the management of City Investing built up its holdings from 0 to 1.7 percent in a decade by these routes. Or the existing control group may make a huge initial stock grant to induce a manager to take over a top executive slot (e.g., Roy Ash on taking the CEO position of Addressograph-Multigraph Corp, bought 300,000 shares worth $2.7 million, half of this sum borrowed from the company itself ["Ash's fringe benefit," *Business Week,* December 6, 1976]).

4 The one exception is Shell, majority controlled by Royal Dutch/ Shell through a subsidiary; but using the format of subsuming Shell under its parent would have required including Royal Dutch/Shell, a foreign company, in our universe of large companies, or excluding Shell entirely as a subsidiary of a foreign company. I have used an

unsatisfactory compromise to keep Shell, an important U.S.-based company, in our universe of large companies.

5 Royal Dutch/Shell appears to be management controlled. See Randall Beaton, *Enterprise in Oil, A History of Shell in the United States* (New York: Appleton-Century-Crofts, 1957), p. 230.

6 In Chap. 5 a revised classification is presented that includes government entities in the 200 largest nonfinancials (see Table 5.1).

7 This was commonly the case in the numerous railroad and other investments made by Jay Gould and professional speculators associated with him; see Julius Grodinsky, *Jay Gould* (Philadelphia: University of Pennsylvania Press, 1945), passim; it was also true more widely of investment in the railroads and urban transit systems of the late nineteenth century. See, for example, Frederick A. Cleveland and Fred W. Powell, *Railroad Finance* (New York: D. Appleton and Company, 1912), Chaps. 2–4; Stuart Daggett, *Railroad Reorganization* (Boston: Harvard University Press, 1908), passim.; Harry J. Carman, *The Street Surface Railway Franchises of New York City* (New York: Longmans, Green, 1919); Burton J. Hendricks, *The Age of Big Business* (New Haven: Yale University Press, 1919), Chap. 4.

8 Lee Preston, testimony in U.S., Congress, Senate, Judiciary Committee, Antitrust Subcommittee, *Economic Concentration*, pt. 1, 88th Cong., 2d sess., (Washington, D.C.: Government Printing Office, 1964), p. 63.

9 Richard Edwards, "Stages in Corporate Stability and the Risks of Corporate Failure," *Journal of Economic History*, June 1975, p. 435.

10 Ibid., p. 429.

11 Alfred D. Chandler, Jr., *The Visible Hand: The Managerial Revolution in American Business* (Cambridge, Mass.: Harvard University Press, 1977), Chap. 11; Alfred D. Chandler, Jr., "The Structure of American Industry in the Twentieth Century: A Historical Overview," *Business History Review*, Autumn 1969, esp. p. 268ff.

12 Chandler, *The Visible Hand*, p. 473.

13 David Mermelstein explains the slowing turnover rate in terms of an alleged "risk aversion" of managers, which makes for greater stability of earnings among large managerial firms. The risk aversion hypothesis itself is unproven, however, and the argument conflicts with the hypothesis that managerial interest makes for a strong growth orientation, which suggests reduced turnover for quite different reasons – high and preemptive growth rates, diversification strategies, and deliberate accumulation of the power and resources that permit growth strategies. David Mermelstein, "Large Industrial Corporations and Asset Shares," *American Economic Review*, September 1969, p. 540.

14 The Rockefellers have not had representation on the major oil company boards or managements for many years; their aggregate hold-

ings (including foundations) have been less than 5 percent, and there does not seem to be a logical basis for any significant residual power based on ownership. Following the Rockefeller proxy victory in 1929, which reestablished a previously weakened position in Standard Oil of Indiana (when the family still had at least 14.5 percent of the stock), the family seems to have gone out of its way to avoid confrontations that would display power, and there have been no such confrontations. Some commentators, who see a continued behind-the-scenes control by the family, do not recognize that an unwillingness to resort to open confrontation seriously weakens bargaining power. That power would have dwindled anyway with the divestments and lack of director/management participation by the family. The Chase Manhattan Bank, still in the Rockefeller orbit, provides the main lever of Rockefeller power vis-à-vis the oil majors, but as can be seen in Table 3.7, by 1976 bank-plus-family holdings in these companies was less than 3 percent and no credible basis for Chase Rockefeller control of these companies has been demonstrated. Compare Peter Collier and David Horowitz, *The Rockefellers: An American Dynasty* (New York: Holt, Rinehart and Winston, 1976), pp. 162–171, 207–210, who are impressed with Rockefeller power over the oil companies in the 1930s, but who conclude that even in 1937, although "No oil man could afford to ignore a Rockefeller, even if he had only just turned thirty [Nelson] . . . the Jersey board was a power in its own right and was not compelled to take his advice" (p. 310).

15 J. Peter Grace dominates W. R. Grace & Company (family holdings are under 5 percent, however) and has been a longtime board member and substantial owner (1.1 percent) of Ingersoll–Rand, another one of the 200 largest. Grace–Phipps interests have been closely associated in Ingersoll–Rand, International Paper Company, and in other ventures. Only W. R. Grace is controlled by this interest group, however; its power in the other two companies has diminished over the years.

George Brown was a major stockholder and board member of two of the 200 largest in 1975 – Halliburton, which absorbed Brown and Root in 1971, and Texas Eastern Transmission, with which Brown was associated from 1947. His holdings in each of these majors was under 5 percent, and with his virtual retirement in the mid-1970s, this impressive but very limited empire was already at an end.

16 According to Ferdinand Lundberg, "There was nothing inherently marvelous about the [Berle and Means] theory; what led to its being given wide currency was that it served to gull an always gullible public with the idea that property was losing its power and that something akin to socialism [but better] was evolving before our eyes. The United States was going to retain private property but at

the same time it was going to have collective nonprofit-oriented professional management in the corporations; if the owners, particularly the big owners, did not like this they would be powerless. As far as that went, big ownership itself was going out of existence. In brief, this was a useful myth in manipulating public sentiment . . ." Ferdinand Lundberg, *The Rich and the Super-Rich* (New York: Bantam, 1968), p. 293.

17 In his attempt to show that family control has been underrated, Philip Burch (*The Managerial Revolution Reassessed*) makes family control identical with the mere holding of an ownership interest sufficient to control, which he defines liberally. He also sometimes finds family control present even when ownership is below his 4 percent standard if individuals have a durable control position (e.g., the Watsons in IBM, with 3 percent of the stock at the time). Because some "family" must have power in a company, this comes close to distilling any meaning out of family control. Although many large family holdings have fallen drastically since 1937–1938, John Blair, in his *Economic Concentration* (New York: Harcourt Brace Jovanovich, 1972), relied entirely on the TNEC data for those years in his discussion of this subject in 1972 (pp. 78–79). Lundberg in his *The Rich and the Super-Rich,* also relies heavily on the 1937–1938 data, arguing that because the great fortunes are well managed and tend to grow, the 1937–1938 percentages for the Rockefellers "must be, if anything, understatements" (p. 186).

18 Dilworth's testimony before The House Judiciary Committee was printed in the *New York Times,* December 4 and 5, 1974.

19 On the split between Alfred and Pierre du Pont in 1915 and the factionalism that followed see James Phelan and Robert Pozen, *The Company State* (New York: Grossman, 1973), pp. 84–89.

20 See the following text on the John Hartford Foundation, and Chap. 4 under "Institutional Investor Behavior."

21 See Edwin P. Hoyt, Jr., *The Guggenheims and the American Dream* (New York: Funk & Wagnalls, 1967), pp. 246–263.

22 Maryln Bender, "The Doubleday Story," *New York Times,* November 19, 1972 sec. 3, p. 1.

23 The 1969 act limited the percentage of stock in founder companies that foundations could own, partly in relation to the percentages held by affiliated individuals. Divestment was required in a series of steps if these percentages were exceeded. Possibly more important was the act's requirement of a 6 percent payout rate (subsequently reduced to 5 percent), which compelled foundations heavy in low-yield founder company stock (Kresge, Johnson & Johnson, Eli Lilly) to encroach on capital or diversify into higher yielding assets.

24 See Chap. 4, Tables 4.8 and 4.9.

25 The Doris Duke Foundation held another 5 percent of Duke Power Company stock.

26 In 1972 J. S. Johnson held 6.1 percent and Esther U. Johnson 0.14 percent of company stock; other family holdings are said by insiders to be small.

27 For a brief account see "Who did the housecleaning at A&P," *Business Week*, December 21, 1974, p. 21.

28 Two advantages that do derive from continued family control, however, are the prestige of continued domination and power and additional material benefits (salaries and other personal benefits, ability to dispense largess to friends and relatives – although possibly at the expense of performance and stock returns!).

29 George Cooper, *A Voluntary Tax? New Perspectives on Sophisticated Estate Tax Avoidance* (Washington, D.C.: Brookings Institution, 1979), p. 82. There was hardly even a nominal estate-gift tax system until the federal legislation of 1932–1935; after that its impact was small but not entirely negligible. In recent years federal estate and gift taxes have brought in $4 to 6 billion per year, the bulk of which is not apparently from very large estates. In addition to Cooper, see also Louis Eisenstein, "The Rise and Decline of the Estate Tax," in *Federal Tax Policy for Economic Growth and Stability*, Joint Economic Committee, (Washington, D.C.: Government Printing Office, November 9, 1955), pp. 827ff.

30 Lundberg, *Rich and Super-Rich*, p. 179.

31 Collier and Horowitz report a John D. Rockefeller gift of $447 million to four foundations over a 12-year period early in the century; *The Rockefellers*, p. 100.

32 Ralph Nelson, *Merger Movements in American Industry, 1895–1956* (Princeton, N.J.: Princeton University Press, 1959), p. 54.

33 Glenn D. Babcock, *A History of the U.S. Rubber Company* (Lafayette, Ind.: University of Indiana, 1966), Chap. 2; testimony of Charles Flint (promoter of the U.S. Rubber Company), *Report of the Industrial Commission* (Washington, D.C.: Government Printing Office, 1901), vol. 13, p. 34.

34 John Moody, *The Truth About the Trusts* (New York: John Moody, 1904), p. 170.

35 See Mace, *Directors*, pp. 62–65.

36 The owner-dominated Carnegie Steel Company was as growth minded, probably more so, than the managerial U.S. Steel Corporation that followed it, and the great owner-dominated industrials of the late nineteenth century such as Singer, American Tobacco, and Swift were incorrigibly expansionist. See Chandler, *The Visible Hand*, pp. 266–269, 299–301, 303–308, 361, and 381–391. Cargill, the only closely held company among the 200 largest in the mid-1970s, is a strongly growth-oriented company, which has diversified rapidly in the last decade (both geographically and into new products). The owners retain 98 percent of net income within

the company. "Cargill: Preparing for the next boom in worldwide grain trading," *Business Week,* April 16, 1979, pp. 71–76.

37 "Profitable growth" may be regarded as a weaker version of the profit maximization concept, with these advantages: It does not assume that the quest for profits is always of constant, unremittingly high intensity but may vary from maximizing to satisficing or worse, depending on challenges, pressures, and individual or organizational special circumstances; and it stresses the expansive and nonstatic nature of the profit quest.

38 Edward S. Herman, *Conflicts of Interest: Commercial Bank Trust Departments* (New York: The Twentieth Century Fund, 1975), Chap. 2.

39 Phantom stock is hypothetically allocated to an officer as an incentive; at some later date the officer will obtain gains paid by the company "as if" the stock had been owned and the capital gain realized.

40 Wilbur G. Lewellen, *The Ownership Income of Management* (Princeton, N.J.: Princeton University Press, 1971), p. 160.

41 Ibid.

42 Robin Marris, *The Economic Theory of "Managerial Capitalism"* (New York: Basic Books, 1964), p. 18. Marris's sole citation is to a *Fortune* article of March 1957 ("How Executives Invest Their Money"), but this article uses the term executive very broadly and provides no details on the distribution of top executives' wealth.

43 Michael C. Jensen, "Miller's Fortune Estimated at $2.4 Million," *New York Times,* January 10, 1978, p. 45.

44 The 16 individuals involved in this study were: Roy Ash (Litton), W. Michael Blumenthal (Bendix), John T. Connor (Merck), Marion Folsom (Eastman Kodak), George Humphrey (National Steel), Robert Ingersoll (Borg Warner), David Kennedy (Continental Illinois National Bank), Neil McElroy (Proctor & Gamble), Robert McNamara (Ford), G. William Miller (Textron), David Packard (Hewlett–Packard), Peter Peterson (Bell & Howell), George Romney (American Motors), C. R. Smith (American Airlines), Thomas Watson, Jr. (IBM), Charles Wilson (GM).

45 Lewellen, *Ownership Income of Management,* p. 11.

46 Wilbur G. Lewellen, "Recent Evidence on Senior Executive Pay," *National Tax Journal,* June 1975, pp. 161–164.

47 Lewellen never differentiated between owner-dominated and management-dominated companies in his analysis of compensation packages. William McEachern, who does this using a method similar to that of Lewellen, found that the compensation packages established in firms with a dominant stockholder were more designed to maximize firm profits and market value than was the case for other firms. See William McEachern, *Managerial Control and Performance* (Lexington, Mass.: Lexington Books, 1975), pp. 58–83. Mc-

Eachern's findings do not, however, prove that these different compensation structures affect managerial behavior. Furthermore, the present author was not able to duplicate some of McEachern's results, using different data and methods, however; see n. 55. See also Robert T. Masson, "Executive Motivations, Earnings, and Consequent Equity Performance," *Journal of Political Economy,* November–December 1971, pp. 1278–1292.

48 Towers, Perrin, Forster, and Crosby, *Short- and Long-Term Executive Incentive Plans* (New York: Towers, Perrin, Forster & Crosby, 1976), p. 8.

49 In the mid-1970s General Electric's plan allocated 10 percent (maximum) of the excess over 5 percent of capital; General Foods used 5 percent of pretax earnings in excess of 14 percent of net capital.

50 Management compensation is increasingly fixed by board committees composed of a majority (or entirely) of outside directors. But the management or management-dominated staff usually provides recommendations and analyses that are rarely challenged by the outside directors on the committee. An officer of a management consulting firm, specializing in executive compensation, described to this author his recent experience as a staff member of a highly respected corporation "advising" the board compensation committee. He gave the committee a reasonably detailed and objective analysis of the bases on which compensation should be fixed, including comparative data, and enumerated some relevant questions that come up in evaluating compensation. The committee members thanked him profusely for providing them with the basis for moving beyond a pure rubber stamp role, which they had played in the past, to the position of being able at least to ask some intelligent questions.

51 See Edward Lawler, *Pay and Organizational Effectiveness* (New York: McGraw-Hill, 1971); Theo. Nichols, *Ownership Control and Ideology* (London: George Allen and Unwin, 1969), Chaps. 9–11.

52 Wilbur G. Lewellen and Blaine Huntsman, "Managerial Pay and Corporate Performance," *American Economic Review,* September 1970, pp. 710–720.

53 Masson, "Executive Motivations."

54 J. W. McGuire, J. S. Y. Chiu, and A. O. Elbing, "Executive Incomes, Sales, and Profits," *American Economic Review,* September 1962, pp. 753–761; Arch Patton, "Top Executive Pay: New Facts and Figures," *Harvard Business Review,* September 1966, pp. 94–97; David R. Roberts, *Executive Compensation* (Glencoe, Ill.: The Free Press, 1959). Despite his conclusion downgrading profits as a factor influencing management compensation, Roberts's own data show profitability a strong second to size in explaining compensation. On the failure of statistical methods as a source of negative findings of a relationship between profits and compensation, see George Yarrow, "Executive Compensation and the Objectives of

the Firm," in Keith Cowling (ed.), *Market Structure and Corporate Behaviour: Theory and Empirical Analysis of the Firm* (London: Gray-Mills, 1972), pp. 157–172.

55 As noted in footnote 44, McEachern carries these analyses forward by differentiating compensation systems according to ownership versus management control. He goes further, breaking ownership control into the dual cases of owner/manager control (OM, where the CEO is also a dominant owner) and control through a hired manager (EC, where the CEO is not a dominant owner, and control is exercised by an external ownership interest). He found that for a three-industry set (16 firms each, 48 total) there was a statistically significant tendency for reward systems to be more oriented toward stockholder welfare variables (market value of stock and profits), than to sales, and these reward systems were also larger in size in cases of external ownership control in contrast with those where management control prevailed. Differences in the same direction were found between owner/manager and management control cases, but less consistently and not always of statistically significant size. These are interesting findings, but several caveats are in order. First, McEachern's company sample is small and his classification into managment control, EC, and OM is dubious in concept and questionable in factual basis in several applications. There are different degrees of remoteness and presence in cases he classes as involving "external control"; for example, the external interest may still be in possession of high office (Dow, with a family member serving as president until 1971; Rohm and Haas, with a Haas chairman of the board although not a CEO; or well represented on the board, or unrepresented on the board and verging on noncontrol). These subtleties are ignored by McEachern, but they should make a difference. As to fact, among other problems, McEachern classed Du Pont as externally controlled in 1969–1972, although a member of the family by marriage was a CEO; and his classification of Merck as externally controlled during those years is also incorrect.

More critical, McEachern only addresses the question of whether there are significant differences *between* the income incentives of owner- and manager-dominated companies, not the actual importance of these incentives as stimuli to performance. He also comes up with the paradoxical result that owner/managers have designed an incentive system more oriented to sales than hired managers (p. 80), which is hard to reconcile with a dichotomy assumed between managerial incentives (sales) and owner incentives (profits).

As regards the overall importance of these compensation variables, this author tested the compensation of the top officer for the years 1972 and 1976 as a dependent variable in a covariance model (described in Appendix C), with independent variables as follows: asset size, industry class, barriers to entry, risk, return on equity, sales growth, and a measure of the form of control (strong versus weak ownership control, each subdivided into EC and OM, versus management control). Asset size was always highly significant for all control classifications, and industrial class was usually significant. Barriers to entry, risk, return on equity, and sales growth never reached significance and displayed no consistent differences as between control classifications. Testing separately for control classes (MC versus EC and MC versus OM), compensation was significantly higher with MC as compared with OM, but there was no significant difference as between MC and EC – in fact, the signs were consistently different from those hypothesized by McEachern (i.e., MC showed higher compensation levels). I used different years, different companies, different variables (asset size, not sales volume, and included a barriers-to-entry variable), a different control classification, and a different statistical method. The variations in results are striking, however, and the issues involved must be said to remain moot.

56 See Isadore Barmash, "Looking for Company Presidents Is Now a Deadly Serious 'Game,' " *New York Times,* May 13, 1978, p. 29, which describes a much more active market for top executives among companies in the apparel and retailing industry, where companies that have grown to substantial size "find themselves forced to search outside." For further discussion and citations see Mc-Eachern, *Managerial Control,* pp. 30–31.

57 According to Douglas Kuehn, "I was not able to get at the precise form of the relationship between objective and constraint because in multivariate analysis I was confounded by the correlations between profits and growth resulting in a high degree of indeterminacy in the estimated equations. The univariate analysis in the present chapter can give no clues to the interactions between the two." See Douglas Kuehn, *Takeovers and the Theory of the Firm* (New York: Holmes & Meier, 1975), pp. 126–127.

58 Edith T. Penrose, *The Theory of the Growth of the Firm* (New York: Wiley, 1959), p. 30. The same point is made by K. D. George, *Industrial Organization* (London: Allen & Unwin, 1972), pp. 26–30. On the bias toward growth based on the cost reduction effects of increasing volume, see M. H. Peston, "On the Sales Maximization Hypothesis," *Economica,* May 1959, pp. 128–136. On the positive relationship between sales and profits, see B. R. Marby and D. L. Siders, "An Empirical Test of the Sales Maximization Hypothesis," *Southern Economic Journal,* January 1967, pp. 367–377. On the positive relationship between market share and profitability, see Bradley T. Gale, "Market Share and Rate of Return" *Review of Economics and Statistics,* November 1972, pp. 412–423; William G. Shepherd, *The Treatment of Market Power* (New York: Columbia University Press, 1975), Chaps. 2 and 4.

59 In a study that does not differentiate between owner and manager control, Crain, Deaton, and Tollison found that executive turnover rates were "positively related in a quite responsive way to profit variations" (sales are negatively related to tenure, but not to a level of statistical significance at a 5 percent test level). The authors conclude that their findings "suggests that nonprofit maximizing behavior in the private sector is not typically tolerated in the market for executive services." W. Mark Crain, Thomas Deaton, and Robert Tollison, "On the Survival of Corporate Executives," *Southern Economic Journal*, January 1977, p. 1374.

60 See Chap. 4, under "Institutional Investor Behavior."

61 See Kuehn, *Takeovers and the Theory of the Firm*, p. 126. See also J. R. Davies and D. A. Kuehn, "An Empirical Analysis of Capital Market Discipline on Poor Performance and Its Implications for the Theory of the Firm," in *Proceedings of the 20th International Conference of the Institute of Management Studies*, June 1973, pp. 642–647.

62 This point is effectively stressed in Theo. Nichols, *Ownership Control and Ideology*, Chap. 9.

63 U.S. corporations planned to finance 90 percent of their 1979 capital expenditures by internal funds. See *Corporate Financing Week* (Institutional Investor), June 18, 1979, p. 2. See also Agit Singh, *Take-Overs* (Cambridge University Press, 1971), p. 4.

64 See Chap. 4, under "Restrictive covenants."

65 Armen A. Alchian and Reuben A. Kessel, "Competition, Monopoly, and the Pursuit of Pecuniary Gain," in *Aspects of Labor Economics* (New York: National Bureau of Economic Research, 1962); Henry G. Manne, "Mergers and the Market for Corporate Control," *Journal of Political Economy*, April 1965, pp. 110–120; Marris, *Managerial Capitalism*, pp. 19–20, 29–45.

66 See Singh, *Take-Overs*, pp. 6–10; J. R. Wildsmith, *Managerial Theories of the Firm* (New York: Dunellen, 1973), pp. 8–11.

67 Agit Singh, "Take-Overs, Economic Natural Selection, and the Theory of the Firm: Evidence from the Postwar United Kingdom Experience," *Economic Journal* September 1975, p. 512.

68 See Federal Trade Commission, *Economic Report on Corporate Mergers* (Washington, D.C.: Government Printing Office, 1969), pp. 54–59; T. F. Hogarty, "Profits from Merger: The Evidence of Fifty Years," *St. John's Law Review*, Spring 1970, pp. 378–391; Samuel Reid, *Mergers, Managers and the Economy*, (New York: McGraw-Hill, 1968), pt. II; "The Great Takeover Binge," *Business Week*, November 14, 1977, pp. 176ff.

69 See Ralph E. Winter, "Takeover Targets: Prosperous Firms Get More and More Offers by Corporate Buyers," *Wall Street Journal*, September 6, 1978. See also "The Great Takeover Binge," *Business Week*, November 14, 1977, which notes the leeriness of acquirers like Ben Heineman of Northwest Industries toward unhealthy com-

panies: " 'It always takes longer than anyone believes to turn a company around,' he explains." Heineman reportedly looks for companies "earning at least 12% on capital and whose markets are growing by 10% a year or more" (p. 179).

70 See Kuehn, *Takeovers and the Theory of the Firm;* Singh, "Take-Overs," and items cited in note 68.

71 Singh, "Take-Overs," p. 510.

72 Ibid., pp. 511–513; Frederic Scherer, in U.S., Congress, Senate, Committee on Banking, Housing and Urban Affairs, *Corporate Takeovers,* 94th Cong., 2d sess. (Washington, D.C.: Government Printing Office, 1976), p. 112. A recent *Business Week* special report, "Can Semiconductors Survive Big Business?" December 3, 1979, notes that 20 absorptions of semiconductor companies have occurred in the last three years, leaving only seven independents out of 36 start-ups since 1966. Most of the absorbed companies were doing well and were small. *Business Week* expresses concern, based on the fact that the great technical successes in the industry have come out of the small entrepreneurial companies concentrating on semiconductors; "the track record for most equipment makers entering the merchant- or open-market place for semiconductors is miserable" (p. 68).

73 "Executives of many companies are relying on the loyalties of large shareholders and, to a lesser extent, of small shareholders to defeat any takeover bid. Says Claude Ganz, president of Dymo Industries: 'We have substantial ownership – I'm talking about 40% – that is vested in four or five parties who are all represented on our board, and we feel an unfriendly take-over wouldn't be feasible as long as these investors are satisfied.' " Quoted from "Sitting Ducks: Company Executives Shore Up Defense Against Take-Overs," *Wall Street Journal,* October 21, 1974.

74 It has been a common view that managerial control will produce a longer planning horizon on the part of corporate leaders (e.g., Chandler, *The Visible Hand,* p. 451), but very little evidence has been adduced in its support. This view has lost favor with the recent declines in relative U.S. productivity gains and international competitiveness, which has shifted attention to an alleged managerial preoccupation with short-term income gains and stock price movements. See Alfred Rappaport, "Executive incentives vs. corporate growth," *Harvard Business Review,* July–August 1978; Robert H. Hayes and William J. Abernathy, "Managing our way to economic decline," *Harvard Business Review,* July–August 1980, pp. 67–76; and the testimony of John De Lorean on the short planning horizon of the top leadership of GM, in J. Patrick Wright, *On a Clear Day You Can See General Motors* (Grosse Point, Mich.: Wright Enterprises, 1979), p. 7, 191, 195–202. See also, "Managers who are no longer entrepreneurs," *Business Week,* June 30, 1980, pp. 74–75.

75 *Forbes Magazine,* for example, has engaged in a steady assault on managements dodging takeover bids for reasons of self-interest. See "Who Is Kidding Whom?" *Forbes,* March 15, 1977, p. 30; Paul Blaustein, "Does Father Know Best?" *Forbes,* March 6, 1978, pp. 31–32; Richard Phalon, "A Modest Proposal," *Forbes,* April 30, 1979, pp. 129–130.

76 This is the value of the equity of the 200 largest firms by market value, not by asset or sales size.

77 On the concentration of institutional holdings, see Chap. 4, Tables 4.5 to 4.11 and associated text. On the distribution of individual stockholdings, Marshall E. Blume and Irwin Friend give "lower boundary" estimates that the wealthiest 0.5 percent of families held 33 percent of all corporate stock at the end of 1972 and that families with stock portfolios valued at $1 million or more owned 40 percent of individually owned stock in 1971. See Marshall E. Blume and Irwin Friend, *The Changing Role of the Individual Investor,* A Twentieth Century Fund Report, (New York: Wiley, 1978), pp. 9–10. Melvin Eisenberg notes that although ownership concentration declines as company size and number of shareholders increases, even with very large companies, normally there are holdings of quite significant size, whose owners will have an interest and expect to participate in structural decisions; the "average shareholder fallacy" consists in ignoring these important substantial holdings. See Melvin A. Eisenberg, *The Structure of the Corporation, A Legal Analysis* (Boston: Little, Brown, 1976), pp. 43–44.

78 The attention paid by top officers to security analysts is impressive. The CEO of Safeway claimed to have attended 59 meetings with security analysts in 1973. See "The top man becomes Mr. Outside," *Business Week,* May 4, 1974, p. 38. For an illustration of commercial bank interest in professional investor attitudes toward their company, see "Remarks at Investor Relations Dinner," First National City Corporation, October 6, 1971, especially the presentation of Chairman Wriston, who refers to the meeting as "an important step in a major effort to improve our communications with the investment community."

79 John Goldethorpe, quoted in Marris, *Managerial Capitalism,* p. 53.

80 A community of which he is a member. This process of socialization is discussed at some length in Nichols, *Ownership Control and Ideology,* pp. 121–133.

81 Alfred D. Chandler Jr., *Strategy and Structure: Chapters in the History of the American Industrial Enterprise* (Cambridge, Mass.: MIT Press, 1962), p. 14 and passim.

82 Oliver Williamson, "Managerial Discretion, Organizational Form and the Multi-division Hypothesis," in Robin Marris and Adrian Wood (eds.), *The Corporate Economy* (London: Macmillan, 1971), pp. 343–386.

83 For a discussion of some of these important exceptions to the frequently idealized portrayal of organizational evolution to the divisional structure, see Richard B. DuBoff and Edward S. Herman, "Alfred Chandler's New Business History: A Review," *Politics and Society*, forthcoming.

84 Richard P. Rumelt. *Strategy, Structure, and Economic Performance* (Boston: Harvard Graduate School of Business, 1974), p. 65.

85 Jay R. Galbraith and Daniel A. Nathanson, *Strategy Implementation: The Role of Structure and Process* (St. Paul, Minn.: West Publishing, 1978), p. 71.

86 Ibid., pp. 71–76 and passim.

87 Of 618 replies from a large company sample in the mid-1960s, only 11 percent did not have profit centers for their various divisions. See John J. Mauriel and Robert N. Anthony, "Misevaluation of investment center performance," *Harvard Business Review*, March–April 1966, pp. 98–105; also, R. D. Buzzell, B. T. Gale, and R. G. M. Sultan, "Market Share – A Key to Profitability," *Harvard Business Review*, January–February 1975, pp. 97–107. A late 1970s update of the study done by Mauriel and Anthony showed a further spread in use of investment and profit centers; a sample of 620 large companies showed only 4.2 percent without either profit or investment centers. James S. Reece and William R. Cool, "Measuring investment center performance," *Harvard Business Review*, May–June, 1978, pp. 28ff.

88 Rumelt, *Strategy, Structure*, p. 84.

89 Ibid., p. 85.

90 J. K. Galbraith, *The New Industrial State* (Boston: Houghton Mifflin, 1967), p. 116.

91 Rumelt, *Strategy, Structure*, pp. 126ff.

92 Williamson, "Managerial Discretion," p. 370.

93 Ibid., p. 380.

94 On the quantitative importance, utility, and disutility of insider advantage in buying and selling stock, see Henry G. Manne, *Insider Trading and the Stock Market* (New York: Free Press, 1966); H. K. Wu, *"Corporate Insider Trading, Profitability and Stock Price Movements,"* Ph.D. dissertation, University of Pennsylvania, 1963; Herman, *Conflicts of Interest*, Chap. 3. See also, Tom Herman, "Mum's the Word: Firms Act to Prevent Leaks as Take-Overs and Mergers Multiply," *Wall Street Journal* June 2, 1976, p. 1; Frederick C. Klein, "Ahead of the News: Merger Leaks Abound, Causing Many Stocks to Rise Before the Fact," *Wall Street Journal*, July 12, 1978, p. 1.

95 U.S., Congress, Senate, Committee on Interstate Commerce. *Investigation of Railroads, Holdings Companies, and Affiliated Companies*, Sen. Rep. No. 714, *The Van Sweringen Corporate System*, 73rd Cong., 1st sess. (Washington, D.C.: Government Printing Office, 1941), pt. 3, p. 1179.

96 This point is made in an article that finds superiority in the performance of owner-dominated companies in Great Britain: "To reach such a size while maintaining owner-control implies that the firm has sacrificed the benefits of full access to the capital market." In addition to high retention rates it is suggested that such firms may have had exceptional management. H. K. Radice, "Control Types, Profitability and Growth in Large Firms: An Empirical Study," *Economic Journal*, September 1971, p. 561.

97 These are the assumptions in R. J. Monsen, J. S. Y. Chiu, and D. E. Cooley, "The Effect of Separation of Ownership and Control on the Performance of the Large Firm," *Quarterly Journal of Economics*, August 1968, pp. 435–451.

98 See Robert E. Wong, "Profit Maximization and Alternative Theories: A Dynamic Reconciliation," *American Economic Review*, September 1975, pp. 689–693.

99 W. J. Baumol, "On the Theory of the Expansion of the Firm, *American Economic Review*, 52, December 1962, pp. 1078–1087; W. J. Baumol, *Business Behavior, Value and Growth*, rev. ed. (New York: Macmillan, 1967), pp. 35–46; Marris, *Managerial Capitalism*, pp. 47ff.

100 Baumol *Business Behavior*, p. 46; Marris, *Managerial Capitalism*, pp. 47ff.

101 Bradley T. Gale, "Market Share and Rate of Return," *Review of Economics and Statistics*, November 1972, pp. 412–423; R. D. Buzzell, B. T. Gale, and G. M. Sultan, "Market Share – A Key to Profitability," *Harvard Business Review*, January–February 1975, pp. 97–107; William G. Shepherd, "The Elements and Evolution of Market Structure," in A. P. Jacquemin and H. W. de Jong, *Markets, Corporate Behaviour and the State* (The Hague: Martinus Nijhoff, 1976).

102 Joseph A. Schumpeter, *The Theory of Economic Development* (Cambridge, Mass.: Harvard University Press, 1934), p. 93.

103 Karl Marx, *Capital* (New York: Modern Library, 1906), vol. I, pt. IV.

104 Marris, *Managerial Capitalism*, p. 10.

105 A similar conclusion is arrived at by Robert Solow – that Marris has not proved his case "against the more standard model of long-run profit maximization anchored by a target rate of return." Robert M. Solow, "The truth further refined: A comment on Marris," *The Public Interest*, Spring 1968, p. 49. Solow's concept of profit maximization is closely akin to the concept of profitable growth.

106 Robert M. Solow, "Some Implications of Alternative Criteria for the Firm," in Marris and Woods (eds.), *Corporate Economy*, pp. 341–342.

107 This is one of the empirical findings of Rumelt, *Strategy, Structure*, p. 126.

108   Such behavior fits many theories of conglomeration and large firm diversification that focus on their short-term financial priorities, their capital mobility, and the very rational (and ruthless) approach they take to investment and divestment. On the latter points, see Barry Bluestone and Bennett Harrison, *Capital and Communities: The Cause and Consequences of Private Disinvestment* (Washington, D.C.: The Progressive Alliance, 1980). For some specific cases, see Ralph E. Winter, "Bailing Out, Corporations Sell Off Some Sagging Units as Profit Picture Dims," *Wall Street Journal*, January 15, 1980; Jeffrey A. Tannenbaum, "Slimming Down, Sliding Earnings Spur Union Carbide Corp. To Big Reform Effort," *Wall Street Journal*, January 3, 1979; Barbara Ettorre, "Colgate Cleans House Speedily," *New York Times*, April 12, 1980, p. 31.

109   See the discussion and citations in Chap. 6 under "Trends in corporate size."

110   The following empirical studies found a significant positive relationship between ROE and ownership control: Kenneth J. Boudreaux, "Managerialism and Risk-Return Performance," *Southern Economic Journal*, January 1973, pp. 366–373; Cynthia A. Glassman and Stephen A. Rhoades, "Owner vs. Manager Control Effects on Bank Profit Rates, Growth, and Costs," in *Proceedings from a Conference on Bank Structure and Competition*, Federal Reserve Bank of Chicago, April 27–28, 1978, pp. 157–170; Philip J. Karst, "The Effect on Performance of the Separation of Ownership from Control," Ph.D. dissertation, Washington University, 1972; Robert J. Larner, *Management Control and the Large Corporation* (New York: Dunellen Publishing, 1970); R. J. Monsen, J. S. Y. Chiu, and D. E. Cooley, "The Effect of Separation of Ownership," pp. 435–451; John Palmer, "The Profit Performance Effects of the Separation of Ownership from Control in Large U.S. Industrial Corporations," *Bell Journal of Economic and Management Science*, Spring 1973, pp. 293–303; H. K. Radice, "Control Type Profitability and Growth in Large Firms: An Empirical Study," pp. 547–562; Miron Stano, "Monopoly power, ownership control and corporate performance," *Bell Journal of Economic and Management Science*, Autumn 1976, pp. 672–679. The five investigations that found no such positive relationships are as follows: J. W. Elliot, "Control, Size, Growth and Financial Performance in the Firm," *Journal of Financial and Quantitative Analysis*, January 1972, pp. 1309–1320; Leon P. Jorgenson, "Separation of Ownership and Control and Its Influence on the Profit Performance of the Large Firm," Ph.D. dissertation, Florida State University, 1972; David R. Kamerschen, "The Influence of Ownership and Control on Profit Rates," *American Economic Review*, June 1968, pp. 432–447; P. David Qualls, "Market Structure and Managerial Behavior," in Robert T. Masson and P. David Qualls (eds.), *Essays on Industrial Organization in Honor of Joe S. Bain* (Cambridge, Mass.: Ballinger

Publishing, 1976), pp. 89–104; Robert L. Sorenson, "Some Economic Implications of the Separation of Ownership and Control in the Large Firm," Ph.D. dissertation, Virginia Polytechnic Institute, 1971.

111 McEachern, *Managerial Control,* Chaps. 4–6.

112 Many classification systems are based on ownership information taken from proxy statements alone, which can lead to serious errors as discussed throughout this text (and in some detail in Burch, *Managerial Revolution Reassessed,* pp. 9–28). There is also little consistency in handling intercorporate ownership.

113 A supplemental analysis was carried out adding a barriers-to-entry variable and a variable differentiating cases where the dominant ownership (1) directly managed or (2) controlled through a hired manager. These additional variables yielded no important changes in the results.

Chapter 4. Financial Control of the Large Corporation

1 Thomas C. Cochran refers to some who had substantial holdings in many ventures and spent a great deal of time supervising their investment as "general entrepreneurs." He notes that several were looked upon by other capitalists as representatives of their genre and were thus able to tap wider resources and exercise commensurate power. Thomas C. Cochran, *Railroad Leaders 1845–1890* (Cambridge, Mass.: Harvard University Press, 1953), pp. 9–11.

2 Ibid., p. 11.

3 Louis D. Brandeis, *Other People's Money, and How the Bankers Use It* (Washington, D.C.: National Home Library Foundation, 1933), originally published in 1914.

4 Report of the Committee Appointed Pursuant to House Resolutions 429 and 504 to Investigate the Concentration of Control of Money and Credit, H. Rept. 1593, 62nd Cong., 3d sess. (Washington, D.C.: Government Printing Office, 1913).

5 Louis D. Brandeis, *Other People's Money,* pp. 16ff.

6 Rudolf Hilferding, *Das Finanzkapital* (Vienna: Wiener Volksbuchhandlung, 1923), originally published in 1910; V. I. Lenin, *Imperialism* (New York: Vanguard Press, 1926), originally published in 1916. Hilferding forecast the subjection of all industry to centralized banker control; Lenin was far more cautious, expecting banks to accelerate combinations, but stressing a fusion of industrial and financial interests rather than clear-cut domination of the latter.

7 Paul M. Sweezy, "The Decline of the Investment Banker," *Antioch Review,* Spring 1941, pp. 63–68; *The Theory of Capitalist Development* (New York: Oxford University Press, 1942), pp. 265–274.

8 Paul M. Sweezy, "The Resurgence of Financial Control: Fact or Fancy," *Monthly Review,* November 1971, pp. 1–33.

9 See the works cited in note 56. See also Edward S. Herman, "Kotz on Banker Control," *Monthly Review*, September 1979, pp. 46–52.

10 Veblen distinguished between "business" and "industry," and "pecuniary" and "industrial" employments – with business and pecuniary encompassing the entrepreneur, divorced from the work process and its immediate direction, as well as from outside financial and speculative interests. See especially, "Industrial and Pecuniary Employments," in *The Place of Science in Modern Civilization and Other Essays* (New York: B. W. Huebsch, 1919).

11 Julius Grodinsky, *Jay Gould* (Philadelphia: University of Pennsylvania Press, 1957), p. 81.

12 Cochran, *Railroad Leaders*, p. 124.

13 William Z. Ripley, *Railroads, Finance and Organization* (New York: Longmans, Green, 1915), pp. 262ff.; George Kennan, *E. H. Harriman, A Biography*, vol. 1 (Boston: Houghton Mifflin, 1922), p. 82.

14 This is often a matter of drawing a somewhat arbitrary balance. In the case of Gould, the extraneous financial interests were always large, the constructive managerial effort was modest, and classification of his controlled entities, as subject to financial control, is plausible. With Harriman, the constructive element was substantial, the manipulative input important but apparently normal for the time, and in Table 3.4 Union Pacific is classed as controlled by minority ownership interests in 1900–1901.

15 Stuart Daggett, *Railroad Reorganization* (Boston: Harvard University Press, 1908), pp. 317–326 (on Moore–Reid and the Rock Island); Harold F. Cox and John F. Meyers, "The Philadelphia Traction Monopoly and the Pennsylvania Constitution of 1874: The Prostitution of an Ideal," *Pennsylvania History* vol. 35, October 1968, pp. 406–423 (on Widener, Elkins, and their associates).

16 *The Van Sweringen Corporate System,* Investigation of Railroads, Holding Companies, and Affiliated Companies, Sen. Rep. 714, pt. 1–3, Committee on Interstate Commerce, 77th Cong., 1st sess. (Washington, D.C.: Government Printing Office, 1941), p. 1183.

17 The basic sources on these practices in the 1920s are the Pecora hearings, *Stock Exchange Practices,* Hearings before the Senate Committee on Banking and Currency, 72nd and 73rd Cong., (Washington, D.C.: Government Printing Office, 1933–1934, pts. 1–17; the Securities and Exchange Commission study, *Abuses and Deficiencies in the Organization and Operation of Investment Companies,* 1940; and the massive Federal Trade Commission study of the utility industry carried out in the 1930s, Federal Trade Commission, *Utility Corporations,* 70th Cong., 1st sess., Sen. Doc. 92(Washington, D.C.: Government Printing Office, 1935), esp. pts. 71A, 72A, and 73A. A good brief introduction to this issue is James Bonbright and Gardiner Means, *The Holding Company* (New York: McGraw-Hill, 1932).

18 The power of Morgan and the other investment banks in the early

years of the century also rested on very close links, including in some cases a control relationship, with the large insurance companies, a very important source of funds for permanent investment at that time. See esp., Pujo Committee report, Committee Appointed Pursuant to HR 429 and 504, pp. 60–83; see also Morton Keller, *The Life Insurance Enterprise, 1885–1910* (Cambridge, Mass.: Harvard University Press, 1963), Chap. 9.

19 See W. Nelson Peach, *The Security Affiliates of National Banks* (Baltimore: Johns Hopkins University Press, 1941), pp. 18–20, 86–89.

20 Thomas R. Navin and Marian V. Sears, "The Rise of a Market for Industrial Securities, 1887–1902," *Business History Review*, June 1955, pp. 105ff.

21 See Harry A. Cushing, *Voting Trusts* (New York: Macmillan, 1927) esp. pp. 10–13, 22–23, 33–34. On June 30, 1894, there were 192 railroads in the hands of receivers, operating 40,818 miles of track with a quarter of the capitalization of all U.S. railroads. William Z. Ripley, *Railroads, Finance and Organization* (New York: Longmans, Green, 1915), p. 376.

22 See esp., Navin and Sears, "The Rise of a Market" passim.; Alfred S. Eichner, *The Emergency of Oligopoly: Sugar Refining as a Case Study* (Baltimore: Johns Hopkins University Press, 1969), pp. 100–113. *The Report of the Commission of Corporations on the Steel Industry* noted that averting a price war "and the coalition of the various consolidations, if successfully financed, would be a tremendous 'bull' argument." pt. I (Washington, D.C.: Government Printing Office, 1911), p. 11.

23 J. P. Morgan and Company either controlled or was in close alliance with Bankers Trust, Guaranty Trust, Chemical Bank, First National Bank of New York, National City Bank of New York, Equitable Life and Mutual Life Insurance Company, plus some other institutions. The alliances were based on extensive interlocks, common ownership of other companies and mutual ownership among these majors, joint participation in underwriting syndicates, and a widely accepted business ethic in which taking an established customer from another firm by competition was not considered "highminded practice" (see Pujo Committee report, Committee Appointed Pursuant to HR 429 and 504, pp. 57–74, 102–104). For an opposing view to the contention that there was a "money trust," see Vincent Carosso, *Investment Banking in America, A History* (Cambridge, Mass.: Harvard University Press, 1970), pp. 151–153.

24 Pujo Committee report, Committee Appointed Pursuant to HR 429 and 504, p. 106.

25 Alfred Marshall, writing in 1919, referred to "the predominating power in American finance, exercised by a relatively small group of men, who have combined the ownership of vast wealth with the ambition to show a Napoleonic faculty in its use." He goes on to

make the odd statement that the fears aroused by these men of power "seems to have been definitely laid by the great Federal Reserve Act of 1913." *Industry and Trade* (London: Macmillan and Company, Ltd., 1919), p. 344.

26 Federal Trade Commission, *Utility Corporations*, 70th Cong., 1st sess., (Washington, D.C.: Government Printing Office, 1935), Sen. Doc. 92, pt. 72A, p. 76.

27 Ibid., p. 115.

28 See Ervin Miller, "Background and Structure of the Industry," in Irwin Friend, et al. (eds.), *Investment Banking and the New Issues Market* (Cleveland: World Publishing, 1967), pp. 92–97.

29 Ibid., pp. 97–101; see also W. E. Atkins, G. W. Edwards, and H. G. Moulton, *The Regulation of the Security Markets* (Washington, D.C.: Brookings Institution, 1946).

30 U.S., Congress, Senate, Committee on Banking and Currency, *Stock Exchange Practices*, Sen. Rep. No. 1455, 73rd Cong., 2d sess. (Washington, D.C.: Government Printing Office, 1934); see also, Ferdinand Pecora, *Wall Street Under Oath* (New York: Simon & Schuster, 1939); Max Lowenthal, *The Investor Pays* (New York: Alfred Knopf, 1933).

31 Miller, "Background and Structure," pp. 138ff.

32 On the linkage between rate of asset growth and external financing, see Neil Jacoby and Raymond Saulnier, *Business Finance and Banking* (New York: National Bureau of Economic Research, 1947), p. 93.

33 There have been claims in recent years that in their search for business, in compensation for the decline in brokerage fees, investment bankers have been so energetic as to have made their own net contribution to merger activity; but the investment banker response is (in the words of Robert F. Greenhill, a partner of Morgan Stanley), "We are simply a service organization . . . we're not running searches looking for sitting ducks." (Quoted in "Greenhill: A new takeover artist," *Business Week*, December 14, 1974, p. 55.)

34 Lazard received almost $4 million in income from ITT from January 1, 1966 through September 5, 1969. See *Investigation of Conglomerate Corporations*, Staff Report, Antitrust Subcommittee, House Judiciary Committee, 92nd Cong., 1st sess. (Washington, D.C.: Government Printing Office, 1971), pp. 156–157.

35 *Investigation of Conglomerate Corporations*, Hearings on Gulf & Western Industries, before the House Antitrust Subcommittee (Washington, D.C.: Government Printing Office, 1969), pt. 1, p. 12.

36 "Ranking America's largest money managers," *Institutional Investor*, August 1976, pp. 79–109.

37 See Lester V. Chandler, "Monopolistic Elements in Commercial Banking," *Journal of Political Economy*, February 1938, pp. 1–22; Jack M. Guttentag and Edward S. Herman, "Banking Structure and Performance," *The Bulletin*, no. 41/43, New York University Grad-

uate School of Business, February 1967, esp. pp. 66–79; Stephen A. Rhoades, *Geographic Expansion of Banks and Changes in Banking Structure,* Staff Studies 102, Board of Governors of the Federal Reserve System (Washington, D.C.: 1979).

38 In late 1980, 52 percent of the domestic commercial and industrial loans of large banks were term loans; i.e., those with a maturity of one year or longer. The bulk of these loans are in the maturity range of four years and under, and in a world of volatile interest rates most of them have rates that "float" by a fixed link to market rates.

39 Medium-grade borrowers have benefited from the fact that competition for the fixed-income securities issued by the top credit risks has been so intense that large lenders have been forced to look hard below this top tier for reasonable yields. For one of the largest insurance companies, 60 percent of the number and 30 percent of the dollar volume of private placements were outside the Fortune 500 list in the late 1970s.

40 See Karen W. Arenson, "Commercial Paper Surge," *New York Times,* February 4, 1979, sec. 3, p. 1.

41 Among them, a probable decline in interinstitutional ownership linkages and explicit collusion, aided by a changed view of the government on price fixing, or perhaps more accurately, the applicability of the antitrust laws to financial institutions since the mid-1940s.

42 Loan agreements of the major airlines, filed as part of airline 10-K reports, are a rich source of joint venture loan information. Data along this line, plus information on interlocks, stock ownership, and so on for selected airlines are given in U.S., Congress, House, Committee on Banking and Currency, staff report of the Subcommittee on Domestic Finance, *Commercial Banks and Their Trust Activities: Emerging Influence on the American Economy,* vol. 1, 90th Cong., 2d sess. (Washington, D.C.: Government Printing Office, July 8, 1968).

43 Using net income as a measure of power, there were seven commercial banks with net income of $100 million or more in 1975, as compared with 91 industrials. Citibank's top bank net income of $350 million was exceeded by 17 industrial companies. The two largest profit makers among industrials, Exxon and IBM, had net incomes ($2.5 and 2.0 billion, respectively) not far short of the aggregate net incomes of the 50 largest commercial banks together ($2.9 billion).

44 A discussion of problem loans in the *Wall Street Journal* notes that the banks go to great lengths to avoid customer bankruptcy, partly because of delays, partly because the costs of the proceedings tend to chop 20 to 30 percent off recoverable assets. "But the key reason for avoiding the bankruptcy courts is 'loss of control,' bankers say. Bankruptcy, after all, is designed to protect the debtor *from* his creditors, not to make sure they get paid." "The Morning After: 'Prob-

lem Loans' That Result from Days of Easy Credit Give Banks Headaches," *Wall Street Journal,* August 20, 1975.

45 Richard Leger, "Taking Charge? Bank of America Moves to Direct Memorex; Company's Problems Viewed as Still Severe" *Wall Street Journal,* March 27, 1973; "Memorex: This is 'the year of restoration,' " *Business Week,* November 10, 1975, p. 100.

46 *The Financial Collapse of the Penn Central Company,* staff report of the SEC to the Special Subcommittee on Investigations, Committee on Interstate and Foreign Commerce, 1972, p. 97.

47 See Edward S. Herman, *Conflicts of Interest: Commercial Bank Trust Departments* (New York: The Twentieth Century Fund, 1975), p. 55.

48 "Pan Am Refinances," *Business Week,* December 15, 1975, p. 34; "Pan American Realigns Management Positions," *Wall Street Journal,* January 28, 1976, p. 12.

49 On the banker role in LTV, see "A Fate Worse Than Bankruptcy?" *Forbes,* August 15, 1970, p. 17; and esp. Rush Loving, Jr., "LTV's Flight from Bankruptcy," *Fortune,* June 1973, pp. 134–138, 220–225; on Grant, see *In the Matter of W. T. Grant, Bankrupt. Morgan Guaranty Trust Company of New York vs. Charles G. Rodman,* Trustee in Bankruptcy of W. T. Grant Company, Bankruptcy No. 75 B 1735, U.S. District Ct., Southern District of New York, esp. Trustee's Answer to Complaint of Morgan Guaranty (September 24, 1976) and depositions of John P. Schroeder, Morgan Guaranty (January 17, 1978). See also "Investigating the collapse of W. T. Grant," *Business Week,* July 19, 1976, pp. 60–62.

50 *Forbes* described Kirby as Burnham's "hand-picked successor" (December 1, 1975, p.30), but other reports and interviews indicate that the issue was only settled as it was by an earnings improvement in the second half of 1974 (*Business Week,* July 20, 1974, pp. 55, 63).

51 See Agis Salpukas, "Townsend Decision to Quit Chrysler Believed His Own," *New York Times,* July 5, 1975, p. 23. On the 1979–80 crisis, see the six-part series by Gary Hector on "The Chrysler Saga," *American Banker,* October 13 ("The Banker's Rebellion"), October 22, November 3, November 10, November 18, and November 25, 1980.

52 For characteristics of such agreements see Edward D. Zinbarg, "The Private Placement Loan Agreement," *Financial Analysts Journal,* July–August 1975, pp. 33–35, 52; Henry H. Fryling, "Private Placement Financing – Lender's Procedural Guide," paper given to Association of Life Insurance Counsel, New York City, December 7, 1964.

53 See for example, *Proposed Merger of Eastern–American Airlines,* House Judiciary Committee, 87th Cong., 2d sess. (Washington, D.C.: Government Printing Office, 1962), pp. 27–31.

54 According to an officer of Prudential Insurance Company, "lenders

make most modifications routinely, with no *quid pro quo* exacted from the borrower unless the proposed corporate action will compromise the lender's margin of safety. My own institution's experience may serve as an illustration. In any given year, we will, on average, receive *one modification request per loan on the books.* In no more than about five per cent of these cases will we refuse the request or even require any *quid pro quo,* because the vast majority of corporate requests are perfectly reasonable and do not increase our risk materially," Zinbarg, "Private Placement Loan Agreement," p. 35.

55 Conference Board, *Corporate Directorship Practices: Membership and Committees of the Board,* Rept. No. 588, 1973, pp. 28–29.

56 Works that are based on this simplistic theory include the following: Robert Fitch and Mary Oppenheimer, "Who Rules the Corporations?" *Socialist Revolution,* July–August 1970 and September–October 1970; Jean-Marie Chevalier, *La structure financière de l'industrie américaine* (Paris: Cujas, 1970); and David Kotz, *Bank Control of Large Corporations in the United States* (Berkeley: University of California Press, 1978).

57 In 1975 Caterpillar Tractor's net income was $398 million; First National Bank of Chicago's net income was $107 million.

58 There were two Morgans in the 1970s, one a commercial bank, the other an investment house, products of the post-Glass Steagall Act separation of such institutions. Only the commercial bank was represented on the General Electric board in 1975.

59 See Robert Sheehan, "A.T. & T. Meet G.T. & E.," *Fortune,* September 1959, pp. 115ff.

60 For example, the 1976 proxy statement of GTE notes that $463,534 in fees were paid to Paine Webber for placing securities.

61 Spelled out in trustee's Answer to Complaint of Morgan Guaranty Trust, In re W. T. Grant Company, Bankrupt, Bankruptcy No. 75 B 1735, District Ct., S. Dist., N.Y. (September 24, 1976).

62 Discretionary holdings refer to those for which the bank is given sole discretion in buying and selling. In other cases the banks have partial or no investment discretion.

63 These data were compiled by Computer Directions Advisors Inc. from the quarterly reports of 13-F institutions – that is, those who must report their holdings to the SEC by virtue of their exercise of investment discretion over equities valued at $100 million or more. The data were summarized in David Tyson, "$1 Billion Holders New Total 100," *The American Banker,* December 18, 1979. Tyson notes in his article that one of the 100, Lional Edie & Co., is a wholly owned subsidiary of one of the other members of the 100, namely, Manufacturers Hanover Trust.

64 See Allan Nevins, *Ford: Decline and Rebirth 1933–1962* (New York: Charles Scribner, 1963), p. 421.

65 The bank control analysts cited in note 56 tend to lump this type of bank holding with others in arriving at bank voting power figures. Peter Drucker, in *The Unseen Revolution* (New York: Harper & Row, 1977), seems to lump all pension fund and ESP holdings into an aggregate that yields "worker control!"

66 See Bert L. Metzger, *Profit Sharing in 38 Large Companies,* vol. 1 (Evanston, Ill.: Profit Sharing Research Foundation, 1975). Also, the periodic volumes issued by Bankers Trust, for example, *1972 Study of Employee Savings and Thrift Plans.* The latter volume showed that in almost a quarter of 216 plans, either the trustee or company voted all the shares. The majority were passed through – this is the trend tendency and characteristic of the plans of very large companies.

67 The same is true of founder company stock owned by the bank under company pension plans, even where the bank has the sole power to vote. See Herman, *Commercial Bank Trust Departments,* pp. 48–49.

68 Wharton School, *A Study of Mutual Funds,* H. Rep. No. 2274, 87th Cong., 2d sess. (Washington, D.C.: Government Printing Office, 1962), Chap. 7; SEC, *Public Policy Implications of Investment Company Growth,* H. Rep. No. 2337, 89th Cong., 2nd sess. (Washington, D.C.: Government Printing Office, 1966), pp. 307–318; *Institutional Investor Study Report of the Securities and Exchange Commission,* vol. 5, Chap. 15, 92nd Cong., 1st sess. (Washington, D.C.: Government Printing Office, March 10, 1971), H. Doc. No. 92–64, Part 5.

69 Herman, *Commercial Bank Trust Departments,* pp. 76–79.

70 In reference to White Motor Corporation, *Business Week* reported that "With the lenders apparently holding the strings now, Knudsen is conducting what adds up to a gradual liquidation of the assets of a company that had $1.4 billion in sales at its peak in 1974 . . . This 'boiling-back' process, as it is called in Cleveland, is being carried out nominally to benefit shareholders." ("How Bunkie Knudsen took on the bankers," *Business Week,* December 13, 1976, p. 72).

71 On the growth of big block trading, paralleling institutional investor expansion, and the efficiency effects of this development, see *Institutional Investor Study Report of the Securities and Exchange Commission,* H. Doc. 92–64, Part 4, 92nd Cong., 1st sess., Chaps. 10–13; Marshall E. Blume and Irwin Friend, *The Changing Role of the Individual Investor,* a Twentieth Century Fund Report (New York: John Wiley, 1978).

72 This rule provided that the mutual funds could not invest more than 5 percent of their own aggregate assets or acquire more than 10 percent of the voting stock of a portfolio company, for 75 percent of their total assets.

73 Legal lists are specific securities designated by state authority as safe and appropriate for investment in fiduciary accounts. These lists are applicable only to the small minority of accounts not covered by agreements between bank and the account founder, which usually give the bank complete or limited investment authority (and implicit exemption from any constraint by legal lists).

74 A 1970 civil suit by the Department of Justice against the Cleveland Trust Company sought to end the practice of bank officials serving on the boards of two or more competitive companies. The case was settled by a consent decree in which Cleveland Trust agreed that it would not allow an officer director to serve on the board of a machine tool company that was in competition with another company that also had a Cleveland Trust officer as a director. See "Bankers on boards," *Business Week*, September 15, 1975, p. 36.

75 See Herman, *Commercial Bank Trust Departments*, pp. 63–72.

76 This was the basis for the suggestion by Morgan Guaranty Trust that it has been looking into ways of getting rid of its voting power, by pass-through arrangements or otherwise. See the statement of Samuel Callaway of Morgan, *The American Banker*, February 7, 1974, p. 1.

77 For case studies of takeover efforts that frequently involved warehousing, see *Institutional Investor Study*, vol. 5, Chap. 15, pp. 2774ff.

78 See Chap. 3, note 78.

79 See Raymond Vernon, ed., *Big Business and the State* (Cambridge, Mass.: Harvard University Press; 1974), esp. George Küster's chapter on Germany; Andrew Shonfield, *Modern Capitalism* (New York: Oxford University Press, 1965). Chaps. 11–12; Richard E. Caves and Masu Uekusa, *Industrial Organization in Japan* (Washington, D.C.: Brookings Institution, 1976), pp. 37–41. For a description of the new groups (*keiretsu*) that have replaced the *zaibatsu* of the post-1945 era with looser but still closely tied interest groups, see "Sumitomo: How the 'keiretsu' pulls together to keep Japan strong," *Business Week*, March 31, 1975, pp. 43ff.

80 For a discussion of the contrast between the "Continental model" and that derived from British tradition and the application of the latter to Canada, see Jorge Niosi, *The Economy of Canada, A Study of Ownership and Control* (Montreal: Black Rose, 1977), pp. 27, 166.

81 See Jonathan Hughes, *The Vital Few* (Boston: Houghton Mifflin, 1966), pp. 424–428, for a survey of Morgan's stature, power, and role in bringing order to the railroads and elsewhere.

82 The best industry studies discuss at length the effects of *government* intervention on airline industry behavior and performance, but they give little attention to any impact of financial institutions. See A. M. Phillips, in William Capron (ed.), *Technological Change in Regulated*

Industries (Washington, D.C.: Brookings Institution, 1971); Richard Caves, *Air Transport and Its Regulators* (Cambridge, Mass.: Harvard University Press, 1962), esp. pp. 112–119. Financial institutions have shown considerable faith in large size and have given occasional encouragement to mergers. See Caves, p. 118; *Proposed Merger of Eastern–American Airlines,* House Judiciary Committee, 87th Cong., 2d sess. (Washington, D.C.: Government Printing Office, 1962), Chap. 5. An exception was forcing Howard Hughes to place his 78 percent of TWA stock in a banker-dominated voting trust as a condition of financing, using the voting trust to reconstitute the TWA board and management, and, with Civil Aeronautics Board assistance, eventually inducing Hughes to dispose of his stock in 1966.

83 William Shepherd, "The elements and evolution of market structure," in A. P. Jacquemin and H. W. deJong (eds.), *Markets, Corporate Behaviour and the State* (The Hague, Martinus Nijhoff, 1976), p. 170.

84 See P. R. Schweitzer, "The Definition of Markets," in *Staff Economic Comment,* Board of Governors of the Federal Reserve System, No. 59, August 1973; Jack Guttentag and Edward S. Herman, *Banking Structure and Performance* (New York: Institute of Finance, NYU Graduate School of Business, 1967), Chap. 2.

85 U.S., Congress, Senate, Committee on the Judiciary, staff report of the Subcommittee on Antitrust and Monopoly, *Bigness and Concentration of Economic Power – A Case Study of General Motors Corporation,* 84th Cong., 2d sess. (Washington, D.C.: Government Printing Office, 1956), p. 55.

86 Banker control of utilities in the 1920s led to heavy finance charges and other forms of abuse, so that in its recommendations for reform the Federal Trade Commission proposed legislative denial of bank power to control. See *Utility Corporations,* pt. 84A, pp. 600–617.

87 Annmarie Hauck Walsh, *The Public's Business: The Politics and Practices of Government Corporations,* a Twentieth Century Fund Study (Cambridge, Mass.: MIT Press, 1978), pp. 6–7.

88 Leger, "Taking Charge? Bank of America Moves to Direct Memorex"; "Memorex: This is 'the year of restoration,' " *Business Week,* November 10, 1975, p. 100; Janice C. Simpson, "Turnaround Artist: Wilson of Memorex Revives Its Profits, Cuts Its Debt Load," *Wall Street Journal,* August 25, 1977. Also Ralph Winter, "Survival Tactics: White Motor Reduces Its Size to Offset a Creditors' Squeeze," *Wall Street Journal,* November 1, 1976; "Investigating the collapse of W. T. Grant," *Business Week,* July 19, 1976, p. 62.

89 Ibid. and see n. 61.

90 Charles F. Adams, Jr., and Henry Adams, *Chapters of Erie* (Ithaca, N.Y.: Great Seal Books, 1956), originally published in 1886; Fred-

erick A. Cleveland and Frṭd W. Powell, *Railroad Finance* (New York: D. Appleton and Company, 1912); Grodinsky, *Jay Gould,* pp. 236–238, 400–410.

91 Grodinsky, *Jay Gould,* p. 354.

92 See esp., *Investigation of Conglomerate Corporations,* staff report of the Antitrust Subcommittee, House Judiciary Committee, 92nd Cong., 1st sess. (Washington, D.C.: Government Printing Office, 1971), pp. 404–411 ("Synergism").

93 For some illustrations, see *SEC* vs. *IU International Corporation,* Civil Action No. 78-0689, U.S. District Court for the District of Columbia, *Complaint for Permanent Injunction* (undated) and also Report of Special Counsel (Arthur S. Lane) to the Board of Directors of IU International, March 1, 1979 (re Seabrook); *SEC* vs. *Rapid-American Corporation,* Civil Action No. 79-, U.S. District Court for the District of Columbia, *Complaint for Permanent Injunction,* August 16, 1979; see summary of litigation in Rapid-American Notice of Annual Meeting of Stockholders, June 25, 1976; Robert J. Flaherty, "The Subject Was Riklis," *Forbes,* November 15, 1976, pp. 29–32. Carol J. Loomis, "Carl Lindner's Singular Financial Empire," *Fortune,* January 1977, pp. 126ff. *SEC* vs. *Gulf & Western Corporation,* Civil Action No. 79-, U.S. District Court for the District of Columbia, *Complaint for Permanent Injunction* (undated); Seymour M. Hersh, "Gulf and Western's Relationship with Banks Is Issue in S.E.C. Study," *New York Times,* July 25, 1977, pp. 1, 34; Seymour M. Hersh, "Gulf and Western Tax Practices Coming Under Wide Examination," *New York Times,* July 26, 1977, pp. 1, 43.

94 There is some bias in these data resulting from the fact that 1900–1901 and 1929 were probably cyclical peaks of control along an uncertain trend line, but there do not appear to have been comparable surges of banker control in the United States over the past three decades.

95 See "Vicious Circle," *Forbes,* May 1, 1974, p. 27.

96 If the bankers occupied the top management positions themselves, or effectively chose the top managers, this would constitute full control, not partial control (i.e., significant influence). This difference is elusive in cases where bankers have real power over management choices, when borrowers are in severe financial difficulty and sometimes in violation of indentures. The classification decision might depend on the exact time of evaluation of control, possibly varying within the course of a year. The arbitrariness of such a classification is substantial. In these uncertain cases, although readily granting the bankers partial control, I assigned them full control only if I could find evidence that they exercised some direct influence, actively choosing, displacing, and installing top executives (as in the Memorex-Bank of America case). On this basis, even Pan Am is classed

here as only partially banker controlled in the mid-1970s, although banker veto power was used during this period to displace top executives. The bankers were merely insisting on a change.

97 Isadore Barmash, "Arlen Realty: A Salvage Job for Arthur Cohen," *The New York Times*, June 24, 1979, p. F3.

98 See "Pam Am Refinances," *Business Week;* "Pan American Realigns," *Business Week.*

99 Applications to specific companies may be seen for the 200 largest in Appendix A.

Chapter 5. Government and the Large Corporation

1 One analyst refers to the recent period of expanding government intervention as having produced a "second managerial revolution," with a shift in corporate decision making "to the vast cadre of government regulators who are influencing and often controlling the key managerial decisions of the typical business firm." Murray L. Weidenbaum, *Business, Government, And The Public* (Englewood Cliffs, N.J.: Prentice-Hall, 1977), p. 285.

2 See esp. G. S. Callender, "The Early Transportation and Banking Enterprises of the States in Relation to the Growth of Corporations," *Quarterly Journal of Economics,* November 1902, pp. 111–162; Carter Goodrich, *Government Promotion of American Canals and Railroads 1800–1890* (New York: Columbia University Press, 1960).

3 A commonly held fallacy is that there has been a steady "200-year trend upward toward more government intervention in the U.S. economy." ("Government Intervention," *Business Week,* April 4, 1977, p. 42).

4 See esp. Louis Hartz, *Economic Policy and Democratic Thought: Pennsylvania 1776–1860* (Cambridge: Harvard University Press, 1948). Goodrich mentions government enterprise but stresses the already prevalent tendency to give primacy to the private sector in joint efforts and to leave really profitable opportunities to the private sector, *Government Promotion,* pp. 279–290.

5 It is hard to measure the value of governmental largess to the railroads, but 79 railroads initially were given 200 million acres of land by the federal government, and six transcontinental railroads were loaned $65 million directly by Congress. See F. A. Cleveland and F. W. Powell, *Railroad Finance* (New York: D. Appleton, 1912), pp. 32–33.

6 Jonathan Hughes, *The Vital Few* (Boston: Houghton Mifflin, 1966), p. 46.

7 This reaction to the rise of big business by smaller enterprise and their resort to government protection are the heart of Alfred Chandler's explanation of the "adversary relationship" between business

and government in the United States. "The adversaries," *Harvard Business Review*, November – December 1979; see n. 24.

8 For a good statement of these attitudes see Richard F. Janssen, "Buddying Up: The Role of Government in Business Might Vault If Nixon Is Reelected," *Wall Street Journal*, April 24, 1972.

9 Vogel argues that a great many businessmen went along with the Cold War and militarization reluctantly, finding its main merit in the political effects of the Red scare. See David Vogel, "Why Businessmen Distrust Their State: The Political Consciousness of American Corporate Executives," *British Journal of Political Science*, January 1978, p. 51. He does not attempt to sort out the various subdivisions of business, however, which might show important groups with a greater commitment to and interest in the Cold War and militarization – such as military contractors and subcontractors, and multinationals with a major external presence and interest. For views suggesting a stronger relationship between business and the Cold War, see the essays by Domhoff, Williams, Gardner, and Eakins in David Horowitz (ed.), *Corporations and the Cold War* (New York: Monthly Review Press, 1969). Explanations of the benign attitude of business toward the large military component of big government fall under the following categories: (1) It provides business profit opportunities without adding government competition as a producer. (2) The vested interests of businesspeople deeply involved in military contracting silences other businesspeople because of reciprocity considerations (cf. Chap. 6). (3) Militarism intensifies nationalistic sentiments, xenophobia, and popular rejection of foreign ideologies such as equalitarianism and socialism. (4) The military establishment has direct value in opening up and protecting foreign markets and investment opportunities. For a classic statement of the merits of an aggressive military posture on internal discipline and ideology see Thorstein Veblen, *The Theory of Business Enterprise* (New York: Scribner's, 1904), Chaps. 8 and 10.

10 For a summary of these business attitudes, see Leonard Silk and David Vogel, *Ethics and Profits* (New York: Simon & Shuster, 1976), pp. 44–61.

11 For a persuasive case that business power remains disproportionately large, see Charles Lindblom's *Politics and Markets* (New York: Basic Books, 1977), Chap. 13, "The Privileged Position of Business." For a rebuttal, see the ad by Mobil Oil, *New York Times*, February 9, 1978, op-ed page, and James Q. Wilson, "Democracy and the Corporation," *Wall Street Journal*, January 11, 1978, editorial page. For a Marxist statement of the case for the autonomy of the state and the special power and interests of its functionaries, see Fred Block, "Beyond Relative Autonomy: State Managers as Historical Subjects," *Socialist Register*, forthcoming.

12 The data presented here are compiled from standard governmental

sources: the *Statistical Abstract of the United States, Survey of Current Business,* and *Historical Statistics of the United States.*

13   Lindblom, *Politics and Markets,* p. 109; Lester Thurow, *The Zero-Sum Society* (New York: Basic Books, 1980), pp. 7–9.

14   U.S. direct investment abroad at the end of 1978 totaled $168.1 billion, with income derived from this investment of $25.7 billion. (*Survey of Current Business,* August 1979, p. 15.) Using the Judd Polk formula, suggesting two dollars of output associated with a dollar of direct investment, the output associated with our direct investment was in the order of $336 billion.

15   For analyses of this relationship see Edward S. Herman and Richard B. DuBoff, "Corporate Dollars and Foreign Policy," *Commonweal,* April 1972, pp. 159–163; David Horowitz, ed., *Corporations and the Cold War* (New York: Monthly Review Press, 1969); Gabriel Kolko, *The Politics of War* (New York: Pantheon, 1968).

16   See U.S., Congress, Joint Economic Committee, Subcommittee on Economy in Government, report on *Economy in Government Procurement and Property Management,* 90th Cong., 2d sess. (Washington, D.C.: Government Printing Office, 1968); Robert J. Gordon, "$45 Billion of U.S. Private Investment Has Been Mislaid," *American Economic Review,* June 1969, pp. 221–238.

17   On the "golden handshake," see Richard F. Kaufman, *The War Profiteers* (Indianapolis: Bobbs–Merrill, 1970), pp. 160–161.

18   H. L. Nieburg, *In the Name of Science* (New York: Quadrangle, 1966), Chaps. 10–12.

19   Alfred E. Kahn, *The Economics of Regulation* (New York: Wiley, 1971), vol. 2, p. 74.

20   Clair Wilcox and William G. Shepherd, *Public Policies Toward Business,* 5th ed. (Homewood, Ill.: Richard D. Irwin, 1975), Chaps. 19–20; Frederic L. Pryor, "Public Ownership: Some Quantitative Dimensions," in William Shepherd (ed.), *Public Enterprise: Economic Analysis of Theory and Practice* (Lexington, Mass.: Lexington Books, 1976), Chap. 1.

21   See Raymond Vernon, ed., *Big Business and the State: Changing Relations in Western Europe* (Cambridge, Mass.: Harvard University Press, 1974). In Italy, government enterprise, mainly in the form of the conglomerate Institute for Industrial Reconstruction, moved boldly into industrial sectors needing rehabilitation (iron and steel) and areas with chronic structural employment, as well as into modern manufacturing and service areas like aviation, telecommunications, and engineering. See Stuart Holland, ed., *The State as Entrepreneur* (White Plains, N.Y.: International Arts and Sciences Press, 1972).

22   Pryor, in Shepherd (ed.), *Public Enterprise,* esp. Table 1-3, p. 11. "Materials sectors" includes utilities, transportation and communi-

cations, construction, manufacturing and mining, agriculture, forestry, and fishing. In Pryor's table the United States had a 5 percent share, tied with Japan, half that of France and less than a third that of Great Britain.

23 On the absence of a left opposition and the reasons therefore, see esp. James Weinstein, *The Decline of Socialism in America 1912–1925* (New York: Monthly Review Press, 1967); Gabriel Kolko, *Main Currents in Modern American History* (New York: Harper & Row, 1976), Chaps. 3 and 5.

24 See Vogel, "Why Businessmen Distrust Their State." Alfred Chandler explains the adversary relationship here, and the contrasting collaborative one abroad, on two grounds. First, the rise of U.S. big business threatened small firms more severely here than abroad, with large producers of consumer goods and railroads inflicting serious damage on small shippers and wholesalers from an early date. This led to a hostile government stance to big business. In England and Japan big business was more heavily concentrated in basic industry and was export oriented. Preexisting internal distribution networks were less threatened. Thus big business needed government more and threatened other indigenous businesses less. Chandler's second point is that government bureaucracy matured late in the United States and absorbed the antibusiness flavor defined by the earlier small-business-based ideology. ("The adversaries," *Harvard Business Review,* November – December 1979, pp. 88ff.) Chandler's first point may have some value; the second adds little to it. Vogel stresses the limited need of big business for government help in the United States (close to Chandler's first point), plus business awareness of the threat posed by a growing government as a power entity capable of being mobilized by other interest groups and the general citizenry.

25 Compare Vernon, *Big Business and the State* pp. 7–8, with Francis X. Sutton, et al., *The American Business Creed* (New York: Schocken, 1962), pp. 195–202.

26 See, for example, U.S., Congress, Senate, Committee on Government Operations, staff study on *Government Competition with Private Enterprise,* (Washington, D.C.: Government Printing Office, 1963). This report was prepared in response to S. 1093, which would establish as a national policy the termination of "all business-type activities engaged in by the Federal Government" with specified exceptions. The report stresses the regular inventories being made of this competition and the steady pressures on government agencies to minimize government production that could be farmed out to private enterprise.

27 See esp. Richard Hellman, *Government Competition in the Electric Utility Industry* (New York: Praeger, 1972), pp. 62ff., 185–186,

228–229; William C. Merrill and Norman Schneider, "Government Firms in Oligopoly Industries: A Short-Run Analysis," *Quarterly Journal of Economics,* August 1966, pp. 400–412.

28   Hellman, *Government Competition* pp. 11–14; Delos F. Wilcox, "Effects of State Regulation upon the Municipal Ownership Movement," *The Annals,* May 1914, pp. 71ff.

29   Quoted in Hellman, *Government Competition,* p. 13.

30   Berle and Means, *The Modern Corporation,* p. 17.

31   Charles L. Dearing, "Turnpike Authorities in the United States," in *Law and Contemporary Problems,* Autumn 1961, pp. 744–745; *The Public's Business,* pp. 4–5.

32   As noted earlier, the national defense component that includes *commodities* such as tanks, guns, planes, uniforms, shoes, gasoline, food, and the like are bought from the private sector. The largest part of social welfare outlays are transfer payments; a much smaller component is the cost of the apparatus of welfare organization and directly rendered services.

33   After 1974, Amtrak and Conrail entered the picture, and with a later benchmark date they might qualify for inclusion. Enormous facilities such as the New York City Transit Authority are not included because their value on either a depreciated historical cost basis or some imputed capitalization of earnings would not be very high. The reproduction cost of such a system would easily qualify – so might its real social value if all positive and negative externalities were employed in the valuation.

34   In 1974 there was still an organization called the Atomic Energy Commission (AEC) with assets of $14 billion reported in Moody's *Governments;* in 1975 the AEC disappeared, to be replaced by two other organizations, including the Nuclear Regulatory Commission, but in the process the $14 billion of AEC assets disappeared.

35   Wilcox and Shepherd, *Public Policies Toward Business,* p. 543.

36   Ibid.

37   Ibid.

38   The Price – Anderson Indemnity Act of 1957, renewed periodically thereafter, limited liability in nuclear accidents to $560 million, partially underwritten by government.

39   See "U.S. Sees No Permanent Disposal of Nuclear Waste Before 1988," *New York Times,* March 16, 1978.

40   See Walsh, *The Public's Business,* pp. 28–29.

41   See John M. Blair, *Economic Concentration* (New York: Harcourt Brace, 1972), pp. 380–385.

42   Hellman, *Government Competition,* pp. 23, 67, 185–186.

43   This is one of the bases of inflation in Weidenbaum's critique of government intervention; see, for example, his discussion of the enormous powers of the Consumer Product Safety Commission,

which omits any mention of extremely modest staff funding and its effect on the level of enforcement of its enormous powers, *Business, Government, and the Public.* pp. 29ff. See also n. 55.

44 See esp. Marver Bernstein, *Regulating Business by Independent Commission* (Princeton, N.J.: Princeton University Press, 1955); Bruce M. Owen and Ronald Braeutigam, *The Regulation Game: Strategic Use of the Administrative Process* (Cambridge, Mass.: Ballinger Publishing, 1978), pp. 9–11; Richard A. Posner, "Theories of Economic Regulation," *Bell Journal of Economics,* Autumn 1974, pp. 335–358; Sam Peltzman, "Toward a More General Theory of Regulation," *Journal of Law and Economics,* August 1976, pp. 211–240. For a broad review of the literature with no particular viewpoint embraced see Barry M. Mitnick, *The Political Economy of Regulation* (New York: Columbia University Press, 1980).

45 As noted by Owen and Braeutigam, "The ideal strategy is to get the agency to endorse 'self-regulation' by the industry so that the industry cartel can manage things under an umbrella of antitrust immunity. Transportation and insurance rate bureaus and the NAB code (limiting quantities of advertisements in TV and radio) are excellent examples of this strategy. The cartel rates of practices thus determined are immune from the usual tendency toward cheating because they carry the force of law, or at least the threat of direct intervention by the agency." (p. 6).

46 See Gabriel Kolko, *Railroads and Regulation 1877–1916* (Princeton, N.J.: Princeton University Press, 1965), and *The Triumph of Conservatism* (New York: Free Press, 1963); Roger Noll, *Reforming Regulation* (Washington, D.C.: Brookings Institution, 1971), pp. 37–39; Wilcox and Shepherd, *Public Policies Toward Business,* Chap. 24; Kahn, *The Economics of Regulation* Vol. 2, Chap. 1, pp. 4–5. Important industry-sponsored regulatory programs of the post-World War I era would include, among others, the oil prorationing and hot oil legislation of the 1920s and 1930s (see Norman Nordhauser, "Origins of Federal Oil Regulation in the 1920s," *Business History Review,* Spring 1973, pp. 53–71); and the new federal regulation of trucking, coal, agricultural prices and marketing, shipping, interest rates on bank deposits, and the labeling and grading of furs and wool. On this last, see Alan Stone, *Economic Regulation and the Public Interest* (Ithaca, N.Y.: Cornell University Press, 1977), pp. 211–231. For a critical review of the emphasis on business sponsorship see Thomas K. McCraw, "Regulation in America: A Review Article," *Business History Review,* Summer 1975, pp. 159–183.

47 Weidenbaum notes that it is this "far-ranging characteristic of the NR that makes it impractical for any single industry to dominate these regulatory activities in the manner of the traditional model." Murray Weidenbaum, *The Costs of Government Regulation of Busi-*

ness, study prepared for the Subcommittee on Economic Growth, Joint Economic Committee, 95th Cong., 2d sess. (Washington, D.C.: Government Printing Office, April 10, 1978), pp. 9–10.

48 U.S., Senate, Committee on Governmental Affairs, *Study on Federal Regulation, Framework for Regulation,* vol. VI, Sen. Doc. No. 96–13, written by Michael Klass and Leonard Weiss (Washington, D.C.: Government Printing Office, 1978), Chaps. 2–3.

49 In this context it is also interesting that much of the new literature focuses almost exclusively on the costs of regulation and downplays or rules out discussion of any benefits (which, as noted, are nonbusiness benefits). This is true of the writings of Murray Weidenbaum, which characteristically begin with statements like "No judgments are expressed on the value of the many regulatory efforts," although Weidenbaum is keen on cost-*benefit* appraisals of regulation. Weidenbaum, *Costs of Government Regulation,* pp. 1, 22–23.

50 For example, the EPA required that unleaded gas be made available by the oil companies by July 1, 1974. For good company statements of (and complaints about) regulatory impact, see the Cities Service 10-K, 1974, pp. 7, 21. See also the Annual Report of Marathon Oil for 1974, p. 1.

51 See, U.S., Department of Energy, *The Effect of Legislative and Regulatory Actions on Competition in Petroleum Markets,* Analysis Report (Washington, D.C.: Government Printing Office, April 1979).

52 Legislation itself is sometimes only possible at all as a result of catastrophic events overcoming industry resistance – for example, the 1938 amendments to the Food and Drug Administration legislation followed 93 deaths in 1937 from Elixir Sulfanilimide; the 1962 Kefauver amendments followed the Thalidomide disaster. See Lawrence P. Feldman, *Consumer Protection: Problems and Prospects* (St. Paul, Minn.: West Publishing, 1976), pp. 13–15; Richard Harris, *The Real Voice* (New York: Macmillan, 1964).

53 Classic illustrations of limits on information gathering powers, closely tied in with constraints on jurisdiction, are the limits on regulatory powers to examine holding companies of regulated affiliates (electric utilities, savings and loan associations, banks, etc.), and the pre-1976 (Toxic Substances Act) lack of obligation of chemical producers and importers, and petroleum refiners, to tell the government what substances they make. Feldman notes that until 1973, manufacturers or food processors were not required by law to register with the Food and Drug Administration, although the FDA was supposed to inspect their operations. Feldman, *Consumer Protection,* p. 60.

Industry-generated information on consumer and occupational hazards is often inaccessible, even to government authorities. A recent discussion of the difficulties encountered by the National Institute for Occupational Safety and Health (NIOSH) states that;

"NIOSH investigators often spend as much time in legal procedures to gain access to medical records as they do in analyzing the material. A study requested by workers at Du Pont Co.'s Belle, W. Va. plant, for example, was held up more than a year until NIOSH obtained a court ruling that the chemical company must turn over medical records for inspection. (A du Pont spokesman says the company wanted a court ruling to clarify du Pont's responsibility for the privacy of living workers' medical records; he adds that medical records of deceased employees were promptly given to NIOSH.)" Gail Bronson, "Ailing Agency: Set Up to Research on Health on the Job, NIOSH Is Sick Itself," *Wall Street Journal*, April 19, 1978.

In addition to inaccessibility, information may be allowed to be presented in a form that renders it useless. A well-known case is the sanctioning by the regulatory agencies of the submission of nominee and record-owner data in required company submissions on their largest owners (instead of data on beneficial ownership). See U.S., Congress Senate, Committee on Government Operations, Subcommittee on Reports, Accounting and Management, *Corporate Ownership and Control*, (Washington, D.C.: Government Printing Office, 1975). Another important illustration is in the requirement that all U.S. oil refiners file monthly reports with the Energy Information Administration on the level of their petroleum product stocks (reports EIA 90 and EIA 87). The information is for what is known as custodial oil, which includes both oil owned by the refinery and oil held for third parties. This latter distinction is important, but such a breakdown is not required in the reports. In shortage situations, when company stock data might be critical in determining whether there is market manipulation or the withholding of supplies, the absence of this division of custodial oil allows company behavior to be camouflaged and renders the data meaningless.

54 A recent analysis of the Federal Advisory Committee Act of 1972 noted that limits on its effectiveness rest in good part on "the ambiguity of the Act itself, ranging from simple lack of clarity, to the absence of requirements, to lack of sanctions for noncompliance." Kit Gage and Samuel S. Epstein, "The Federal Advisory System: An Assessment," *Environmental Law Reporter*, February 1977, reprinted in *Congressional Record*, March 11, 1977.

55 In 1972 the Consumer Product Safety Commission was given jurisdiction over the safety of more than 11 thousand consumer products produced by 2.5 million companies, with responsibility for protecting consumers from unsafe products, developing safety standards, providing consumer information on product safety, and promoting safety research – all with a budget of under $40 million and a staff of nine hundred. See *Federal Regulation and Regulatory Reform*, report by the Subcommittee on Oversight and Investigations of the House Committee on Interstate and Foreign Commerce (Moss Subcom-

mittee), 95th Cong., H. Doc. 95–134, 1st sess., (Washington, D.C.: Government Printing Office, October 1976), pp. 198–208. See also "Dictating product safety," *Business Week,* May 18, 1974, pp. 56ff.

56 Stone, *Economic Regulation,* p. 207. On the favorable economics of lengthy delays in the regulatory process, Mark Green has good discussions of Geritol and Panalba in his *The Other Government, The Unseen Power of Washington Lawyers* (New York: Grossman, 1975), pp. 99–131.

57 An active Government Accounting Organization (GAO) looking too closely at defense contractors, at the behest of the then Secretary of Defense Robert McNamara, led to a famous investigation of the GAO; "asking Congress to clip GAO's wings, the spokesmen of the contractor community made it clear that their real concern was with the combined impact of the McNamara reforms, aided and abetted by GAO audits." Nieburg, *In the Name of Science,* p. 374. An aggressive stance on conflict of interest lending by savings and loan associations on the part of the Federal Home Loan Bank Board (FHLBB) in the late 1950s and early 1960s led to a congressional investigation, hearings, and recommendations that resulted in an FHLBB shakeup and a paralysis of the regulation of conflict of interest for an extended time. See Edward S. Herman, "Conflict of Interest in the Savings and Loan Industry," in Irwin Friend (ed.), *Study of the Savings and Loan Industry* (Washington, D.C.: Federal Home Loan Bank Board, 1969), pp. 924–927 and references cited therein.

58 When EPA threatened serious regulation of pesticides, the agriculture-pesticides industry lobbies moved quickly: (1) A bill was put forward and barely defeated in the Committee on Agriculture to require the consent of the secretary of agriculture before any official antipesticide action. (2) H.R. 8841 was passed in a form requiring notification of the secretary of agriculture and a newly created Scientific Advisory Panel prior to any antipesticide action. These pressures had an effect on EPA regulation of pesticides even before passage of H.R. 8841. See *Federal Regulation and Regulatory Reform,* pp. 136–145.

59 In 1979 the Senate Commerce Committee voted unanimously to bar the Federal Trade Commission from adopting rules on unfair commercial advertising and to forbid it from investigating the insurance industry and various other matters. The House voted to prohibit the Federal Trade Commission from enforcing the antitrust laws dealing with farm coops or to attempt to regulate the funeral industry. See Larry Kramer, "Industry Winning War of Attrition as Congress Moves to Disarm FTC," *Philadelphia Inquirer,* December 2, 1979, p. 3-H; "FTC's Authority Would Be Cut By Senate Panel," *Wall Street Journal,* November 21, 1979, p. 4.

60 A great many bills have been proposed to curb OSHA's powers, for example. Recently, a bill was introduced to exempt 90 percent of presently eligible workplaces from regular OSHA safety inspections. See Urban C. Lehner, "Senate Gets Bill Aimed at Curbing Of OSHA Rules," *Wall Street Journal*, December 20, 1979, p. 6.

61 See Martin G. Glaeser, *Public Utilities in American Capitalism* (New York: Macmillan, 1957), p. 249.

62 Hellman notes that at a time when the Federal Power Commission (FPC) was in sharp conflict with private power companies, siding with public power company buyers claiming price discrimination, the U.S. Chamber of Commerce put in an appearance before the House Appropriations Committee pushing for a cut in the FPC salary budget. Hellman, *Government Competition*, p. 42.

63 William Cary, *Politics and the Regulatory Agencies* (New York: McGraw-Hill, 1967), p. 11.

64 *Federal Regulation and Regulatory Reform*, p. 208.

65 See, for example, Barry Cole and Mal Oettinger, *Reluctant Regulators: The FCC and the Broadcast Audience* (Reading, Mass.: Addison-Wesley, 1978). pp. 12–13.

66 "Pesticide Safety Program Held Lax," *New York Times*, January 3, 1977, pp. 1–2.

67 Quoted in Ralph Nader, *Unsafe at Any Speed* (New York: Grossman, 1972), p. xlix.

68 For a discussion of this and other interventions by the Carter economists see Mark Green and Norman Waitzman, *Business War on the Law: An Analysis of the Benefits of Federal Health/Safety Enforcement* (Washington, D.C.: The Corporate Accountability Research Group, 1979), pp. 84–86.

69 Roger Noll, Merton Peck, and John McGowan, *Economic Aspects of Television Regulation* (Washington: Brookings Institution, 1973), p. 123. Most of the remaining 12 out of 33 commissioners went into retirement.

70 On the extent of the revolving door see *Congressional Oversight of The Regulatory Appointments Process*, Vol. I of *Study of Federal Regulation*, Committee on Government Operations, Sen. Doc. No. 95–25 (Washington, D.C.: Government Printing Office, 1977), pp. 66ff, 154–168.

71 Cole and Oettinger, *Reluctant Regulators*, p. 10.

72 Ibid., pp. 10–13; Cary, *Politics and the Regulatory Agencies*, pp. 63–64.

73 Noll, *Reforming Regulation*, p. 43.

74 Victor Kramer, speaking before a joint congressional committee in 1976, quoted in Cole and Oettinger, *Reluctant Regulators*, p. 6.

75 A recent senate study showed that in more than half of a large sample of regulatory proceedings there was no organized public interest group participation at all; and in those cases where there is such

participation, it is small relative to that of the affected industry. In 1976 the direct outlays of the major airlines in proceedings before the Civil Aeronautics Board (CAB) was over $3 million; the outlays of the only public interest group focusing on the CAB was $20,000. *Public Participation in Regulatory Agency Proceedings,* vol. III of *Study on Federal Regulation,* Senate Committee on Governmental Affairs, Sen. Doc. No. 95–71, 95th Cong., 1st sess. (Washington, D.C.: Government Printing Office, 1977), p. 19.

76 In the spring of 1978 General Motors Corporation sued the EPA for violating GM's constitutional rights, by attempting to spot check new cars rolling off assembly lines; a suit that "if successful, could strip away from government regulators one of their main methods for trying to determine whether new cars meet pollution rules after they are on the road." Leonard M. Apcar, "GM Sues EPA to Bar Spot-Checks of Cars to Predict Adherence to Pollution Rules," *Wall Street Journal,* May 1, 1978, p. 4.

77 Business completely dominated political funding until the 1930s. See Louise Overacker, *Money in Elections* (New York: Macmillan, 1932), pp. 375–376; Herbert Alexander, *Political Financing* (Minneapolis: Burgess, 1972), p. 19. In recent decades, union political contributions have been of the same order of magnitude as those reported for political action committees (PACs) of business entities and groups. But there are many routes through which raw economic power makes itself felt in the political process, and unions are no match for corporate business in basic measures of resource access. Trade union aggregate assets and receipts in 1973 were each on the order of $3 to 4 billion; corporate assets and receipts were on the order of $2 to 4 *trillion;* and corporate *net* income exceeds the *gross* income of all unions by a factor of better than 20 to one. The Watergate years revealed the extent to which large amounts of corporate money had entered the political process *sub rosa.* Single corporation contributions, such as those of Exxon in Italy and Lockheed in Japan and Western Europe, and slush funds, such as those of Gulf and Northrop, exceeded the aggregate of union contributions in election years; and although these funds were used mainly for pay-offs abroad and were spread over a number of years, they demonstrate capacity and will to achieve political ends through the use of money. The Watergate revelations also showed the great ingenuity of corporate donors in finding ways to channel money where needed. It has yet to be proved that the law can contain the application of raw economic power when vital interests are at stake.

The rise of "advocacy advertising" and grassroots lobbying in recent years also reveals the fungibility of corporate resources under perceived political threats. The sums involved here dwarf official figures of campaign contributions. According to S. Prakash Sethi,

"My own figures and estimates by congressional subcommittees and the General Accounting Office place current business outlays for advocacy advertising and other forms of grassroots lobbying at $1 billion per year. According to surveys conducted by the *Public Relations Journal*, U.S. corporations and associations spent a combined total of $410.4 million on institutional advertising in six major media during 1976 . . ." "Grassroots Lobbying and the Corporation," *Business and Society Review*, November–December 1979, p.8.

78 For a powerful statement of business' capacity to mold public opinion through its role as sponsor see Eric Barnouw, *The Sponsor* (New York: Oxford University Press, 1978).

79 In trying to fix a new fuel economy standard for light trucks and vans, the National Highway Traffic Safety Administration had to contend not only with the usual pressures on the White House and Congress but also with a threat by Chrysler to shut down a Detroit plant employing two thousand workers, which led to vigorous attacks on the standard by several civil rights groups and a major letter-writing campaign. The new standard was sharply curtailed by higher political authorities. Deborah Baldwin, "Wheeling and dealing in Washington," *Environmental Action*, March 25, 1978, pp. 4–8.

80 Walter Mossberg notes that "The agency's reputation for nit-picking has also spawned inaccurate but damaging stories. Last month, for example, *Business Week* magazine reported that, at Dow Chemical Co., 'it cost 60,000 per plant to lower railings from 42 inches to the OSHA-required 30 inches to 34 inches although Dow studies found the higher level was safer.' In fact, Dow Chemical didn't lower any railings, didn't spend any money on railings, and wasn't ordered by OSHA to change any railings." "Safety Agency Will Tighten Regulations on Health Hazards, Drop Trivial Rules," *Wall Street Journal*, May 19, 1977, p. 48. *Business Week* itself quotes the head of OSHA asking, "How do you fight back when you are being killed by a myth?" "Why Nobody Wants to Listen to OSHA," *Business Week*, June 14, 1976, p. 64.

81 Lawrence J. White, "The automobile industry," in Walter Adams (ed.), *The Structure of American Industry* (New York: Macmillan, 1977), p. 196; Ralph Nader, *Unsafe at Any Speed* (New York: Grossman, 1969), Chap. 2.

82 Deborah Baldwin quotes Chrysler engineer Charles Heinen to this effect, "In every single case where we have said we couldn't do anything, we have been granted some relief . . . ," Baldwin, "Wheeling and Dealing in Washington," p. 8.

83 *Federal Regulation and Regulatory Reform*, p. 133.

84 Ibid., p. 134. Another example is the evolution of automobile safety

rules under the auspices of the National Highway Safety Administration since 1966. See Nader's 1972 edition of *Unsafe at Any Speed,* pp. xiv–lxxii.

85 Noll, *Reforming Regulation,* pp. 40ff. and works cited therein.

86 Ibid., pp. 37ff.

87 James M. Landis, *Report on Regulatory Agencies to the President-Elect,* Senate Judiciary Committee, 86th Cong., 2d sess. (Washington, D.C., Government Printing Office, 1960), p. 11.

88 Senator Warren Magnuson's objection to Robert Morris's nomination to the FPC is illuminating: It was that *all five* commissioners ought not to be industry oriented. See *Federal Regulations and Regulatory Reform,* p. 168.

89 Les Gapay, "Agencies and Industries Show Persistent Signs of Cozy Relationships," *Wall Street Journal,* November 1, 1974, p. 1.

90 Owen and Braeutigam, *Regulation Game,* p. 2.

91 See esp. Almarin Phillips, in William Capron (ed.), *Technological Change in Regulated Industries* (Washington, D.C.: Brookings Institution, 1971), pp. 213–215; Kahn, *Economics of Regulation,* Vol. 2, pp. 209–220; Richard Schmalensee, *The Control of Natural Monopolies* (Lexington, Mass.: Lexington, 1979).

92 See Gellman, in Capron (ed.), *Technological Change,* pp. 166–196; Anne F. Friedlander, *The Dilemma of Freight Transport Regulation* (Washington, D.C.: Brookings Institution, 1969).

93 Hellman, *Government Competition.* As Owen and Braeutigam observe, "Regulation greatly reduces the risk of bankruptcy from causes other than competition. And, while regulation may make very high rates of return difficult to achieve, it does virtually guarantee a steady stream of adequate profits." Owen and Braeutigam, *Regulation Game,* p. 2.

94 Owen and Braeutigam argue that regulation is a rational choice of "voters," who by their votes (or those of their representatives) show a willingness to trade some efficiency loss for the benefits of reduced risk and the improved equity implicit in the shift from market to the administrative process (pp. 1–2 and passim). The political assumptions required for this contention are hardly realistic – "logrolling" or interest group bargaining models would easily show a deleterious macro result to ordinary (and a majority of) voters emerging out of micro trade-offs by special interest groups; and a variety of other more realistic political assumptions regarding voter knowledge and the workings of the democratic and administrative processes (some discussed by Owen and Braeutigam) make their inferences about voter choice dubious.

95 *Business Week,* June 14, 1976, p. 65.

96 Charles R. Perry, in Herbert Northrop et al., *The Impact of OSHA* (Philadelphia: Wharton School, University of Pennsylvania, Industrial Research Unit, 1978), pp. 230–231.

97 "A tough – but acceptable – toxic chemicals law," *Business Week,* October 25, 1976, p. 106.
98 Jonathan Spivak, "Why Does the FDA Fall So Short?" *Wall Street Journal,* May 20, 1971, editorial page.
99 See note 55.
100 "The U.S.' Unnaturalized Citizens," *Forbes,* November 1, 1975, p. 31.
101 For an excellent statement of this position see Lindblom, *Politics and Markets,* Chap. 13.
102 For a good discussion of the case for the independence of the state and its managers see Fred Block, "Beyond Relative Autonomy: State Managers as Historical Subjects," *Socialist Register,* forthcoming.
103 Jonathan D. Aronson, *Money and Power: Banks and the World Monetary System* (Beverly Hills, Cal.: Sage, 1977); Richard J. Barnet and Ronald E. Muller, *Global Reach* (New York: Simon & Schuster, 1974), Chap. 10; Stephen Hymer, *The Multinational Corporation* (Cambridge: Cambridge University Press, 1979), pp. 50–53, 66–74, 87–88; U.S. Congress, Committee on Finance, *Implications of Multinational Firms for World Trade and Investment and for U.S. Trade and Labor,* Report Submitted by U.S. Tariff Commission (Washington, D.C.: Government Printing Office, 1973).

Chapter 6. The Centralization of Corporate Power

1 See Charles A. Beard, *The Economic Origins of Jeffersonian Democracy* (New York: Macmillan, 1915); Vernon L. Parrington, *Main Currents in American Thought* (New York: Harcourt, Brace, 1930); James Madison in *The Federalist* (New York: Modern Library, 1941); and *United States v. Aluminum Company of America,* 148 F. 2d 416 (2d Cir. 1945).
2 See esp. Joe S. Bain, *Industrial Organization,* 2nd ed., (New York: Wiley, 1968) pp. 100–111 M.A. Adelman, "The Measurement of Industrial Concentration," *Review of Economics and Statistics,* November 1951; G. W. Nutter, *The Extent of Enterprise Monopoly in the United States, 1899–1939* (Chicago: University of Chicago, 1951); Paulo Sylos-Labini, *Oligopoly and Technical Progress* (Cambridge, Mass.: Harvard University Press, 1962), esp. Introduction and Appendix; Federal Trade Commission, *Economic Report on Corporate Mergers* (Washington, D.C.: Government Printing Office, 1969); Stanley Lebergott, "Has Monopoly Increased?" *Review of Economics and Statistics,* November 1953; *Economic Concentration,* Hearings Before Senate Antitrust Subcommittee, pt. 1, Overall and Conglomerate Aspects, 88th Cong., 2d sess. (Washington, D.C.: Government Printing Office, 1964), esp. statements of Gardiner Means, John Blair, Lee Preston, and J. Fred Weston; William H. Shepherd,

Market Power and Economic Welfare, (New York: Random House, 1970), pt. II.

3 A classic statement of the advantages of size is in Corwin Edwards, *Maintaining Competition* (New York: McGraw-Hill, 1949), pp. 97–108; see also Federal Trade Commission, *Economic Report on Corporate Mergers,* Chap. 6.

4 See Robert F. Hoxie, *A History of Labor in the United States* (New York: Russell & Russell, 1966); Michael Reagan, *The Managed Economy* (New York: Oxford University Press, 1963), pp. 161ff.; J. K. Galbraith, *American Capitalism, The Concept of Countervailing Power* (Boston: Houghton Mifflin, 1952), Chaps. 9–11.

5 Real estate is also a decentralized sector, obscured by the fact that it is combined with banking, which is concentrated and has large asset totals.

6 Manufacturing plants with 1,000 or more employees rose from 18 percent of manufacturing employment in 1914 to 24.4 percent in 1929, to 28.7 in 1972. The share of value added of plants with 2,500 employees or more rose from 17.3 percent in 1947 to 21.8 percent in 1963. J. Blair, *Economic Concentration* (New York: Harcourt Brace Jovanovich, 1972), pp. 98–99, and U.S. Bureau of the Census, *Statistical Abstract of the United States: 1975* (Washington, D.C.: Government Printing Office, 1975), p. 736.

7 Betty Churchill, "Size Characteristics of the Business Population," *Survey of Current Business,* May 1954, pp. 15–24.

8 U.S. Department of Commerce, *Historical Statistics of the United States, Colonial Times to 1957* (Washington, D.C.: Government Printing Office, 1960), p. 571.

9 F. M. Scherer, *Industrial Market Structure and Economic Performance* 2nd. ed. (Chicago: Rand McNally, 1980), p. 75. The concept of industry used in the text is based on a so-called three-digit definition of industry as given in the Standard Industrial Classification (SIC) system developed by the Census Bureau. In this system, which extends to seven digits, one digit (e.g., 2) is used to designate the broad category of manufacturing; two-digit industries covers categories like "Food and Kindred Products" (20) and "Tobacco Manufactures" (21). Three-digit industries encompass subdivisions like Meat Products (201), Beverages (208), and Cigarettes (211). See Ibid., pp. 59–70 for a fuller discussion of the SIC classification system.

10 Ibid., p. 49.

11 The term seems to have come into wide usage about 1969, particularly in studies by the staff of the Cabinet Committee on Price Stability, the Federal Trade Commission's *Economic Report on Corporate Merger,* and some antitrust cases. See Betty Bock, *Concentration, Oligopoly, and Profit: Concepts vs. Data,* Report No. 556 (New York: Conference Board, 1972), p. 44.

12 Ibid, pp. 57–67; Betty Bock and Jack Farkas, *Relative Growth of the "Largest" Manufacturing Corporations, 1947–1971,* Report No. 583 (New York: Conference Board, 1973), pp. 43ff.

13 Blair, *Economic Concentration,* Chaps. 2, 3, and 5; Charles H. Berry, *Corporate Growth and Diversification* (Princeton, N.J.: Princeton University Press, 1975); Alfred B. Chandler, Jr. *The Visible Hand* (Cambridge, Mass.: Harvard University Press, 1977), Chaps. 9–11; Michael Gort, *Diversification and Integration in American Industry* (Princeton, N.J.: Princeton University Press, 1962); Richard P. Rumelt, *Strategy, Structure, and Economic Performance* (Boston: Harvard Business School Division of Research, 1974).

14 Richard E. Caves, "International Corporations: The Industrial Economics of Foreign Investment," *Economica,* February 1971, pp. 1–27; Lawrence G. Franko, *The European Multinationals* (London: Harper & Row, 1976); Mira Wilkins, *The Maturing of Multinational Enterprise* (Cambridge Mass.: Harvard University Press, 1974); M. V. Yoshino, *Japan's Multinational Enterprises* (Cambridge, Mass.: Harvard University Press, 1976).

15 See Adelman "Measurement of Industrial Concentration"; Nutter *Enterprise Monopoly;* Shepherd, *Market Power and Economic Welfare,* p. 73.

16 Willard F. Mueller and Larry G. Hamm, "Trends in Industrial Market Structure, 1947 to 1970," *Review of Economic and Statistics,* November 1974, pp. 511–520.

17 Scherer, *Industrial Market Structure,* p. 67. William Shepherd, in a valiant attempt to correct raw concentration ratios for geographic size of market, gives a higher estimate – the average concentration ratio for the largest four sellers in manufacturing rises from 39 percent to 60 percent, over 60 percent of manufacturing volume is accounted for by industries with concentration ratios in excess of 50 percent, and nearly half of manufacturing activity is in industries with concentration ratios of 70 percent or more with "quite a few major industries" verging on monopoly or duopoly. Shepherd, *Market Power and Economic Welfare,* pp. 106–113.

18 Mueller and Hamm, "Trends in Industrial Market Structure," p. 513. For all 166 manufacturing industries studied, the average unweighted concentration change 1947–1970 was from 40.9 to 42.7 percent; for consumer goods industries, 36.3 to 42.4 percent; for producers goods, from 44.1 to 42.8 percent; and for highly differentiated consumers goods, from 49.6 to 62.3 percent.

19 See Neil Borden, *The Economic Effects of Advertising* (Chicago: Richard D. Irwin, 1942), pp. 34–35, 48–49, 602–605; Chandler, *The Visible Hand,* pp. 334–336, 374–375, and Chaps. 7, 12; William S. Comanor and Thomas A. Wilson, *Advertising and Market Power* (Cambridge, Mass.: Harvard University Press, 1974).

20 This has come about not so much from economies in scale in pro-

duction as from the advantages of vertical integration, size, diversification, and economies of scale in selling and product and process
innovation. See Joe S. Bain, *Barriers to New Competition* (Cambridge, Mass.: Harvard University Press, 1956); Chandler, *The Visible Hand,* pp. 363–376; Shepherd, *Market Power and Economic Welfare,* pp. 5–9.

21 Arthur R. Burns, *The Decline of Competition* (New York: McGraw-
Hill, 1936); George Stocking and Myron Watkins, *Monopoly and
Free Enterprise* (New York: The Twentieth Century Fund, 1951),
Chaps. 10–11; Scherer, *Industrial Market Structure,* Chaps. 13–14;
Ralph Cassady, Jr., and William F. Brown, "Exclusionary Tactics
in American Business Competition: An Historical Analysis,"
UCLA Law Review, 1961, pp. 88–134.

22 See Almarin Phillips, *Market Structure, Organization and Performance*
(Cambridge, Mass.: Harvard University Press, 1962), Chap. 2.

23 Louis D. Brandeis, *Other People's Money, and How the Bankers Use It*
(Washington, D.C.: National Home Library Foundation, 1933), p.
35.

24 Phillips, *Market Structure,* pp. 25–29.

25 Ibid., pp. 28–34; Scherer, *Industrial Market Structure,* Chap. 6.

26 U.S., Congress, Senate, Committee on Governmental Affairs, Subcommittee on Reports, Accounting and Management, staff study
on *Interlocking Directorates Among the Major U.S. Corporations* (Washington, D.C.: Government Printing Office, 1978), pp. 482–484,
968–979, 988.

27 In the paper industry alone there were three judgments for price
fixing in 1975–1978, and 100 suits were still pending in 1978 against
industry members on the same grounds; see Timothy Schellhardt,
"Cozy Competitors: Price Fixing on the Rise in Paper Industry Despite Convictions," *Wall Street Journal,* May 4, 1978. More generally, George A. Hay and Daniel Kelley, "An Empirical Survey of
Price Fixing Conspiracies," *Journal of Law and Economics,* April
1974, pp. 13–38; Scherer, *Industrial Market Structure,* Chap. 6.

28 Phillips, *Market Structure,* pp. 29–30.

29 See the discussion of the elaborate machinery of coordination used
in the electrical manufacturers' price-fixing activities, Scherer, *Industrial Market Structure,* pp. 170–171.

30 "A price war is of benefit only to the consumer, and the maintaining
of a certain price level would be to the advantage of all competitive
companies." From a 1934 letter by I. G. Farben Industries to Win-
throp Chemical Company, cited by Corwin Edwards in *Economic
and Political Aspects of International Cartels,* Subcommittee on War
Mobilization, Senate Committee on Military Affairs (Washington,
D.C.: Government Printing Office, 1946), p. 12.

31 Brandeis, *Other People's Money,* p. 35.

32 If Morgan Guaranty and Citibank are indirectly connected by the

fact that each has an officer on the board of Phelps Dodge, this may suggest some banker weight vis-à-vis Phelps Dodge, but hardly a route whereby the two banks can exercise power over each other (as opposed to communicating with each other).

33 This is the number of linkages exclusive of those involving inter-locks with subsidiaries. If the universe is defined as the 250 largest plus their giant subsidaries (those with assets of $5 billion or more, which number 11), the number of interlocks would rise to 1,132.

34 David Bunting, "Corporate Interlocking, Part IV – a New Look at Interlocks and Legislation," *Directors & Boards,* Winter 1977, p. 43.

35 These data are for the universe of the 250 largest corporations plus their large subsidiaries.

36 See esp. Victor H. Kramer, "Interlocking Directorates and the Clayton Act After 35 Years," *Yale Law Journal,* June 1950, p. 1274.

37 Bunting, "Corporate Interlocking," p. 45.

38 John Schroeder of Morgan, Tilford Gaines of MHT, and Edward Palmer of Citibank.

39 *Interlocking Directorates Among the Major U.S. Corporations,* p. 27. An earlier FTC study also disclosed a very large number of indirect in-terlocks among ostensible competitors; see Federal Trade Commis-sion, *Report on Interlocking Directorates* (Washington, D.C.: Govern-ment Printing Office, 1952), passim.

40 *Interlocking Directorates Among the Major U.S. Corporations,* p. 77.

41 Ibid., p. 92.

42 Ibid., p. 100.

43 See Federal Trade Commission, *Control of Iron Ore,* a report pub-lished by the House Judiciary Committee, December 1952, pp. 9–10.

44 It is extremely difficult to get reliable information on joint ventures, as SEC disclosure rules do not require information if the venture is not a controlled subsidiary or is small. Companies generally dis-claim control in the case of 50/50 ownership with another company, and the size requirement is unspecific. Some companies also fail to name the venture partner(s) even when the existence of a joint ven-ture is acknowledged.

45 See Michael Tanzer, *The Political Economy of International Oil and the Underdeveloped Countries* (Boston: Beacon Press, 1961), pp. 319–326; Robert Engler, *The Politics of Oil* (Chicago: University of Chicago Press, 1961), pp. 202–212.

46 U.S., Congress, Senate, Foreign Relations Committee, Subcom-mittee on Multinational Corporations, *Hearings on Multinational Pe-troleum Corporations and Foreign Policy,* 93rd Cong., 2d sess. (Wash-ington, D.C.: Government Printing Office, 1974), pt. 7, pp. 18–25.

47 Ibid., p. 25.

48 The U.S. government has initiated many antitrust suits against members of the oil industry. The number of such suits may be said

to demonstrate the quasi-autonomy of important governmental agencies. The uniform failure of such actions since 1914, and the collaboration of government in numerous important anticompetitive activities of the industry (cartels, joint ventures with inherently restrictive characteristics, prorationing), may be said to show that industry power has been sufficiently great to convert apparent governmental threats into merely tiresome harassment and symbolic action. As Adams and Dirlam have noted, since writing the depletion allowance into the IRS Code in 1926, "the government has done for the oil companies what they could not legally do for themselves without clear violation of the antitrust laws." "Private Planning and Social Efficiency," in A. P. Jacquemin and H. W. deJong (eds.), *Markets, Corporate Behaviour and the State* (The Hague: Martinus Nijhoff, 1976), p. 226.

49 Quoted from industry documents in John Blair, *The Control of Oil* (New York: Pantheon, 1976), p. 38.

50 Ibid., pp. 40–41.

51 Ibid., pp. 39–40.

52 Table 6.6 shows 186 joint ventures between Shell and Exxon outside of the United States. This table and the discussion of oil joint ventures draw heavily on two Ph.D dissertations from the University of Oklahoma: James Sturgeon, *Joint Ventures in the Petroleum Industry: Exploration and Drilling*, 1974 and John R. Munkirs, *Joint Ventures in the International Petroleum Industry: Production and Pipelines*, 1973. These theses examined joint ventures outside the United States and the Communist bloc for the period 1957–1971.

53 Quoted from a 1946 Socal internal memorandum, in Blair, *Control of Oil*, p. 38.

54 FTC, *Control of Iron Ore*, pp. 38, 77–78. There is also a large amount of iron ore provided on the basis of long-term contracts with steel companies.

55 European Economic Community, *Seventh Report on Competition Policy*, Brussels, 1978, pp. 116–117.

56 See Stanley E. Boyle, "An Estimate of the Number and Size Distribution of Domestic Joint Subsidiaries," *Antitrust Law & Economic Review*, Spring 1968, pp. 86–87.

57 Walter J. Mead, "The Competitive Significance of Joint Ventures," *Antitrust Bulletin*, Fall 1967, pp. 838–846.

58 "Joint Venture Activity, 1960–1968," *Economic Review*, Federal Reserve Bank of Cleveland, June 1969, p. 22; Jeffrey Pfeffer and Phillip Nowak, "Patterns of Joint Venture Activity: Implications for Antitrust Policy," *Antitrust Bulletin*, Spring 1976, pp. 315–337.

59 Pfeffer and Nowak, "Patterns of Joint Venture Activity"; Boyle, "Size Distribution of Domestic Joint Subsidiaries," pp. 89–90; Malcolm W. West, Jr., "Thinking Ahead," *Harvard Business Review*, July–August 1959, p. 32.

60 Pfeffer and Nowak, "Patterns of Joint Venture Activity," p. 322.

61 Richard E. Caves and Masu Uekusa, *Industrial Organization in Japan* (Washington, D.C.: Brookings Institution, 1976), p. 44.

62 Blair, *Control of Oil*, p. 228.

63 See John Wilson, "Market Structure and Interfirm Integration in the Petroleum Industry," *Journal of Economic Issues*, June 1975, pp. 319–335.

64 Burns, *Decline of Competition*, p. 45.

65 Ibid., p. 73.

66 Charles R. Stevenson, quoted in Stocking and Watkins, *Monopoly and Free Enterprise*, p. 236.

67 *National Trade and Professional Associations of the United States and Canada and Labor Unions*, 12th ed. (Washington, D.C.: Columbia Books, 1977), p. 9.

68 *Interlocking Directorates Among the Major U.S. Corporations*, pp. 968–985.

69 "The risk in GE's proposed merger," *Business Week*, December 29, 1975, p. 27.

70 "Business' most powerful lobby in Washington," *Business Week*, December 20, 1976, pp. 60–63.

71 G. William Domhoff, *The Higher Circles: The Governing Class in America* (New York: Vintage, 1970), Chaps. 5–7.

72 Ibid., Chap. 4.

73 Ibid., Chap. 1; G. W. Domhoff, *The Bohemian Grove: A Study in Ruling Class Cohesiveness* (New York: Harper & Row, 1974).

74 Robert Engler, *The Politics of Oil* (Chicago: University of Chicago Press, 1959), p. 225.

75 Ibid., pp. 289–291; *Advisory Committees*, U.S. Congress, Senate, Committee on Government Operations, Hearings before the Subcommittee on Budget, Management . . ., 93rd Cong., (Washington, D.C.: Government Printing Office, November 1973–February 1974), p. 118.

76 Diana Roose, "Top Dogs and Brass Hats: An Inside Look at a Government Advisory Committee," in G. W. Domhoff (ed.), *New Directions in Power Structure Research*, special issue of *The Insurgent Sociologist*, Spring 1975, p. 53.

77 Roose quotes Pentagon cost analyst A. Ernest Fitzgerald as describing the Industry Advisory Council as "the board of directors of the military industrial complex." Ibid., p. 55.

78 Federal Advisory Committees, *Eighth Annual Report of the President* (Washington, D.C.: Government Printing Office, 1980), p. 15.

79 Roose, "Top Dogs and Brass Hats," p. 61.

80 *Advisory Committees*, testimony of Rodgers and Malek, pp. 81–84, 125–127.

81 Engler, *Politics of Oil*, p. 67.

82 *Advisory Committees*, p. 67.

83 Bank trust department holdings of 5 percent or more of the voting stock, with sole bank voting rights, would be included, but there were no cases of such holdings by a single bank in two oil companies or in two of the 20-company sample.

84 Report of the Committee Appointed Pursuant to House Resolutions 429 and 504 to Investigate the Concentration of Control of Money and Credit, H. Rept. 1593, 62nd Cong., 3d sess. (Washington, D.C.: Government Printing Office, 1913), p. 131.

85 Ibid., p. 132.

86 National Resources Committee, *The Structure of the American Economy, Part 1, Basic Characteristics* (Washington, D.C.: Government Printing Office, 1939), pp. 306–317.

87 Terry Robards, "The Chase and David Rockefeller," *The New York Times,* February 1, 1976, p. D-1.

88 In a major congressional investigation of these ties in 1951, Republic Steel and Cleveland Cliffs had the following connections: (1) reciprocal ownership, with a 7 percent holding by Cleveland Cliffs in Republic; (2) two officers of Cleveland Cliffs on the board of Republic; (3) the same law and accounting firms; (4) extensive business dealings in ore property and ore; and (5) several joint ventures. See U.S., Congress, House, Committee on the Judiciary, Subcommittee on Monopoly Power, *Study of Monopoly Power: Steel,* Serial 14, pt. 4A, 81st Cong., 2d sess. (Washington, D.C.: Government Printing Office, 1950), pp. 223–247.

89 For purposes of this discussion, Citibank and Citicorp are looked upon as a single entity, as are Morgan Guaranty Bank and J. P. Morgan & Company, because each bank is owned by a holding company and the boards of each pair substantially or completely overlap.

90 When AT&T was threatened with divestment in an antitrust suit of the late 1940s and early 1950s, a director of New York Telephone, who was a personal friend of Attorney General Brownell, was mobilized and effectively solicited Brownell's help in undermining the Justice Department proceeding. See *Consent Decree Program of the Department of Justice,* Report of the Antitrust Subcommittee of the House Judiciary Committee, 86th Cong., 1st sess. (Washington, D.C.: Government Printing Office, January 1959), pp. 51–57.

91 The Bell system had a huge $22 billion in pension money in mid-1979, about $12 billion in stock. But most of this money was handled by managers for the Bell system, with a heavy stress given to their investment performance. The system had 107 outside money managers in June 1979. In-house management of pension assets by AT&T amounted to only about $150 million and, in 1979, was deployed in an experimental random selection fund.

92 Scherer, *Industrial Market Structure,* p. 490.

93 *Bank Mergers and Concentration of Banking Facilities,* Staff Report to

Subcommittee No. 5 of the House Judiciary Committee, 1952; *Corporate and Bank Mergers*, Interim Report of Antitrust Subcommittee, 1955; David and Charlotte Alhadeff, "Growth of Large Banks, 1930–1960," *Review of Economics and Statistics*, November 1964, pp. 356–363.

94 Samuel Talley, "Recent Trends in Local Banking Markets," Staff Economic Studies 89 (Washington, D.C.: Board of Governors of the Federal Reserve System, 1977).

95 FTC, *Economic Report on Corporate Mergers*, pp. 184–185.

96 Howard H. Hines, "Effectiveness of 'Entry' by Already Established Firms," *Quarterly Journal of Economics*, February 1957, pp. 132–150.

97 Franko, *The European Multinationals*, pp. 157–160.

98 Ibid., pp. 92–100; George W. Stocking and Myron W. Watkins, *Cartels in Action* (New York: The Twentieth Century Fund, 1947), pp. 4–11. The latter stated: "Our tentative findings indicate that 87 percent by value of mineral products sold in this country in 1939, 60 percent of agricultural products, and 42 percent of manufactured products were cartelized" (p. 5).

99 Raymond Vernon, *Storm over the Multinationals* (Cambridge, Mass.: Harvard University Press, 1977), p. 82.

100 See esp. Richard E. Caves, "International Corporations: The Industrial Economics of Foreign Investment," *Economica*, February 1971, pp. 1–27; K. D. George and T. S. Ward, *The Structure of Industry in the EEC* (Cambridge, Mass.: Cambridge University Press, 1975); J. H. Dunning, *American Investment in British Manufacturing Industry* (London: Ruskin House, 1958), pp. 155–157; Stephen Hymer and Robert Rowthorn, "Multinational Corporations and International Oligopoly: The Non-American Challenge," in C. P. Kindleberger (ed.), *The International Corporation: A Symposium* (Cambridge, Mass.: MIT Press, 1970); Frederick T. Knickerbocker, *Oligopolistic Reaction and Multinational Enterprise* (Boston: Harvard Graduate School of Business, 1973).

101 Vernon, *Storm over the Multinationals*, pp. 73–82.

102 EEC, *Second Report on Competition Policy* (Brussels, April 1973), p. 161.

103 EEC, *Seventh Report on Competition Policy* (Brussels, April 1978), p. 250.

104 Commission of the European Communities, *A Study of the Evolution of Concentration in the Food Industry for the United Kingdom*, vol. 1 (Luxembourg: Office for Official Publications of European Communities, 1975), pp. 122, 183.

105 Vernon, *Storm Over the Multinationals*, p. 82.

106 For a description of the process of denationalization associated with multinational expansion, and the high concentration and market power in markets occupied by multinationals in Brazil and Mex-

ico, see Richard S. Newfarmer and Willard F. Mueller, *Multinational Corporations in Brazil and Mexico: Structural Sources of Economic and Noneconomic Power,* Report to the Subcommittee on Multinational Corporations of the Senate Foreign Relations Committee (Washington, D.C.: Government Printing Office, August 1975), esp. pp. 53–63, 105–117.

107 See Keith Griffin, *International Inequality and National Poverty* (New York: Holmes & Meier, 1978); Newfarmer and Mueller, *Multinational Corporations;* Vernon, *Storm Over the Multinationals,* pp. 77–80; David Felix, "Economic Development: Takeoffs into Unsustained Growth," *Social Research,* Summer 1969, pp. 267–293. For a good discussion of the overall impact of economic penetration, with all of its corollaries, on a less-developed country, see Jan K. Black, *United States Penetration of Brazil* (Philadelphia: University of Pennsylvania Press, 1977), passim.

108 Olivier Pastré, *Le Capital Financier International,* Doctoral Thesis in Economics, University of Paris XIII-Villetaneuse, March 21, 1978, pp. 23–28.

109 The Bilderberg group is a private group of individuals, heavily involved in business and politics, which first met in 1954, and which seems to have been organized to help harmonize relations in the West by personal contacts and discussion. Its 1956 Steering Committee of 39 individuals included 15 from the United States, all members of the Council on Foreign Relations. See Eugene Pasymowski and Carl Gilbert, "Bilderberg: The Cold War Internationale," reprinted in *Congressional Record,* (Washington, D.C.: Government Printing Office, September 15, 1971), pp. 32052ff.

110 The International Energy Agency was formed in 1974 to plan oil supply coordination among (eventually) 19 consuming countries. Three industry advisory bodies were formed to aid in planning and to supply data used by IEA; one, the Reporting Company Group, has representatives from 31 majors. The Federal Trade Commission is responsible by law for monitoring the activities of the IEA to see that competition is not impaired. Federal Trade Commission, Fifth Report to the Congress and the President, Pursuant to Sec. 252 (i) of the Energy Policy and Conservation Act of 1975, revised January 1979, pp. 2–4. Also, Wilfred L. Kohl, "The International Energy Agency: The Political Context," in J. C. Hurewitz (ed.), *Oil, the Arab–Israeli Dispute, and the Industrial World* (Boulder, Colo.: Westview Press, 1976), pp. 246–257.

111 According to Bernard Wysocki, Jr., "Technological innovation accounts for much of the success of plastics. Over the past several years, research men have found new ways to package food at high speeds on machines that form and fill plastic easily and economically." See his "Container War: Plastic Food Packaging Makes Deeper Inroads On Paper, Metal, Glass," *Wall Street Journal,* May 8, 1978.

112 Paul Gibson, "Proctor & Gamble: It's Got a Little List," *Forbes,* March 20, 1978, pp. 33–34.
113 "Federal Judge Rules Against GTE in Suit by ITT on Buying," *Wall Street Journal,* March 2, 1978, p. 19.
114 "Westinghouse Greed Alleged by Gulf Oil," *New York Times,* December 2, 1977; Anthony Parisi, "Gulf Suit Charges A-Fuel Monopoly to Westinghouse," *New York Times,* May 10, 1978.
115 "Zenith Radio, Sony Agree on Settlement in Suit over Trade," *Wall Street Journal,* April 27, 1977, p. 33.
116 Paul Ingrassia, "Home Grown Woes: Zenith's Own Actions as Well as Imports Prompted Its Troubles," *Wall Street Journal,* October 25, 1977.
117 Gibson, "Proctor & Gamble."
118 "AT&T Intends to Order 85 IBM Computers," *Wall Street Journal,* May 5, 1977. The article states that the value of this order would be about $300 million.
119 "Inside IBM's management," *Business Week,* July 14, 1973, p. 48. This article summarizes some of the documents released in the antitrust suit brought by Telex Corporation against IBM.
120 "Communications: Regulated AT&T vs. competitive IBM, Who will supply the office of the future?" *Business Week,* July 27, 1974, p. 44.
121 *United States v. National City Lines,* 186 F. 2nd 562 (7th Circuit Court of Appeals, 1951); Walter Adams and Joel Dirlam, "Private Planning and Social Efficiency," pp. 218–219.
122 Ibid., p. 220.
123 Henry E. Kariel, *The Decline of American Pluralism* (Stanford, Cal.: Stanford University Press, 1961); Emil Lederer, *State of the Masses,* (New York: Norton, 1940); Theodore Lowi, *End of Liberalism* (New York: Norton, 1969).
124 This point is discussed further in the "Final comments" of Chapter 7.

Chapter 7. Power, Responsibility, and Conflicting Imperatives

1 Traditional microeconomic analysis assumed technology and product as givens. On these static assumptions, the most important form of nonprice competition was advertising. Price competition reduces prices and is unquestionably beneficial to the consumer; advertising, which inflates costs and prices while increasing seller marker power, is not. On more dynamic assumptions, however, which admit technology and product as important competitive variables, nonprice competition takes on more positive aspects, potentially able to reduce costs and enlarge buyer options. Rapid technical and product change can be associated, however, with substantial monopoly power, as small sellers are driven from this more dynamic market,

and rapid product change is favorable to consumers' interests only on special assumptions. Nevertheless, given the clear importance of technical change in a dynamic (and realistic) context, at a minimum nonprice competition loses its exclusively negative properties.

2 In his *The Visible Hand, The Managerial Revolution in American Business,* (Cambridge, Mass.: Harvard University Press, 1977), Alfred Chandler, Jr., pays very little attention to the extent of ownership interests of the control groups of large enterprises. His focus is on the organizational changes brought about by changes in size and the demands of strategic business planning.

3 This is only fully true for 100 percent ownership. If minority interests exist, then the resources of the corporation are not the owner-manager's, even if he or she owns 75 percent of the stock. The legal position of the large owner, short of 100 percent, is thus constrained, but it, and the owner manager's moral position, are stronger than that of a nonowner/manager.

4 Where the controlling ownership interest is not active in the management but instead hires a manager, such hired managers should have even less discretion than controlling nonowner/managers.

5 *Some* market power may be necessary for significant managerial abuses to be realized, but with given levels of market power, managerial abuse will be related to the degree of managerial control, hence to corporate size and diffusion of ownership.

6 Tax avoidance by large firms may be greater in scale and far more significant in dollar terms than tax evasion. For example, large firms take advantage of international tax rate differentials and litigate or lobby on tax laws and Internal Revenue Service (IRS) tax rulings. An important illustration of this point is the secret ruling by the IRS, allowing the U.S. oil companies who were members of Aramco to classify their payments to Saudi Arabia as tax payments to a foreign government instead of as royalty payments. See Robert Engler, *The Politics of Oil* (Chicago: University of Chicago Press, 1959), pp. 232ff.

7 Daniel M. Berman, *Death on the Job* (New York: Monthly Review Press, 1978); Samuel S. Epstein and Richard D. Grundy, eds., *Consumer Health and Product Hazards – Cosmetics and Drugs, Pesticides, Food Additives* (Cambridge, Mass.: MIT Press, 1974); K. William Kapp, *The Social Costs of Private Enterprise* (New York: Schocken Books, 1971); E. J. Mishan, "The Postwar Literature on Externalities: An Interpretive Essay," *Journal of Economic Literature,* March 1971, pp. 1–28.

8 "Positional goods" are those that are "either (1) scarce in some absolute or socially imposed sense or (2) subject to congestion or crowding through more intensive use." Fred Hirsch, *Social Limits to Growth* (Cambridge, Mass.: Harvard University Press, 1976), p. 27. An essential feature of positional wealth is that although the ap-

petite for such goods grows with rising productivity, and at a better than average rate, "in the aggregate, it is an appetite that cannot be satisfied" (p. 26). Rationing will occur by means of relatively more rapid price advances for such goods and less convenient access.

9 Barry Bluestone and Bennett Harrison, *Capital and Communities: The Causes and Consequences of Private Disinvestment* (Washington, D.C.: Progressive Alliance, 1980), passim.; Harry Braverman, *Labor and Monopoly Capital* (New York: Monthly Review Press, 1974); Richard C. Edwards, *Contested Terrain* (New York: Basic Books, 1978); Santosh Mukherjee, *Restructuring of Industrial Economics and Trade With Developing Countries* (New York: International Labor Organization, 1978); David F. Noble, *America by Design* (New York: Knopf, 1977).

10 See Chapter 5, n. 102.

11 Hyman P. Minsky, "Financial Instability Revisited: The Economics of Disaster," in Board of Governors of the Federal Reserve System, *Reappraisal of the Federal Reserve Discount Mechanism,* vol. 3 (Washington, D.C.: Board of Governors of the Federal Reserve System, 1972), pp. 95–136; Wilbur Silber, *Financial Innovation* (Lexington, Mass.: Lexington Books, 1975); John Wenninger and Charles M. Sivesind, "Defining Money for a Changing Financial System," *Quarterly Review,* Federal Reserve Bank of New York, Spring 1979, pp. 1–8.

12 See, for example, John H. Goldethorpe, "The Current Inflation: Towards a Sociological Account," in Fred Hirsch and John Goldethorpe (eds.), *The Political Economy of Inflation* (Cambridge, Mass.: Harvard University Press, 1978), pp. 186–213.

13 See Alva Myrdal, *The Game of Disarmament: How the United States and Russia Run the Arms Race* (New York: Pantheon, 1977); Emma Rothschild, "Boom and Bust, Department of Defense Annual Report, Fiscal Year 1981," *New York Review of Books,* April 3, 1980, pp. 31–34; Ruth L. Sivard, *World Military and Social Expenditures* (Leesburg, Va.: World Military and Social Expenditures Publications, annual volumes); Herbert F. York, *Race to Oblivion, A Participant's View of the Arms Race* (New York: Simon & Schuster, 1970).

14 Irma Adelman and Cynthia Taft Morris, *Economic Growth and Social Equity in Developing Countries* (Stanford, Cal.: Stanford University Press, 1973); Gunnar Myrdal, *Economic Theory and Under-Developed Regions* (London: Duckworth, 1957); Barbara Ward, *Program for a Small Planet* (New York: Norton, 1979).

15 In the 1950s and 1960s, U.S. government-sponsored arms sales to the Third World were relatively small, averaging $230 million per year. In fiscal 1978 they amounted to $11 billion, or 81 percent of the total U.S. arms sales of $13.5 billion. The backlog of undelivered orders under the U.S. Foreign Military Sales program rose to $48 billion at the end of 1979. Third World military expenditures in

1979 amounted to $86 billion, or 5 percent of GNP. Council on Economic Priorities, "Weapons for the World/Update III," *Newsletter,* April 14, 1980, p. 1; NARMIC – American Friends Service Committee, *Arming the Third World* (Philadelphia: American Friends Service Committee, 1979), p. 2; Sivard, *World Military and Social Expenditures,* 1979 ed., p. 20.

16 S. Sideri, "Prospectives for the Third World," *International Spectator,* March 1971, pp. 488–493; Aart Van de Laar, *The World Bank And The Poor* (The Hague: Martinus Nyhoff, 1980).

17 On the possible benefits of "distance," see David Felix, "Economic Development: Takeoffs Into Unsustained Growth," *Social Research,* Summer 1969, pp. 267–293.

18 This view is accepted by Thomas Watson, Jr., who says: "Bigness itself is a relatively new phenomenon in our society. Even if nothing else had changed, the vast concentrations of power in our society would demand that businessmen reconsider their responsibilities for the broader public welfare." Thomas Watson, Jr., *A Business and Its Beliefs* (New York: McGraw-Hill, 1963), p. 80.

19 R. H. Tawney, *Religion and the Rise of Capitalism* (New York: Harcourt, Brace, 1926), p. 253.

20 Thomas C. Cochran, *Business in American Life: A History* (New York: McGraw-Hill, 972), p. 237.

21 Ibid.

22 This view is expounded even by liberal business leaders such as Henry Ford II. See Jerry M. Flint, "Ford Says Company Profit Is Its Social Responsibility," *New York Times,* May 12, 1972.

23 Cochran, *Business in American Life,* pp. 186–191.

24 Baer, president of the Philadelphia and Reading Railroad, and spokesman for the coal operators, made this statement in response to a letter from W. F. Clarke, a photographer living in Wilkes-Barre. In the press, Clarke's communication received wide publicity as the "divine right" letter and helped swing public opinion in favor of the miners. The letter was disseminated by Rev. J. J. Curran, an important protagonist of the miners. See Catherine Ann Cline, "Priest in the coal fields: the Story of Father Curran," *Records of the American Catholic Historical Society of Philadelphia,* June 1952, pp. 73–75.

25 On John D. Rockefeller's view of himself in this regard see Peter Collier and David Horowitz, *The Rockefellers: An American Dynasty* (New York: Holt, Rinehart and Winston, 1976), pp. 48–49.

26 Cochran, *Business in American Life,* p. 238.

27 Andrew Carnegie, *The Gospel of Wealth* (New York: Century, 1900), p. 13.

28 See James Weinstein, *The Corporate Ideal in the Liberal State: 1900–1918* (Boston: Beacon Press, 1968), esp. Chaps. 1 and 2.

29 See esp. Stuart D. Brandes, *American Welfare Capitalism, 1880–1940* (Chicago: University of Chicago Press, 1976).

30 Ida M. Tarbell, *Owen D. Young, A New Type of Industrial Leader* (New York: Macmillan, 1932), pp. 153–157.

31 This was a theme of a popular book by James D. Mooney and Alan C. Reiley, *Onward Industry!* (New York: Harper & Bros., 1931), p. 342.

32 For a study of the common developments among the fascist and nonfascist business leaderships in doctrines of trusteeship and appropriate social and economic policy see Robert A. Brady, *Business as a System of Power* (New York: Columbia University Press, 1942), passim.

33 Frank Abrams, quoted in Edward S. Mason, "The Apologetics of 'Managerialism,' " *Journal of Business,* May 1963, p. 11.

34 Watson, *A Business and Its Beliefs,* p. 103. Watson noted that only 14 percent of the work force at that time was employed by the *Fortune* 500 companies.

35 Ibid., pp. 81–82.

36 Ibid., pp. 96–97.

37 Thornton F. Bradshaw, "Corporate Social Reform: An Executive's Viewpoint," in S. P. Sethi, ed., *The Unstable Ground: Corporate Social Policy in a Dynamic Society* (Los Angeles: Melville, 1974), p. 24.

38 Ibid., p. 26.

39 Ibid., p. 31. Although he says that the rules change, Bradshaw also quotes a social critic admonishing him: "We have changed the rules, and you are still playing the same old game." To which Bradshaw replies: "Well, if the game has been changed, no one has let us know about it. My company is still judged by its return on investment, its earnings per share, and its growth track record."

40 The first state statute explicitly providing that chartered corporations could give to charities without specific charter provision was passed in 1917 (in Texas); by the 1970s, 48 states had passed such legislation. The first court decision that discarded the "benefits" (to the corporation) test with real impact did not occur until 1953; *A. P. Smith Manufacturing Co.* v. *Barlow*, 13 N.J. 145, 98 A. 2d 581, appeal dismissed, 346 U.S. 861 (1953). This case involved a $1,500 corporate donation to Princeton University. For discussion and further citations see Phillip I. Blumberg, "Corporate Responsibility and the Social Crisis," *Boston University Law Review,* Winter, 1970, pp. 157ff.

41 Rumelt notes that "policies designed to affect corporate behavior that are not translated into profit goals by the firm's control system will have little chance of influencing behavior." Richard P. Rumelt, *Strategy, Structure, and Economic Performance* (Boston: Harvard Graduate School of Business, 1974), p. 158. See also Robert W. Acker-

man, "How companies respond to social demands," *Harvard Business Review*, July–August, 1973, pp. 88–98.

42 Berle and Means, *The Modern Corporation*, pp. 254–255.

43 Ibid., p. 356.

44 A. A. Berle, Jr., *The Twentieth Century Capitalist Revolution* (New York: Harcourt Brace, 1954), p. 73.

45 A. A. Berle, Jr., *Power Without Property* (New York: Harcourt Brace, 1959), p. 110.

46 William Hazlitt, *Table Talk* (London: Everyman Edition, 1952), p. 264.

47 J. Patrick Wright, *On a Clear Day One Can See General Motors* (Grosse Pointe, Mich.: Wright Enterprises, 1979), p. 164.

48 Bluestone and Harrison, *Capital and Communities*, Chap. 5; Richard E. Caves, "International Corporations: The Industrial Economics of Foreign Investment," *Economica*, February 1971, pp. 1–27; Stephen Hymer, "The Internationalization of Capital," *The Journal of Economic Issues*, March 1972, pp. 91–111.

49 William N. Carley, "One Step Ahead: Many Companies Work to Avoid Local Taxes – With Great Success," *Wall Street Journal*, July 17, 1972; "The second war between the states," *Business Week*, May 17, 1976, pp. 1–27; Ed Kelly and Lee Webb, eds., *Tax Abatements* (Washington, D.C.: Ohio Public Interest Campaign and Conference on State and Local Policies, 1979); Barnet and Muller, *Global Reach*, pp. 273–288.

50 Berle, *Power Without Property*, p. 118.

51 James F. Harris and Anne Klepper, *Corporate Philanthropic Public Service Activities*, Conference Board Report 688, 1977, p. 5; William Baumol, "Enlightened Self-Interest and Corporate Philanthropy," in William Baumol, et al. (eds.), *A New Rationale for Corporate Social Policy* (New York: Committee for Economic Development, 1970), pp. 5–11.

52 See Bluestone and Harrison, *Capital and Communities*, Chaps. 2–4; Barnet and Muller, *Global Reach*, Chap. 11; Iver Peterson, "States Seeking to Curb Impact of Closing Industrial Plants," *New York Times*, March 16, 1980.

53 Bluestone and Harrison, *Capital Communities*, p. 44.

54 Ibid., p.50.

55 Eric Mergenthaler, "Cleanup Clash: U.S. Steel, EPA Fight Long Running Battles Over Plants' Pollution," *Wall Street Journal*, August 9, 1975.

56 Reserve Mining, a joint venture of Armco and Republic Steel, has been involved in a major environmental battle, challenging its right to dump mineral tailings, including asbestos, into Lake Superior. See Paul Brodeur, *Expendable Americans* (New York: Viking, 1974), p. 268.

57 On Union Carbide, see "How Union Carbide Has Cleaned up Its

Image," *Business Week,* August 2, 1976, p. 46. On GM, see Ralph Nader's account of GM's long resistance to pollution control in *Unsafe at Any Speed* (New York: Grossman, 1964), Chap. 4. On Hooker Chemical, see Michael Brown, *Laying Waste: The Poisoning of American by Toxic Chemicals* (New York: Pantheon, 1980).

58 Council on Economic Priorities, "Paper Profit: Pollution in the Paper and Pulp Industry," Economic Priorities Report, December–January 1971, pp. 13, 24.

59 J. Preston Levis was chief executive officer of the company from 1950 until 1968, after which he remained on the board until his death in 1973. Robert Levis was on the board from 1963. The Levis family holdings were reported by the company to be under 2 percent in 1975; what they were in 1968, I do not know.

60 Ibid., p. 24.

61 Brodeur, *Expendable Americans,* gives a full account.

62 Ibid., pp. 142 and passim.

63 Ibid., pp. 187–188.

64 Willard S. Randall and Stephen D. Solomon, *Building 6* (Boston: Little, Brown, 1977).

65 See Joseph A. Page and Mary-Win O'Brien, *Bitter Wages* (New York: Grossman, 1973), pp. 59ff.

66 Nader, *Unsafe at Any Speed,* pp. 96–103.

67 John De Lorean claims that "At General Motors the concern for the effect of our products on our many publics was never discussed except in terms of cost or sales potential." See Wright, *On a Clear Day,* p. 5. De Lorean describes in some detail a case where a Chevrolet assembly plant to be located in Detroit – justified by his staff on both purely economic and social grounds – was vetoed by the top management on arbitrary personal choice grounds, pp. 226–227.

68 In 1963 James C. Bowling of Philip Morris (PM) said that "We believe that there is no connection [between smoking and cancer], or we wouldn't be in the business." John T. Landry, another officer of PM, said that "I think if it were proved I would give up smoking, I also think if it were proved I'd get the heck out of this business." See *The New Yorker,* November 30, 1963, pp. 93, 96. PM is still in the business and Bowling and Landry are both still top officers of PM.

For a good discussion of the remarkably successful recent push of the tobacco companies into Third World markets, see Albert Huebner, "Exporting Cancer: Making the Third World Marlboro Country," *The Nation,* June 16, 1979, pp. 717–720.

69 According to De Lorean, "The people running General Motors today tend to be short-term, professional managers. They are in the top spots only a short time, less than 10 years. In a sense, they just learn their job about the time they have to leave. So the concern at the top today is for the short-term health of the company. These

professional managers want to produce a good record while they are in office." See Wright, *On a Clear Day,* p. 217. See the further citations and discussion in Chap. 3, note 74 and associated text.

70 For an important illustration, see Barry I. Castleman, *The Export of Hazardous Factories to Developing Nations* (Washington, D.C.: Environmental Defense Fund, 1978).

71 IBM's position on proper behavior in South Africa has been very similar to other U.S. companies with significant sales and investments in that country. That is, it has argued strongly for business as usual, on grounds both of benefits to South African blacks and the absence of any positive effects that would follow from an IBM withdrawal. See David Vogel, *Lobbying the Corporation,* (New York: Basic Books, 1978), pp. 120–121. An estimated one-third of IBM's sales in South Africa are to the government; see Lawrence Litvak, Robert DeGrasse, and Kathleen McTigue, *South Africa: Foreign Investment and Apartheid* (Washington, D.C.: Institute for Policy Studies, 1978), pp. 50–52.

72 Thomas Hayes, "Complying With E.P.A. Rules, How Allied Chemical Manages Safety Standards," *New York Times,* January 16, 1980, p. D1.

73 Exclusive of government intervention and pressures applied by labor unions in collective bargaining.

74 A public interest group seeking a directorship with Northern States Power Company received 14 percent of the votes in 1973, enough to elect a director under the company's cumulative voting arrangements. But the company sent out, at company expense, a second proxy request and succeeded in reducing the dissident candidate's vote to 4 percent, and defeat. See the discussion in Vogel, *Lobbying the Corporation,* pp. 89–94.

75 Ibid., pp. 71–89; also the 1970 and 1971 issues of *Economic Priorities Report* by the Council on Economic Priorities, "Minding the Corporate Conscience" and "The Movement for Corporate Responsibility;" Donald E. Schwartz, "The Public Interest Proxy Contest: Reflections on Campaign GM," *Michigan Law Review,* January 1971, pp. 421–445.

76 These abortive efforts are discussed in Vogel, *Lobbying the Corporation,* pp. 213–215.

77 See Charles R. Halpern and John M. Cunningham, "Reflections on the New Public Interest Law . . ." *Georgetown Law Journal,* May 1971, pp. 1095–1126; David Vogel, "Promoting Pluralism: The Public Interest Movement and the American Reform Tradition," paper given before the American Political Science Association, August–September 1978.

78 Both the Interfaith Center on Corporate Responsibility (ICCR) and the Investor Responsibility Research Center, Inc. (IRRC) have for some years published summaries of public interest proxy resolutions

and their disposition. The ICCR publishes an annual volume of resolutions it has submitted.

79 Jeffrey M. Berry, *Lobbying for the People* (Princeton, N.J.: Princeton University Press, 1977), pp. 13–14.

80 Vogel traces church stockholder activism to 1963. Vogel, *Lobbying the Corporation,* pp. 161–163.

81 These estimates are taken from Chap. 4, Table 4.4 and ibid., p. 162.

82 The boycott against Dow's Saran Wrap in 1967 resulted in sales 6.5 percent larger than those anticipated by the company. See Vogel, *Lobbying the Corporation,* p. 46.

83 See ibid., pp. 115ff.

84 ICCR, *The Corporate Examiner,* June 1978.

85 This account draws mainly on the following: James E. Post and Edward Baer, "Demarketing Infant Formula: Consumer Products in the Developing World," (draft, 1978); James W. Kuhn, "The Role of the Market in Infant Nutrition: The Role of Nestle in Infant Formula," (draft, case study, 1978); Leah Margulies, "A Critical Essay on the Role of Promotion in Bottle Feeding," *PAG Bulletin,* vol. VII, Nos. 3–4, September–December 1977, pp. 73–83; ICCR proxy submission to American Home Products Corporation, March 20, 1978.

86 *Statement of the Sisters of the Precious Blood and Bristol-Myers Company on Infant Formula Marketing Practices Overseas* (undated), p. 1.

87 Ibid., p. 10.

88 Margulies, "A Critical Essay," p. 81.

89 This discussion rests heavily on the following: Litvak et al., *South Africa;* David M. Liff, *U.S. Business In South Africa: Pressures from the Home Front* (Washington, D.C.: IRRC, 1978); IRRC, *Corporate Activity in South Africa* (Washington, D.C.: IRRC, 1976); U.S., Congress, Senate Foreign Relations Committee, *U.S. Corporate Interests in South Africa,* 95th Cong., 2d sess. (Washington, D.C.: Government Printing Office, 1978).

90 Derek Reveron, "Pamphlet Power: Small Group of Activists Puts Pressure on Big Firms to Get Out of South Africa," *Wall Street Journal,* February 23, 1978.

91 Ibid.

92 John Buras, "U.S. Links Widen in Pretoria Scandal," *New York Times,* March 19, 1979, p. A3; Wendell Rawls, Jr., "Group Says South Africa Put $11 Million into U.S. News Media Deals," *New York Times,* June 20, 1979.

93 SEC rules provide that if a proposal receives less than 3 percent of the votes cast at an annual meeting, it cannot be resubmitted to the same company for five years. The second year a proposal must receive 6 percent of the vote to qualify for resubmission, the third year, 10 percent.

94 On the coordination of the companies' lobbying activities with

South African interests, and the vehicles of this lobbying, see Litvak et al., *South Africa*, p. 62; Barbara Rogers et al. *The Great White Hoax* (London: African Bureau, 1977), p. 77.

95 According to one South African economist, "We have learnt that our large economic relations are our best shield in a world which has chosen us as scapegoats." Quoted in Litvak et al., *South Africa*, p. 63.

96 "GM bids to soften apartheid's sting," *Business Week*, April 15, 1972, p. 36.

97 Michael C. Jensen, "The American Corporate Presence in South Africa," *New York Times*, December 4, 1977, sec. 3.

98 Litvak et al., *South Africa*, pp. 68–69.

99 Ibid., pp. 75ff.

100 Despite its difficulties of several years ago (Dita Beard; Chile), ITT's Big Blue Marble Children's program and good-deeds commercials helped raise its public image as a caring company; see Eric Barnouw, *The Sponsor* (New York: Oxford University Press, 1978), p. 86. See also the Council on Economic Priorities Report, "Corporate Advertising and the Environment," September–October 1971, which shows huge spending for ads (many misleading and timed to correlate with lags in meeting environmental standards), extolling corporate environmental efforts.

101 See Ralph Nader, Mark Green, and Joel Seligman, *Taming the Giant Corporation* (New York: Norton, 1976), p. 158.

102 See Vic Reinemer, "Corporate Ownership and Control: A Public Policy View," in Harvey J. Goldschmidt (ed.), *Business Disclosure: The Government's Need to Know* (New York: McGraw-Hill, 1979), pp. 142–175.

103 F. M. Scherer, "Segmental Financial Reporting: Needs and Trade-offs," in Goldschmidt (ed.), *Business Disclosure*, pp. 3–57.

104 Possibly the most significant factor in the slow recognition and treatment of occupational diseases and hazards has been the quite understandable tendency of companies to "play dumb." This includes not collecting and maintaining medical records, not cooperating with and showing interest in studies of occupational hazards, and not recognizing or denying allegations and studies that show hazard. Important light is thrown on this matter in three books previously cited, Brodeur, *Expendable Americans;* Randall and Solomon, *Building 6*; and Page and O'Brien, *Bitter Wages*. See also Samuel Epstein, *The Politics of Cancer* (San Francisco: Sierra Club, 1978), Chap. 10.

105 This is called "kitchen-sinking" in the lingo of Washington lawyers; see Mark Green, *The Other Government: The Unseen Power of Washington Lawyers* (New York: Grossman, 1975), p. 230.

106 See Barnouw, *The Sponsor,* passim.

107 William O. Douglas, "Directors Who Do Not Direct," *Harvard Law Review,* June 1934, pp. 1305ff.

108 Roderick Hills, "Views on how corporations should behave," *Financial Executive,* November 1976, p. 33.

109 See U.S., Congress, Committee on Interstate and Foreign Commerce, *Public Policy Implications of Investment Company Growth,* H. Rept. 2337, 89th Cong., 2d sess. (Washington, D.C.: Government Printing Office, 1966), pp. 10–13 and passim.

110 At the height of the bribery scandal period, Commissioner Philip Loomis noted in an address that self-reform was urgently required to "avoid the need for additional federal regulation" and "to strengthen public confidence." See his "Remarks before the National Conference of the American Society of Corporate Secretaries," June 19, 1976 (SEC News Release).

111 Questionable practices may be hidden from the top officers as well as from the other directors, partly for legal protection. See Christopher D. Stone, *Where the Law Ends: The Social Control of Corporate Behavior* (New York: Harper & Row, 1975), pp. 61ff.

112 A variety of possibilities is considered in Gerry Hunnius, G. David Garson, and John Case, *Workers' Control: A Reader on Labor and Social Change* (New York: Vintage, 1973); also, David L. Ratner, "The Government of Business Corporations: Critical Reflections on the Rule of 'One Share, One Vote,' " *Cornell Law Review,* November 1970, pp. 1–49.

113 Peter Brannen, Eric Batsonne, Derek Farchett, Philip White, *The Worker Directors: A Sociology of Participation* (London: Hutchison, 1976), p. 218.

114 James Furlong, *Labor in the Boardroom* (Princeton, N.J.: Dow Jones, 1977), p. 9.

115 "Co-determination: When workers help manage," *Business Week,* July 14, 1975, p. 133–134.

116 Ibid.

117 Furlong, *Labor in the Boardroom,* p. 3.

118 Ibid., p. 43.

119 Ibid.

120 Brannen et al., *Worker Directors,* p. 216.

121 Ibid., pp. 228–230.

122 "Sweden: Worker participation becomes the law," *Business Week,* June 21, 1976, pp. 42–43.

123 For an optimistic view of the new system of labor participation, see H. G. Jones, *Planning and Productivity in Sweden* (London: Croom Helm, 1976), Chaps. 9 and 12; for the evolution of the Swedish system see Martin Schnitzer, *The Economy of Sweden, A Study of the Modern Welfare State* (New York: Praeger, 1970).

124 On the Tennessee Valley Authority, see Wayne King, "T.V.A., a

Major Polluter, Faces Suit to Cut Sulfur Dioxide Fumes," *New York Times,* July 4, 1977. On the businesslike character of much of government enterprise, see William G. Shepherd, *Public Enterprise: Economic Analysis of Theory and Practice* (Lexington, Mass.,: Lexington Books, 1976), pp. 104 and seq.; Annmarie Hauck Walsh, *The Public's Business: The Politics and Practices of Government Corporations* (Cambridge, Mass.: MIT Press, 1978), pp. 5–6, 26, 332–334.

125   Herman Schwartz, "Governmentally Appointed Directors in a Private Corporation – The Communications Satellite Act of 1962," *Harvard Law Review,* December 1965, p. 355.

126   Ibid., p. 352.

127   Wallace D. Farnham refers to the government of the time of the Union Pacific directorships as an "annex of the marketplace," and he asserts that the governing statutes "took on whatever meaning interested persons chose for them." " 'The Weakened Spring of Government': A Study in Nineteenth-Century American History," *American Historical Review,* April 1963, p. 666.

128   Quoted from the 1869 Report of the Government Directors, p. 63, by Schwartz, "Governmentally Appointed Directors," pp. 358–359.

129   Herman, *Commercial Bank Trust Departments,* pp. 76–78.

130   Stone, *Where the Law Ends.*

131   Ibid., pp. 174–183.

132   Ibid., p. 180.

133   Ibid., pp. 203–227.

134   This is also the view of Harold Geneen, longtime CEO of ITT, who explained to a group of reporters that "The U.S. economy is so big and so diverse that whatever direction it's moving in, there is very little that government can do to change it." Robert J. Flaherty, "Harold Geneen Rests His Case," *Forbes,* June 15, 1977, p. 47.

135   In principle, even a nonproducing government could seize control of business and regulate or nationalize it, and negative business confidence effects could be offset by appropriate monetary and fiscal actions. But a limited function government starts from a smaller power base and would have to assume more risks of economic and political failure. Its actions would precipitate a political struggle between business and its political representatives against those in government espousing the controversial policies. Given the uncertainties of the negative confidence effects, the lags and imperfections in monetary/fiscal processes, and the possibilities of a political policy stalemate, it is by no means certain that monetary/fiscal offsets would fully compensate for the negative business reactions.

136   The famous confrontation between President John F. Kennedy and

the steel industry was over the government's right to constrain prices and wages by informal guideline procedures, versus industry's right to ignore such efforts at moral suasion. The government won this particular struggle, which demonstrated the government's power to influence a specific major business decision when this was deemed important. But this was a special case and did not constitute a fundamental challenge. The main thrust of Kennedy antirecessionary policies in 1960–1963 was not a big stick but, on the contrary, a large and juicy carrot. See Hobart Rowen, *The Free Enterprisers: Kennedy, Johnson and the Business Establishment* (New York: G. P. Putnam, 1964), p. 43 and E. Ray Canterbery, *Economics on a New Frontier* (Belmont, Cal.: Wadsworth, 1968), p. 140.

137 A bill first introduced by Senator Adlai Stevenson at the time of the huge oil price increases, in 1974, proposing the establishment of a government-owned oil company to develop federally owned oil reserves and to provide a new competitive element in the oil market, has never gotten out of committee.

138 On the roots of this phenomenon, see Alexis de Tocqueville, *Democracy in America* (New York: Harper & Row, 1966), originally written in 1835; Richard Slotkin, *Regeneration Through Violence: The Mythology of the American Frontier, 1600–1860* (Middletown, Conn.: Wesleyan University Press, 1973); C. Wright Mills, *White Collar* (New York: Oxford University Press, 1956), Chap. 15, "The Politics of the Rear Guard"; Gabriel Kolko, *Main Currents in Modern American History* (New York: Harper & Row, 1976), Chaps. 3–5; Kerner Commission, *Report of the National Advisory Commission on Civil Disorders* (New York: Bantam Books, 1968); Arnold A. Rogow, *The Dying of the Light* (New York: G. P. Putnam, 1975).

139 See Cochran, *Business in American Life*, Chap. 13; Matthew Josephson, *The Politicos, 1866–1896* (New York: Harcourt Brace, 1938), passim.; Lincoln Steffens *Autobiography* (New York: Harcourt Brace, 1931); Robert H. Wiebe, *Businessmen and Reform* (Cambridge, Mass.: Harvard University Press, 1962). On business' adversary relationship to government, see Chandler, "The adversaries," and Vogel, "Why Businessmen Distrust Their State."

140 In his famous Federalist Paper Number X, Madison describes the central problems of the new Union as how to reconcile liberty with the tendency "of an interested and overbearing majority" to deprive minorities of their rights. The minority whose rights were most threatened, in Madison's view, arose out of "the various and unequal distribution of property." The threat of factions to "the permanent and aggregate interests of the community" Madison thought would be protected under the Constitution by the use of indirect rule and by the great size of the population and country,

which make for divisiveness and inaction. See Henry Cabot Lodge, ed., *The Federalist* (New York: G. P. Putnam, 1888), originally published in 1787, pp. 51–60.

141 Lindblom, *Politics and Markets,* Chap. 13. On the use of Red Scares, see Robert K. Murray, *Red Scare: A Study in National Hysteria, 1919–1920* (Minneapolis: University of Minnesota Press, 1955); William Preston, Jr., *Aliens and Dissenters: Federal Suppression of Radicals, 1903–1933* (Boston: Harvard University Press, 1963); Alex Carey and Trudy Korber, *Propaganda and Democracy in America* (forthcoming).

142 As noted by Edward A. Jesser, Jr., chairman of the United Jersey Banks, in a speech to the American Bankers Association: "Quick and tough decisions can be made in a relatively short time in a country such as Brazil compared to the difficulty there is in reaching agreement on what actions to take in a democracy." *American Banker,* November 28, 1975, p. 13. For a good account of the wide dissatisfaction of U.S. businesspeople with the workings of democracy see Leonard Silk and David Vogel, *Ethics & Profits: The Crisis of Confidence in American Business* (New York: Simon & Schuster/Conference Board, 1976). Chap. 2; see also Michael J. Crozier et al., *The Crisis of Democracy,* Report on the Governability of Democracies to the Trilateral Commission, esp. Chap. 3, "The United States," by Samuel Huntington (New York: New York University Press, 1975)

143 Noam Chomsky and Edward S. Herman, "Why American Business Supports Third World Fascism," *Business and Society Review,* Fall 1977, pp. 13–21.

144 In the Goldwater and Nixon years this was explicitly formulated as "the Southern strategy." See Richard Rovere, "A Reporter at Large, The Campaign: Goldwater," *The New Yorker,* October 3, 1964, pp. 201–243; William D. Phelan, Jr., "The Authoritarian Prescription, Nixon's Southern Strategy," *The Nation,* November 3, 1969, pp. 467–473.

145 Lloyd Gardner, *Economic Aspects of New Deal Diplomacy* (Madison, Wisc.: University of Wisconsin Press, 1964); Walter LaFeber, *America, Russia, and the Cold War, 1945–1966* (New York: Wiley, 1967); Gabriel and Joyce Kolko, *The Limits of Power, The World and United States Foreign Policy, 1945–1954* (New York: Harper & Row, 1972), esp. Chap. 12; see also the works cited in n. 141.

146 Peter Steinfels, *The Neo-Conservatives* (New York: Simon & Schuster, 1979); Irving Kristol, *Two Cheers for Capitalism* (New York: Basic Books, 1978); Norman Podhoretz, *The Present Danger* (New York: Simon & Schuster, 1980). It is interesting that the historian Élie Halévy, in his pessimistic assessment of twentieth-century trends, noted a contradiction similar to that described in the text:

"The internal contradiction from which European society suffers can, then, be defined as follows. The conservative parties call for the almost unlimited strengthening of the state with the almost unlimited reduction of its economic functions. The socialist parties call for the unlimited extension of the functions of the state and, at the same time, for the unlimited weakening of its authority. The compromise solution is 'national socialism.' " Élie Halévy, *The Era of Tyrannies* (Garden City, N.Y.: Anchor, 1965), p. 267. Original ed. 1938.

147 The *Wall Street Journal* reported in late 1980 that "business lobbyists, flushed with success in Congress, lay plans for 1981. They will work hardest for business tax relief . . . Another top goal: reduction of the power of the regulatory agencies, including OSHA, the SEC, the EPA." *Washington Wire,* September 19, 1980, p. 1. No other regulatory agencies were specified by name as business targets. On the divergent business responses to the old and new regulation, see Chap. 5, on "Government regulation."

148 *Barrons* and the *Wall Street Journal* have been warmly supportive of the New Chile since 1973; *Forbes Magazine* and *Business Week* have also been increasingly appreciative of the merits of the new "stability." See most recently, Norman Gall, "How the 'Chicago Boys' Fought 1,000% Inflation," *Forbes,* March 31, 1980 and Jerry Flint, "More Cubas in the Making," *Forbes,* March 31, 1980. Influential businesspeople like William Simon, David Rockefeller, and John Connally have been enthusiastic about developments in Chile, Argentina, and Brazil. For further citations, see the works cited in notes 142 and 143.

149 Thorstein Veblen, *The Theory of Business Enterprise* (New York: Scribner's, 1904), pp. 391, 393.

150 The "frustrated intellectual" has provided a popular contemporary scapegoat for otherwise inexplicable opposition to the status quo in neoconservative analyses of the 1970s. Among other problems, however, these analyses disregard the facts that most intellectuals are conventional, sharing the main premises of their social order, and that large numbers of them are tied to the business community through research grants and as paid consultants. An explicit strategy carried out on a large scale by regulated businesses is referred to by Owen and Braeutigam as "coopting the experts." They note that "AT&T has made a major investment, for instance, in very high grade economic talent over the past decade." Bruce M. Owen and Ronald Braeutigam, *The Regulation Game* (Cambridge, Mass.: Ballinger, 1978), p. xv. An inkling of the extent of this cooptation is provided by the list of consultants to AT&T and the payments made to them shown in the Annual Report Form M of AT&T to the Federal Communications Commission. The Report for De-

cember 31, 1978, lists direct corporate payments to 104 named social scientists and 215 small consulting organizations manned by intellectuals (many still attached to academic institutions).

In interrogating economist William Baumol on the reasons for the wide agreement among his fellow economists on a principle espoused by Baumol, Chester Kamin, representing MCI Communications Corporation in a suit against AT&T, asked Baumol what these economists cited by him had in common. Baumol replied that they were eminent. Referring to AT&T Form M, Kamin showed that another common characteristic was that every one of them was employed by AT&T. See Stephen Aug, "Regulators Ease Businesses' Disclosure," *Washington Star,* May 11, 1980, p. A-13.

151 Although Ronald Reagan promised a massive increase in the military budget during his 1980 presidential campaign, much of his wide business support derived from the belief that he would reduce the size of government. Thus Walter Scott, president of Investors Diversified Services, noted that "Reagan seems more dedicated to a philosophy of reducing government." See Thomas C. Hayes, "Executives Favoring Reagan," *New York Times,* October 27, 1980, p. D-1. In this usage "government" is implicitly redefined to exclude that segment of government looked upon benignly or with favor by business.

152 M. I. Finley, *The Ancient Greeks* (New York: Viking, 1964), pp. 29–30. Finley traces these developments back to eighth century B.C. Greece.

153 On the growing potential for international monetary destabilization and the importance of the absence of an international lender of last resort, see Jack Guttentag and Richard Herring, "Financial Disorder and Eurocurrency Markets," *Proceedings of a Conference on Bank Structure and Competition* (Chicago: Federal Reserve Bank of Chicago, May 1980 [forthcoming]); Jack Guttentag and Richard Herring, "Lender of Last Resort in an International Context," (draft manuscript, November 1980).

Index

A&P. *See* Great Atlantic and Pacific Tea Company, Inc.
Abrams, Frank, 254
Accounting, 157, 191, 278. *See also* Auditing
ACOA. *See* American Committee on Africa
Acquisition of corporations. *See* Mergers of corporations; Stocks, acquisition; Takeovers of corporations
Active power. *See* Power, definition
Activists, 3–4, 184, 251, 256, 257, 268–270, 276, 277, 281
Adams, Charles Francis, Jr., 6–7
Adams, Walter, 239
Advertising, 1, 178, 194, 270, 272, 273
AEC. *See* Atomic Energy Commission
Aerospace industry, 167
Aetna Insurance Company, 230
Aggregate concentration, 12, 16, 83, 145, 190, 191–192, 194, 240, 248
Agriculture, 1, 166, 171, 172, 188, 230, 240, 250
Airlines, 155, 156, 167, 176, 182. *See also* Civil Aeronautics Board; specific airlines, e.g., Delta Airlines, Inc.
Alcoa. *See* Aluminum Company of America
Alinsky, Saul, 266
Allied Chemical Corporation, 21, 202, 262, 264
Aluminum Company of America (Alcoa), 41, 220
Amax, Inc., 41
American Airlines, 24, 41
American Bankers Association, 168
American Committee on Africa (ACOA), 273–274

American Cyanamid Company, 41, 84
American Enterprise Institute, 214
American Express Company, 202
American investments in South Africa. *See* South Africa, American investments in
American Management Association, 44
American Petroleum Institute, 214
American Telephone and Telegraph Company (AT&T), 20, 50, 200, 201, 203, 219, 221, 227, 230, 236, 238, 291
American Tobacco Company, 231
AMK Corporation. *See* United Brands Corporation
Amtrak. *See* National Railroad Passenger Corporation
Anaconda Company, 50, 101
Antitrust: actions, 30, 51, 150, 196, 220, 236–237; law, 163, 167, 173–174, 195, 204, 216, 230 (*see also* Clayton Act; Sherman Act)
Apartheid, 273, 274, 276, 277
Arabian American Oil Company (Aramco), 204–205
Aramco. *See* Arabian American Oil Company
Arco. *See* Atlantic Richfield Company
Arlen Realty and Development Corporation, 160, 227
Armand Hammer, 24
Armco Inc., 221
Armour and Company, 69
Asbestos. *See* Toxic substances
Assets of corporations. *See* Corporations, assets
Astor, John Jacob, 252
AT&T. *See* American Telephone and Telegraph Company